American Views of Soviet Russia, 1917-1965

American Views
of
SOVIET RUSSIA
1917-1965

edited by

PETER G. FILENE
University of North Carolina at Chapel Hill

1968

THE DORSEY PRESS
Homewood, Illinois

© THE DORSEY PRESS 1968

First printing, March, 1968

Library of Congress Catalog Card No. 68-14880

Printed in the United States of America

FOR JEANETTE

ACKNOWLEDGMENTS

In the process of writing this book I received invaluable help from several sources. The librarians of Harvard University, Lincoln University (Mo.), and the Missouri State Library were always patient and cooperative. William G. Rosenberg of the University of Michigan gave me the benefit of his expert criticism. And as always, my wife Jeanette offered suggestions and reassurance whenever I needed them.

INTRODUCTION

When a small band of revolutionaries seized control of Russia in November, 1917, and proclaimed the victory of the Bolshevik Revolution, they jolted the course of history with tremors which have not yet subsided. Those were indeed, as John Reed exulted, "ten days that shook the world."

It is fitting that an American journalist should have invented that famous phrase, for Soviet Russia immediately exerted a special impact on the thinking of Americans. In 1917 the American people also were trying to shake the world. Under President Wilson they were fighting a war to "make the world safe for democracy," to secure in the Old World the principles which they had developed in the New. Suddenly the Bolsheviks rose up on the ruins of Russia's autocracy with a strident challenge to "bourgeois democracy," with a revolutionary appeal to the workers of the world, with a claim to the destiny of history. The significance was unmistakable: Americans confronted a rival to their ideals and perhaps to their national existence.

But the rivalry was not so simple as "us" against "them," "good" against "evil." It was more ambiguous and more interesting than that. True, the Communists' doctrine of class conflict leading to international revolution and dictatorship by the proletariat; their animosity to private property and profit; their outspoken commitment to atheism—all these contradicted the basic values of most Americans. They provided some of the reasons why four United States Presidents withheld diplomatic recognition from the Soviet regime for 16 years. Nevertheless, many Americans found much to admire in the USSR. The labor unions' voice in factory management, the special benefits to working mothers, the free medical care—these were forms of "democracy" which the Soviet dictatorship provided and the American democracy did not. In this perspective the boundary between vice and virtue blurred.

During the 1920's, most Americans scorned so tolerant a perspective; basking amid the unprecedented economic boom, they saw no

ix

need for self-doubts. Capitalism was the wave of the future, they boasted to the Communist leaders. After the Wall Street stock market crash, however, the Soviet-American comparison became more intricate and uncomfortable. For while millions of persons in the United States walked the streets jobless and went to bed hungry, the Moscow regime was implementing a Five-Year Plan which eliminated unemployment and sent industrial production soaring to dizzy records. The stark juxtaposition forced upon Americans the dilemma of whether the freedom to starve was preferable to the Russian people's lack of political and personal freedoms.

The decade of the thirties also introduced another factor into the Soviet-American relationship. As Adolf Hitler became increasingly shrill and menacing, German Fascism more and more displaced Russian Communism as the "menace" to international peace. Indeed, once the Third International ordered the various Communist parties in Europe and the United States to form a "Popular Front" with socialist and liberal groups against the Nazi threat, many Americans hailed the Soviet Union as the leading defender of world democracy. By contrast, the appeasement policies of England and France and the isolationist policies of the United States made the capitalist nations seem feeble, even villainous.

But again the contrast blurred. As hundreds upon hundreds of leading Bolshevik officials were convicted for treason in the Moscow purge trials of 1936–38 and were executed or imprisoned, American sympathizers stirred uneasily. Was the exiled Leon Trotsky right after all, when he warned that Stalinism would strangle the original ideals of the Revolution? In 1939, these sympathizers still were debating that question when news of the Nazi-Soviet nonaggression pact broke upon them with stunning force. Did this alliance of autocrats prove that the polar ideologies of Nazism and Communism shared the common ground of tyranny, that they were equally despicable?

The pace of international events gave little time for reflection upon ideological dilemmas such as these. Less than two years after the Nazi-Soviet pact, Hitler's armies suddenly invaded Russia; six months later, after the bombing of Pearl Harbor, the United States and the USSR were allies. It was indeed a "strange alliance" and, as victory approached, also a strained one. For without the emergency of war, the differences between the two powers began to reassert themselves. The focus of immediate dispute was in Eastern Europe, but the implications were global.

Soon after World War II ended, Americans began to realize that the world was not at peace and probably would not be for a long, long time. As Communist expansionism annexed or menaced nations along most of the huge Soviet frontier from northern Europe to eastern Asia, Americans debated what to do. The alternatives covered a broad spectrum: outright war with Russia, "liberation" of the Soviet satellites, military alliances with non-Communist nations, foreign aid, and negotiations with the Soviets. Infusing the debate with special intensity was the awareness that the United States—and then the USSR, too—possessed nuclear weapons which, if used in war, might virtually destroy civilization. Strategy and anxiety competed as Americans sought to deal with Soviet Russia.

In this way the cold war was more ambiguous than ordinary wars. It became still more so after Stalin died. Preaching "peaceful coexistence," Stalin's successors continued the conflict with capitalism with all methods short of military warfare. As crisis and "thaw" succeeded each other in sporadic fashion during 1953-63, American hopes for accommodation with the Soviets fluctuated wildly. And as the range and destructiveness of nuclear weapons became more and more awesome, some Americans began to ask whether it wasn't preferable to be red than dead. Still another dimension of ambiguity was added with the emergence of Communist China as a rival to the USSR and with the emergence of the Asian, African, and Latin American nations as a "third world" potentially uncommitted to the cold war.

Thus, ideological ambiguities combined with economic, military, and political events to complicate American views toward Soviet Russia between 1917 and 1965. At the same time, the fundamental clash between the two nations' sets of beliefs animated these views with keen emotion. In newspapers, books, magazines, and meetings, the dispute over the Soviet phenomenon raged ceaselessly. Fundamental principles were at stake; the meaning and success of American values were involved. When talking about the USSR, Americans were really talking about their own nation and themselves.

The Soviet Union was more than a topic; it was a place. President Wilson sent troops to Russia, John Reed died there, the Ford Motor Company built a factory in Nizhnii-Novgorod, hundreds of engineers took jobs under the Plan, and thousands of tourists visited "the Red experiment." For those who encountered at first hand—with their own eyes and ears and noses—the nation and people ruled by a rival ideology, the act of judgment became especially difficult. No newspaper editorial or platform speaker arranged the evidence for them. Instead, they had only their senses (and, of course, their prejudices) to instruct them, to tell them whether to believe their exuberant guide, whether to generalize from a bug-ridden hotel room, whether to trust that old woman who whispered of tortures. The tourists' mental tension between a bewildering flux of evidence and their own preconceptions forms a particularly fascinating aspect of American responses to the USSR.

The following pages attempt to convey the variety, intensity, and drama of these themes. Obviously the selections offer only a small slice of the mountain of relevant material (more than 200 books, for example, were written by Americans about Soviet Russia during 1917-45 alone). But that slice is at least fairly representative. Literary critics, journalists, Senators, housewives—all kinds of Americans responded on all levels of sophistication to the Soviet phenomenon. The materials vary accordingly. Although magazine editorials and articles predominate because they took positions most succinctly and clearly, there are also speeches in Congress, manifestoes by groups of intellectuals, travelogues by casual and not so casual tourists, and personal letters. Had the public-opinion pollsters begun their work earlier, we could also have dug down more extensively to the inarticulate public. Unfortunately, for the most part we must stay on the verbal surface—but that is interesting enough.

February, 1968   Peter G. Filene

TABLE OF CONTENTS

I. WAR AND REVOLUTION, 1917–1920
the question of who makes the world
safe for what kind of democracy

II. FROM NEP TO THE PLAN, 1921-1932
the question of capitalism

III. THE PURGES AND THE PACT, 1933-1940
the question of freedom

V. THE COLD WAR, 1946-1952
the question of containment

VI. THE COLD WAR, 1953-1965
the question of coexistence

I

WAR AND REVOLUTION
1917-1920
the question of who makes the world safe for what kind of democracy

The First Revolution

After a week of riots, strikes, and troop mutinies in Petrograd, Tsar Nicholas II abdicated his throne on March 15, 1917.[1] The Russian Revolution had taken place. A week later, President Woodrow Wilson announced that the United States was the first nation to extend diplomatic recognition to the Provisional Government, whose leaders promised to institute representative and liberal rule. On April 2, the President asked Congress to declare war on Germany.

This juxtaposition of revolution and war is significant. During the next two years, Americans rarely discussed Russian events apart from the World War, because the United States depended on Russia to uphold the Eastern Front. Consequently, the Russian Revolution held for Americans a special interest—namely, national self-interest—and therefore earned especially intense reactions.

An editorial in The Nation *conveys the tone in which most of the American public greeted the first news of the Russian Revolution. Several days later, President Wilson's war message to Congress*

---

[1] According to the Old Style calendar, the Revolution occurred during the last week of February. Russia did not adopt the New (Western) Style until early 1918.

1

directed attention to Russia's new regime and its relationship to American participation in the World War.

1   RUSSIA DEMOCRATIZED*

Not since August 1, 1914, has anything come out of Europe to stir the pulse and fire imagination like the news from Russia. Wherever there are men of liberal minds, wherever there is a belief in democracy, people are rejoicing wholeheartedly that the Russian autocrat, disgraced by innumerable cruelties and massacres perpetrated during his reign, has been driven from his throne, and with him the whole crew of pro-German intriguers who have been paralyzing Russia by selfishness, greed, and bureaucratic inefficiency. One must go back at least to 1848, when all Europe was seething in revolt, to parallel the thrill that this word will bring to struggling men everywhere. It is the first visible sign of that democratization of the world which must come if civilization is to profit by the unparalleled bloodshed of this terrific world-war. This spectacle of a nation rising to free itself from mediaevalism, with a foreign foe at the door, must quicken every one's faith in humanity, as it brings visions of a Russia enlightened, modernized, freed from its fortress of St. Peter and St. Paul that has been the tomb of its patriots, and from that Siberia which has spelled for all the world supreme suffering for freedom—the last word in crushing, autocratic domination of an aspiring, liberty-seeking people.

2   RUSSIA AN ALLY†

A steadfast concert for peace can never be maintained except by a partnership of democratic nations. No autocratic government could be trusted to keep faith within it or observe its covenants. It must be a league of honour, a partnership of opinion. Intrigue would eat its vitals away; the plottings of inner circles who could plan what they would and render account to no one would be a corruption seated at its very heart. Only free peoples can hold their purpose and their honour steady to a common end and prefer the interests of mankind to any narrow interest of their own.

Nation, Vol. CIV (March 22, 1917), p. 327 (editorial).
†Woodrow Wilson, War Message to Congress, April 2, 1917, *Papers Relating to the Foreign Relations of the United States, 1917, Supplement I, The World War,* p. 200.

Does not every American feel that assurance has been added to our hope for the future peace of the world by the wonderful and heartening things that have been happening within the last few weeks in Russia? Russia was known by those who knew it best to have been always in fact democratic at heart, in all the vital habits of her thought, in all the intimate relationships of her people that spoke their natural instinct, their habitual attitude towards life. The autocracy that crowned the summit of her political structure, long as it had stood and terrible as was the reality of its power, was not in fact Russian in origin, character, or purpose; and now it has been shaken off and the great, generous Russian people have been added in all their naïve majesty and might to the forces that are fighting for freedom in the world, for justice, and for peace. Here is a fit partner for a league of honour.

The Bolshevik Revolution

Because they relied on Russia to maintain the Eastern Front against Germany, Americans watched anxiously as the socialist Petrograd Soviet (Council of Workers' and Soldiers' Deputies) challenged the Provisional Government with cries for a revision of war aims along the lines of a "general democratic peace" without annexations or indemnities. A radical minority within the Soviet, the Bolsheviks, proclaimed still more drastic goals. Following the return of Vladimir Lenin from exile, the Bolsheviks adopted his so-called "April Theses": all power to the Soviets, immediate withdrawal from the war, nationalization of the land, and control of industry by workers' committees.

The clash between the Provisional Government and the Soviet increasingly disabled the Russian war effort. In July the Bolsheviks took control of a spontaneous popular uprising but failed to overthrow the government. At the same time, Prince Lvov resigned in favor of Alexander Kerensky, a socialist, as head of state. But Kerensky too could not stabilize the political situation. In September another coup erupted, this time by General Lavr Kornilov in favor of stronger measures against the socialists and stronger prosecution of the war. Again the coup failed, but it left Kerensky in a feeble position, disliked by both conservative and radical forces, discredited by Russia's economic, political, and military deterioration.

By October of 1917, the Bolsheviks had gained a large following

*among the factory workers and military garrisons in Petrograd and
had secured a majority in the Soviet. The time was ripe, Lenin decided, for a seizure of power. On the night of November 6, the
Bolsheviks easily captured control of Petrograd, while Kerensky fled.
On the next evening the Second All-Russian Congress of Soviets formally approved the coup and transferred power to the Bolsheviks.
The second Russian Revolution had taken place. All power belonged
to the Soviets—or, more accurately, to Lenin, Leon Trotsky, and the
other leaders of the Bolshevik party.*

*Many of the numerous Americans in Petrograd on November 6
subsequently wrote eyewitness accounts of the Bolshevik uprising.
One of these was Bessie Beatty, a correspondent for the San Francisco* Bulletin. *The letters by Pauline Crosley, the wife of a temporary attaché in the American Embassy, provide another perspective
on the same events.*

3   AN AMERICAN IN PETROGRAD*

At daybreak a company of Red Guards from the Viborg factory
district—men whose only military equipment was a rifle slung over
the shoulder, and a conviction that the hour of the proletariat had
come, and that they were the defenders of the cause of the workers
of the world—came to a halt on the north bank of the Neva. The
bridges were guarded by cadets from the Engineers' School, placed
there the night before, when Kerensky had ordered them opened. At
the point of their guns, the factory workers ordered the officers to
close them again. The engineers obeyed, and the street-cars started
blithely on their way back and forth across the river, just as if nothing had happened.

At the same moment, two detachments of Bolshevist soldiers and
sailors, acting under orders from the Military Revolutionary Committee, took possession of the telephone exchange and the General Staff.
It was all done so swiftly and so quietly that the Bolshevik battle
was half won before Petrograd awoke to the knowledge that civil war
was on.

It was nine o'clock when Petroff brought me tea and word that the
Bolsheviki had that minute taken possession of the hotel. Petroff's

*Bessie Beatty, *The Red Heart of Russia* (New York: Century, 1918), pp. 185–205,
209–22. Copyright, 1918, The Century Company. By permission of Appleton-Century, af-
filiate of Meredith Press.

astounding news sent me hurriedly into the hall, and into the arms of a squad of soldiers. The young officer in command detained me.

"Amerikanka Korrespondent," I explained, and indicated a desire to go downstairs.

"Pazhal'sta, pazhal'sta!" he said, bowing low, and motioning his men to let me pass.

At the head of the winding staircase groups of frightened women were gathered, searching the marble lobby below with troubled eyes. Nobody seemed to know what had happened. Each floor was crowded with soldiers and Red Guardsmen, who went from room to room, searching for arms, and arresting officers suspected of anti-Bolshevik sympathies. The landings were guarded by sentries, and the lobby was swarming with men in faded uniforms. Two husky, bearded peasant soldiers were stationed behind the counter, and one in the cashier's office kept watch over the safe. Two machine-guns poked their ominous muzzles through the entry-way. My letter of credit was inside the safe, and the only other money I had was an uncashed check for eight hundred rubles.

I started for the National City Bank on the slender chance of finding it open. I was just in time. Within the hour the Bolsheviki captured the State Bank, and all the others promptly closed their doors.

On my way back I walked through the Dvortsovy Square. Four armored cars were drawn up under the shadow of the mighty granite shaft in front of the Winter Palace, their guns pointing significantly at the palace windows. Flaming red flags were freshly painted on their gray sides, and on one in huge letters was the word "Proletariat." A crowd of perhaps twenty mechanics and chauffeurs tinkered with guns and engines, making ready for instant action. Occasionally a man looked up from the nut he was tightening to offer some comment on the situation. The whereabouts of Kerensky was the chief topic of the moment.

"He is not there now," said one of them, pointing with his wrench in the direction of the palace. "He ran away to Finland in the night."

"He is not in Finland," said another scornfully. "He went away to get troops. He is coming back to fight us."

"They say he escaped to the front disguised as a Red Cross nurse," said a third, with a sneer that produced a loud burst of laughter from his companions.

Inside the palace, seated around the mahogany table in the great council chamber, where the Tsar of all the Russias had spoken commands that made an empire tremble, fifteen members of the Provisional Government grimly waited. In the hall outside the door ten military school cadets kept watch. These, the women's regiment, and a company of cadets encamped on the lower floor, were all that stood between them and the rising army of the workers. To them the whereabouts of Kerensky was no secret. He had gone in search of loyal troops who would rise to the protection of the Provisional Government, and upon his success or failure they must stand or fall.

It was noon when I returned to St. Isaac's Square. The Marinsky Palace, where the Council of the Republic was meeting,—once the home of the Council of the Empire, mouth-piece of absolutism in old Russia,—was surrounded by sailors, soldiers, and Red Guardsmen. The palace guards offered no resistance when a crowd of sailors demanded admission. They swarmed through the entrances, and appeared simultaneously in various parts of the hall. A sailor, a tam-o'-shanter on the back of his head and long ribbon streamers flying out behind, stepped up to President Avksentieff.

"Stop talking. Go home," he said. "There is no Council of the Republic!"

Avksentieff and his followers demurred for a moment; then, looking around the room at the men in blue, they adjourned, and filed into the square. The Council of the Republic, hope of Tseretelli, Cheidze, and those other moderate Socialists who were trying so desperately to stave off the final break, was at an end.

The more radical Socialist members went to Smolney Institute, where the delegates from all parts of Russia were flocking to the second All-Russian Congress of Soviets.

At three o'clock I started for Smolney, a little old revolutionist whom we Americans all called "Daddy R.," trotting beside me. We walked down the Morskaya toward the telephone exchange. Just opposite we halted. Coming toward us, in regular marching formation, was a company of military cadets, strapping, handsome fellows from the officers' school. Before they reached the building, the commander halted them. Half of the number walked deliberately past the armored car, turned, and approached from the other side. A volley of rifle fire broke the stillness, and the crowd scurried to the cover of doorways and side streets. A gray-bearded, benevolent-looking *dvornik* dragged me inside a courtyard, where a dozen other people sought shelter, and clanged the great iron door shut behind us. A beggar, with legs cut off at the knees, hobbled beside me.

"Crack! Crack!" went the rifles again—then a moment of breathless silence. The *dvornik* cautiously opened the door a few inches,

and I put my head out. The street was deserted. The cadets were crouched in kneeling positions on the sidewalks against the wall, guns pointing at the telephone office.

The *dvornik* pushed the door shut again, and this time he locked it and motioned us to follow. We crossed a courtyard, and turned into a dark, narrow tunnel, through which we picked our way over piles of debris and up and down stone steps till we came into the open a block below.

By another route Daddy R. and I made our way back to the Morskaya. I stepped to the middle of the street to see what was happening, but a Russian officer motioned me away.

"They will fire again in a minute," he said. "They are trying to take the telephone exchange from the Bolsheviki."

He had no sooner finished speaking than the front of the building began to belch lead in a shower that sent the cadets hurrying in search of shelter. An armored car hove in sight from the opposite direction, opened fire, and completed the rout of the attacking force.

We hurried toward the Nevsky. The bridge across the Moika was bristling with guns. Four armored cars barred the way, and a crowd of soldiers and sailors worked rapidly, throwing up a barricade across the street. One man was stretched flat on the wooden pavement, prepared to fire a machine-gun from the protection of a telegraph-pole. The Red Guards waved the passengers back from the bridge, but the tracks were left open, and the cars went back and forth unhindered. We tried to make our way through the old France Hotel, which wanders all over the block between the Morskaya and the Moika, and out on to the canal by another entrance. Again we were turned back. Another volley of gunshot sent us scurrying to the shelter of a basement shop.

It was nearly five when we reached the entrance of Smolney. The great building, until a few months before a private seminary where the feminine flower of Russian aristocracy was cultivated in seclusion, had suddenly become an arsenal, bristling with guns and swarming with armed men.

Upstairs the Workmen's and Soldiers' Deputies were gathering for the Congress of Soviets. They were coming together to decide whether the Bolshevik demand of "All power to the Soviets" should be granted. It was a question already being answered by the voice of the guns.

The meeting was to open at five. At nine the crowd in the great, chaste white assembly room was still waiting for action. Outside, in the dimly lighted corridors, hundreds of men with muddy boots tramped back and forth, in and out of committee rooms. Soon after nine, a delegate from the Menshevik group[1] announced that his party was still in caucus, unable to come to an agreement, and asked for another hour's delay. A murmur of disapproval ran through the room. Nerves were at trigger-tension. For once, Russian patience seemed to be about to reach its limit.

Another hour passed. Suddenly through the windows opening on the Neva came a steady *boom! boom! boom!*

"What's that? What's that?" asked the sailor of the soldier, and the soldier of the workman.

A man with pale face and blazing eyes fought his way through the crowd on to the platform.

"The cruiser *Aurora* is shelling our comrades in the Winter Palace. We demand that this bloodshed shall be stopped instantly!" he shouted.

"It's a lie!" said one of them.

"It's just another trick of the bourgeois to divide our forces!" said a second.

A few men hurried from the hall; but the crowd had received too many startling rumors that day to be much disturbed by another one.

Again came the *boom! boom! boom!* from the direction of the Neva. Again the murmur of question.

"It's a motor-lorry cranking up in the courtyard below," some one ventured.

"The people upstairs are moving tables around," another suggested.

That moment the attention of the crowd was diverted by the arrival of a man of medium height, square-shouldered, lean, dark, and tense-looking. His face was white, and his black hair brushed back from a wide forehead, black mustache, and small black beard, his black jacket and flowing black tie, still further emphasized the alabaster whiteness of his skin. He stood within a few feet of me, one hand in his pocket, and with sharp, quick glances took the measure of that strange sea of faces.

"Here's Trotzky!" whispered the man beside me. "Come, I want you to meet him."

Before I had time to acquiesce or protest, I found a lean hand grasping mine in a strong, characteristic handshake. We stood there

---

[1]Mensheviks: a socialist party which, as compared to the Bolsheviks, favored less dictatorial leadership and more moderate tactics for gaining power. Until the Bolsheviks broke away in 1912, both groups were joined in the Social Democratic party. [Ed.]

for a few moments, talking of inconsequential things, but all of us charged with the tensity of the hour. There was keen intelligence here, nerve, a certain uncompromising streak of iron, a sense of power; yet I little suspected I was talking to the man whose name within a few brief weeks would be a familiar word on every tongue— the most-talked-of human being in an age of spectacular figures.

At twenty minutes to eleven our conversation was abruptly cut short by the appearance of Dan,[2] who opened the meeting. It was Dan's swan-song. Only a few weeks before, in this gathering, his voice would have been law; but with the swing of the workers to the left his power was gone. The mass had broken with its leaders, and every comment from the crowd indicated more definitely the irrevocability of that break.

Dan announced that he would not make a speech, declaring that the hour in which his comrades were being shelled in the Winter Palace, and self-sacrificingly sticking to their posts, was not the hour for oratory. He said that five hundred and thirteen delegates had been seated, and the new presidium of twenty-five members would contain fourteen Bolsheviki.

The spokesmen of the various parties then announced the names of their representatives. Leaders of the social patriotic groups, of the Mensheviki, and Socialist Revolutionists refused to take their place in the presidium, and the Menshevik Internationalists declared they would delay joining the presidium until certain questions were settled.

The Bolsheviki, with Nicolai Lenin and Zenovieff at their head, climbed to the platform. A great cheer went up from the Bolshevik supporters. Lenin and Zenovieff, who had been in hiding since the July riots, had that day come out of their holes to take a historic part in this new Revolution.

When the ovation had died down, Dan briefly stated the object of the meeting before relinquishing his place to Trotzky.

"The business of the Convention," said he, "divides itself into three heads: a governmental crisis, the question of war and peace, and the Constituent Assembly."

"Take up the question of peace first," shouted a soldier in the crowd.

It was all that was needed to set the indignation of the Mensheviki flaming.

---

[2]F. I. Dan, a Menshevik. [Ed.]

"Tavarischi, forty minutes have passed since we announced that our comrades were being shelled in the Winter Palace, and the cruiser *Aurora* is still firing. We demand that this bloodshed be stopped immediately."

"A committee has already been sent out," some one else declared.

Martoff, perhaps the ablest of the Menshevik Internationalists, took the platform, and in a voice ringing with indignation demanded immediate settlement of the governmental crisis.

"If this convention wants to be the voice of revolutionary democracy, it must not sit idly by before the rapidly developing civil war that may result in a disastrous explosion of the counter-revolution," he said. "When the question of the organization of the government is being settled by the conspiracy of a single one of the revolutionary parties, we are challenged by only one problem; the immediate warding off of this impending civil war."

He proposed the appointment of a committee for negotiating with other Socialist parties and organizations to stop the rapidly developing clash.

The resolution was passed; but, instead of immediately appointing a committee, Trotzky permitted the convention to listen to the opinions of delegate after delegate on a number of subjects not pertaining to the question.

It was a critical moment in the history of the Russian Revolution. Perhaps it was some bitter memory of insults he had suffered at the hands of these other leaders, perhaps it was simply the natural inability of the Russian to compromise, or a combination of these and other motives, that made Trotzky delay action, and thereby toss away his opportunity for compromise. Probably even he himself could not say.

Meanwhile the guns on the Neva continued their eloquent *boom! boom! boom!*

Kharash, a delegate from the Twelfth Army, got the floor.

"While a proposition for peaceful settlement is being introduced here, a battle goes on in the streets of Petrograd," he said. "The Winter Palace is being shelled. The specter of civil war is rising. The Mensheviki and Socialist Revolutionists repudiate all that is going on here, and stubbornly resist all attempts to seize the government."

"He does not represent the Twelfth Army!" cried a soldier from the ranks. "The army demands all power to the Soviets."

Twenty others were on their feet the same instant:

"Staff! Staff! He comes from the Staff! He is not a soldier!" they shouted angrily, shaking their fists at the delegate from the Twelfth.

Pandemonium broke loose. The shouts of the men inside the building drowned the boom of the guns outside. In the midst of it a man demanded and got the floor.

"We are leaving the convention," he said. "We can stand no more! We are going unarmed to die with our comrades in the Winter Palace."

A hush fell over the crowd. It was broken only by the sound of shuffling feet as the speaker led the way to the door, followed by a hundred or more of the conservative revolutionists, who filed quietly out.

At midnight, with three fellow correspondents, I left the atmosphere of that memorable meeting, gray with smoke and charged with battle, and went in search of passes that would permit me to go to the Winter Palace.

. . .

However much the rest of Petrograd talked that night, there was one spot in the storm-tossed city where no words were wasted. This was the office of the Voina Revoliutsiony Komitlet (Military Revolutionary Committee), sprung suddenly and quietly into an existence shrouded in deep mystery.

Alex Gomberg, Russian product of New York's East Side, with an American habit of providing against emergencies, suggested that it would be useless to attempt to get through the Bolshevik lines without a pass from this committee. . . . As a friend of Trotzky, known to the members of the all-powerful committee, he undertook to arrange the necessary permits.

He led the way down the dimly lighted corridor to the farther end. A young fair-haired boy met us in an outer office, took our names and request, and disappeared into the next room, shutting the door behind him. We stared curiously after him. Beyond that door were the men who were directing the siege and capture of Petrograd— directing it so efficiently that in the days that followed, the enemies of the Bolsheviki insisted the committee was composed of Germans, because Russians were incapable of such perfect organization.

When the inside door opened again the fair-haired boy reappeared with the passes in his hand. Mine was typewritten on a bit of paper torn from a scratch-pad, numbered "Five," and stated simply:

"The Military Revolutionary Committee of the Council of Workmen's and Soldiers' Deputies allows Miss Bessie Beatty free passage all over the city."

That scrap of paper was to prove the open sesame to many closed doors before the gray dawn of morning. It bore the blue seal of the committee, the only signature capable of commanding the slightest sign of respect from a Russian bayonet that night.

The Smolney Institute is excellently located to provide seclusion for a young women's seminary, but in the middle of a cold night it seemed a long dark way from anywhere. Walking down the stairs, we speculated upon the improbability of finding an *izvostchik* abroad at such an hour.

Down in the courtyard a huge motor-truck was cranking up for departure. Its only occupants were three sailors, a young Cossack soldier with a cape of shaggy black fur that hung to his heels, and a Red Guardsman. We hailed them, and Mr. Gomberg shouted a request to be taken to town. It was drowned by the sound of the engine. He repeated it in louder tones. The sailor looked dubiously at me and at Louise Bryant, the other woman member of the party.

"It's a dangerous trip," he said. "We are going out to distribute proclamations, and we are almost certain to be shot at."

We looked at one another for a moment, considered that it was probably our only chance to reach the Winter Palace, and asked to be allowed to take the risk. Two strong hands came over the side to pull me up, and two sailors sitting on a board across the body of the truck arose to give us their seats. They held a hurried consultation, then asked us to stand again. They had decided that this exposed position would be too dangerous for women. The Cossack lad in the shaggy cape spread some proclamations on the floor of the car.

"Sit here," he said, "and when the shooting begins you can lie flat on your backs and keep your heads low."

A bundle of rifles lay on the floor under my knees, and as we started off over the cobbles I grabbed a chain and held fast to keep from being bumped out. The streets were like black cañons. Apparently there was not a human being abroad; yet every time the sailor tossed a handful of white leaflets into the air, men came darting mysteriously from doorways and courtyards to catch them.

The Cossack towered above me, rifle in hand, with eyes searching the dark for signs of danger. At the street intersections we slowed up, and groups of soldiers gathered around the bonfires crowded close to the truck for news from Smolney. They peered with curious and startled eyes into our unexpected faces, then hurried back to the circle of light around the blazing birch-wood logs. During one of these pauses Mr. Gomberg grabbed a proclamation and read it to us:

TO RUSSIAN CITIZENS

The power has gone over to the organ of the Petrograd Council of Workmen's and Soldiers' Deputies, the War Revolutionary Committee, which is at the head of the Petrograd proletariat and garrison.

The cause for which the people strive: immediate democratic peace, abolition of *pomieschik* property on land, workmen's control, the creation of a Soviet government—this business is done.

Long live the Revolution of workmen, soldiers, and peasants.

WAR REVOLUTIONARY COMMITTEE

It was one by the clock in the steeple of the Nicolaievski Station when we turned into the Nevsky. The great circle was deserted. Earlier in the day there had been fighting here, but no trace of it was visible now. . . .

[Blockades by Bolshevik soldiers created temporary difficulties in going to the Winter Palace.] It was quarter of three when we halted in the shadow of the great red arch and peered cautiously out into the dark square. There was a moment of silence; then three rifle shots shattered the quiet. We stood speechless, awaiting a return volley; but the only sound was the crunching of broken glass spread like a carpet over the cobblestones. The windows of the Winter Palace had been broken into bits.

Suddenly a sailor emerged from the black.

"It's all over!" he said. "They have surrendered."

We picked our way across the glass-strewn square, climbed the barricade erected that afternoon by the defenders of the Winter Palace, and followed the conquering sailors and Red Guardsmen into the mammoth building of dingy red stucco. On the strength of our blue-sealed passes, they permitted us to enter unquestioned. A commissaire of sailors motioned us to a bench beside the wall. A squad of sailors mounted the stairs to the council chamber, and placed the Provisional Government under arrest. Above us we could hear the sound of doors being broken open, while a searching squad went from room to room looking for hidden prisoners.

The rifles taken from the military cadets were stacked in a heap in the hall, and a solid line of victorious sailors filed in and out of the palace. The desire for souvenirs, trophies of the hour, seemed to have seized them; but the palace apparently offered little choice. One sailor came down the stairs with a coat-hanger in his hand, and another carried a sofa cushion. The best a third could find was a candle. The commissaire stopped them at the door.

"No, no, tavarisch!" he said, holding out his hand. "Pazhal'sta, pazhal'sta, you must take nothing from here."

He talked to them in a patient, reasonable tone, as one would speak to a child, and like children they gave up their plunder. One man, a soldier who had taken a blanket, protested.

"But I am cold," he said.

"I can't help it, tavarisch. If you take that, they will say we came to loot. And we did not come for loot: we came for revolution."

At that moment there was a clatter on the stairs, and I turned to see the members of the Provisional Government file slowly down. . . .

Some of them walked with defiant step and heads held high. Some were pale, worn, and anxious. One or two seemed utterly crushed and broken. The strain of that day of anxious waiting, and that night under the capricious guns of the cruiser *Aurora,* coupled with the weeks when Cabinet crisis had followed Cabinet crisis, had proved too much for them.

They marched silently off across the square, and headed for the Fortress of Peter and Paul, rising grimly out of the darkness beyond the Neva.

I sat there silently watching them go, and wondering what this night's work would mean in the future of Russia and the world. The *commissaire* who had motioned us to the seat indicated that we might now go upstairs, and we passed quickly to the council chamber. We made our way through the shattered rooms, blazing now with a million lights from the twinkling crystal chandeliers. The silk curtains hung in shreds, and here and there on the walls was the ugly scar of a recent bullet. On the whole, the destruction was much less than we had expected to find it. The attacking force had gone about its work, determined to take the palace, but to take it with as little bloodshed as possible, and in the lulls between storms they had made frequent attempts to break the resistance by fraternization. None of the defenders had been killed, but six of the sailors who had fought in the open square had paid with their lives for their revolutionary ardor, and many others had been wounded. . . .

With the surrender of the Winter Palace, the victory of the Bolsheviki was complete. The dictatorship of the proletariat had become a fact. The only power in Petrograd at dawn that morning was the power of the People's Commissaries, headed by Nicolai Lenin and Leon Trotzky, and backed by the Russian fleet, the bayonets of the Petrograd garrison, and the Red Guard rifles. . . .

Absolute quiet reigned in the city that day and the next, and such order as Russia had not known since the days immediately following the March Revolution, when the entire populace was lifted into a state of exaltation in which selfish desires played no part. Every soldier had been told that the honor of the new Revolution was in his hands. Every member of the Red Guard had been warned that provocation in all the time-tried Russian forms would be used by monarchists, counter-revolutionists, and German agents to discredit the cause of the workers. They were admonished to refrain from violence themselves, and to prevent looting wherever the slightest indication of it was found. Placards were posted upon the buildings urging precautions against disorder, and soldiers were on patrol duty at every street corner. . . .

The masses had swung away from their leaders. They had their own very definite ideas as to what they wanted. The sailors were protesting violently that the Centrabalt[3] did not represent the rank and file of the navy, and it was finally dissolved by order of the Military Revolutionary Committee. Soldiers from the ranks were charging their committees with counter-revolution, and shouting with fire in their eyes that their executives were putting off the army elections week after week because they knew they no longer had the faith of the men in the trenches and could not be reëlected. The same split had come between the peasants and their executives, and every rumor from the remote corners of Russia indicated that little villages, towns, and cities were following the lead of Petrograd, and rising in massed revolt.

The Bolsheviki had achieved a degree of success greater than they suspected. The leaders, exhausted by lack of sleep, depressed by the rejection of the *Intelligentzia,* and conscious of their inadequacy for the mere physical task of bringing bread to keep Petrograd alive, failed utterly to realize their strength. A heavy pall of discouragement settled on Smolney.

Word had come that the Cossacks were marching on the city, and that the citadel of the workers would be attacked the following morning. Petrograd poured out to fight. The factory gates opened wide, and that amazing army of the Red Guard, ununiformed, untrained, and certainly unequipped for battle with the traditional backbone of the Russian military, marched away to defend the "revolutionary capital" and the victory of the proletariat.

Women walked by the side of men, and small boys tagged along

---

[3]The Centrabalt (Central Committee of the Baltic Fleet) was organized by the Bolsheviks before July, 1917. [Ed.]

the fringes of the procession. Some of the factory girls wore red crosses upon the sleeves of their thin jackets, and packed a meager kit-bag of bandages and first-aid accessories. More of them carried shovels with which to dig trenches. The fire of the Crusaders was in their eyes, and the faith of the Christian martyrs in their souls, as they marched down the Nevsky, singing as they went, oblivious to the bitter cold that blew in from the Baltic waters, and unafraid for the first time of that foe whose very name had been a terror to countless generations of beaten, broken human beings.

4   VIEW FROM THE EMBASSY*

8 French Quay
Petrograd
November 7, 1917

My Dear —————,

NOW, my dear, there *is* some excitement, and as I write the atmosphere is punctuated by all kinds of shots—rifle, pistol, machine guns, field pieces and large guns aboard ships!

Walter and Miss Gueradhy are at the telephone getting reports from various parts of the city and I am putting down my impressions while they are fresh in my mind. It is midnight, but I am not sleepy!

Yesterday Walter was at the Admiralty, making his routine visit, when his friend there advised him to get home quickly, saying: "They are going to try again, these people!" On his way home he heard much shooting and saw the bridges being opened to prevent the Anarchists from crossing them. He came to the Lazaret for me and advised the other ladies to get home as quickly as possible, further advising them to come to our house if unable to get home.

After we reached our apartment we telephoned to all Americans we could reach, advising them of the trouble. There was street fighting, but not serious, and by midnight all seemed quiet, though there was an occasional shot.

. . .

We all prepared for bed, when very heavy guns were heard, and we learned by telephone that the Russian Cruiser *Aurora* is in the

*Pauline S. Crosley, *Intimate Letters from Petrograd* (New York: E. P. Dutton, 1920), pp. 201–13, 219–20. Copyright, 1920, by E. P. Dutton & Co., Inc. Reprinted by permission of the publishers.

river, bombarding the Winter Palace. We can see the Fortress of Peter and Paul from our front windows and the flashes of field guns there, apparently also firing at the Winter Palace.

Fortunately for the information we so desire, Walter has many friends in different parts of the city to whom it has been his custom to telephone in cases like this, and tonight the system is working so he is getting reports from all of them. They indicate that fighting is general all over the city, but hardest about the Winter Palace, where it seems the most of the Ministers of the Provisional Government have taken refuge. We have been promised this uprising for several days, in fact I wrote you last July that it would come, but, believing the Government knew as much as I did, it seemed they would be prepared for it, but the city has again fallen an easy prey to the better organized anarchists, who have had some German assistance this time in their organization.

We now have a considerable store of provisions in the house and will not suffer if forced to remain indoors, though it is another item of interest here that no one stays at home simply because there is street fighting! We even go to the ballet and opera, dodging those sections of the city where we hear shooting, both going and returning. I had another large dinner party here and no one stayed away because of the fighting.

We are wondering tonight if all the various threats of the anarchists, made in their speeches during the past few months, will be carried out! The threats included making as much misery as possible for those they do not like, and I believe they have the desire and intention to do that very thing. I have not heard of any threat or plan to really better conditions, except that it has been threatened that those who live in large handsome homes must give up some of their rooms to those less fortunate. If it comes to that I hope I may have some choice as to my boarders!

You should have seen us hiding our precious canned fruit, vegetables, condensed milk, cocoa, etc., we received from the States!

It will take a search party a long time to locate all of it; not even our domestics know where it is. . . .

Germans are thick in Petrograd now. They have offices and are "advising" the Bolsheviki, who, by the way, have taken the most famous girls' school in the country, Smolney Institute, for their Headquarters. I suppose it is no secret that the Germans are here for I met one quite openly at a tea recently.

Just now I hear no shooting, and I *am* sleepy, so I will stop. There will certainly be many people leaving here now, so I will have this ready to send by the first one of whom I learn.

You need not worry about us for we will be safe as long as any one is, and there will be foreigners in Petrograd for a long time yet.

Until next time,

Yours faithfully,

8 French Quay
Petrograd
November 12, 1917

My Dear ————,

The letter I wrote you the night of the heavy firing got away the next day, but I am not making it a matter of record who took it, because no one knows who will see *this* letter, or whether or not it will reach you! I shall keep on writing, and take advantage of all opportunities to send something out. Such chances will decrease from now on.

The heavy firing above mentioned was at "The Battle of the Winter Palace"! Said Palace was defended by a few women soldiers and some military cadets, only. Walter says he has never before seen a revolution in which the government put out of office has been defended by armed women and children alone! A few were killed and the place surrendered, all Ministers being arrested, *except Kerensky*, who fled early in an automobile commandeered from an American! He said he was going for loyal troops and would be back soon to recapture Petrograd. I will be surprised if we see him again, for *Kerensky is finished.* This is no "demonstration" such as we saw in July and I believe these people are here for a long time to come. Then there was much parading and showing of force on the streets; this time the force was here, but it was sprung suddenly in many parts of the city at the same time, with no parading at all.

There has been constant fighting since I last wrote you, but no general fight in which large numbers took part; simply fights for the possession of points desired by each side, such as the great favorite, the telephone exchange, and the various public buildings. . . .

Again there has been no government in Petrograd; no one with whom foreigners could do business; the city has been in the possession of armed soldiers, sailors and workmen, many of them intoxicated, and there was a total inability to detect who, in any given group, is the leader thereof. There *appears* to be no organization, no responsibility, though of course a great deal centers in Smolney, which is a very busy place, bristling with machine guns and others.

Walter does not go there but his "scouts" do, so we know what it looks like.

As an example of the armed bands: This morning one of these was strolling up the Quay when a Russian officer came along; nothing was said, but one of the band raised his rifle, fired, and the officer fell dead.

The band moved on without comment and without even a glance at the corpse! My friend who saw it and related the incident to me is not certain murder was intended, but is certain there was no good reason for the crime. Think of Petrograd being in the hands of such a heartless mob! . . .

The name of Lenine is prominent, as before, but also one Trotzky (Bronstein) is now in the limelight. He has been "elected" Foreign Minister, and his strong point seems to be making bloodthirsty speeches. We have a good friend who has been in the Foreign Office for some years and he tells me the following: Trotzky arrived at the Foreign Office (State Department) one morning and announced that he was the new Minister for Foreign Affairs; as he does not look like one, everybody laughed; then he felt he must make them a speech to preserve his dignity, which he did. Upon the conclusion of the speech every one except the messengers who live at the Foreign Office put on his coat and left for home! Another strike!

This is now the sixth day of the revolution, and it is still a success, with no sign of any one to really combat it. The street fighting now going on is not real opposition; it is mostly for the purpose of instituting and maintaining terror. . . .

Always affectionately,

No. 8 French Quay
Petrograd
November 20, 1917

My Dear ————,

A friend has promised this will "go out" tomorrow, so I will bring "the situation" up to date.

Each day is considerably like the one before it; street firing is less general, but continues; the weather is vile, with snow frequently; politics are worse than the weather but present nothing as clean looking as snow! . . .

"Smolney" has voted to make Lenine a Dictator! (He was already all of that.) They "vote" there with the readiness with which a hungry horse eats grass! How I wish I could keep or remember all of their "decisions"—one must read them to believe they were made—I have not seen any one with an imagination extravagant enough to believe what they decide so readily.

Some one objected to the term "menace" I used in connection with the Bolsheviki, and asked, "A menace to what?" My answer was (and will remain) "A menace to civilization; to art; to education; to beauty, morality and to life!" (If I have left out anything you consider important you may add it, because I have not discovered anything attractive in their platform *as it works out.)*

Intervention

The Soviet government quickly set about applying its program. Instituting the policy known as "War Communism," Lenin divided landlords' estates among the peasants; then nationalized the land as well as all banks and the largest industrial enterprises; repudiated the national debt; and confiscated Church property.

As for the war, the new regime made an armistice with the Central Powers and called on all belligerents to seek a democratic end to the fighting. Meanwhile, Trotsky met German representatives at Brest-Litovsk in order to negotiate a separate peace. After bitter bargaining, the two sides on March 3 finally signed a treaty by which Poland, the Ukraine, and the Baltic provinces were surrendered to German control. These were harsh terms, but they freed the Bolsheviks from a costly war effort. In any case, Lenin reassured his followers, proletarian revolutions in Germany and elsewhere would undo the work of Brest-Litovsk. (This program of world revolution soon took the institutional form of the Third International, or Comintern, an administrative and propaganda agency directing Communist parties in all countries.)

The Bolshevik Revolution and its aftermath aroused growing hostility in the United States. While the Wilson Administration refused to grant diplomatic recognition to the new regime, public spokesmen bitterly condemned Russia for her "treacherous" withdrawal from the war and her demand that the Allies revise their war aims. In a more complex fashion than before, the Russian Revolution and the World War blended together in American thinking.

Opposition to Soviet rule also developed quickly within Russia. By the beginning of 1918, General Kornilov and other "White" leaders had started to organize troops for counterrevolution. In response, Trotsky formed the Red Army to suppress the rebels. During the next two years Russia struggled through a bloody civil war, armies clashing on fronts along almost the entire perimeter of the huge country. And after an attempted assassination of Lenin, the newly created secret-police organization (Cheka) instituted the bloody Red Terror against suspected traitors among the civilian population.

In the spring of 1918, England, France, and Japan offered support to the White forces and exerted heavy pressure on the United States to participate in sending troops to eastern Siberia and northern Russia. Such a move, they said, would hasten the defeat of Germany by helping to restore the Eastern Front. The American public soon favored armed intervention with growing enthusiasm. For months President Wilson resisted these diplomatic and popular pressures; then in July a new development changed his mind.

A contingent of Czech deserters from the Austro-Hungarian armies, who had fought on the side of Russia until the Bolsheviks withdrew from the war, had arranged with Soviet authorities to travel to the Western Front via the Trans-Siberian Railroad and a global journey. After Bolshevik officials tried to disarm them, however, the Czechs joined with the White forces, seized various cities along the Trans-Siberian, and appealed to the Allied governments for help in rescuing their compatriots in the Russian interior. The Czech appeal reached Washington on July 2. Within a month the Administration officially announced that it was sending American troops, in conjunction with British and Japanese forces, to northern Russia and eastern Siberia.

More than abstract ideals was now involved in the Soviet question; the lives of sons and brothers and husbands were at stake. During the second half of 1918, American attitudes toward Russia reached a new pitch of hostility. But this feeling changed quickly after Germany signed the November armistice ending the World War. As American soldiers came home from the battlefields of Europe, the continued presence of American troops in Russia provoked more and more dissatisfaction in the United States. War weariness undermined the former support for intervention.

Among American liberals, this general dissatisfaction acquired a specially cutting edge, for it joined their increasing antipathy toward Wilson's policies. Most liberal supporters of the President had already been unhappy with his anti-Soviet policy. They soon became frankly indignant at the terms of the Versailles peace treaty, which they regarded as a betrayal of the Wilsonian ideals for which the United States had fought the war.

The first two selections—editorials from The Outlook *and* The Nation*—illustrate the typical terms in which the public debated intervention during the spring of 1918. The third selection is taken from the so-called* aide-mémoire *in which Wilson informed the Allied ambassadors of his decision to sponsor joint military intervention in Russia. (Public announcement of the decision occurred two weeks later.)*

The last two selections convey the profound disillusionment among many of Wilson's supporters after the war ended. The editors of The Dial *synthesized the prevailing attitude among liberal dissidents toward the President's Russian policies. Lincoln Steffens' letter indicates that this antipathy soon extended to Wilson's achievements at the Paris Peace Conference. Steffens was one of three men whom the Administration sent to Moscow early in 1919 to arrange for a conference among Western, Bolshevik, and White Russian representatives in order to end the civil war. The project fell through, but Steffens returned with vivid opinions about both the Soviet Revolution and Wilson's policies at Versailles.*

5   HELP FOR RUSSIA*

Sympathy for Russia's dreadful fate and hope and faith in a future Russia which shall be democratic in the true sense are universal in America. Assuredly, in the forward march of civilization Russia is bound in time to become a strong democracy. The Russian people in large numbers, probably in an actual majority, know that the rule of the Bolsheviki is not an extension of democracy, but a class absolutism which is at the same time weak and cruel.

But it is not enough to hope and believe in the future. What material aid can we give Russia now? The first reply is that the way to help Russia is to beat Germany. Today Russia is under German bonds. Vast and valuable parts of Russia are under actual German control and subject to German demands. These divisions, such as the Ukraine and Finland, are even more vassals of Germany today than are Austria and Turkey. What Germany wills in these countries must be done. The rest of western Russia is nominally under Bolshevik

---
*"Help for Russia," *Outlook*, Vol. CXIX (June 12, 1918), pp. 251–52.

rule. Practically, Germany is in a position to enforce any demand she may make. It would be exceedingly difficult for the United States to send soldiers, munitions, provisions, or money to Russia by any avenue of approach through Russia's northern or western or southern borders. These avenues are closed and marked *"Verboten."*

The only other way of approach is from the east. Japan must inevitably take a large part in any such action. Japan has the men, the ships, and the financial means, and Japan is near by. But Japan does not desire to act alone. She has said officially that she would act only with the consent and aid of her allies. The one course open to aid Russia and balk Germany is for the Allies to combine wholeheartedly in such a movement. It is quite possible for us to send a small army to the Siberian coast of the Pacific from our western coast. To this might be added British forces (a small British force is already in Vladivostok), possibly also some French and Italian forces. The combined army might be increased by a force not inconsiderable in number by gathering together from the East the Russians hunted out of their own country by the Bolsheviki, while in America itself there are thousands of Poles, Russians, and other Slavs who might be recruited in a separate body. Thus a joint expeditionary army might be formed in which the Japanese soldiers would be in the majority, but which would have for its purpose the protection of Russia, the encouragement of those hundreds of thousands of Russians in the eastern part of the Empire who are bitterly opposed to Bolshevist rule, and, as a secondary motive, the annoyance of Germany in the rear of its present military activities. This army might before long become the nucleus of a great revivified Russian army. This plan is believed by many students of the situation to be sound in principle and practical in detail. It cannot be carried out without the approval and active co-operation of the United States. If there is any better plan for getting material and military aid to Russia, it remains to be put forward. . . .

If there remains yet in this country any feeling that Russia as a nation can be helped by aiding the Bolsheviki, it is a mistaken belief based on a total misconception of the political nature of Bolshevik rule. Careless thinkers who believe that the cure for the ills of democracy is more democracy have wrongly regarded Bolshevism as an extension of democracy. It is just the reverse. The Bolsheviki are not the exponents of a new, peculiarly Russian, type of democracy. They would bring about—and have already brought about—class war and despotism by the proletariat. The rule of the unfit—the domination of all other classes by the class that is least enlightened—is not democracy. It is not even Socialism. It is class tyranny of the worst conceivable sort, and so long as it prevails there is no hope for Russia.

This is true whether we regard the leaders of the Bolsheviki as conscious agents of the German autocracy or not. There is evidence that some of them have received pay from the Imperial German Government. . . .

Aside, however, from any such evidence, the Bolsheviki have, by their course, proved themselves the enemies of popular liberty.

When, before the French Revolution, the nobles tried to disperse the States-General, it was not because the members of that assembly who represented the people were improperly chosen; it was because the nobles feared any representation of the people. When, likewise, the Russian Soviets threw the first and only legal national Constituent Assembly out of doors, it was not because its delegates were not fairly elected; if it had been, the Soviets would have proceeded to institute new elections for delegates. It was because the Bolsheviki and their tools had a minority of the delegates in the Assembly. The Bolsheviki, in short, insisted that, not the majority, but the minority, should rule. Lenine, Trotsky, and the other prophets of the new philosophy hate the *bourgeoisie* worse than they do the capitalists; they even call a peasant who owns a bit of land a *bourgeois*. Lenine declared, not merely that the proletariat should rule, but that no one outside the proletariat should have anything to do with the Government or be allowed a seat in the Constituent Assembly. All this is as far as the North Pole from the South Pole from anything resembling democracy; it is purely and simply despotism by a single class.

It is to rid Russia of this despotism and to help put her on the road toward democracy that America's help is sorely needed.

6   HOW NOT TO HELP RUSSIA*

A military expedition to Russia has become the topic of heated discussion in the last few weeks. The advocates of this measure see in it a way of restoring Russia to "normal" conditions and of making her a fighting force. A military expedition consisting of English, Japanese, and American soldiers, it is argued, would rally around itself the sound and sane elements of the Russian people; the Bolshevist usurpers would easily be overthrown, and the prostrate country would awaken to new vigorous life.

* "How Not to Help Russia," *Nation*, Vol. CVI (June 1, 1918), pp. 639–40.

That such a scheme should find even a moment's consideration only shows the extent of popular ignorance in matters concerning the Russian revolution, and the popular belief in quick remedies against fundamental social evils. The advocates of an expedition imagine the Bolsheviki to be an insignificant group of hot-headed agitators who tricked the country into disaster. Remove these pernicious individuals, they argue, and the social organism of Russia would quickly recover. The question, however, presents itself as to why the "better" elements of Russia have so little succeeded in counteracting the influence of Bolshevism, why the Bolsheviki have succeeded in holding their power far longer than any of the provisional governments after the downfall of Nicholas Romanov, and why the Bolsheviki have so easily defeated the conservative Russian generals, among whom were such popular leaders as Kaledine and Kornilov.

The obvious reason is that behind the Bolsheviki are the Councils of Workingmen, Peasants, and Soldiers, known as the Soviets, and behind the Soviets are the masses of the Russian people. The Bolshevist Government has proved to be the most stable since the collapse of the monarchy because the Bolshevist programme fitted best the ideas and inclinations of the Russian masses. These ideas may be erroneous, and many a wild Bolshevist dream has turned out to be an actual calamity for Russia. This, however, does not alter the fact that the Soviets are vitally connected with the bulk of the plain Russians. The Russian peasant, the Russian factory worker, and the other elements of laboring Russia do not believe in Milukov and do not believe in Kerensky, but they do believe in their own Soviets.

If a military expedition were now to come and start a movement to overthrow the Soviets, it would amount to declaring war against the Russian masses. However liberal the promises of the Powers behind the expedition may be, the masses will not believe them. The masses will see in the expedition an attempt to destroy their freedom. Civil war under such conditions becomes imminent. Siding with the Allied military forces we should find many of the former landlords, Cossacks, factory owners, and other conservative elements, who form a minority of the nation. Russian radicals and Socialists of an anti-Bolshevik character would hardly lend their assistance to a military expedition destined to punish Russia for the excesses of her revolution, while the Soviets would certainly call the masses to resist Allied invasion. The outcome would be deplorable in every way, Russia would be plunged into a deeper chaos of misery and destitution. The work of reconstruction now planned by the Soviet administration would become impossible. German penetration of Russia would not be stopped, and the Entente Allies would have to be charged with preventing Russian democracy from working out its own forms of life.

The advocates of military intervention in Russia overlook the fact that it is not the Soviets that have destroyed Russian transportation and the normal course of Russian industrial production; not the Soviets that have caused the wearing down of machines, tools, and implements which cannot be reproduced in Russia; not the Soviets that have ruined the financial system, the currency, and the exchange. All this was inherited by the present Government from the old régime and is, primarily, a result of the war and the backward economic condition of the country. A military dictator would not be able to provide Russian railroads with locomotives and rolling stock, Russian peasants with scythes and threshing machines, Russian industries with the equipment and instruments which they used to import from England, America, and other countries. A Government headed by Milukov or Guchkov or Grand Duke Nikolai Nikolaievitch would be no less helpless than the Government of Lenine and Trotzky; it might be even worse off, being confronted with embittered millions who would meet its decisions with contempt, scorn, and resistance.

Military intervention in Russia is the worst of all possible ways to relieve the Russian situation. Back of the plan lies the conviction that the Russian masses are hordes of savages who can be driven at will by a masterful hand. The history of the present revolution proves the fallacy of this conviction. The Russian masses lack education, culture, and habits of organization; yet they have manifested a remarkable love of freedom and a conscious tendency towards realization of industrial democracy. We must give up the idea of solving Russian problems *for* the Russian people *against* the wish of the Russian masses.

7   WILSON ON INTERVENTION*

It is the clear and fixed judgment of the Government of the United States, arrived at after repeated and very searching reconsiderations of the whole situation in Russia, that military intervention there

*Woodrow Wilson, Aide-memoire to Allied Ambassadors, July 17, 1918, *Papers Relating to the Foreign Relations of the United States, Russia,* Vol. II, pp. 288–90.

would add to the present sad confusion in Russia rather than cure it, injure her rather than help her, and that it would be of no advantage in the prosecution of our main design, to win the war against Germany. It can not, therefore, take part in such intervention or sanction it in principle. Military intervention would, in its judgment, even supposing it to be efficacious in its immediate avowed object of delivering an attack upon Germany from the east, be merely a method of making use of Russia, not a method of serving her. Her people could not profit by it, if they profited by it at all, in time to save them from their present distresses, and their substance would be used to maintain foreign armies, not to reconstitute their own. Military action is admissible in Russia, as the Government of the United States sees the circumstances, only to help the Czecho-Slovaks consolidate their forces and get into successful cooperation with their Slavic kinsmen and to steady any efforts at self-government or self-defense in which the Russians themselves may be willing to accept assistance. Whether from Vladivostok or from Murmansk and Archangel, the only legitimate object for which American or Allied troops can be employed, it submits, is to guard military stores which may subsequently be needed by Russian forces and to render such aid as may be acceptable to the Russians in the organization of their own self-defense. For helping the Czecho-Slovaks there is immediate necessity and sufficient justification. Recent developments have made it evident that that is in the interest of what the Russian people themselves desire, and the Government of the United States is glad to contribute the small force at its disposal for that purpose. It yields, also, to the judgment of the Supreme Command in the matter of establishing a small force at Murmansk, to guard the military stores at Kola, and to make it safe for Russian forces to come together in organized bodies in the north. But it owes it to frank counsel to say that it can go no further than these modest and experimental plans. It is not in a position, and has no expectation of being in a position, to take part in organized intervention in adequate force from either Vladivostok or Murmansk and Archangel. It feels that it ought to add, also, that it will feel at liberty to use the few troops it can spare only for the purposes here stated and shall feel obliged to withdraw those forces, in order to add them to the forces at the western front, if the plans in whose execution it is now intended that they should cooperate should develop into others inconsistent with the policy to which the Government of the United States feels constrained to restrict itself.

At the same time the Government of the United States wishes to say with the utmost cordiality and good will that none of the conclusions here stated is meant to wear the least color of criticism of what the other governments associated against Germany may think it wise to undertake. It wishes in no way to embarrass their choices of policy. All that is intended here is a perfectly frank and definite statement of the policy which the United States feels obliged to adopt for herself and in the use of her own military forces. The Government of the United States does not wish it to be understood that in so restricting its own activities it is seeking, even by implication, to set limits to the action or to define the policies of its associates.

It hopes to carry out the plans for safeguarding the rear of the Czecho-Slovaks operating from Vladivostok in a way that will place it and keep it in close cooperation with a small military force like its own from Japan, and if necessary from the other Allies, and that will assure it of the cordial accord of all the Allied powers; and it proposes to ask all associated in this course of action to unite in assuring the people of Russia in the most public and solemn manner that none of the governments uniting in action either in Siberia or in northern Russia contemplates any interference of any kind with the political sovereignty of Russia, any intervention in her internal affairs, or any impairment of her territorial integrity either now or hereafter, but that each of the associated powers has the single object of affording such aid as shall be acceptable, and only such aid as shall be acceptable, to the Russian people in their endeavor to regain control of their own affairs, their own territory, and their own destiny.

It is the hope and purpose of the Government of the United States to take advantage of the earliest opportunity to send to Siberia a commission of merchants, agricultural experts, labor advisers, Red Cross representatives, and agents of the Young Men's Christian Association accustomed to organizing the best methods of spreading useful information and rendering educational help of a modest sort, in order in some systematic manner to relieve the immediate economic necessities of the people there in every way for which opportunity may open. The execution of this plan will follow and will not be permitted to embarrass the military assistance rendered in the rear of the westward-moving forces of the Czecho-Slovaks.

Washington, July 17, 1918

8   WITHDRAW FROM RUSSIA!*

Following the Bolshevik success, what the whole course of events and policy has shown is that for the first time in the history of the modern world we are confronted with an economic revolution instead of a merely political revolution. The Soviet Government might have been captured by any one of the many political parties of Russia, the Mensheviki, the Right Social Revolutionary Party, even the Left Communist Party (which accuse both Lenin and Trotzky of being "reactionaries"!), and so on. It was as a matter of fact carried by the Bolshevik Party, which, in spite of reports to the contrary, gained in strength as time went on and today, after over a year of its rule, has behind it the majority support of the Russian people and can actually hope in the coming spring to have a Red Army of perhaps three million soldiers ready to lay down their lives in its defense. Why? What is the vital principle of the Bolsheviki that keeps them so long in power? From what background do they spring? What do they want?

Although these questions deserve detailed answers, we wish to state, for the sake of clearness, our belief concerning the chief points. Russians regard us, as well as many others in Western nations, as political infants. They are not content with what we glibly call democracy. Their hopes and aspirations are centered on a greater experiment than merely representative government. They are intensely communistic, more so than the people of any other country. They want actually to abolish the whole institution of private property. They want to create a government which is entirely a people's government, a government of the workers and the poor peasants. They will, if they can, abolish the capitalist class. Contrary to report, they bear no ill will against the intellectuals as a class, although they recognize the basic truth of the psychology of the intellectual class; that is, they regard the intellectuals as parasites on the so-called capitalist class. Yet they hold the professions and the arts in high honor. Their program for universal education is extensive, and is not confined to merely vocational training. The Soviet Government has encouraged individual artists, subsidized theaters and the ballet and the opera. It has reprinted the great classics of literature in inexpensive form for everybody. It recognizes the need for technical experts and for discipline of all kinds. Fundamentally, however, it is interested in

---

* "Withdraw from Russia!" *Dial*, Vol. LXV (December 14, 1918), pp. 525–28.

maintaining a workers' government, supported, as Lenin so eloquent-
ly phrased it in a speech before the Moscow Soviet, by "the regular
march of the iron battalions of the proletariat."

One point more, perhaps, needs emphasis. The universality of the
stories in the daily press about the "Red Terror" and the mass murder of the bourgeois class demands corrective. In the first place, there
was no "Red Terror" before the invasion of Russia by Allied troops.
In the second place, the executions are not irresponsible murders,
but deliberate measures of self-defense, such as any government in
similar circumstances, threatened both by internal and external enemies, invariably adopts. In the third place, the number of them has
been grossly exaggerated. In the fourth place, they do not begin to
equal the indiscriminate slaughter of Soviet officials practiced by the
invading troops (principally the Czecho-Slovaks) whenever they are
successful in overthrowing a local Soviet. In the fifth place, plots
against the Central Soviet Government have been persistent and unscrupulous, both on the part of the disgruntled Russians who have
been expropriated or who have a political axe to grind and on the
part of foreign governments, desirous of the overthrow of the present
regime. In a word, the Soviet Government has adopted the conven-
tionally harsh method of suppressing the attempts to instigate civil
war in Russia. Had the Allied Governments recognized the Soviet
Government instead of attacking it, and had they given it the cooperation and assistance which it asked, it is safe to assume that fully
nine-tenths of the present "Red Terror" would not have occurred.
Recently, moreover, thanks to Allied intervention, the Bolsheviki
have become so strong in their internal grip on the situation that
they are now in a sufficiently secure position not to need to employ
the harsher measures of the "Red Terror." The brain worker and the
petit bourgeois are no longer to be oppressed, but propitiated. The
further the armies of the Allied Governments march into Russia the
stronger becomes the movement towards reconciliation within the
country. It is an ancient phenomenon. Before the foreign enemy
domestic differences vanish—all become Russians. Well could Trotzky
state that he could have afforded to pay one hundred thousand
roubles for every Japanese soldier landed on Russian soil. The blundering policy of the Allied Governments has not only evoked the
Bolsheviki—if continued, it will make all Russia support them.

And yet this mad policy has been followed in spite of the many
attempts that the Soviet Government has made to cooperate with
the Allied Governments. There was always what one might call an

undercurrent of flirtation with the Allied Governments. For us there was open friendship: even the more fanatical recognized the difference between a medieval autocracy like Germany and a liberal republic like ourselves. . . . Time after time the Soviet Government made direct and indirect offers of commercial cooperation. And usually they signified their complete willingness to renew the war against Germany (for they never hesitated to describe the treaty of Brest-Litovsk as no other than a robber's peace) as soon as the army could be reorganized and supplied with necessary munitions and equipment. Not one of these many offers was acknowledged, much less accepted. There seemed to be a preconcerted plan not to recognize the Soviet Government under any circumstances and no matter what they offered. Since the armistice with Germany they have themselves offered an armistice to the Allied nations. More: according to the Daily News of London, Litvinoff, the representative until recently of the Soviet Government in England, has formally offered any concessions to the Allied nations including payment on the national debt by what gold is in Russia and by liberal concessions—in return for recognition of the Soviet Government by the Allied nations—and peace. But so far the consistently and sincerely friendly advances of the Soviet Government have been ignored.

Possibly one reason for this has been the star chamber method of conducting our diplomatic relations with the Soviet Government. If public opinion in the various Allied countries—ourselves included—had ever had any opportunity whatever to discuss any of these offers, the situation today might be different. But the news from Russia, particularly since the Bolsheviki have had control, has been notoriously false. The stories of massacre and anarchy are, of course, largely for effect, and are not to be taken seriously. . . . It is also well known that the various governmental censorships, principally the British, have suppressed actual news messages sent by accredited correspondents of accredited news associations from Moscow and Petrograd—messages sent by men who were not themselves Bolsheviki at all, but simply honest journalists. And many are the stories of events by "eye-witnesses" who saw no more than the inside of a hotel in Stockholm. Not a word of the constructive work being done by the Soviet Government has been given out by the press. . . . All that we are allowed are silly stories about new decrees on marriage and free love, issued (where rarely authentic) by irresponsible groups striving to put the Soviet Government in a false light. When a really first-rate analysis of what the Soviet Government is doing is published—like The Soviets at Work by Lenin—we are informed by Post-master General Burleson that it is unmailable. But the worst of all is the fashion in which the news about Allied intervention is distorted. We are led to believe that Allied troops landed in Vladivostok to restore "law and order," to put down the rule of an anarchical minority and to substitute a democratic government. It is false. There was quiet and the best of law and order at Vladivostok when Allied troops landed. The Soviet had the support and affection of the people. The Allied troops did not set up a democratic government: they set up a reactionary dictatorship. We are prepared to prove that in every case where Allied troops have invaded Russian soil they have overthrown the popular government and set up a temporary government resting for its support on foreign bayonets, a government reactionary and in some cases even frankly monarchist. It is safe to say that the average American citizen would be thoroughly shocked at knowing the kind of imperialistic and anti-democratic game which is being played by our own and our Allies' armies in Russia. These are facts and we think it high time that they be told. We do not believe that our own Government wants the restoration of the monarchy in Russia or that it would support a demonstrably unpopular government forever. The American Government would like to see in Russia a liberal and commercial republic like ourselves—a quiet, respectable government with which we could do business. Undoubtedly. But what we should like and what we are as a matter of cold fact getting are two widely different things. It is no secret that powerful parties in Japan are advocating the unostentatious annexation of large sections of Siberia, and that they have no interest in seeing any stable popular government arise east of the Urals. It is no secret that England trembles for Persia, Afghanistan, and India, and that the Tory party would gladly crush the Russian Revolution if it exhibited any tendency towards proselytism in foreign countries (as it has). It is no secret that a certain section of French governmental opinion cares not a fig what sort of a reactionary government there is in Russia, provided only it is a government that will immediately repay the foreign loan. In a word, our intervention in Russia may have been undertaken with the best of intentions, *but the practical situation with which we are faced today is either to support reaction and imperialism or—to withdraw our troops.* Russian intervention has become for America a tragic anachronism since the defeat of Germany. We have neither a national nor an international interest which today legitimately sanctions the presence of our troops on Russian

soil. It is false to our traditions to be fighting a workingman's republic, even if we do not approve of its form or its manners. It is not in
accordance with any doctrine of American national policy for us to
be engaged in crushing a revolution or in crucifying the hopes and
aspirations of a great and mighty people. It is really difficult to
believe that this is the same country which in Washington's time
almost had a civil war because this government refused to intervene
in the French Revolution, *on behalf of the revolutionists.* And not
even the most severe critics of the present leaders of the Soviet Government have said one-tenth as bitter things as were said of Robespierre and Marot in their day. No; to help crush a revolution is not
in accordance with the real American tradition.

For that reason we demand of our Government that our troops
now in Russia be immediately withdrawn. We are asking no more
than British Labor and French Labor and Italian Labor have already
officially demanded of their governments. We are asking no more
than President Wilson has again and again promised to the Russian
people- "We are fighting," said the President in his communication
to the Provisional Government of Russia on June 9, 1917, "for the
liberty, the self-government, and the undictated development of all
peoples, and every feature of the settlement that concludes this war
must be conceived and executed for that purpose." We are asking no
more than would ask, if they knew the facts, and do ask, those who
are aware of them, the soldiers who entered this war inspired by an
honest ideal to defeat the menace of German autocracy and to bring
freedom to the oppressed peoples of the world. Those who have
given their lives on the battlefields of France will rise to reproach us
if we are now false to our trust. We have fought for freedom, and as
the President has said, the undictated development of all peoples. We
demand that Russia have her fair chance at that freedom and self-
development, and that if we are in no position to direct or guide the
actions of other nations with respect to her *we* at least shall leave her
free to work out her own destiny. Let a war which has not been declared by the nation we are fighting, or by ourselves, cease. And let
those representatives of Russia who speak for the majority of the
Russian people and not for interested cliques of intriguers have a
voice and a hearing at the peace conference.

We demand that freedom of communication with Russia be at
once restored, and that the whole truth be permitted to appear without let or hindrance in our periodicals; that the motives back of intervention, be they either political or economic or what not, be given

to the American people in order that they may have full knowledge and may of themselves determine whether or not they are willing to back up the present intervention in Russia and what is the logical further activity implied by that intervention. We demand that the open diplomacy for which the President has declared be practiced with respect to Russia. We demand, in a single word, *the truth.* We have lived for the last year in a poisonous atmosphere of lies and slander and intrigue and double-dealing. As Americans, who honestly believe that we speak for the sober second thought of this country and for those who have no organ of publicity or appeal, we demand that once and for all the clean wind of the truth be allowed to sweep away the false conceptions and interested propaganda which have infected the country. We demand of our Government a clear formulation and simple, honest statement of its Russian policy. We demand that that policy be based on the facts and not on lies, that that policy be American and American alone.

9   SPREAD OF CLASS WAR INEVITABLE*

Paris, April 13, 1919

My Dear Allen:

. . . We are going to have a League of Nations, weak, wrong, capable of great abuse; and we shall get a peace also, full of dynamite which will burst into war,—unless,—there is something else in sight. The rulers of the world have sat here with the problem of human living before them, laid out on their table by the tragedy of war. That should have opened their minds and hearts too and led them to tackle the job in some new, big way. They wanted to. There was good-will here. But their old bad habits of mind, their fixed attention upon things they do not really want, their age, their education,—these have made it impossible for them to do their work. Even Wilson couldn't. Even he did not have knowledge enough, and of the right kind, to proceed to the removal of the causes of our troubles.

So they have failed. They have the appearance of success, but,— they have failed. And it does not matter. The problem will be solved. Other, newer men, with a fresher culture,—the men I have seen lately,

*Lincoln Steffens to Allen H. Suggett, April 13, 1919, *The Letters of Lincoln Steffens,* Ella Winter and Granville Hicks (eds.) (2 vols., New York: Harcourt, Brace, 1938), Vol. I, p. 466. Copyright, 1938, by Harcourt, Brace & World, Inc.; renewed, 1966, by Ella Winter and Granville Hicks and reprinted by permission of the publishers.

—they will have their turn now. And they are on the job. Their minds are clear of all the trash which blinds these Paris Conferees. They know that liberty, democracy, fraternity,—all these lovely old desires can come only after men have made sure that there is food enough to eat, safety for themselves and their children, warmth, shelter, work and full pay. And these are the things they are after. They know what the price may be: sickness, death, civil war. How we have been working for the past two weeks to break the line of that civil war! Well, we haven't done it. We still may. But I begin to doubt it. I think now that the stupid class war is inevitable all over Europe.

Len

Red Scare

The Soviet question not only contributed to the widening split between Wilson and many liberals during 1919. It also played a key role in a nationwide antiradical hysteria known as the Red Scare. Before the tumult subsided in mid-1920, Attorney General A. Mitchell Palmer had arrested almost 5,000 allegedly Communist aliens in 33 cities and had deported 249 of them to Russia.

During a speech to the Senate, Henry L. Myers of Montana described the relationship between domestic radicalism and Soviet Communism in the following terms.

10 SYMPATHY TOWARD BOLSHEVISM WIDESPREAD*

The widespread sympathy or semi-sympathy in this country with the Soviet Government of Russia is alarming. It appears to pervade all classes of people and all ranks of society. It appears to have some hold in colleges and schools. It has adherents in the ranks of fashion. It has some adherents among the well-to-do and intelligent. It is astounding that some people who appear to be educated, intelligent, native Americans will express more or less sympathy with the Soviet Government of Russia. I have encountered some of it which has amazed me. . . .

_____

*Congressional Record, 66th Cong., 2nd sess. (April 28, 1920), pp. 6207–12.

Sympathy with bolshevism seems to be getting a hold in the public-school system of parts of the country. There are sporadic instances of it which should serve as a warning of what may be found more extensively under cover. It is reported that about a year ago a teacher in one of the public schools of Washington, in talking on current topics to her pupils, expressed a tolerant feeling for bolshevism, and undertook to give "the other side," the pleasing side, of bolshevism, and instead of unsparingly condemning it, warned her pupils that they should not be too quick to condemn bolshevism. To my mind this is horrible, shocking. So far as I know, this charge has never been denied. The school board of the District of Columbia took cognizance of it and undertook to discipline that teacher for her shockingly indiscreet expressions. . . .

There are hundreds of publications in the United States which are openly praising the Soviet Government of Russia or advocating the overthrow of our Government, or doing both. Many of them are printed in foreign languages and circulate among the ignorant, prejudiced, easily misled class of foreigners, most of whom can read no language other than their own and rely upon their foreign-language papers for all of their information and guidance. It is impossible to know what these foreign-language periodicals are publishing unless their articles are translated into English. To keep track of their publications and translate their every utterance is a tremendous task. Department of Justice officials, I believe, undertake it, but it imposes an undue burden on them. The publishers should be required to print their publications in English or suspend. There is in my State a daily paper which, I am informed, continually praises the Soviet Government of Russia and holds it up as a model. . . .

I believe there are many people who express feelings of leniency for or sympathy with the Soviet Government of Russia who do not know anything about it, do not know what it is. I believe there are millions of people in this country who are indifferent to it, who have no knowledge whatever of the character of that Government.

All the while emissaries in this country of that Government are "boring from within" and injecting the insidious poison of their virus into the veins of our body politic, misleading credulous people and doing incalculable harm. I think the American people need to be aroused. The people appear to be asleep to the dangers that are in their very midst and which are daily growing. I think the people of the United States should be awakened from their lethargy and made to know something of the Government which is daily being loudly

Gale in the Los Angeles Times

On the Threshold!

praised in this country as superior to our own time-tried and tested Government. Let us see what kind of a Government it is they have in Russia which we are being daily advised is the model Government. . . .

It appears that the Government of Russia, under the general supervision of those criminal despots and anarchists, Lenin and Trotski, is divided into different jurisdictions, much as this country is divided into the different jurisdictions of the several States of the Union. Instead of being called States there they are called soviets. The proletarians of each city of any considerable size, together with the surrounding country, more or less extensive, tributary to the city and controlled by its forces, constitute a soviet or local government. Those within that jurisdiction who are permitted to take part issue the decrees which constitute the laws of that soviet or jurisdiction. Thus the laws of different soviets differ to some extent. Some are worse than others, although all are bad enough. Let us see what some of them are. Vladimir is the capital of the Province of the same name, 75 miles from Moscow. A decree issued by the soviet of the city of Vladimir follows:

> Any girl having reached her eighteenth year and not having married is obliged, subject to the most severe penalty, to register at the bureau of free love of the commissariat of surveillance.
>
> Having registered at the bureau of free love, she has the right to choose from among the men between the ages of 19 and 50 a cohabitant husband.
>
> Remarks—(1) The consent of the man in the said choice is unnecessary. (2) The man on whom such a choice falls has no right to make any protest whatsoever against the infringement.
>
> The right to choose from a number of girls who have reached their eighteenth year is also given to men.
>
> The opportunity to choose a husband or wife is to be presented once a month.
>
> The bureau of free love is autonomous.
>
> Men between the ages of 19 and 50 have the right to choose from among the registered women, even without the consent of the latter, in the interests of the State.
>
> Children who are the issue of these unions are to become the property of the State.

It appears that in the jurisdiction of that soviet "marriage," such as it is, is contracted to last but a month, and that at the end of a month either party may dissolve it at will, without cause or formality, by contracting another "marriage" for a month with another partner, and that this performance may be repeated ad infinitum once a month. Children resulting from such cohabitant state become the property of the State. . . .

Mr. President, could anything be more horrible and shocking? It is astounding and beyond comprehension that such a state of affairs can exist in the world of today, in any country which has ever claimed to be even semicivilized. It is shocking beyond expression to every sense of decency. It is worse than the practices of the most barbarous tribes of darkest Africa. Even among them a sort of mating of the sexes, a crude form of matrimony, is recognized and upheld. This beats the heathen. This is recognized, legalized, universal prostitution. It sinks to a lower depth than dumb brutes. Russia is a disgrace to the world. . . .

They have utterly destroyed marriage, the home, the fireside, the family, the corner stones of all civilization, all society. They have undertaken to destroy what God created and ordained. They defy alike the will of God, the precepts of Christianity, the decrees of civilization, the customs of society. It is hard to realize that such things exist and are tolerated by the civilized world.

The time has come when we should use plain, unvarnished language, when naked facts should be stated. The time has come when the men and women of this country who are loyal should be told the plain truth about the Soviet Government of Russia, which is being eulogized and defended in this country and declared to be a better government than ours, even though the telling cause decency to falter and bring the blush of shame to those who tell and to those who hear or read.

This, in brief, is a description of the government which is daily being held up in this country as an example for us, and which is declared by some to be superior to our form of government. This is the character of government which some people in our midst would have established in this country. This is the government toward which some fairly respectable people in this country exhibit a lenient and tolerant feeling. This is the government of which there is some talk of recognition by this country. There are people in this country who declare our Government should recognize the Lenin and Trotski government of Russia as a reputable government, and that we should appoint an ambassador to it and receive an ambassador from it and with which we should, they say, conduct generally diplomatic negotiations and business, and to which we should extend full diplomatic recognition. That has been suggested by high authority in this country. . . .

The despots of Russia are doing their best to spread their vile system of anarchy to the entire world. They boast of it. Their minions have invaded this fair country and their seed sown here is bearing fruit.

In the last few months 3,000 arrests of radical Reds, agitators, and undesirable aliens have been made by agents of the Department of Justice, with a view to their deportation. I have no doubt all of them are highly undesirable and are guilty of disloyal activities. I have no doubt this country would be better off if all of them were deported to the countries from which they came or tied in bags and dumped into the middle of the ocean. The Department of Justice claims to have adequate evidence against all of them and claims all of them are just subjects of deportation. A recent statement issued by the Department of Labor, which by an anomalous arrangement of law is given the power of passing judgment in deportation cases, shows that of the 3,000 persons arrested only 390 have been ordered deported, while 933 have been dismissed. The remainder doubtless are out on bail or have had their cases otherwise disposed of without any penalty. That less than 400 of 3,000 have been ordered deported, after months of investigation and resistance of the processes of the law, it seems to me is an unsatisfactory condition of affairs. That the Department of Justice would cause to be arrested twenty-six hundred people in a few months, with a view to their deportation, with no adequate evidence against them, is to me unbelievable. The Department of Justice gets the evidence before making arrests. There appears to be in the Department of Labor a marked reluctance to deport these disturbers of the Government which I think lamentable and alarming.

The activities of those who would undermine and overturn our Government are undoubtedly increasing. They appear to go on with little check or hindrance. In my opinion the country is honeycombed underneath the surface with the vicious activities of hydraheaded monsters and cunning plotters, who are scattering the poison of their malignant virus and working day and night for the overthrow of the best Government which the world has ever seen, where more liberty is given to the masses, more freedom to its citizens, more rights to its workingmen, more privileges to the whole populace than in any other Government under the sun. In my opinion this country is reeking and seething with the machinations of disloyalty, sedition, and bolshevism. Their proponents are becoming bold. They have defenders and sympathizers in high places.

What is the remedy? The Attorney General of the United States says there is not sufficient law to combat these conditions, to prevent their growth, to punish such deadly malefactors. He says the country is in need of more efficient and drastic laws to enable the Government to fight its insidious foes and preserve its safety. Very well; I say, then, let us enact more law. Let us have laws that are adequate and sufficiently drastic. Self-preservation is the first law of nature as applied to nations as well as individuals. Months ago the Senate passed a bill known as the Sterling sedition bill, to give the officials of the Government more power in suppressing and punishing sedition and disloyalty, intended to save us from those in our midst who are, with safety to themselves, "boring from within." The House of Representatives has not yet passed that bill nor any other of its kind. I hope it may yet do so, but time is fleeting and the danger grows. What the Congress of the United States needs is some of the backbone evinced by the New York Legislature when it expelled from its membership five men who had been proven to the satisfaction of the legislature disloyal to their country. I honor the New York Legislature for its brave and patriotic act. . . .

It is said by some who oppose the proposed legislation that it would be a blow at liberty; that it would invade the right of free speech and the right of freedom of the press. I believe in liberty and in freedom of speech and press, but I do not believe in that liberty or that freedom of speech or press which is license to advocate the overthrow by force or violence, plotting or scheming, of the best and freest Government ever established by man.

However, with this combined class opposition, with the very pronounced opposition of leaders of organized labor, and with the great masses of the American people lethargic and indifferent, I regard it exceedingly doubtful if the Attorney General of the United States will be given the power and the legislation which he says is necessary to protect this Government from its enemies within. The Congress of the United States is too subservient to the decrees of organized labor. Some people say we should placate these enemies of our Government, these disturbers of the peace, these radical agitators, and reds by giving them what they want and removing the cause of their unrest. Some people in high places advocate this. Well, that is one way of removing unrest. Of course, if a man is going to rob a bank you can keep him from robbing it by giving him all the money there is in the bank. That would temporarily remove the unrest of the would-be robber, but it would not give a very restful feeling to the depositors and stockholders of the bank. If a man wants possession of my house and home and threatens to burn it down and kill me unless he gets it, I can placate him by moving out and letting him move in. I suppose that would temporarily remove his unrest, but it would be paying a pretty high price for the cure. It would be pretty hard on me and my family. There has been too much yielding to the demands of this element. . . .

The truth is, for Bolshevism there is neither cause nor justification. It can not be remedied by human agencies. Bolshevism is simply hell in the hearts of men and women; it is hell in the hearts of people who are natural criminals. It can not be removed from their hearts by human means. The only effective eradicator of the seeds of Bolshevism in the hearts of people there can be is by act of God. What this country needs and what the world needs more than anything else is a great revival of religion. If men and women everywhere had in their hearts the spirit of the Savior of mankind, there would be no Bolshevism.

That, though, can not be brought about by legislation. However, legislation can, by gripping the situation and providing drastic laws for prevention and punishment, deter people from acts of Bolshevism, disloyalty, and sedition, and from teaching their vile doctrines, or punish them after committing such acts or teaching such doctrines, and thereby keep within the bounds of safety this criminal spirit. Many people are kept good only through fear of the law. Many a man would commit acts of robbery or other lawlessness if not deterred by fear of punishment at the hands of the law. Nobody but God can take out of a wicked man's heart the criminal instinct, but the law can prevent him from exercising it, or, as a deterrent to others, punish him if he does exercise it.

Congress should take hold of this situation firmly, without fear or favor. It can remedy it. The conditions of which I speak will continue and will increase unless our Government takes hold of them with a firm hand and adopts stern repressive measures for its own protection, especially the legislative branch of the Government. We whipped the redskins to obtain possession of this country, we whipped the Red Coats to achieve its independence, and we must not let the red-hearted and red-handed overthrow it. "Down the reds" has been our practice. It should now be our motto. These red malefactors and enemies of good government should be made to feel the stripes and see the stars—the stripes and stars of the glorious American flag.

Nonrecognition

By mid-1920, popular attitudes and official policies toward the Soviets settled into a more temperate condition. Once it was clear that Lenin's regime had overcome the counterrevolutionary armies, the United States government withdrew all its troops from Russian soil. At the same time, however, it reaffirmed in unmistakable terms its refusal to recognize the Soviet rulers.

On August 10, 1920, Secretary of State Bainbridge Colby publicly defined the official United States policy toward the Bolshevik regime.

11 DEFINITION OF OFFICIAL POLICY*

Washington, August 10, 1920

From the beginning of the Russian Revolution, in March, 1917, to the present moment, the Government and the people of the United States have followed its development with friendly solicitude and with profound sympathy for the efforts of the Russian people to reconstruct their national life upon the broad basis of popular self-government. The Government of the United States, reflecting the spirit of its people, has at all times desired to help the Russian people. In that spirit all its relations with Russia, and with other nations in matters affecting the latter's interests, have been conceived and governed.

The Government of the United States was the first government to acknowledge the validity of the Revolution and to give recognition to the Provisional Government of Russia. Almost immediately thereafter it became necessary for the United States to enter the war against Germany and in that undertaking to become closely associated with the Allied Nations, including, of course, Russia. The war weariness of the masses of the Russian people was fully known to this Government and sympathetically comprehended. Prudence, self-interest and loyalty to our associates made it desirable that we should give moral and material support to the Provisional Government, which was struggling to accomplish a two-fold task, to carry on the

---

*Secretary of State to Italian Ambassador, August 10, 1920, *Papers Relating to the Foreign Relations of the United States, 1920,* Vol. III, pp. 463–68.

war with vigor and, at the same time, to reorganize the life of the nation and establish a stable government based on popular sovereignty.

Quite independent of these motives, however, was the sincere friendship of the Government and the people of the United States for the great Russian nation. The friendship manifested by Russia toward this nation in a time of trial and distress has left us with an imperishable sense of gratitude. It was as a grateful friend that we sent to Russia an expert commission to aid in bringing about such a reorganization of the railroad transportation system of the country as would reinvigorate the whole of its economic life and so add to the well-being of the Russian people.

While deeply regretting the withdrawal of Russia from the war at a critical time, and the disastrous surrender at Brest-Litovsk, the United States has fully understood that the people of Russia were in no wise responsible.

The United States maintains unimpaired its faith in the Russian people, in their high character and their future. That they will overcome the existing anarchy, suffering and destitution we do not entertain the slightest doubt. The distressing character of Russia's transition has many historical parallels, and the United States is confident that restored, free and united Russia will again take a leading place in the world, joining with the other free nations in upholding peace and orderly justice. . . .

That the present rulers of Russia do not rule by the will or the consent of any considerable proportion of the Russian people is an incontestable fact. Although nearly two and a half years have passed since they seized the machinery of government, promising to protect the Constituent Assembly against alleged conspiracies against it, they have not yet permitted anything in the nature of a popular election. At the moment when the work of creating a popular representative government based upon universal suffrage was nearing completion the Bolsheviki, although, in number, an inconsiderable minority of the people, by force and cunning seized the powers and machinery of government and have continued to use them with savage oppression to maintain themselves in power.

Without any desire to interfere in the internal affairs of the Russian people, or to suggest what kind of government they should have, the Government of the United States does express the hope that they will soon find a way to set up a government representing their free will and purpose. When that time comes, the United States will consider the measures of practical assistance which can be taken to promote the restoration of Russia, provided Russia has not taken itself wholly out of the pale of the friendly interest of other nations, by the pillage and oppression of the Poles.[1]

It is not possible for the Government of the United States to recognize the present rulers of Russia as a government with which the relations common to friendly governments can be maintained. This conviction has nothing to do with any particular political or social structure which the Russian people themselves may see fit to embrace. It rests upon a wholly different set of facts. These facts, which none dispute, have convinced the Government of the United States, against its will, that the existing regime in Russia is based upon the negation of every principle of honor and good faith, and every usage and convention, underlying the whole structure of international law; the negation, in short, of every principle upon which it is possible to base harmonious and trustful relations, whether of nations or of individuals. The responsible leaders of the regime have frequently and openly boasted that they are willing to sign agreements and undertakings with foreign Powers while not having the slightest intention of observing such undertakings or carrying out such agreements. This attitude of disregard of obligations voluntarily entered into, they base upon the theory that no compact or agreement made with a non-Bolshevist government can have any moral force for them. They have not only avowed this as a doctrine, but have exemplified it in practice. Indeed, upon numerous occasions the responsible spokesmen of this Power, and its official agencies, have declared that it is their understanding that the very existence of Bolshevism in Russia, the maintenance of their own rule, depends, and must continue to depend, upon the occurrence of revolutions in all other great civilized nations, including the United States, which will overthrow and destroy their governments and set up Bolshevist rule in their stead. They have made it quite plain that they intend to use every means, including, of course, diplomatic agencies, to promote such revolutionary movements in other countries.

It is true that they have in various ways expressed their willingness to give "assurances" and "guarantees" that they will not abuse the privileges and immunities of diplomatic agencies by using them for this purpose. In view of their own declarations, already referred to, such assurances and guarantees cannot be very seriously regarded. Moreover, it is within the knowledge of the Government of the United States that the Bolshevist Government is itself subject to the

[1] This is a reference to the Russo-Polish War of 1920–21. [Ed.]

control of a political faction, with extensive international ramifications through the Third Internationale, and that this body, which is heavily subsidized by the Bolshevist Government from the public revenues of Russia, has for its openly avowed aim the promotion of Bolshevist revolutions throughout the world. The leaders of the Bolsheviki have boasted that their promises of non-interference with other nations would in no wise bind the agents of this body. There is no room for reasonable doubt that such agents would receive the support and protection of any diplomatic agencies the Bolsheviki might have in other countries. Inevitably, therefore, the diplomatic service of the Bolshevist Government would become a channel for intrigues and the propaganda of revolt against the institutions and laws of countries, with which it was at peace, which would be an abuse of friendship to which enlightened governments cannot subject themselves.

In the view of this Government, there cannot be any common ground upon which it can stand with a Power whose conceptions of international relations are so entirely alien to its own, so utterly repugnant to its moral sense. There can be no mutual confidence or trust, no respect even, if pledges are to be given and agreements made with a cynical repudiation of their obligations already in the mind of one of the parties. We cannot recognize, hold official relations with, or give friendly reception to the agents of a government which is determined and bound to conspire against our institutions; whose diplomats will be the agitators of dangerous revolt; whose spokesmen say that they sign agreements with no intention of keeping them. . . .

The policy herein outlined will command the support of this Government.

Accept [etc.]   *Bainbridge Colby*

II

FROM NEP TO THE PLAN
1921-1932
the question of capitalism

NEP

By the end of 1920, the Moscow regime had suppressed the last of the organized counterrevolutionary movements. Soviet Russia was safe, but it also was devastated. Four years of world war, two years of civil war, and Allied intervention and blockade had ruined the country's economy. The policy of "War Communism" had also produced economic deterioration by inciting the peasantry to destroy its crops rather than surrender them to government requisitions. Finally, a severe drought magnified the food shortage still further. Angered, hungry, and desperate, the peasants and factory workers staged numerous riots.

Toward the end of February, 1921, the naval garrison at Kronstadt mutinied in a violent expression of discontent with Communist policies. The Soviet government suppressed the uprising after much bloodshed, but Lenin concluded from this evidence, as well as from the general economic crisis in Russia, that socialization had been imposed too quickly. On March 17, therefore, he announced to the Tenth Communist Party Congress a New Economic Policy (NEP). Calling a halt to the rigid policies of War Communism, the Soviet premier proposed a much larger degree of internal private trade and enterprise, although maintaining state ownership of the basic produc-

*tive industries. The new economic system was termed "state capital-
ism." As Lenin explained, the NEP was only a "strategic retreat"
preparatory to a more gradual return to socialism.*

*This basic shift in policy produced enormous impact on American
observers of the Soviet scene. During the next few years, commentators excitedly evaluated the significance of the NEP, both in terms
of Russia's future and in terms of Soviet-American relations.*

*Americans responded to the NEP in diverse ways, including con-
sternation, confidence, and sarcasm, according to their ideological
premises. Floyd Dell, a staff member of the pro-Soviet journal,* The
Liberator, *analyzed the reactions among left-wing intellectuals. In an
interview with a* New York Times *correspondent in Riga, Senator
Joseph I. France of Maryland expressed a very different sort of view.
Lastly,* Time *magazine synthesized the attitudes of many, perhaps
most, Americans toward the Soviet "strategic retreat."*

12 THE TIME OF DULL REALITIES*

"Revolutions have their periods of poetry and their periods of
prose. The Russian Revolution has entered now into its prose period.
The time of revolutionary glory, tragic and beautiful, has passed; and
the time of revolutionary work, sober and stern, has begun. The time
of wonderful dreams is over, and the time of dull realities has come."

So say many of our friends, who shared with us here as dazzled
onlookers the poetry and the glory and the dream of that revolutionary dawn, when it was bliss to be alive, and to be young was very
heaven. And now, when we ask them to share with us, again as onlookers only, for that as yet is all the part assigned us by destiny, the
sober, realistic, everyday triumphs of the revolution in its prose period, they turn to us and ask: "Is this reality enough to satisfy you,
after those great dreams? Don't you feel a little fooled? Was it all
worth while? Is this what you wanted? Or—speak candidly now!—is
the Revolution, after all, a failure? Inevitably so—nobody's fault—the
best that could be expected—nothing to cry about—but still, different
from what we all did expect—in short, pretty small potatoes, after
such tremendous hopes! How about it?"

We may fairly ask ourselves that question. Are we disappointed?
Is this prose Russia worth all our dreams?

---

*Floyd Dell, "The Russian Idea," *Liberator,* Vol. V (January, 1922), pp. 26–27.

To ask that question is, to begin with, to set a pretty high price on dreams. I do. The bourgeois world today is spiritually bankrupt because it paid out too much in dreams, no less than in money, in the late war, and got nothing in return. If it were true that our revolutionary dreams had been betrayed by the realistic facts of Soviet Russia today, then that would mean the spiritual bankruptcy of the revolutionary movement for many a long day. But is it true?

This, I think, is true: That all the unfulfilled ideals of the eighteenth century, all the magnificent dreams of Rousseau and Tom Paine and Blake and young Wordsworth, all the large promises of Jefferson and Danton for a new and free and happy social order—all the hopes that culminated in the American and French Revolutions, and were travestied and betrayed so tragically in subsequent history— those beautiful Utopian dreams have somehow, in the minds of some of us onlookers, got entangled with the specific promises of the revolutionary Communists of Russia. I think the dead who died in vain to create a free America and a French Republic and a beautiful and orderly and happy new society have a right to sit up in their graves and laugh sardonically at the America of Rockefeller and Gary and Harding, at the France that plots to restore Czardom in Russia, at the whole modern capitalist world of unemployment, misery and war. They were fooled: it was not so nominated in the land of the Declaration of Independence and the speeches of Robespierre. Nothing was said by the prophets and poets who whooped it up for the bourgeois revolution about strikes and panics and militarism and the twelve-hour day in Pittsburg. But if we blame Lenin because he has not created a Utopia, that is our own mistake. It was not Lenin, it was Rousseau and Jefferson who promised us that. We cannot present the unfulfilled dreams of the last century to Lenin to be paid off. He said nothing about creating a Utopia in Russia. He knew better.

From the first he said nothing about absolute "freedom" to be ushered in at once. He called it what it is—a bourgeois dream. Instead, he talked of work, of discipline, of machinery, of the factory-system, of electrification.

He said nothing about absolute "happiness" except the happiness that comes in a devoted and unceasing struggle against tragic odds, and the useful and creative happiness that will come to the world of labor when Communism is at last established.

Those who are disappointed in Russia for failing to create the freedom and happiness promised a century and a quarter ago by the deluded prophets of the rising bourgeoisie, are simply a little mixed.

Nevertheless, there is a difference between prose and poetry. In these days of revolutionary prose, it is a good thing to turn back to its poetic period, to remind ourselves of the glory of that dawn, and to try our confidence in the sober realities of today by the glorious hopes of yesterday.

Albert Rhys Williams has written a book which recovers for us, in all its tragic and immortal loveliness, the poetry of that yesterday. It is called "Through the Russian Revolution." As everyone knows, Albert Rhys Williams went through the revolution not only as an onlooker, but as an active participant. He actually saw more of its central and critical events than anyone else, Russian or foreigner. And he has, not hastily, but as a devoted and deliberate labor of love, made a record of these events that will stand as an enduring memorial of them to other generations than ours. He has captured, in his ringing prose, the dramatic soul of that revolutionary time—its hopes, its tragedies, its triumphs, are all here, set down with love and faith and tenderness. It is bright with all the fires that burned in the revolutionary heart of Russia. It is, for all the sad and terrible things it tells of, a happy book—all the happier in that among its pages are many bright-colored revolutionary posters in which one can see the hopes and daring and creative faith of Russia pouring itself out in magnificent defiance of the disasters by which it is hemmed in on every side. It is the book of the Russian Revolution—the book of its achievement and its promise.

I turn in this book to one of the pages of retrospect in which Albert Rhys Williams, in this day of the prose of revolution, casts a glance backward over the whole course of events, and I find this passage:

> Nearly everyone in this book is now in his grave. Here is the way some of them died:
> Volodarsky—Assassinated in the general plot to kill all Soviet leaders.
> Neibus—Executed on the Kolchak front.
> Yanishev—Bayonetted by a White Guard on the Wrangel front.
> Woskov—Died of typhus on the Denikin front.
> Tunganogi—Shot at his desk by White Guards.
> Utkin—Dragged from motor car and shot.
> Sukhanov—Led into the woods in the early morning and clubbed to death with rifle butts.
> Melnikov—Taken out of prison, shot and bludgeoned.
> . . . They went to their death in order that the Revolution might live.

And he asks: "Is the Revolution worth these sacrifices?"

He gives an answer to the question, an answer in honest revolutionary prose, mentioning such everyday things as farms, factories, schools and libraries; and one thing which is not familiar and everyday—the breaking of the spell of past over a great people. But the whole book is the answer to that question. In its pages we see these men not only die for the Revolution, but live for the Revolution—and their lives are a testimony that if they could look from their graves at the sober triumph of the Revolution today they would not feel that they had died in vain.

For in their lives there was no such distinction as, for the purpose of this argument, we have permitted our idealistic friends to make, between the poetry and the prose, the dreams and the realities, of revolution—not even such a distinction as appears to the most sympathetic of us at a distance. "They were," says Comrade Williams, "at once dreamers and hard workers, idealists and stern realists—the flower of the Revolution. The incarnation of its dynamic spirit." They had then the same sober, practical tasks as these in which Soviet Russia is engaged today—the manifold problem of bringing Communist order out of the chaos of Czardom. And over that work today there broods the same dream, the same hope, as yesterday. Blockade, war, pestilence and famine have not broken the Russian spirit. Abandoned by the workers of other lands, Russia fights alone. Factories may be nationalized or de nationalized; there may be government monopoly, or free trading; these are incidents of the day's work—experiments, resolutely tried, candidly abandoned, to be used again to-morrow, or not, as circumstances may dictate. Our idealistic friends see in these incidents a forsaking of the ideal, a relapse into the accustomed ways of the world. But we do not see Russia as yet welcomed into the comity of capitalist nations—*they* can tell the difference between Lenin and Judge Gary, even if our idealistic friends cannot.

There are, I am sorry to note, idealists in Russia who evince their disappointment in the un-Utopian character of the Soviet State by throwing bombs at its officials, by blowing up bridges, by plotting with emigres and foreign adventurers, by spreading lies about Russian affairs among credulous foreign visitors. But they are not called idealists in Russia—they are called counter-revolutionists.

These belated idealists among us onlookers deserve no such opprobrious term. There must be revolutionists before there can be counter-revolutionists. I certainly have no right to throw the first stone—or even the first mud—at them. But I think they might be quietly reminded that this is not their revolution. Their revolution happened back at the end of the eighteenth century. Their glorious dreams of freedom and happiness—not ours—have been mocked by history. Our dreams are coming true in Russia, day by day. . . . And when, some day, they come true in America, they will come by the same hard, idealistic road—and they will be made to come true by those who want something more definite, something better, something more real, than the eighteenth-century bourgeois dream of "freedom and happiness."

Perhaps, when that day comes, our idealistic friends will not like it—at all! But I must confess that I, for one, don't really very much care whether they do or not.

13   A CASE FOR RECOGNITION*

"Russia is reverting to capitalism inevitably, by the play of relentless natural forces. The Bolshevik leaders, far from attempting to impede the process, recognize its inevitability and are framing their laws accordingly. The revolution itself was not the outcome of communist action, but the result of the same natural forces which are now swinging the pendulum back from communism to capitalism."

These are the three main points in Senator France's impressions after a four weeks' visit to Russia, which terminated with his arrival on Latvian soil yesterday morning.

. . . [T]he Senator is optimistic about the future of Russia. And by that he means the future of Russia under Soviet rule, for he believes that the present Government, though it may and probably will be greatly modified in policy or personnel by coming changes, is founded upon a basis so broad and strong that it cannot be overthrown. That basis is the Russian peasants, who constitute nearly 90 per cent of the population. . . .

Senator France admitted that his personal experience had been confined to Moscow and an area, say, of 100 miles around the capital. Whether that can be taken as a representative cross-section of all Russia . . . is a question. The Senator maintains that it can, and it is on this assumption that he bases his argument, whose three main points are set forth above. Briefly, he outlined his reasoning as follows:

New York Times, August 1, 1921. Copyright 1921 by The New York Times Company. Reprinted by permission.

Though the return of Russia to capitalism is the most important feature of the situation, I must preface my reference thereto by a brief explanation of the revolution itself, as given me by the Moscow leaders. The pivot of the whole thing is this: The revolution was not directed by them or any one else on lines laid down beforehand, or even devised to meet the occasion. It proceeded on its irresistible course as naturally as an avalanche reaches the bottom of a mountain valley by gravity.

You see, before the revolution, all Russian land was held in fee simple by the Czar, the nobility and the Church—in other words, by the Czarist regime. Once that regime was overthrown, the land became ownerless. All the millions of the Russian peasantry felt that the time had come to take possession of the land they tilled. The Bolsheviki rode into power on the crest of that wave of universal sentiment. Once country estates were seized, it was natural and logical that urban property, from the mansions of the nobility to the factories, should be seized also. From that to the confiscation of banks, &c., was but a brief step. Thus you have the state of affairs in Russia, say, two years ago.

But by their very action in legitimatizing the seizure of land by the peasants the Bolsheviki laid a new and infinitely broader foundation for the capitalism they were striving to overthrow. They see that now themselves and are prepared to act accordingly.

On that point Senator France is particularly insistent. He declares that the principal Soviet leaders — Lenin, Trotzky, Tchitcherin and others—now recognize the realities of the situation. They have abandoned the Marxian Utopia, he says, for the earth as it is. They are open-minded—this epithet recurred constantly in the Senator's conversation—they will not try to dam or even swim against the flood of natural forces. There are people in Moscow—the Old Guard of the Marxian doctrines—who oppose this change of policy, this betrayal, as they see it. But the Senator believes that their efforts will be totally unavailing.

He continued:

It is on the Russian peasantry—now a people of small land owners—that the strength of the Soviet rule rests. True, I saw only a limited area, but throughout it the peasants were working hard and appeared thoroughly contented. One doesn't need to know Russian or Russia to see whether farmers are working and gauge their general sentiment. I was told—and I believe it—that this was not a show area, but fully representative of non-famine Russia. . . . Why shouldn't it be, when everywhere the peasant, who throughout the centuries has been little better than a slave, is now an owner and capitalist in his own right, with small, easy taxation in place of monstrous, intolerable taxation—and without vodka, that kept him so brutalized as never to have the spirit to rebel?

Naturally these peasants want to sell their produce in order to buy things they need and desire. On that universal want, capitalism must return and is returning. There is the whole matter in a nutshell. . . .

When asked how he suggested that the Russian problem should be handled, the Senator replied:

The first step should be universal recognition of the Soviet Government, which is the Government de facto, founded on the will of nearly the whole Russian nation. This would remove a great part of Soviet suspicion and hostility toward the outer world, which is not to be wondered at in view of the numerous attempts at counterrevolution that have been fomented and aided in foreign capitals.

Then Russia should be lent money for her immediate needs—to buy food, means of transport, agricultural machinery and other needed manufactured goods. . . .

But, first and last, my message to the American people is this: Give these folks a chance; they haven't had one yet.

14   CAPITALISM INEVITABLE*

Last week's despatches told a simple story and, like many such, its significance was great. The story was that Bolshevik Russia had reformed its internal trade policy, permitted private capitalists to operate, begun what was known as the " 'Newest' Economic Policy."

In 1921, Lenin the Late promulgated his N.E.P. (New Economic Policy)—inviting foreign capital to exploit Russian concessions sharing profits with the Government—which virtually marked the receding of the waves of Communism from the shores of Capitalism. It was a fearless step to save Russia from economic ruin. It showed that Moscow Communists, whatever else they were, were not afraid to admit their errors and rectify them; but the Party held many diehards, notably ex-War Lord Trotzky. The N.E.P. was kept in force until 1923. Private traders began to gain confidence. The Government flirted with foreign Powers. The Russian Bear began to raise itself on its bony haunches.

At the end of 1923, the Communist intransigents triumphed, began a drive against the capitalists. The N.E.P. went largely by the

---

*"'Newest' E. P.," *Time,* Vol. V (April 13, 1925), p. 8. Courtesy Time; copyright Time Inc. 1925.

board. The drive was chiefly a political movement, readily understandable, since the rise of Capitalism, even in an attenuated form, must eventually spell the fall of Communism. The capitalists had been restoring Russia to economic ability, themselves to power. It was this latter factor that caused the Moscow oligarchy to attack.

Following this reaction, the year 1924 in Russia was economically and politically rotten. The country went from bad to worse. Cooperative trading between town and village broke down; industrial unrest assumed alarming proportions at Leningrad and Moscow; the peasants stuck more closely than ever to their hoarded grain; the capitalists, such few as there were, were hounded into inactivity. On top of this, came heavy frost in the autumn before the first snowfall, with incalculable damage to the sown grain. Abroad, Communism saw an intractable U.S., a change of Government in Britain, that could hardly be looked upon as favorable to Russia. It secured recognition in Italy, France, some other countries,[1] but no appreciable benefits. . . .

But where recognized, where unrecognized, Russia secured few real advantages, and Communism was seemingly drifting to Never Never Land. The Russian Bear sank down exhausted on its empty belly. Starvation was once more a reality. Discontent was growing more difficult to control. Elaborate propaganda failed to screen the actualities of a situation that was not far from desperate.

Last week, came acknowledgment of blunder, speedy reforms, promises of more, assurances that the change of the Government's policy was "meant seriously and for a long period." Under the Newest Economic Policy, private capitalists will enjoy the same privilege as Government monopolies, trusts and cooperatives. Bolshevik banks will extend credit, taxes will be lowered, private property restored. Practically all administrative and economic pressure on internal trade was removed.

One step leads to another. Seemingly, it cannot be long before a New Foreign Policy will open the way to the reëstablishment of Russia in the comity of nations, with resultant prosperity for the world. The embarrasing question: Can Communism compromise with Capitalism and yet be Communism?

---

[1] These are the countries which have recognized the Bolshevik Government given in order of recognition: Esthonia, Lithuania, Latvia, Finland, Persia, Afghanistan, Turkey, Poland, Germany, Great Britain, Italy, Norway, Austria, Greece, Sweden, China, Denmark, Mexico, Hungary, France, Japan.

Burgeoning or Bankrupt?

The leaders of American capitalism took a particular interest in the NEP. They also reached particularly divergent conclusions, as the following two articles indicate. The first was written by the editor of an influential financial newspaper, the New York Journal of Commerce, *during his tour through Russia in 1926. The second was written by the president of the United States Chamber of Commerce, Julius H. Barnes, for that organization's official publication.*

15   A GREAT EXPERIMENT*

Moscow, May 12

Perhaps there are few topics in the modern economic world that are as little understood as the economic policy which modern Russia is pursuing. . . .

Russia has a definite national, economic policy which is being carried forward with tenacity and very considerable consistency. Its central thought is the development of national resources under a single control and their use in promoting trade with other nations according to a single unified plan.

If the idea can be carried out with ability and success, it is likely to attain somewhat the same results that are gained by a large, ably-managed business enterprise which is competing with a good many smaller concerns—well-directed also but with much narrower powers, and occasionally suffering from internal controversy or difference of opinion. . . .

BASIS OF RUSSIAN ORGANIZATION

The basis of present Russian organization is not, as many suppose, purely Communistic, and is not so regarded by the more discriminating minds among those who are today responsible for it. The term "State capitalism" is more fairly and accurately applied to it. As a base, this State capitalism accepts the idea of national ownership of all resources. These are classified and assigned to certain types of organizations; either productive or trading, (wholesaling or retailing).

*New York Journal of Commerce, June 4, 1926.

Trade as such is divided between foreign and domestic trade; and a set of organizations appropriate to trade with the various countries is then evolved. So, about eleven trading organizations, ten conventions or price and pooling agreements, and some eighty or more "trusts" or productive organizations have been established. There is a possibility of conducting trade with others or of the existence of private business carried on by others, in these same fields in Russia, but such possibilities are so closely hemmed in and hedged about that there is small probability of their attaining any substantial development. None believes that private competition will ever accomplish much in the way of competition with the Government-owned enterprises so long as the present regime is maintained.

It is to these Government enterprises, and practically to them alone, that the nation looks for the actual management of its production and trade. Each is attaining a high degree of organization. It is estimated that there are in Russia today about 400,000 members of boards of directors of business enterprises. Everything is being highly organized on the capitalistic basis, and in each branch of business or trade there is something approximating a military style of discipline. . . .

QUESTION OF EFFICIENCY

It does not need much argument to indicate the various advantages of this type of organization and operation. They have already often been set forth, in the case of the various "trusts" and combinations, which are found in most of the Western nations and include the savings common to large scale business, the elimination of competitive wastes and the general increase in possible efficiency due to central control.

Now, can Russia, by her national policy, realize these savings? That is still to be seen. But enough has already been done to raise the serious fear of excessive "overhead" charges. Already Russians themselves recognize the existence of over organization and of high unit costs resulting therefrom. Prices in Russia are high and the cause ascribed for high prices by many local commentators is exactly this high cost of management. A bureaucratic system of distribution is rigidly enforced and there is a specified course of movement from producer to wholesaler, from wholesaler to general co-operative establishments and from general co-operative to retail co-operative, which is rigidly prescribed.

HIGH COSTS HAMPER RUSSIA

At each step there must be a profit; and this profit and (underlying it) the cost of management and distribution must be apportioned to each item and added to the price. All this means high charges and, for the time being, corresponding difficulty in competing with foreign countries. Russia today is distinctly non-competitive. It furnishes supplies of foodstuffs, such as grain and raw materials, such as ores and the like, to many countries as a basis for their manufacturing. Russia imports almost all highly machined products and such manufactured goods as she produces are turned out with the aid of machinery which is largely obsolete and in plants which are far behind the times in general organization. Wages are low and hours, in spite of the Socialist philosophy of the Government, are as long as those in capitalistic countries. A rigid protective system and a semi-military control of foreign trade cuts off all possibility of dangerous outside competition, keeps all plants working at high speed, most of them with two or more shifts a day, and compels the worker and peasant to buy the goods produced by home institutions instead of comparing prices with foreign countries.

So far as finding a compulsory market and compelling the consumption of goods is concerned, the system works like the traditional "charm," and in so doing it provides employment for all who can in any way be used with the number of machines actually set up and available. But the test of international competition shows that thus far the system has not produced efficiency. Even with Government regulated and controlled prices the price level is today close to 190 per cent as compared with pre-war, and while the situation is no doubt partly due to obsolete machinery and other obvious factors, no small element in it is, of course, the high cost of overhead, the multiplicity of organizations through whose hands the goods must pass and the general lack of the impetus to saving and economy which comes from competition.

FOREIGN CAPITAL

Many of these difficulties are quite fully understood and recognized by the managers of Russia's commercial policy. . . . But those who thus recognize the defects of the system believe that they would largely disappear if national industry could be placed upon a sufficiently broad base and conducted upon a large enough scale. In that case unit costs would be cut and high overhead would be largely distributed and "thinned out" so that it would not constitute the handicap it offers at the present time.

To attain this larger base for production and to manufacture both on a broader scale and a cheaper cost footing there has grown up an intense desire for foreign capital. Strangely enough, as it seems at first sight, the Government does not, however, seek to borrow this capital itself—at least not at present. What it wants is to insure foreign investment and foreign management under the "concessions" system.

The theory is that in this way the best outside technical skill, as well as the outside capital that is needed will be enlisted and that after the necessary period of private operation involved in the "concession" the whole undertaking will revert to the Government and be operated by it as part of its great industrial system. . . .

COMPETITIVE PLACE OF RUSSIA

All this is preparation for the new competitive place which Russia expects to occupy. The future to which her administrators and business men are looking is distinctly one of industrial achievement. First, independence of foreign countries, then, probably ability to defeat them if necessary on their own ground will be the order of development. It is not well to keep the eye fixed merely on the present position of Russia. For the first time in her history she has developed a consistent plan of growth. What her industries and businesses are to do has been planned ahead for five years and her tentative projects extend much further into the future even than that. She has laid the foundation by working out a semi-military industrial organization in which every man has his place and is compelled to fill it.

Granted the presence of good ability always at the head, there is no reason why the plan should not be successful in exploiting the immense natural resources of Russia, introducing modern capitalistic methods and producing the most powerful competitive mechanism in existence. It is a prospect to which other nations may well give thoughtful attention, for while such experiments on a smaller scale, it is true, have usually broken down of their own weight in the past, it by no means follows that this experiment will necessarily do likewise. Should it go on and succeed, the result may be a great transformation of industrial methods as well as of social and economic organization in other countries. The prospect may be viewed as a menace to existing industrial society or as an experiment in national management of business, from which many lessons will necessarily develop—according to the bias or predisposition of the observer.

ATTITUDE OF OTHER NATIONS

Some inkling of what is really going on in Russia in an economic way, some notion that the days of the military communism are already far behind and that the country has embarked upon a great capitalistic experiment—perhaps the greatest of modern times—has been gradually taking possession of the minds of foreign Ministers as well as of business men in other European countries. Some of both groups are still for standing aloof, but the majority without trying to look too far into the future, are chiefly desirous of sharing in the possible economic reorganization and exploitation which they foresee in Russia.

Moscow is coming to be a center of interest for Germans, French and Scandinavians. American business men come occasionally, but most of them are indisposed to run counter to the desires of the Washington Government or what they suppose to be its wishes. So they are on the point of losing their opportunity and only the great resources of the United States and its unique ability to supply capital and credit is still preserving this remarkable field for them—if they choose to take the trouble to occupy it.

16   THE FACTS THAT ANSWER TROTSKY*

In his book, "Whither England?" Leon Trotsky supplies a special "Preface for America," in which he says in part:

"By exerting pressure on its debtors or giving them an extension, by granting or refusing credit to European countries, the United States is placing them in a gradually tightening economic dependence, in the last analysis an ineluctable situation, which is the necessary condition for inevitable social and revolutionary disturbance. The Communist International, viewed in the light of this knowledge, may be considered an almost conservative institution as compared with Wall Street. Morgan,

*Julius H. Barnes, "The Facts That Answer Trotsky," *Nation's Business,* Vol. XIII (November, 1925), p. 20.

Dawes, Julius Barnes—these are among the artificers of the approaching European revolution."

Which led Mr. Barnes to answer:

Sick Russia prescribes its patent nostrums for robust America.

An ancient civilization one hundred million strong, living today just above the verge of utter barbarism, attempts to instruct orderly America, busy with its expanded economic life and social opportunities, typified by its eighteen million automobiles and its towering skyscrapers.

Tyrannized Russia, barred from free speech and free press, its ignorance of world progress typified by its scanty six pounds per capita newsprint consumption per year, preaches to America where 150 pounds newsprint consumption per capita makes the printed page the universal medium of information, where current world events show nightly on the screens of thousands of motion-picture theaters, where music and uttered thoughts enter every home through the universal radio.

Bankrupt Russia, pleading for foreign credits, seizing the product of its wooden-plow farms at Government-dictated prices—only thus acquiring the means for overseas purchase of scanty necessities—instructs America in the errors of a policy which in twelve years has raised the savings account of America from six billion to twenty billion dollars.

Communistic Russia, destroying the individual productive impulse until this great agricultural country recently escaped millions of famine-deaths only by the bounty of capitalistic America, prescribes its futile rules for America, where individual opportunity and fair play have raised the common standard of living to be the admiration and despair of other peoples.

The lessons of the most splendid quarter century of material progress in the world's history bear no message to this fanatic mind.

These recent years, science and invention produced the automobile, the aeroplane, the submarine, the motion picture, the X-ray and the radio. New industries raised the average employment and earnings until the American worker's home today possesses universally the bath-room, the gas range, electricity, the phonograph, the telephone, the radio and the automobile.

Iron, coal, copper, oil and timber lie valueless until orderly government and enterprising industry shape them for human use and they become national wealth that makes more secure living standards which preserve health and lengthen life.

America's great contribution to human progress has been this: Intelligently directed industry takes from nature its treasures of field, forest and mine, fabricates these into the thousand articles of human use by mastery of nature's electric energy, and enormously increases the production of every single man.

America's hundred million people and their achievement is the open record to inspire the effort of sixteen hundred million other humans in the world. Fast or slow, other peoples—seeing what in America the average man may aspire to accomplish and own—will follow.

Yet, when America proposes to develop thus in the far corners of the world, among other less fortunate peoples, old and new, the same magical process of production and transportation, which means individual opportunity and individual content and happiness,—this mind of Trotsky's can see nothing but a selfish effort to preserve American industry against the competition of rival countries.

The great menace to this social progress is such tyranny as that in Russia today, where great treasures of coal, iron, copper, oil, timber and idle labor lie useless because of the economic and political fallacies which maintain one hundred million people in dense ignorance and which play on their credulity with such cheap cries as "exploitation" and "world revolution."

The Red Experiment

The United States enjoyed during the Twenties a fantastic economic boom and a succession of three Republican Presidents. Under these circumstances, popular interest in Russia declined sharply, but not entirely. A growing number of Americans—primarily social workers, educators, social scientists, and journalists—braved rigorous conditions in order to visit the "Red experiment" and recall the ideals of the Progressive era.

One of these tourists was Oswald Garrison Villard, editor of the influential liberal organ, The Nation. *In the last of a series of reports on his trip through the USSR in 1929, Villard drew a portrait of Soviet society which implicitly judged his own society as well.*

17 THE SOVIETS AND THE HUMAN BEING*

I. THE SOVIETS AND THE PEASANT

The Soviets and their individual subjects—here is perhaps the greatest paradox of all. For with the complete denial of political liberty, of the right to dissent and to oppose, yes, even to hold conflicting economic opinions in plain view, one still has while in Russia the feeling that it is a land of greater individual freedom than most others. This is in large part due to a recognition of the tremendous advance in the position of the Russian worker over his situation in the Czarist period, and also to the smashing of certain outworn taboos, to the frank recognition of some human conditions as to which other states and societies shut their eyes. If the day ever does come when genuine political liberty prevails in Russia it will without doubt be the freest of all countries, especially as it has been spared the curse of Anglo Saxon hypocrisy. . . .

Despite all I have written of the hardships and forced alterations in the life of the peasant, his is a far better situation than ever before. He may have over him some harsh and overbearing Soviet officials, and possibly occasionally a corrupt one, but none to compare with the brutal, arrogant, and crooked officials of the Czarist regime, from whom nothing could be obtained without a bribe. The driving out of the landlords was the first step toward individual freedom; the disestablishment of the lazy, ignorant, and autocratic priests the second. And in this respect let no man weep if there are today many villages without orthodox churches. If they are without such churches it is because they care so little for their religion that they will not support them. It is far better, in my judgment, that the churches should all be closed than that they should be continued as the handmaidens of ignorance, as teachers of degradation, of superstition, of fetish- and image-worship.

II. COMMUNISM AND THE CHURCHES

No self-respecting state, and no decent one, could do else than strike from the peasants the shackles the orthodox Russian church placed upon their spirits and their entire mental development, at the behest of the Czarist system. Some ethical training will, it is to be

*Oswald Garrison Villard, "Russia from a Car Window: V. The Soviets and the Human Being," *Nation,* Vol. CXXIX (December 4, 1929), pp. 654–57.

hoped, be given in the schools, but if there is none whatsoever the peasant will still be far better off morally than under the religious control of the past. True, he will not be allowed under the Soviets to beat his wife and children as freely, maltreat his animals as cruelly, steal as regularly, get drunk as frequently as in the old days, but for this in the years to come the Russian peasant will yet devoutly thank the atheistic Soviets. No honest man can deny that in Russia the religion of the state church was the opiate of the people—one of the opiates that prevented rebellion at least a hundred years ago. In setting their face against a state church—and a crooked one—the Soviets struck a tremendous blow for individual freedom and set a splendid example to Italy, Poland, Spain, and other priest-ridden countries.

This is not, however, to be taken as condoning the present persecution of minor sects by the Soviets. To muster out a corrupt medieval state church and free men's minds from religious bigotry and the dread of a man-conjured hell is one thing. But to strike at all forms of worship and not even to do it openly and honestly, that is surely unworthy of any group of rulers who claim to be enlightened. There is no doubt whatever that in the past year, as part of the general swing-back toward extreme communism, those who are affiliated with sects such as the Unitarian, Methodist, Baptist, and Christian Scientist are feeling the despotic hand of the government. In Moscow I was offered from a trustworthy source a list of one hundred persons affiliated with churches who have been exiled to Siberia or otherwise punished, within a year, on one trumped-up charge after another, often the all-embracing one of counter-revolution; for the Soviets are careful enough not to exile men purely because of their religious activities. . . . By contrast with the freedom which the government grants the citizen in other matters of personal life, its interference with religious activities is deserving of vigorous censure. . . .

III. THE HEALTH OF THE WORKER

As for the workingman, a proletarian state should be able to present a remarkable list of achievements for him, and it does. Here are some of the benefits conferred upon the men and women who carry on the Soviets' industries: free drugs, free doctors, free dentists, free hospitals, free accident insurance, free health insurance, free old-age pensions, and two weeks' vacation each year. In addition there are provided clubhouses, reading rooms, educational courses, theaters, athletic grounds for the worker and his children, and the best homes that are being built in Russia. If he is still illiterate, there are teachers in plenty to teach him so that he may have access to books and daily newspapers. The wonderful old floors of the picture galleries and the former palaces of the Czar are being worn out by the great troops of men and women workers personally conducted through them. If the worker is taken ill every consideration is given to him—he may even be sent to the beautiful Caucasus for recovery in one of the countless sanitariums maintained for the workers. In every city through which he passes in the Caucasus, perhaps in every city of western Russia, he will find the former homes of the rich and the aristocratic turned into hospitals and refuges for the sick poor. At Stalingrad we entered the grounds of the old iron works. We were asked if we cared to see the mansion of the former head of the plant, which had been owned by French capitalists. We assented and entered, only to find the place a sanitarium for consumptives, with each bed filled. It was not an ideal place for tubercular invalids; but somehow it typified the revolution in social emphasis which the Soviets have brought about. Formerly nobody cared about a tubercular worker; now the finest house available is his home until he dies or recovers.

Coming to the workingmen's clubs, we saw one costing $750,000 at Kanavino, next to Nizhni Novgorod, with a superb theater in it. Some of our party demurred. Was it not too big and too costly for so small a city, someone asked the head of the Nizhni Novgorod Soviet the next morning? "Well," was his reply, "if what the manager says about the attendance at the club is true we shall have to build four more like it during the next five years." The clubhouse was well kept, well run, and well attended by people of all ages; some of the children were extremely well dressed, all were neat and clean. Never have I seen so many checker- and chess-tables under one roof. There were two large auditoriums beside the theater, one fitted for movies. On the ground floor was an excellent cafeteria where cheese sandwiches cost eleven copecks (5½ cents) and a "hot dog" twenty-five (12½ cents); apples cost ten copecks; cakes twelve; and coffee five.

Across the street was a maternity hospital; after visiting, quite unannounced, some workers' apartments, we burst, also unannounced at eleven at night, into the hospital, which was finished last spring, and inspected it from top to bottom. Eighty beds are provided, the whole being paid for by the city and out of the social insurance funds. Not one of the patients, not one of the dozens of healthy little babies being wheeled on trucks to their mothers for their night meal, becomes liable for a cent. It is the mother's right and the child's right to have the best care without cost. Nine doctors, one in charge of the laboratory, twenty-five nurses earning $25 to $30 a month, and fourteen general employees carry on the work. Those who were on duty gazed wide-eyed at the sudden intrusion of these strange, inquisitive Americans. We asked if this was built for the use of working people. "Most assuredly," was the head physician's answer. "Are others taken, too?" "Anyone who applies." "But what if the hospital were full save for one bed and the wife of a worker, the spouse of a bourgeois, and the life-partner of an aristocrat should apply for that bed?" The chief physician looked at us in amazement. "We should take the first that came. This is a humanitarian enterprise and we know no social or class differences here."

IV. PUBLIC AMUSEMENTS

Much has been written about the various "parks of culture." These are efforts to give the people education and amusement combined. The great one in Moscow is a sort of refined and vastly improved Luna Park. Here are movies, theaters, and concert halls, with municipal bands, picture galleries, rifle-shooting ranges, opportunities for military drill, a model kindergarten with highly trained workers, manual training for older children, tennis courts, ball grounds, gymnastic apparatus—all together. One seated group was making music with balalaikas, guitars, violins, harmonicas. The sign said that these seats were reserved for that purpose and that visitors were welcome. The leader assured me, in English, that if I would come regularly he would help me to acquire a balalaika even to financial help! Our young American boys and girls found themselves in no time playing ball with teams of young Russians, tossing the ball over a net in a game of skill the name of which they never learned. Everywhere there was quiet, peace, content; no loud voices, no wrangling, no public hugging as at Coney Island; no toughs, no rowdies, no papers scattered around. Everything was, like Moscow itself, as orderly as could be, and nowhere in this park of culture did a single policeman or even a uniformed employee cross my sight. These "parks of culture," like the races in which the government pitted its own horses against one another and permitted betting, are a significant part of the Soviet program. The Russian leaders do not intend that communism shall make the lives of the proletariat grim and dull and void of pleasure. They wish to bring beauty and happiness, coupled with more knowledge, into the workers' lives, and they have much still to do to change the grim somberness of the adults of Moscow.

It is the government that keeps up the wonderful ballet, the superb opera, the fine theaters; that insists that the workers shall be brought into contact with the masterpieces of art. If the people are soberly clad, that is not because the government wishes it; it is compelled to suffer this for the present, it asserts, for the sake of larger things. It is the government which urges the people to travel, to go to the country for holidays, as hundreds of thousands do from Leningrad and Moscow—perhaps to bootleg some food—and come back laden with flowers and as happily tired as similar crowds returning to Berlin or New York. It is the government which sends out those vacation boats which go up and down the Volga on two weeks' cruises crowded with happy people in scant bathing suits, as eagerly in search of actinic rays as the bathers on our own American beaches. No; whether the Soviet leaders do so to keep the masses content, or whether they do it because it is part of their program of enriching the lives of their workers, they are putting into life all the privileges and all the color they can. They provide short working hours; they have broken up the week so that Sunday disappears and there can be no one regular rest day or churchgoing day, but they plainly desire to fill the rest days with amusements which shall educate when they do not restore physically. Even the lunch hour at the factories is filled with music or lectures or communistic exhortations.

V. THE COMMUNIST CHALLENGE

"But," I hear it said, "there is not one thing in all this which the workers could not get under a capitalist government. We have factories which give their workers the best of care, give them amusements, good pay, and retiring pensions. There is nothing in the Soviet treatment of its workers which is distinctively communistic or a part of communism, nothing that could not be provided by American employers and municipalities working together." Precisely. This was the belief that came to me in Russia whenever I inspected what was being done for the welfare of the individual worker. We *could* have finer parks of culture than they; we *could* supply fine theaters and decent amusements and ideal labor conditions if we would. But, the communist points out, we *don't*. Our American legislatures do not free the worker from the dread of sickness; do not give him the dentists he needs and can never afford. They are only just beginning to provide old-age pensions; they have not tackled the question of un-employment; they are not concerned because millions of our workers are born, live, and die in our mill towns or cities without once having a glimpse of country life. . . . Any capitalist state could, if it wished, give all the benefits listed above to the workers if it could bring itself to the belief that the workers, and not those who are already rich and privileged, are the chief concern of an enlightened state. The Russian communist insists that this will not come to pass elsewhere until the rich and privileged are subordinated or wiped out, until each state declares that the meek and lowly, namely the workers, shall inherit the earth and shall not be limited to such of the good things of life as they can procure with their scanty wages. Here is the most serious communist challenge to capitalist society. It will have to be answered some day; perhaps before so very long, if the Soviets should make a great success of their "immortal gamble."

VI.   WHAT OF THE BOURGEOISIE?

And the Russian bourgeoisie and the aristocrats meanwhile—what of them? They cower in garrets, live as best they can, starve if need be. They, too, can visit the parks of culture, the theaters and other amusements, if they have the money. But they are intellectually des-titute, cut off from social intercourse, and never free from the espio-nage of the G.P.U., the dreaded Soviet secret police. Anyone is free to accuse or denounce them. They do not dare to be seen together in numbers lest they be charged with counter-revolution. The mem-bers of the diplomatic corps and the foreign colony in Moscow fear to associate much with the remnants of what are now the submerged classes lest the Soviet police trail the friends they visit. It is a cause of suspicion if a bourgeois sees much of foreigners; when diplomatic relations with England were broken off dozens of persons, some say hundreds, who had had contacts with the British Embassy were ar-rested and a number shot by the Soviets, whose leaders seemed for the moment fear-struck. Even today the government cares not a whit about the sufferings of the former aristocrats and bourgeoisie. Unless they are suspected of plotting, they may live in complete obscurity and die off as rapidly as possible. . . . So freedom in Russia plainly is not for the bourgeois nor the aristocrat; they are prisoners on suffer-ance; their children who have fled to foreign states may not come to them, nor may they cross the borders to see their offspring once more before they die.

VII. WOMEN IN SOVIET RUSSIA

Freedom, by contrast, has come to all Russian women—freedom and equality. No longer is a peasant's wife no better than his ox or his ass. No longer is the worker's wife at a disadvantage before the law and in industry; no longer is she tied down for life through economic necessity to a brutal, dissolute husband. No longer is she denied entrance to the professions or the right to rise politically. She may live her own life, and if she desires no children the facts as to birth control are at her service, while abortion is no longer illegal. Divorce is free and marriage easy—some of us witnessed both processes in Moscow. It must not be overlooked, too, that the complete equality of Russian women extends to industry. At the head of a great oil refinery in the Baku district is a woman. At Dnieprostroy we were introduced to a woman engineer who had been called away from a dinner party a couple of evenings previously to superintend the replacing of an engine upon its track. She is a charming and brilliant woman. . . . There is no sex bar anywhere and no sex prejudice among the workers. This Soviet society has determined to profit by all the creative talent and executive ability available. It has learned from the history of capitalist states not to deprive itself, as civilization did for centuries, of the mental talents of one-half of the human race.

VIII. MARRIAGE AND SEX

Let no one believe that woman has been degraded by any act of the Soviets; quite the contrary. . . . So far as extra-marital relations are concerned, Russia is no different from what it has been. The present government does not care who lives with whom out of wedlock, and neither did the Czarist government. By contrast with the latter the present rulers of Russia are really Puritans. While they believe that it is nobody's business what relationships men and women have to one another, they are strenuously opposed to promiscuity and anything approaching prostitution. They have cleaned up the cities not a little—Nizhni Novgorod, for instance, which during its famous fair was a center of prostitution and gambling. All the Russian cities I saw were cleaner and more decent to the eye than French and Italian or Spanish towns.

In the Soviets' refusal to regulate private morals by law there is wisdom, justice, and common sense; for such matters belong in the domain of public opinion. I much prefer the Russian frankness and laissez-faire policy to our own American hypocrisy which turns back men and women at Ellis Island because they have lived together unmarried before coming here, just as if there were not next door to Ellis Island, on Manhattan, a hundred or more thousand couples living in extra-marital relations. The Soviets, no more than the American government, would favor a white-slave traffic; the difference between the two is that the one seeks by communism to do away with the economic misery which produces white slaves and the other creates a law to deal with the case which merely victimizes the innocent and enriches hundreds of blackmailers. . . .

Curious it is how ready we are to jump at conclusions. "Don't talk to me about those people," said a respected member of our delegation in Russia after viewing the nude bathing on the Volga and other rivers. "A people which has sunk so low as to have deprived their women of all modesty is beyond the pale." I mildly asked him if he was aware that nude bathing had been practiced on this river and most of the other great rivers of the world for centuries. It had never occurred to him. He thought the Soviets had introduced it! Nor had he ever heard of the historic bathing together in the nude of the sexes in Japan, Sweden, Norway, and elsewhere. I asked him if he believed that there were bathing-suit factories on the shores of Galilee when Christ was alive. He was inclined to doubt it, but I am afraid that he is still telling people that Russian women are totally without modesty, and that the Soviets are responsible for it. I am sure that still others who were with us hold to the opinion that if we could really search far enough we should find clear evidence of the nationalizing of women in some portions of Russia. . . .

Within the limits of public order the individual should be left absolutely free. It is in this direction that I feel that the Soviets desire to move. I heard, for instance, nothing while I was in Russia of a censorship of literature. I know that there is a censorship of political matters, and there is certainly a strict censorship of the press, and of what the foreign correspondents in Moscow wish to send out. One of them, for instance, was not allowed to telegraph that there was official evidence that the ruble is slipping in value. On the other hand, the censor has freely passed the reports of the shocking increase in executions, even allowing Mr. Duranty[1] to say in one dispatch that on one day the "bag of revolutionists and kulaks [rich peasants] was fifty"—by bag he meant executions. Here, too, one

---

[1]Walter Duranty, Moscow correspondent for the *New York Times.* [Ed.]

must hope that if the Soviets last and become more firmly established they will do away more and more with the restrictions which now hedge around the freedom of the individual Russian. Important as they are, and often harassing and cruel, as, for instance, the refusal to permit the free movement of individuals beyond the frontier, I still believe that when one is in Russia one does feel personal freedom in the air and this despite the nationalization of all private property and despite the state's assumption that it is to say how much property a citizen shall have and what he shall not acquire. It is an anachronism and a paradox, I admit. But, as I cannot say too often, Russia is a conglomeration of contradictions, paradoxes, and anachronisms.

Crash

Toward the close of the Twenties, the terms of the Soviet-American comparison changed suddenly and drastically. In 1929 the American bubble of prosperity exploded under the impact of the stock market crash. A year earlier, the Soviet Union had discarded the NEP in favor of the Five-Year Plan Operating through a central agency, Gosplan, the government pursued a goal of rapid industrialization by setting production quotas for each factory. At the same time, the regime set out to socialize agricultural production by ordering peasant farms to be collectivized and the wealthier farmers (kulaks) to be "liquidated as a class."

As the paralysis of depression spread through the American economy, the Five-Year Plan attracted more and more attention. With industrial production steadily sinking, with unemployment inexorably soaring, with shabby men and women waiting patiently outside soup kitchens, Americans began to take a new interest in the "Red experiment." There, they were told, factories were producing at record rates and no one lacked a job. A flood of articles and books about the USSR appeared during 1930 and particularly 1931, contrasting vividly with the relative lack of interest during the Twenties.

The following article by the well-known author, journalist and literary critic, Edmund Wilson, produced an immense commotion within liberal and radical circles.

18 AN APPEAL TO PROGRESSIVES*

Today there are in the United States, according to the census director, something like nine million men out of work; our cities are scenes of privation and misery on a scale which sickens the imagination; our agricultural life is bankrupt; our industry, in shifting to the South, has returned almost to the horrible conditions of the English factories of a hundred years ago and the fight of the unions there for recognition is all to begin again; so many banks are failing that the newspapers do not dare to print the truth about them. And when we look to Europe west of Russia or to South America, we see only the same economic chaos, the same lack of will or capacity to deal with it and the same resultant poverty and suffering. May we not well fear that what this year has broken down is not simply the machinery of representative government, but the capitalist system itself?—and that, even with the best will in the world, it may be impossible for capitalism to guarantee not merely social justice but even security and order? May we not fear lest our American society, in spite of its apparently greater homogeneity, may not eventually collapse through sheer inefficiency and corruption as ignominiously as the feudal regime in Russia or France? . . .

[I]t seems to me that at the present time the optimism of the Americans is flagging, that the morale of our society is weak. The faith and energy for a fresh start seem not forthcoming: a dreadful apathy, unsureness and discouragement seem to have fallen upon our life. It is as if people were afraid to go on with what they have been doing or as if they no longer had any real heart for it. I want to suggest that the present depression may be nothing less than one of the turning points in our history, our first real crisis since the Civil War. The Americans at the present time seem to be experiencing not merely an economic breakdown but a distinct psychological change. From the time of the Civil War on, all our enthusiasm and creative energy went into the development of our tremendous resources. This development had two aspects: one was the exploration of the continent and the engineering feats involved in reclaiming it, and the other the amassing of gigantic fortunes. Today the discoveries have all been made: we no longer look toward the West, as the Europeans looked to America in the Renaissance, as toward a world of untold treasures

*Edmund Wilson, "An Appeal to Progressives," *New Republic,* Vol. LXV (January 14, 1931), pp. 234–38. Reprinted by permission of The New Republic, copyright 1931, Harrison-Blaine of New Jersey, Inc.

and wonders—and the excitement of mastering new rivers, forests, prairies, mountains and coasts seems now completely spent. This was already true at the time of the European War (when incidentally we were running into a business depression) but the War gave us a new objective — new discoveries, the discovery of Europe; new heroic stunts of engineering to accomplish, the transportation of our army to France. Since the War, however, we have had nothing to excite us and carry us along except the momentum of money-making. We have been trying still to find in it the exhilaration of the money-making of our period of expansion, which had been in reality largely the exhilaration of the richness, wildness and size of the continent—the breaking it into the harness of the railroads, the sudden finds of gold and silver mines. But during these last years our buoyancy, our hope, our faith has all been put behind the speed of mass production, behind stupendous campaigns of advertising, behind cyclones of salesmanship. It has been a buoyancy which has been becoming hysterical. And the reaction from a hysterical exhilaration is a slump into despondency and inertia. What we have lost is, it may be, not merely our way in the economic labyrinth but our conviction of the value of what we are doing. Money-making and the kind of advantages which a money-making society provides for money to buy are not enough to satisfy humanity—neither is a social system like our own where everyone is out for himself and devil take the hindmost, with no common purpose and little common culture to give life stability and sense. Our idolization of our aviators—our extravagant excitement over Lindbergh and our romantic admiration (now beginning to cool off) for Byrd—has been like a last desperate burst of American idealism, a last impulse to dissociate our national soul from a furious progress which was leading from automobiles and radios straight through electric refrigerators to Tom Thumb golf courses.

The old American ideal and legend of the poor boy who gets to be a millionaire, which gradually came to take the place of the legend of the poor boy who got to be President, has today lost all its romance. Not only do people not hope to be Hoover—they do not even hope so often as they did to be Henry Ford. The romance of the legend of the poor boy was the romance of democracy, of the career open to the talents—but the realities of a millionaire society have turned out to be the monstrosities of capitalism: the children of the successful poor boy get lazy and sick on their father's money and the poor boys who afterwards arrive on the scene discover, with the crippling of the grain market, the elimination of the factory worker by the improvement of the machine and the decimation of the white-collar class, even when apparently well on their way to millionaire-dom, by enormous business mergers, that the career is no longer open to the talents to the extent which had originally been hoped. What began as the libertarian adventure of eighteenth-century middle-class democracy seems to have ended in the *cul de sac* of capitalism. And capitalist-minded as the Americans have become, they seem to feel they are in a *cul de sac*—they do not really seem to dare to go on. In spite of the fundamental stupidity and absurdity of so much of what we have been doing, we are better educated and more intelligent than we were, and since the War we have been closer to Europe. The Buicks and Cadillacs, the bad gin and Scotch, the radio concerts interspersed with advertising talks, the golf and bridge of the sub-urban household which the bond salesman can get for his money, can hardly compensate him for daily work of a kind in which it is utterly impossible to imagine a normal human being taking satisfaction or pride—and the bond salesman is the type of the whole office class in our society. The brokers and bankers who are shooting themselves or jumping out of windows are disheartened by the precariousness of their profession—but would they kill themselves if they loved it? Who in the United States today really loves our meaningless life. . . ?

We liberals have professed not to love it, yet we have tried to believe in it, none the less. Living in a country where money changes hands so often and social position fluctuates so easily, where the minds of the working class have seemed largely to have been absorbed into the middle-class psychology, we have been unable to believe in the Marxian doctrine that capitalism must eventually give rise to class warfare, and we have perhaps never taken sufficiently seriously Marx's prediction that for many years to come the stupid automatic acquisitive instinct of humanity would still be so far ahead of its capacity for intelligent and disinterested behavior that capital-ism would never even be able to drive itself with enough foresight to avoid a wreck. . . .

[T]he truth is that we liberals and progressives have been betting on capitalism—and that most of our heroes and allies: heterodox pro-fessors like Dewey and Beard, survivors of the old republican tradi-tion like Woodrow Wilson and Justice Holmes, able and well educated labor organizers like the officers of the Amalgamated, intelligent journalists like Lippmann and Chase, though all sincere and out-spoken democrats, have been betting on capitalism, too. And now in the abyss of bankruptcy and starvation into which the country has fallen and with no sign of any political leadership which will be able to pull us out, liberalism seems to have little to offer beyond a recommendation of the public ownership of water-power and certain other public utilities, a cordial feeling that labor ought to organize in a non-social-revolutionary way and a protest, invariably ineffective, against a few of the more obviously atrocious jailings, beatings-up and murders of the working class by the owners.

Doesn't this program begin at last to seem inadequate? We have always talked about the desirability of a planned society—the phrase "social control" has been our blessèd Mesopotamian word. But if this means anything, does it not mean socialism? And should we not do well to make this perfectly plain? It may be objected that at the present time to propose socialism in America is utopian. But with such administrations as we have been getting, do not all our progressive proposals, however reasonable or modest, seem utopian? Is it not obvious that our present kind of government . . . is incapable of acting in good faith in even the simplest matter of preserving the water power which is supposed to be operated for the general benefit from being exploited by private profiteers? Our society has finally produced in its specialized professional politicians one of the most useless and obnoxious classes which has perhaps ever disgraced human history—a class which seems to be unique among governing classes in having succeeded in being corrupt, uncultivated and incompetent all at once. We know that we are not even able to depend on them to protect us against the frankly disreputable race of blackmailers, thieves and assassins who dominate our municipal life. . . .

Yet, as I say, it may be true that with the present breakdown we have come to the end of something, and that we are ready to start on a different tack. If we look back through the depressions of the last fifty years, we see that through every one of them there was always something for which the Americans could still legitimately feel ambition or enthusiasm, something to appeal to the national imagination: after 1885, there was still the West and the consolidation of the railroads; after the prolonged depression of the nineties, the final consolidation of great industries such as United States Steel and the Rooseveltian crusade against the corporations in the interests of the increasing class of those who were being injured by the process of consolidation, and Rooseveltian imperialism; after the depression during the first years of the War, our entrance into the War; and after the depression which followed the War, the motor-car and aviator period I have described. Today the further consolidation of business ruins more people even than in Roosevelt's time and there is no sign of a Roosevelt or a Wilson to revive our political imagination and to persuade the people out of luck that something is about to be done for them. It may be that the whole money-making and spending psychology has definitely played itself out, and that the Americans would be willing now for the first time to put their idealism and their genius for organization behind a radical social experiment. The future is as blank in America today as the situation is desperate: the President seems so torn between different cowardices that it is practically impossible for him to act, and when he tries to he is deadlocked by Congress; nor have the manufacturers or the financiers come forward with any constructive proposal. Yet the very blindness of the present outlook may mean that things are going to break in a new quarter. I have a feeling that just at present the people who don't deal in ideas professionally are doing more thinking than the ideologues: the man in the electric-refrigerator business who predicts a world upheaval within eighteen months "because revolutions usually happen in the spring"; the lawyer and real-estate dealer who says that the stock market ought to be "wiped out"; the provincial bank president who never believed in Coolidge prosperity, had been expecting the crash two years before it came and says that we shall never collect our debts from Europe; the New Yorker in the luxury trade who wants to get away from his job and go to Russia; the mother of the Middle Western family who says indignantly that the motor-car business has been trying to "lift itself by its bootstraps" and that industry ought to be controlled—are all people one can meet any day, though in the America of twenty years ago one could hardly have met them at all.

The minds of such people, furthermore, have been affected by the example of Russia far more than the professional intellectuals, who are accustomed to assuming that they are the only people who understand the Soviets and that everyone else is stupidly prejudiced against them, are readily able to grasp. During the N.E.P. period in Russia the capitalist world was able to feel the comforting assurance that the Russians had recognized the impossibilities of Communism and were inevitably relapsing into capitalism again. But with the inauguration of the Five Year Plan to eliminate capitalist business in Russia, the aspect of things changed. The apparent success of the Five Year Plan has affected the morale of all the rest of the world— and of the Americans surely not least. In the course of this winter of our capitalist quandary, the Soviets have emerged from the back pages of the newspapers and are now to be seen all over the place—even to interviews with Stalin's mother. And behind the reports of even the reactionary papers one feels as much admiration as resentment. After all, the Communist project has almost all the qualities that Americans glorify—the extreme of efficiency and economy combined with the ideal of a herculean feat to be accomplished by common action in an atmosphere of enthusiastic boosting—like a Liberty Loan drive—the idea of putting over something big in five years. Furthermore, the Russians are studying our methods—they have imported a thousand American engineers and put them at the head of enormous industrial and engineering enterprises with practically a free hand, and one would not be at all surprised to hear that Eddie Bernays[1] had been in Moscow at the time of the recent trial. We have already, in spite of the Treasury regulation, been doing a great deal of important trading with Russia, and an important New York bank was at one time on the point of advancing to the Soviets that loan which The New Republic has been advocating but which the government in this case forestalled.

The Communists in the United States do not believe that American business or government can possibly imitate or ally themselves with the Soviets. They believe that a war against Russia is inevitable. They believe, furthermore, that they themselves constitute a small, trained, compact minority who, when American capitalism inevitably breaks down and is left helpless in its ignorance and anarchic selfishness, will be able to step in and man the works. This idea has always sounded to us absurd, but who will say that it is entirely fantastic today when the machine is obviously badly in need of repairs and there seems no political group in a position of power with either a sensible plan or good intentions? I believe that if the American radicals and progressives who repudiate the Marxian dogma and the strategy of the Communist party hope to accomplish anything valuable, they must take Communism away from the Communists, and take it without ambiguities or reservations, asserting emphatically that their ultimate goal is the ownership of the means of production by the government and an industrial rather than a regional representation. What we need in this country is a genuine opposition, and it is a long time since the liberals have been one. A genuine opposition must, it seems to me, openly confess that the Declaration of Independence and the Constitution are due to be supplanted by some new mani-

---

[1] Edward L. Bernays was a noted public relations counsel. [Ed.]

festo and some new bill of rights. It must dissociate its economics completely from what is by this time a purely rhetorical ideal of American democracy, though it has since the first days of the Republic been inextricably bound up in our minds with the capitalist system. If we want to prove that the Marxian Communists are wrong and that there is still some virtue in American democracy, if we want to confute the Marxian cynicism, the catastrophic outcome of whose "economic laws" is predicted, after all, only on an assumption of the incurable swinishness and inertia of human nature, an American opposition must not be afraid to dynamite the old shibboleths and conceptions and to substitute new ones as shocking as possible. Who knows that they may not seem less shocking to other people than to us shibboleth experts ourselves? . . . The extreme illiberalism of the post-Wilsonian period has had the effect of discouraging liberals: we have gone on making our complaints and proposals, but with a vigor which has tended to diminish in proportion as we became increasingly conscious that no one was paying attention to us. Who knows, however, that if we spoke out now with confidence and boldness, we might not find our public at last?

The Plan: Two Tourists' Views

Americans did not simply observe Soviet Russia from a distance of thousands of miles; in swelling numbers they visited the land of the proletariat in person. During 1930 approximately 5,000 American tourists traveled through the USSR, twice the total of the year before. In 1931 the figure climbed perhaps as high as 10,000.

Most of these visitors brought with them the same question which increasingly preoccupied their countrymen in depression-blighted America: Was the Five-Year Plan succeeding and, if so, should it be imitated by the United States?

Will Durant, the celebrated author of The Story of Philosophy, *reported to* Saturday Evening Post *readers what he and his wife had seen during a Russian journey in the summer of 1932. Later he published the articles under the title,* The Tragedy of Russia. *A visiting journalist, Maxwell Stewart, painted a strikingly different scene.*

19 A TRAGEDY*

. . . [I]n our [train] car we struck up acquaintance, through our halting German, with a Russian doctor and a Jewish engineer. The Jew told of the pogroms he had seen in the days of the Tsars, and spoke gratefully of his people's freedom under the Soviets. The doctor was a giant who liked the hardships he was encountering in his work among the construction camps; he smiled at our American comforts, and preferred Siberia; "there are heroic things to be done here," he said, magnificently. Together they sang for us the latest revolutionary songs. Their spirit infected us, and we began to thrill with the tempo of this enterprise, the promise of this reborn land.

When we arrived at our first destination we were already enthusiastic Bolsheviks. We prepared cheerfully to leave the train and plunge into the midst of Siberia. Here at Omsk, where Dostoievski had spent his years of exile in the House of the Dead, we would breathe the fresh air of Russia's liberation, and study at closer range these sturdy people who were bearing short rations gladly while they built Utopia.

The station was vast and impressive; as we entered it I thought of the thousands of exiles who had passed through it before and after the Revolution. But my historical fancy was distracted by present sensation. This spacious waiting-room was quite literally covered with people; not merely the benches, but every foot of the floor; people squatting, sitting, standing, leaning, reclining, lying down, on and amidst their forlorn baggage of boxes, sacks, baskets and bags; people of all ages, but of only one condition—poverty final and complete. We had never seen poverty like this, not even in China or India; for there the poor are naked, and the human body, barring deformity, has a redceming dignity not possessed by the pitiful rags that covered these spiritless bodies, the torn boots that covered a few of these feet. We had seen filth like this, at Canton or Benares, but nowhere worse filth than these faces encrusted with the soil, these hairs thick and tangled with dust, these eyes half closed with dirt. Everywhere in the station they lay, like fish squirming in a box; we needed the help of broad porters' shoulders to find a pathway through them; and when we emerged by another door into the street, the crowd was there too, at least two hundred more, making seats

---

*Will Durant, *The Tragedy of Russia: Impressions from a Brief Visit* (New York: Simon & Schuster, 1933), pp. 11–21. Copyright 1933 by Will Durant; copyright renewed 1961. Reprinted by permission of Simon & Schuster, Inc.

and beds out of the mud of the road. What were they doing here? We learned the reason later: they were waiting—a day, a week, or a month—for their chance to get a train out of Omsk. But the trains were rare, and the cars were almost full when they reached Omsk; these people had to take their turn. Why did they wish to leave Omsk? We should not ask that question tomorrow.

The guide-book had spoken of taxis, and had given their rates; but there were no taxis, there were only moribund cabs, old *droshkies* whose listless drivers announced that it would cost us one hundred and twenty rubles—that is, sixty dollars—to transport ourselves and our five pieces of baggage three miles to the hotel. My young vocabulary was soon exhausted upon them; failing to understand one another, we piled into the cabs nevertheless, trusting to a *fait accompli* to clarify for us the murky metaphysics of the ruble. Over the uneven cobbles and the mud-puddles of the streets we passed precariously to the town. Some of the houses were shacks, some were modest but presentable little structures one story high; they were all of wood, and obviously dated from the ancient régime. The only new buildings were the well-constructed factories, and the offices of the Grain Trust. Main Street was here a thoroughfare of small and gloomy stores, in which hardly any customers could be seen. On the rough sidewalks and the curbs sat a good part of the population of this city of 116,000 souls; they squatted wherever the earth would receive them, and offered their little wares, or waited idly for paradise. They were almost as shabby and destitute as the derelicts at the station. Through them we picked our way into the hotel to which Intourist, official travel bureau for the Soviet Government, had sent our request for a room.

On the letter-rack stood our reservation, long since delivered, but still unopened because addressed in English. Nevertheless, there were rooms; and we chose one furnished with a table, two simple wooden chairs, and frail little iron beds covered only with thin historic comforters pungent with age. The lady in charge timidly informed us that this room would be ours for a night for the small sum of thirty-six rubles—eighteen dollars. We inquired into the whereabouts of food, and were told that we might eat in the neighboring *stolovaia* at ten rubles per person per meal. We calculated the cost of this one day in Omsk: it would come to a hundred dollars. We had but twenty rubles with us, and our American money, which we had been told would find ready currency in Russia, was refused on every hand; it was illegal for a Russian to take it, and even the State Bank would change it only at the rate of 1.94 rubles per dollar. The Government insisted that its rubles were worth fifty-three cents; but when it sold its products or services, its rubles bought the equivalent of from two to five cents—in Omsk it was nearer two. This was our first taste of Soviet finance.

I was in despair, and flung mispronounced Russian words about me in the effort to explain that this frenzied finance was incredible; but the *izvoshchiki* and the landlady stared at me mutely — they would have their rubles. It was Ariel, my traveling companion, who saved me, as she was to do so many times on this chaotic trip. She stalked every person she could find in the hotel, and confronted each of them with the challenge: *Sprechen Sie Deutsch?* One answered *Ja;* Ariel gripped him with firm hands and brought him to our salvation. He was a buying agent for a Soviet Government organization which we shall designate under the initials N.A.R. He was tall and thin, quiet and strong; his boots were the cleanest we had seen in Russia, and his leather jacket marked him out as a man of some prosperity and power. Ariel explained our situation to him in German almost as bad as my Russian; he took it in swiftly, and cleared the air with a word and a bundle of rubles. With the help of our own little batch he paid the cabmen, paid the hotel-keeper, and sent out for some food to a station nearby. When it came—chopped meat, tapioca and black bread—he sat down to share it with us; and pledging us to secrecy, unburdened his soul.

"Let us arrange," he said, softly, "that if anyone enters the room we shall be talking of the virtues of Stalin."

We agreed; and assured by our innocence that we could not possibly be spies, he answered our questions with a candor that shocked us.

"Are the people of Omsk better off," we asked him, "than before the Revolution?"

He smiled bitterly.

"In those days some of us were poor, others were neither poor nor rich, others were rich. Now we are all poor—all but the N.A.R., for printing is cheap." (He was to refuse more than five dollars for all the rubles he spent on us.) "In those days we had food to eat; today the people starve."

A moment later a maid knocked at the door, and brought us tea. We handed her a borrowed ruble, but she refused it. Then, pointing to a piece of bread, she begged for it humbly, and striking her stomach whispered (even without interpretation we could understand her):

"I am starving."

We could hardly believe her. We handed her the slice of bread; she bowed almost to the floor, and rushed out, leaving the worthless ruble behind.

"Promise me," said the N.A.R. agent, "that when you return to your country you will report truthfully what you have seen: this maid, those people in the street, those at the station, this organized starvation."

He went on passionately, for he had suffered. Condemned to ten years in Siberia for "speculation"—that is, for selling things which only the State might sell—he had many times been near death through much labor and little food. He had worked his way out of imprisonment into a place of comfort and power; and yet he hated this communism as the enemy of all freedom and happiness.

"But," we protested, "we have been told that the people voluntarily accept this restraint, and these short rations, in order to industrialize their country, and make it secure in case of war."

"It is not so," he said. "Eighty per cent of us despise the Soviet Government. It is turning us all into slaves."

"If the people despise the Government why don't they overthrow it?"

Through the window came the dull rhythm of marching feet. Every second it grew stronger, until we saw in the street below a squad of soldiers pounding by with heavy boots.

"Every hour they pass by," said the man from the N.A.R. "They do not enjoy it; but they have to remind us, every hour, that we have no guns, and must obey. If it were not for that army. . . ."

"If the people despise the Government, why do they join the army?"

"In order not to starve." . . .

Having found the privy unusable because of the poor eyesight of the Russians, we persuaded the landlady to clean it. She agreed with a weary smile. We understood her smile the next day, when we found conditions as before.

That afternoon I stood in the rain for an hour, with our friend of the N.A.R., waiting for a bus to take us to the station, where I was to present to the commandant an order from Intourist for a *coupé* to Moscow on the Friday train. Across the street a red banner announced the progress of communism in China, and its approaching victory throughout the world. Nearby was a fine statue of Lenin receiving Dora Kaplan's bullet; a bird, not having read *Das Kapital,* sat on his forehead and voided its waste on his nose. A gigantic Mongol, waiting with us, grew tired of standing, and lay down full length in the mud of the rain-soaked road. The little bus came, and we fought for standing room in it; the place I won was behind a lucky peasant who carried some naked fish under his arm, tickling one neighbor with their heads, and myself with their oily tails.

At the station we waited three hours for the station-master, while around us half a thousand paupers moved noisily among their bags, mothers scolded, and children cried. At seven o'clock the commandant returned to his office, read my letter, and informed me that all places on the Friday train were taken, and that we should have to wait until Monday. The thought of keeping Ariel five days instead of two in the midst of this destitution horrified me; and I, who had entered Russia by the back door in the hope of remaining unnoticed and unescorted, was driven to the expedient of showing a letter of introduction from the most famous of American senators. The commandant melted a little, and promised that tickets would be ready for me in his office at three o'clock the following afternoon. I began to learn that the most terrible of all things in Russia is the difficulty of getting out.

Waiting for the bus that was to take us back, I saw a little more of the station crowd. Children hunted in the bags of their parents and found hard crusts of bread, which they munched feverishly. One man scratched a bone out of the road, brushed away some of the dirt with his sleeve, and bit hungrily into the rotten meat. A hay-wagon passed, on which a man lay prostrate, rolling helplessly; soon, surely, his head would be caught in the wheel. My N.A.R. guide smiled at my concern.

"Don't worry about him," he advised me. "Can't you see that he's dead—dead of starvation? It happens too frequently to bother about it."

Yes, Omsk itself was dying. Its population was falling day by day; within the year it had been surpassed by Novo-Sibirsk, the new capital of Siberia. In the old days it had been a busy center of trade, full of merchants and goods; there was no place or function for it now, since the stores were half empty and the State controlled all the commerce of the land. Perhaps the Soviet remembered how Kolchak had made Omsk his counter-revolutionary capital; what difference did it make, to a stoic rebuilder of nations, that a few decrepit souls, or cities, died? . . .

20 THE PLAN IN ACTION*

All are agreed that Soviet Russia's Five-Year Plan is one of the most interesting and significant developments of modern times. But at this point agreement stops completely, for the Plan is so tremendous and many-sided, so challenging to the basis of life as we have always known it that it is difficult to find two persons who will interpret it alike. . . . Everything depends upon what qualities of human life we hold most important, for the amazing achievements of the Plan have been at the expense of many values which we Americans have long considered absolutely basic.

It came as a start to the writer the other day to read of the tenth anniversary of the inauguration of state planning in Russia. For although we are accustomed to think of the announcement of the preliminary figures for the Piatiletka—the Five-Year Plan—in 1927 as marking the beginning of state planning, the Soviet State Planning Commission was actually organized in February 1921 and started the preparation of control figures in the key industries the year which marked the bottom in the post-war decline in Russian industry. The first seven years were, however, largely years of reconstruction, the primary aim being simply to restore the comparatively low pre-war standard of productivity. This was achieved only in the year ending September 30, 1927. It was at this time that the decision was first made to order the nation's economic life by attempting to draw up a careful plan of national requirements five years in advance. The revised Five-Year Plan was finally approved by the Congress of Soviets in 1928 and put into operation on October 1 of that year.

The basic principles of the Piatiletka are simplicity in themselves. In order to transform Soviet Russia from a predominantly agricultural country into a first-rate industrial nation, a five-year building and construction program costing over three and a half billion dollars has been entered into which involves a much more rapid rate of industrial development than has ever been achieved in any country. In order to accomplish this, a definite plan has been prepared covering every phase of the national economy. It is unnecessary to point out that this requires that the program of every industrial operation and every building project must be correlated with each of the many others upon which it depends, both as to time and as to quantity. This tremendous undertaking has not been achieved without some

*Maxwell S. Stewart, "Russia's Five-Year Plan in Action," *Survey,* Vol. LXVI (July 1, 1931), pp. 337–40.

very serious mistakes, but the experience of the seven previous years proved sufficient to prevent any catastrophic error such as conceivably might have occurred.

For the close of the five-year period the increase in the gross agricultural output was set at 151 per cent over that of the year 1927-28, that of all industries 181 per cent, pig-iron production was to be trebled, and the national income was to be doubled. While every line of industry was to be expanded, especial emphasis was given to those industries engaged in the manufacture of production-goods and tools at the expense of industries producing goods for immediate consumption. The former enterprises, the so-called heavy industries, were to be increased 255 per cent while the output of light industry was to grow by 181 per cent. This discrepancy, of course, was made necessary because of the backwardness of Russia's pre-war industry, but it has meant that the Russian people have been forced to curtail consumption in order to further the Plan. Some idea of the pace which is being maintained may be gathered from the fact that during 1931 the revised control figures call for an increase of 58 per cent in the total production of heavy industry within the twelve months while light industry is to increase but 27 per cent. This tremendous gain is being made possible by the opening of a whole series of new factories which have been constructed during the past two years. The opening of two huge new tractor plants, for example, is expected to increase the tractor production by 240 per cent during the present year.

One should not however get the impression that the Five-Year Plan is a fixed schedule which binds the nation to a certain regime irrespective of changing conditions. As a matter of fact the control figures which are fixed annually have differed widely from those of the original Five-Year Plan and changes have often been made during the course of the year. The adjustments have been mostly upwards, made necessary by uncalculated demands resulting from the growth of some dependent branch of industry.

It is also incorrect to think of the Piatiletka as a more or less rigid theoretical plan foisted on industry from above. It is perfectly clear that such a scheme would not have the least chance of success. The Plan is built from the ground up. In the beginning the workers of every factory and working-unit meet in their trade unions to discuss their particular share in the plan for the coming year. The shop committee in each establishment submits its tentative schedule for each department, and the workers criticise it and make their suggestions. The writer has attended such meetings and can testify to the thoroughness and seriousness of the consideration given. A large proportion of the workers took part in the discussion and they did not mince words in their criticisms of current inefficiencies. While in some cases young workers are carried away by an unjustified enthusiasm concerning the possibilities of the coming year, one can say that each worker in a sense determines his share in the general Five-Year Plan.

After the local factory group has threshed out the problems, the plan as worked out is forwarded to the trust of which the factory is a part. It finally reaches the planning committee of the Supreme Economic Council which has charge of practically all Russian industry. At last the State Planning Commission, the Gosplan, after due consultation with the other bodies, formulates the control figures for the year on the basis of the carefully worked out data obtained from these other groups. At times rather fundamental readjustments are made at the last minute by the Gosplan, usually on the side of prudence. . . .

. . . [D]uring 1930 the various industries of the Soviet Union produced, according to official figures which may be considered as reasonably reliable, twice as much as in 1913—an increase which had been wholly achieved since 1927 when the pre-war level of production was finally reached. There was an increase of 40 per cent in the heavy industries during the last year, and if the quota set forth by the control figures for 1931 is attained, 98 per cent of the Five-Year Plan for these basic industries will have been reached by the end of the present year—three and a quarter years after the beginning of the Plan. . . .

But in spite of the rather general success of the Piatiletka, a number of serious weaknesses have been revealed which illustrate both the dangers involved in economic planning as such and especially of trying to force the rate of economic development at too great a pace. Due to the tremendous pressure put on heavy industry, there has been a very serious shortage of ordinary consumption goods of all kinds, particularly of footwear and clothing. The whole Plan has threatened to break down because of a miscalculation of the amount of coal and wood which would be required as fuel. For although coal-mining has progressed more than called for by the original Five-Year Plan, there is still an acute shortage. The overcrowding of the arteries of transportation has proved to be an even more critical problem. . . .

As the breakdown of transportation would bring to naught the entire program, the Soviet leaders have acted with unusual alacrity in taking measures to remedy the situation. A year ago Ralph Budd, president of the Great Northern Railway, visited the Soviet Union as consultant for the reconstruction of the railways. This year Charles A. Gill, chief engineer of the Baltimore and Ohio Railroad, has been engaged together with a large staff of experts, to give advice on the reorganization of the Soviet railways along American lines. The present plans call for doubling the 50,000 miles of track now in operation within the next few years. In addition to the technical assistance employed from abroad, the Soviet Government has taken extraordinary measures to increase the staff of skilled railway workers. A decree was issued at the beginning of the year ordering every industrial concern to release all of its ex-railway employees for return to railway service.

In fact it has been the deficiency of skilled workers in every field of industry which has constituted the greatest single obstacle to the fulfillment of the Piatiletka. Two years ago Soviet Russia, like most of the rest of the world, was suffering from relatively widespread unemployment. As recently as the beginning of 1929 there were over a million and a half unemployed, including a certain reserve of skilled workers in most lines. But with the progress of the Five-Year Plan all of these and more have been absorbed into industry and construction work. As the only possible source of further supply consisted of raw peasant youths totally unaccustomed either to the discipline of factory life or to the use of modern machinery, the Soviet Government has established special industrial training schools with a capacity of 800,000 a year. Even this measure has proved insufficient for providing the one million six hundred thousand new workers required during 1931. The scarcity is most felt, however, not among ordinary factory workers, but among the specialists and engineers necessary to carry through the tremendous amount of new construction provided by the Plan and to operate the factories along modern lines. Thousands of experts have been brought in from Germany and the United States, and technical schools have put on double pressure to turn out as many technical experts as possible in the shortest possible time. Obviously this has been accomplished at the expense of thoroughness and the dearth of well-qualified technical leadership is undoubtedly hindering the full achievement of the plan according to schedule.

This lack of qualified specialists is evidenced in the failure to meet the specifications of the Five-Year Plan regarding greater industrial efficiency. During the first year the decrease in the cost of production was only 5 per cent instead of the 7 per cent which had been provided by the Plan. . . . It is often difficult to say whether slowness in adopting modern methods is due to stupidity, conservatism or out and out sabotage. Unquestionably all three factors have played important parts. There is no doubt in the mind of any close observer that deliberate sabotage has been widespread and that such practices have greatly retarded the progress of the Five-Year Plan.

Similarly there can be no doubt that much of the increase in industrial output has been achieved at the expense of quality. Those who have lived for years in the Soviet Union complain bitterly over the inferior quality of present-day goods as compared with those of a few years ago. This is particularly true in the case of woolen and leather goods where a shortage of raw materials has necessitated the utilization of inferior products. However lest this emphasis on the decline in quality be misconstrued, the writer would like to give his personal testimony on the two or three Soviet-made articles which he has used long enough to give them a fair trial.

I have found, for example, that Soviet-made overshoes will wear more than twice as long as American overshoes of the same price and keep the feet much warmer during the winter months. Moreover I purchased a pair of ordinary high shoes for eight roubles ($4.00) some six months ago and have worn them steadily since then but they show no undue signs of wear. I have also found Soviet-made woolen hose to be far superior to hose of similar price in the United States. My impression is that when Soviet industry can secure good raw materials the products will compare favorably with the best elsewhere. On the other hand, Russian-made suits and women's clothing are tremendously expensive—judging by gold prices, and the finer qualities simply do not exist at present.

While the difficulty of evaluating the Five-Year Plan as a whole has already been indicated, from a purely economic view—if there can be such a thing as "pure economics"—it has undoubtedly been a success. There has been an astounding increase in both agricultural and industrial production. Foreign and internal trade have shown tremendous gains. The experience of the last two and a half years has rather conclusively demonstrated the feasibility and practicability of social planning. It is almost a foregone conclusion that the Plan will be almost completely fulfilled by the end of 1932 instead of the original date, September 30, 1933.

But if we look at it from the standpoint of the greatest welfare of the Russian people, the situation is badly confused. The advances which have been made have been at the expense of serious psychological and physical sacrifices. Personally, the writer is inclined to discount the importance of the latter. The Russians are a healthy, vigorous people; in spite of the shortage, they are reasonably well dressed. At least there is food enough for all. Housing conditions are bad, however, and overcrowding is almost universal throughout the Union, but I see no other reason for concern over the physical wants of the population. Such discomforts as are felt are counterbalanced by the elimination of unemployment. There is work, food and clothing for all, which is more than we can claim for our own country despite its much greater wealth.

The writer must confess, however, that he is at a loss to say categorically what the psychological effect of all these years of strain will be. For the time being the youth of Russia is gloriously enthusiastic. They have something to live and work for. But one is sceptical about the final fruit of this seemingly unnatural stimulation. It may be that the Russians have uncovered new possibilities within the souls of men—it often appears so; but then again it may only be war-time psychology operative on an unprecedented scale which is bound to collapse as the Wilson idealism of 1918 evaporated leaving the "back to normalcy" of Harding.

The challenge of the Five-Year Plan is moral as well as economic. It is a direct challenge to the smugness and complacency which characterize American thinking on our own chaotic system. It is not unlikely that when historians of the future review our age they will look upon the organization of the diverse and complex economic activities of man under planned social control as the most significant single achievement of our day. This value, of course, will stand irrespective of the outcome of the Five-Year Plan, but Russia has staked her entire future upon its success.

The Plan: Two Engineers' Views

Besides transient tourists, another sort of American visited the USSR. These were the engineers working for the Five-Year Plan. They went to Russia either as free agents or as employees of American firms which had made technical assistance contracts with the Moscow regime. As of 1931, more than 1,000 American technicians

were working for the Soviets. By 1933, 600 were working in auto-
mobile and tractor plants alone. If any Americans could achieve a
thorough and accurate opinion of the Red experiment, presumably
it would be these men living among the Russian people for ex-
tended lengths of time. Yet they too arrived at starkly contrasting
conclusions.

In a letter to Mining and Metallurgy, *an engineer in Moscow angrily*
corrected the journal's dour view of conditions confronting American
technicians in the USSR. Clarence T. Starr, on the other hand, found
little to praise in his experiences as a mining engineer for the Plan.

21 WORKING FOR RUSSIAN PROGRESS*

Moscow, U.S.S.R., Oct. 21, 1930

To The Editor:
I have just received the October number of *Mining and Metallurgy*
and note your editorial comments on *conditions of American engi-*
neers in Russia. While food conditions here are difficult enough, it
seems as if the time were approaching when the press of the United
States, especially the technical press, should begin to take notice of
something else than the *lack of luxuries in Russia.*
    Many of the American engineers here are managing to get along.
Many of those with a desire to render to the U.S.S.R. some return
for their usually generous remuneration and who have a touch of the
pioneering spirit manage to carry on and are even enthusiastic as to
the ultimate results. It is true that it is difficult for an engineer used
to foreign service with any number of subservient natives at his command. There is nothing subservient about the average Russian today;
he doesn't step to the gutter to allow a well dressed foreigner to pass,
as many of those foreigners can testify, but they are *eager to learn,*
almost pitifully eager it seems to one who has tried to get close to
and understand them.
    Why not mix with your critical comments a few of the high lights—
pouring of concrete on the Dneiprostroi project, 80,000 cu. meters
in September and 5,280 cu. meters in one day. A world's record, I
am told, for all time or any country. Also the coal production in the
Donetz Basin district, admittedly 10 per cent less than the five-year

*Julius H. Gillis [Letter to the editor], *Mining and Metallurgy,* Vol. XI (December, 1930), p. 593.

plan calls for, but for all that, 33 per cent greater than any time in Russian history before or after the revolution.

The prices you state are ridiculous as far as they apply to the American engineer. Such prices are charged by profiteers in the open market to their fellow brethren and other unfortunates who have not as yet accepted the status of a worker, but as an American engineer we pay 70¢ per lb. for butter, 14¢ per lb. for sugar, 2½¢ a loaf for bread, chickens are $2 to $5, according to the size.

During the summer my wife and I traveled from Moscow more than half way across Siberia and back. She has also taken short trips alone and with my two daughters, and on all of these, while luxuries were entirely missing, at no time was there serious discomfort. There is no reason why a spirited and self-reliant American cannot come over here and do himself and Russia some good, if he but have a sympathetic attitude toward the struggle of Russia to attain higher things. If he hasn't that feeling, together with a considerable measure of patience or is suffering from an inferiority complex, I agree that it is better both for himself and Russia that he stay away. Of course, one can refuse to learn the language or to find out what can be had and can take trips into strange districts with no thought as to what might be found to eat there, but the Soviet cannot be blamed for that. Shipments go astray here also; but only yesterday I returned to the U.S. Government eight official documents intended for various citizens in different parts of that efficient republic which were enclosed by mistake with mine, but which will be long overdue when they are finally delivered at their proper destinations. And then as to apartments which have not been provided as contracted by the Soviet. I cannot forget a few years ago when a prominent copper company in Montana hired many draftsmen and engineers for the purpose of putting over one of their big programs. Living conditions were to be excellent and prices nominal. Those draftsmen and their families who spent that winter in tents can probably still testify as to the abundance and nominal cost of fresh Montana air, and I sincerely believe that the officials of that company did not share their shivers or lose much sleep worrying about the justice of the situation which was entirely beyond the capacity of their newly imported employees to correct. But why bring that up? Such a thing could not have happened in Russia. Not while two could sleep where only one had slept before.

I seem to have written at some length and have gone beyond my subject; perhaps, as a lawyer would say, most of it is irrelevant and has no bearing on the case, but your "costs" were so unqualified and so far from the truth that I couldn't let them go unchallenged.

My family are having a very interesting and not especially uncomfortable time. As I write this they are discussing an evening to be spent in the near future at the opera. They will not pay $9.90 a seat. The talent will be nearly, if not quite, equal to anything they could see in New York and they will not come home feeling that nearly everyone else in the world can afford better clothes than they.

I certainly appreciate your having read this and hope you will dig up some really interesting and accurate facts in the near future for your editorial notes and comments on conditions in U.S.S.R.

Julius H. Gillis

22 A DEAD HAND HOLDS RUSSIA BACK*

My first experience with the engineers of Soviet Russia was in Pennsylvania several years ago. I had been engaged by the firm with which I subsequently became the Russian partner to take a group of Russian engineers through the mines in the anthracite field.

We were in the underground workings of a mine with which I was only slightly familiar and had come to the top of a plane when one of the visiting Russians asked:

"What is the grade on this haulage road?"

I didn't know but, after studying it for a minute, I gave him an approximate answer.

"What size locomotive do they use to bring the cars up?" he asked.

Again I expressed my lack of exact information but under the conditions as I saw them I thought a six-ton loco would be about right.

"How many cars does it pull each trip?" was his next question.

Again I thought for a minute and said that, on such a grade, I figured a six-ton loco could easily handle four cars to a trip and could handle five but, in the latter case, it would make rather hard going.

The mine superintendent subsequently confirmed these statements. However, as we continued our inspection of the mine, I noticed my Russian friend at every opportunity was figuring in a little note book. Finally, several hours later, he exclaimed:

*Clarence T. Starr, "A Dead Hand Holds Russia Back," *Nation's Business,* Vol. XIX (August, 1931), pp. 25–27, 101.

"But you are right. A six-ton locomotive is the size needed to pull a four car trip up that slope. Won't you tell me how you figured it so quickly? It took me several hours to figure and check the calculation while you did it mentally. Won't you please tell me what formula you used that enabled you to make the calculation in five minutes?"

"That is where you are wrong," I answered. "I didn't do that in five minutes. It took me 25 years."

Perhaps, as well as any, that anecdote illustrates the Russian's constant search for, and dependence on, formulae and rules. This search is dictated by necessity and conviction. In business, or perhaps I should say in government, since they are the same thing in Russia, there can be little opportunity for individual initiative. Every activity—coal mining, building, selling shoes, running a taxi—is not only supervised and directed by the government, it *is* the government. Quantities that can be produced or bought, qualities, prices, methods of selling, producing, bookkeeping, packing, everything, are laid down by the state, through its Supreme Economic Council, or one of its dependent agencies. These rules are iron clad.

DEPEND ON BOOKS AND FORMULAE

What the Russian in office- and everyone, engineers and all, is more or less in office—wants is an authority. If he prepares a plan, and can cite Professor Soandso's book or formula, then he's safe. The government has recognized the book or formula as the authority and the engineer who relies on it has a ready alibi if anything happens.

If, however, the engineer varies an accepted formula from his own experience or tries a new idea without approval, one of two things may happen: He may be right or he may be wrong. If he's right, there's little coming to him in the way of reward or promotion, for in government, whether it be in Russia, or elsewhere, such things move in a fixed groove. If he's wrong he cannot take refuge in saying that he thought the new idea worth trying. A mistake is a serious thing, a crime, and is severely punishable. But a mistake made on authority, in accordance with accepted practice, is pardonable.

This acceptance of authority, this working by rule and formula is not confined to engineering alone. It runs through the whole Russian economic system. The Five-Year Plan itself is a part of it. . . .

My firm's contract in Russia, at the beginning, called for redesigning the workings and buildings for certain coal mines. Any American business man will instantly visualize a rather simple procedure. The steps would be, in general, a survey and study, preparation of the general plans with an estimate to be submitted to a Board of Directors. If the plans and estimate were acceptable, we would expect an order to go ahead with a comparatively free hand within limitations of time and money.

In Russia it is a different story. Such direct action is impossible because of the division of authority and responsibility. To get a proper appreciation of the procedure in Russia it is necessary to keep in mind that the coal trusts, like all other industrial units, are governmental institutions functioning within limits prescribed by the Supreme Economic Council which in turn is controlled by the requirements of the Five-Year Plan.

Each coal trust (there were five such trusts when I left Russia) is given its orders by the Supreme Economic Council for tonnage required the next year and must get it out. The trust upon receipt of its orders presents the problem to another trust also an agent of the Supreme Economic Council responsible for such things as plant design. This trust, known as the projecting department, is the department with which we worked most closely and from whom we received our assignments.

CONSULTANTS FOR THE PROJECTING TRUST

On completion of an assignment the first step was to present our general or schematic plans and recommendations to the group of technical experts employed by the projecting trust as consultants. This group was expected to express and did express its conclusions as to the correctness of design and so on. Its approval was not final nor were its decisions mandatory. Such authority is vested in another group known as the Supreme Technical Council, called the S.T.C., the immediate agency of the Supreme Economic Council.

For every industry in Russia there is a technical council before whom the engineer must *defend* his proposals. I use the word "defend" not only because it is an accurate translation of the Russian word but because the engineer who submits the plans is literally under attack. The presumption seems to be that something must be wrong with his plans. He doesn't explain, assuming that his employers have faith in him, he "defends."

IRKSOME EXPERIENCE

To the experienced American engineer of known reputation accustomed to having his opinions and recommendations considered primarily on the basis of practical experience this session with the Supreme Technical Council sometimes proved a decided ordeal. I have in mind the experience of the president of one of the best known firms of coal plant designers in the United States. With the assistance of a Russian Commission sent to America to expedite the work, his firm prepared plans and estimates for three large units, requiring about a year for the work. The president, however, spent an additional nine months in Russia defending his plans before they were finally approved by the S.T.C.

Each man on this council is supposed to be an expert in some particular field. He is probably the author of some treatise or the originator of the formula on which calculations must be based. The council as a whole takes its responsibilities seriously and members appear unhappy if they cannot pull the recommendations to pieces. Every detail is gone into most carefully as each man must be convinced that everything done in his field is according to approved formula both as to technical detail, and its relation to the general scheme of Russian Economy.

This adherence to formulae, in addition to irritating the practical-minded American, is costly. Russia has largely accepted German practice and the formulae are built on German foundations. As an illustration, it is German practice to enclose electric transformers in buildings. It was extremely difficult to persuade them to use the American practice of open air transformer stations even though this would mean a saving of several hundred thousand dollars in building construction for a single station. . . .

I have no desire to belittle the Russian engineer nor to suggest that engineering is to be learned by rule of thumb and not from the literature of the profession. Russia has many able engineers but they are held down by the fear that, if they deviate from government rule and the deviation is not successful, the punishment will be severe. . . .

FORMULAE THAT MAY FAIL

One young Russian engineer came to me one day and asked:

"How much sand per day will be used by a certain type of engine pulling so much weight up such and such a grade?"

I had been in Russia long enough to know there was something behind the query, so before beginning the guessing contest I questioned my interrogator and discovered that he had worked out a formula. After looking it over I asked him:

"Have you figured out what wet rails do to your figures?"

No, he hadn't, nor what a flat wheel or any of several other unknown factors might do. He wasn't discouraged but went right ahead and got his formula accepted as a standard. If a "lokey" stalls because my engineer didn't take into account several different factors, the engineman is out of luck. First, he doesn't get any more sand that day without several conferences. Second, if he didn't take the theoretically correct amount, he will probably lose his job or be suspected of sabotage. If, however, he did take the correct amount he is absolved from all blame. So is the author of the formula since the Technical Council approved it. . . .

Standardization is an excellent thing, both in theory and in practice, but it can be carried to a point where all adaptability is lost. Let me describe an instance, and here I'm telling a story which parallels, but not exactly, a situation we met in Russia.

In one building some 15 different motors were needed. To do exactly the work required, one should have been 9.5 horsepower another 10.25 and so on, but to build or buy a different motor for each task might well be an extravagance. On the other hand, to fit the same powered motor to every task would be a great waste of power.

Somewhere there would be to us with American training a common-sense halfway point which should neither try to procure an individual motor exactly suited to each particular task nor to make over the job to fit a particular motor. We should have asked, "What will make the mine pay?" "How can we get coal out with the least cost in view of all existing conditions?"

But to the Russian under government control there could be no half way. There must be a rule. Standardization was either all right or all wrong.

One of the handicaps Russia is facing in her industrial problems right now is in her leap to standardization. Mines of similar tonnage must have exactly the same equipment, mine cars, fans, head frames, preparation plants, regardless of physical conditions of the property.

This reliance on theory, this obedience to law is due partly to industrial inexperience, partly to the pressure to get into production as quickly as possible, but the most important cause is the Russian ideal of government.

When the Communists assumed power, there were no industrial facilities but there was a crying need for thousands of things. There was an urge to build in a few years an industrial system equal to that of Great Britain or Germany or the United States which had taken years to build. There was no time to accumulate experience to try plans by success or failure. Some one—and that some one was the government—must settle what was right and all must follow it.

And with that goes the inherent weakness of all government in business, the suppression of the individual, the denial of the reward of initiative. If we set out to build a nation on the theory that each man is as good as his neighbor then we may well ask ourselves, "Will all men end up on the level of the best or on the level of the worst?"

What seems to me more likely to happen is that all men will end up on a dead level of mediocrity.

III

THE PURGES AND THE PACT
1933-1940
the question of freedom

Heretics from the Faith

The First Five-Year Plan imposed enormous hardships on the Russian people. In the drive to build up heavy industry and to collectivize agriculture, the regime sacrificed the comforts of consumers and the freedom or even lives of resistant peasants. Only by the mid-1930's, with the Second Five-Year Plan underway and approximately 75 per cent of peasant farms collectivized, did economic conditions become easier.

Political repression grew increasingly harsh, however. The assassination on December 1, 1934, of Sergei Kirov, a high Communist official and a close friend of Stalin, incited the government to execute scores of persons before the actual assassin was apprehended. (Two decades later, Premier Khrushchev claimed that Stalin himself had ordered Kirov's death.)

These Soviet developments aroused surprisingly little attention in the United States. Just as the prosperity of the Twenties distracted Americans from Russia, so the New Deal increasingly distracted them between 1933 and 1939. The volume of books and articles about the USSR declined drastically during this period, except for a flurry when President Roosevelt granted diplomatic recognition to the Moscow regime late in 1933.

Only among liberal and radical sympathizers did interest continue at the same height as before. Indeed, the Soviet question became almost monopolized by those on the ideological Left, particularly those who claimed that capitalism was dead and who dismissed the New Deal as incoherent improvisations. In line with Edmund Wilson's advice in his 1931 "appeal to progressives," these left-wingers were wondering how or whether to "take Communism away from the Communists." Incessantly they argued about the meaning and merits of Stalin's policies. Inevitably their discussion created a virtual symposium on the meaning of freedom.

The career of Eugene Lyons personifies starkly the substance as well as the turmoil of this debate. Lyons climaxed a lifetime of ardent political radicalism by serving from 1928 to 1934 as the United Press correspondent in Russia. He ended his "assignment in utopia" filled with a sour disillusionment.

Max Eastman, the versatile editor, poet, and critic, followed a roughly parallel ideological course. He began as an enthusiast of the Bolshevik Revolution; in the 1920's he became an ardent Trotskyite; and by the 1930's he was becoming progressively convinced not only that Stalin had betrayed the Revolution, but that Marxism itself was morally and rationally untenable.

Lyons' explanation of his break with the Communist faith, written soon after leaving the USSR, anticipated the much fuller account in his autobiography, Assignment in Utopia (1937). The reaction among pro-Soviet circles to such heresy is suggested by Lincoln Steffens' review of Max Eastman's Artists in Uniform.

23 TO TELL OR NOT TO TELL*

I

"Whatever happens," I pledged in my own mind on my way to Soviet Russia, "I shall never attack the Soviet regime. No matter how disappointed I may be in the Bolshevik reality, I shall keep the disappointment to myself."

I knew the bitterness in my own heart against the Emma Goldmans and other "renegades" who had turned against the socialist fatherland. I had myself, a dozen times over, heaped abuse upon those American radicals who had gone to the new Russia to pray

---

*Eugene Lyons, "To Tell or Not to Tell," *Harper's,* Vol. CLXXI (June, 1935), pp. 98–112. Copyright 1935, by Harper's Magazine, Inc. Reprinted by permission of the author.

and emerged to scoff. They were white-livered, bourgeois-minded backsliders, namby-pamby liberals, tired radicals, if not actually on the payroll of Wall Street. Did the idiots think that a revolution could be made without terror and bloodshed? Their "objective" reports, their self-righteous horror, their lugubrious pity for the sufferings of the Russians—just transparent masks of their treachery to the cause.

No, I vowed that I would not allow myself to be maneuvered into their company. I steeled myself against possible shock, assuring myself morning and night that I did not expect too much from a revolution only ten years old in a culturally backward country, a revolution whose energies had been diverted by civil war and intervention and famine. Of course I should find shortage and suffering, self-seeking bureaucrats and innocent victims. That was the price exacted by history. One could not sniff and choose—this I like and that I don't. It was revolution, good, bad, and indifferent. The working class in power for the first time in human history.

The fact, however, that I pledged myself in advance to silence was proof that doubts gnawed at the core of my faith. The very speed and heat with which I consigned critics of the new Russia to the outer darkness of impotent liberalism and foul renegacy showed that I dreaded their corroding effects upon my untarnished beliefs. The same doubts and dreads, I may have suspected, bothered other American intellectuals of the left. . . .

I was prepared for the trenches. My post, as correspondent for a great American news agency, was particularly strategic. I should be in a position to shoot the lies about Russia in the capitalist press full of holes. I knew that truth does not consist of so-called facts; that a picture may be true and "objective" in detail yet compose into a nightmare lie in its entirety. I would devote myself to the underlying truths rather than to the misleading surface facts.

Mine would be the larger objectivity of history in the making.

II

I reached Moscow in February, 1928. The date is significant. The Soviet Union three months earlier had celebrated a decade of power. Joseph Stalin had just sealed his triumph over all political opposition by sending Trotsky, Zinoviev, Radek, Kamenev, Rakovsky, Preobrazhensky, and their supporters into Siberian or Arctic exiles. "Nep"— the New Economic Policy of a socialist-capitalist compromise insti-

tuted by Lenin in 1921—was groggy on its legs from the blows of a
new socialist drive. The Five Year Plan of national industrialization
was on the political horizon, and the offensive against the growing
influence of the better-to-do peasants (kulaks) demanded by Trotsky
was about to be launched by Stalin.

The country, in short, was on the brink of a second revolution, as
costly and thoroughgoing as that of 1917. The class war was being
resumed on all fronts. An electric awareness of impending battles was
in the air. "Nepmen" and kulaks and "former people," intellectuals
of the pre-Soviet generation and Communists of the easy-going "idealistic" school were scurrying for cover in a panic. There would be
no more room for word-mongers and romantics, no more nonsense
about democracy and fair play in the ranks of the ruling party. A
disciplined, monolithic, hard-boiled army was starting to build socialism in one country!

My initial reactions to the physical scene were distressingly unsatisfactory. The sense of depression engendered by dirt, rags, drabness,
beggary seemed a betrayal of the cause, and I hastened to fight it
down. The sympathy stirred by the spectacle of suffering—even the
suffering of social outlaws and class enemies—seemed an alarming
symptom of ideological weakness, and I held on grimly to slogans of
ruthlessness. Real Bolsheviks, I observed, were not merely indifferent
to this suffering but took a perverse pride in it, as a sort of testi-
monial to their strength of purpose. . . .

Within a few days I realized . . . that I was myself, as a bourgeois
correspondent, among the untouchables. I pointed out meekly that
John Reed had also arrived as a bourgeois correspondent, though
now his ashes rested on Red Square. I tried to remind people that I
had accepted the role of capitalist reporter with the knowledge and
consent of Communists in New York and Moscow. To no avail. I
was asked not to call on American friends in the Hotel Lux, headquarters of the foreign Communists, because "it is embarrassing to
associate with a bourgeois representative." Russians who had been
my friends in New York were frightened speechless by my voice over
the telephone in Moscow. But I adjusted myself even to the fact of
political and social outlawry. What is personal discomfiture against a
great revolution?

I still had my strategic position on the world front of the class
war and my duty to perform—a strategic position but not a comfortable one. My job, after all, was to flash Russian news to American readers. . . .

III

The first fruits of the Five Year Plan . . . were very bitter. Opposition inside the ruling party against the speed of industrialization and the methods and tempo of agrarian collectivization was squelched with unprecedented vigor. Even the relative democracy that had made an open political controversy in the party possible until then, as in the Trotsky-Stalin battle, became unthinkable. . . .

The kulaks were "liquidated as a class" in one of the most brutal episodes of such dimensions in all modern history. Millions of peasant homes were destroyed, their occupants packed into cattle cars and dumped in the frozen North or parched Central Asia. These kulaks of course were not the bloated exploiters of propaganda posters. I saw batches of these wretched men, women, and children at railroad sidings, peering out of air-holes in the cattle cars like caged animals. By pre-revolutionary standards, let alone Western standards, they were themselves poverty-stricken. In practice, moreover, economic status became secondary in the choice of victims; whoever opposed the forcible collectivization became officially a kulak, and if he were too utterly poor for such a label to stick he was called a "kulak agent" and liquidated anyhow.

More than half the nation's livestock was slaughtered by desperate peasants. Foodstuffs and other consumers' goods dwindled disastrously. The purchasing power of the national currency slid to new depths every month. Standards of living went down instead of up. The rise in food consumption, increase in living space, and other everyday improvements specifically promised by the Plan were no longer mentioned. . . .

Terror became a tangible presence. Prison camps multiplied, executions without trial became so commonplace that they lost their "news value." Wives whose husbands were rounded up on vague suspicion never saw them again; bodies are not given up by the G.P.U. Vast construction and industrial undertakings were placed under the G.P.U., or secret service, and scarcely any major construction job was without its quota of prisoners. Fear and mutual distrust spread everywhere, including the ranks of the Communists themselves. Art was harnessed to industrialization and whipped mercilessly if it balked.

Inventoried in this fashion, the pressures and fears of that period sound like a neat page of ancient history. For me, immersed in these events, using them as the raw material of my everyday work, they were not historical generalizations. They were passionately human and intimate. The great tragic themes of peasant liquidation, persecution of intellectuals, tightening food shortage were bodied forth in hundreds of individual tragedies, the continuous impact of sights and sounds, numberless minor episodes in the press and in life. . . .

All that too was news, and I sweated in earnest determination to balance every present-tense event with a future-tense promise. I was trying to convince myself, as much as my readers, of this balance. Endlessly I explained that it was all part of the price of a new system in birth. Bloodily, expensively, in a sort of national panic, new factories did go up and more machines did begin to function between breakdowns. The industries related to war were especially successful. Decades of industrialization, I repeated after *Pravda* and *Izvestia,* were being crowded into a few hectic years. The one socialist land was being made impregnable in a military sense against its capitalist neighbors. New industrial giants were rising where once was empty steppe. The deeply rooted private-property sense of the peasantry was being weeded out with bayonets and agriculture was being industrialized on a collective foundation. The more that doubts assailed me, the more that unorthodox pity for the victims flooded my being, the louder I apologized. There was something soothingly anaesthetic about the metaphors of class war—economic fronts, agrarian fronts, socialist fortresses, victories and defeats.

When I paused to consider my own state of mind, I was dismayed. The certainties I had brought with me had somehow lost their firm texture. My stomach was not strong enough to digest the Soviet reality. The spectacle of disaster, oppression, arbitrary power, pain, and death all around me could not be reduced to simple Bolshevik arithmetic of price-paid-for-the-future. The news that forty-eight professors and specialists had been shot without trial at one clip for alleged sabotage of the food industry reached me while I was inspecting the new tractor plant in Stalingrad; try as I would I could not check off one against the other as orthodox bookkeeping demanded. "They'll never solve the meat problem by slaughtering professors," I said bitterly. . . .

A suspicion was breaking through the walls of my prejudice in favor of everything Soviet—the suspicion that much of what was happening had not the slightest relation to socialism. I began to ask indeed whether it was not defeating socialism. The excesses of kulak liquidation had brought food shortage in its train and that, in turn, was working havoc with productivity of labor. . . .

IV

I returned to America for a visit early in 1931. All the way across Europe and the Atlantic I wrestled with the problem of how much of what I had seen and what I had thought I should tell. I was no longer so certain that a recital of Soviet actualities constituted an attack on the proletarian revolution. What if the revolution at this stage needed the defense of exposure to world opinion? What if the concentration of autocratic power in the fists of a few leaders needed the corrective of public responsibility for their deeds?

Communists and Soviet sympathizers the world over, from Trotsky down, were trying to solve this problem without doing violence to their intellectual integrity. Some of them had decided that history could not be falsified and that the Stalin regime was not necessarily synonymous with Communism and revolution. A few went farther and insisted that the world revolution must not be burdened with the mistakes and failures of the Soviet Union, but must dig the grain of socialism out of the Soviet land and renounce the dirt and dross. The rest held steadfastly to the theory that it was all a family affair, to be hidden from strangers and hidden especially from the working classes; that victories must be exaggerated, failures denied, and the vision of a socialist fatherland nurtured at all costs. . . .

I could not fix the precise point in time when the Hamletian alternative, to tell or not to tell, had first presented itself. In the beginning I had felt guilty *toward the revolution* whenever I reported anything uncomplimentary about the Soviet scene. Later I had begun to feel guilty *toward the Russian people* when I concealed or toned down such things. It was this recognition of the Russians as human entities, with certain minimal human rights and a capacity for human pain, quite aside from their historical function as experimental material, that signalized the change in me.

In America the old inhibitions, the anxiety to save face for the revolution, were victorious in my mind. In private conversation I voiced doubts and fears. . . .

But when I faced an audience in public I uttered few of these things. I had returned to an America of depression and millions of unemployed, in which the ruling group still boasted of its rugged individualism. For millions the epic of a Russia where unemployment had been abolished spelled hope. Its slogans of national planning were penetrating even bourgeois economic thought. I took the easiest and pleasantest course of sustaining these hopes. Although my former radical friends had thrown me over, the general public, where it knew me at all, regarded me as a supporter of the Soviets. A super-patriotic society with headquarters in Chicago sent advance notices to the communities where I appeared warning them that I was a low Bolshevik propagandist. . . .

V

The years after I returned to Russia, in May, 1931, were in some ways the most brutal since the revolution. The extraction of grain and other foodstuffs from sullen peasants became each year a more practiced campaign of force. The death penalty was not only decreed but enforced for crimes which had not been thus punished since the Middle Ages. The fact that the victims were indiscriminately called "counter-revolutionists" did not make the business any less barbarous in my eyes. No one dared challenge the divine right of the G.P.U. to destroy any life it pleased without the formality of a legal accounting. The excesses of preceding years were being paid for in food shortage. Russians talked to me of the "good old days of 1927 and '28." Passportization, one of the most hated instruments of Tzarist tyranny, was re-introduced in even more onerous forms.

No correspondent could have written of these things with complete freedom and retained his job. Besides, I had not yet answered the Hamletian riddle, to tell or not to tell. I had adjusted myself instead to a compromise. I readily admitted the industrial progress, the extension of elementary education, and in dispatches made the most of every new "victory" on any "front." But these victories did not reconcile me to the price being paid. I could not bring myself to subscribe to the theory that the end justifies the means, when under my eyes were proofs that the means determine the end.

Two developments of those years confirmed these deepening prejudices against official lawlessness and government by terror. The first was the arrest and torture, in the larger cities, of tens of thousands of men and women suspected of possessing *valuta*—foreign money, gold, silver, and precious stones. The unsavory job was entrusted to a special "valuta department" of the G.P.U. and it set new records in the story of man's inhumanity to man. The second of course was the fearful famine which killed several millions in the Ukraine, North Caucasus, and Kazakstan in the winter and spring of 1932-33. These facts were of a piece with the general policy of those years. Yet they appeared to me as a culmination, as the quintessence of the guinea-pig theory of revolution. . . .

In later years I came to blame myself for not having reported these gruesome aspects of the Soviet reality more sharply. But perhaps I was not wholly at fault. The kind of facts one could prove in black-on-white to an irate censor could not be obtained without endangering the freedom of Russians. The victims of the valuta division of the G.P.U. were pledged to silence under threat of a return to the torture chambers, although the essential facts were a matter of general knowledge. Throughout the duration of the famine in southern Russia all correspondents were strictly forbidden to leave Moscow without official permission, so that an eye-witness story was out of the question. Only one foreign writer had ventured to visit a Northern prison camp, a Canadian girl, and she was quickly expelled from the Soviet Union.

In addition, I had by no means decided to tell everything I knew. Old loyalties stronger than any logic dogged my every step.

The brutalities of Hitlerism in Germany momentarily provided a post-factum justification for their counterpart in Russia. I visited Hitler's Reich several times and found a scaled-down version of the practices which had horrified me in Russia. The German Jews were being treated to a regime roughly equivalent to that endured by "class enemies" in Russia. Concentration camps, purgings, arbitrary arrests, and executions—all the machinery of unbridled dictatorship—were being installed. The Nazis made no secret of the fact that they modelled their political household upon Bolshevik patterns. Nazi firmness, like Bolshevik firmness, covered a multitude of excesses. I asked myself: must one choose between two sets of frenzied cruelties?

VI

Early in 1933 I sent out a dispatch about the exile of the entire population of several Cossack towns *(stanitzas)* in the Kuban region of North Caucasus, men, women, and children, innocent and guilty alike, as a warning to other recalcitrant peasant districts in the famine area. The story was confirmed by the other correspondents. This chastisement of the Cossacks was no worse than had been inflicted on millions of peasants for years. But the melodramatic nature of the sweeping exile of entire communities attracted world-wide attention. The Soviet authorities were infuriated. My crime was deepened by a series of articles, sent by mail earlier but published about the same time as this dispatch, summarizing a few of the more evident signs of famine and intensified political pressure. Though I erred in the direction of understatement and circumlocution, these articles were perhaps the most outspoken I had written up to that time.

My ambiguous intermediary status in the official rating of foreign newspapermen was thereupon ended. I was definitely branded as "unfriendly." The head censor summoned me into his august presence and threatened expulsion. "The proper authorities," he pontificated, "are considering your case. I do not know what action they will take, but your unfriendly tendencious dispatches have put the Press Department in a position where it cannot and will not intervene in your behalf."

I realized that my tenure of office was nearing its finish. The miracle is that I managed to remain some ten months longer. Toward the end of the year Commissar Litvinoff and the head censor, who were then in the United States, obtained my recall. . . .

VII

I returned to the United States in April, 1934. More sharply than ever I faced the dilemma: to tell or not to tell.

By 1934 exaggerated faith in the Soviet experiment had become the intellectual fashion among the people for whose good opinion I cared most. It was clear to me what sort of account of Russia the intellectual élite preferred to hear.

The editors of a liberal weekly invited me to a staff luncheon. It would have been the polite and kindly thing to bolster up their eager misconceptions. I was given an opening to denounce books about Russia that had told too much. News had just come through that the G.P.U. had been converted into a Commissariat for Internal Affairs. By stretching my conscience, I might have assured them that a new era of liberalism had dawned under the Soviets. But the imprint of the Ukrainian famine, the valuta horrors, the death decrees and heresy-hunts still smarted in my memory. I alluded to a few of these things. A chill seemed to come over the luncheon; apparently I had committed the offense of puncturing noble illusions. The Olympian irony of the situation—I could not help thinking it—was that these men, their exact kind, were being stamped out in the Soviet land like so many insects. They fitted perfectly into the hated category of pre-revolutionary intellectuals, who must hide in dark cracks, praying for only one boon—not to be noticed.

Other intellectuals were no less frightened of the truth. They asked questions about Russia and appeared horrified if I failed to give the prescribed answers. Indeed, it seemed to me that these men and women, insulted to the marrow by the iniquities of bourgeois society, were wiping out the insult Japanese fashion by committing intellectual hara-kiri. They might survive as revolutionaries (at least until the revolution comes) but they were committing suicide as reasoning creatures. . . . Mental integrity was confused with "impotent middle-of-the-road liberalism." These intellectuals, thrown into a panic by the depression and the apparent advent of fascism, forgot that they might take a vigorous position and defend it even more effectively without chloroforming their minds and hearts. . . .

The desire to "belong," not to be a political dog in the manger, was a powerful inducement to silence, or at least to cautious understatement. There were other lowly personal motives drawing me in the same direction. In six years I had sunk roots in the Russian soil. I had grown to love Russia and Russians: much of my resentment flowed from that love. Besides, I must continue to make a livelihood by writing, and it would be useful to return to the Soviet land occasionally, as others do, to renew my status as an authority on that sector of the globe. Yet I knew for a certainty that the Soviet gates, inscribed with the slogan "Workers of the world unite, you have nothing to lose but your chains," would be locked against me if I did not chain my tongue.

These personal considerations I settled easily enough. The social considerations, however, were not so easy to assay and to act upon. Forces of fascism and reaction, anti-semitism and know-nothingism were unquestionably at work in America. The new Russia had come to symbolize for many the opposition to these forces. The symbol was fantastically unlike the reality I had seen and felt and tasted. But was it not more desirable to leave it intact all the same?

Intellectually, I answered the question in the negative. I had come to believe that every defense of Bolshevik *Schrecklichkeit* was also a defense of Fascist *Schrecklichkeit,* on which reaction fattened and grew strong. It was encouraging a method of thinking, I had become convinced, in which human values were secondary to dehumanized slogans and, therefore, deepened the pestiferous swamps in which wars and hatreds and dictatorships bred. . . .

I argued that the Soviet regime must accept the consequences of its actions in the full limelight of public opinion, especially working class opinion, the world over. Outside criticism by the friends of a better world and not by the reactionaries is to-day the only brake on the most centralized monopoly of power in history. Inside Russia no one, least of all a Communist, dares criticize—dares even refrain from shouting hurrah and kissing the knout. . . .

24 SWATTING FLIES IN RUSSIA*

There is something the matter with this work of art. Max Eastman has set out to give some "Soviet ideas on literature," to recount some of the tragedies that have overtaken literary men in Russia. He explains the suicide of two gifted poets—explanations that any interne in psychiatry would hesitate to be quite so sure about. He explains why poor Boris Pilnyak wrote about Tadjikistan—and other "humiliations." He gives resolutions and dicta of extremist groups repudiated by the Russians themselves. He takes the pre-revolutionary artist-bohemians and shows the marks left by the straitjacket of the Stalinist whip-bureaucracy upon their tender flesh. He says: "These excited children (artists) came flocking to Moscow each with his solemn-sure idea of what the art and poetry of the new era was to be," and then shows how dreadfully they made other artists suffer for these ideas. It is, in Max's words, "a sad story of the regimentation of the creative spirit."

But what is sad is not the regimentation. No; there is something else the matter with this work of art. It makes the right people glad and it makes the left people furious, as the author evidently labored with delight to do. And, as was also planned for about five years, the joy and the rage aroused were misdirected by the artist for his own sweet sake; not art's. To him art seems to be a weapon. And the fault in this book of propaganda lies not in the thesis, not in the argument and not even in the facts. Most of these are only a little wrong, a teeny-weeny bit off the correct line; just enough to gather in the goats-got. . . .

No. This book, as books go, is all right enough. It is the author that's the matter. If the stuff in "Artists in Uniform" had been written by some poetic philosopher-critic as handsome and as humorous as, say, Max Eastman—our old pre-revolutionary Revolutionary—it might have been more—well, more scientific. He, our Max, would have reported what the Revolution did to some art, artists and philosophers, as but one of the many devastations of the complete

*Lincoln Steffens, "Swatting Flies in Russia," *New Republic*, Vol. LXXIX (June 20, 1934), pp. 161–62. Reprinted by permission of *The New Republic*, copyright 1934, Harrison-Blaine of New Jersey, Inc.

Change; and why; and whether we could not spare our part in the
terror? We want to know that; Lenin once asked to know that. Some
scientist will tell us that, some day. There was a time when Max
Eastman might have told us.

But now, Russia revolutionized remains what the Great Liberal
called it and fell for: it's the acid test of liberals. And it begins to
look as if the present author of the book before us were one of that
large party of revolutionary pilgrims to the great Revolution who
were waiting at the station for a local—remember?—when that express went by, and not only did not stop for them, but threw dust
and smoke all over them and their baggage. Their baggage! Maybe
that's the matter with Max.

Let's examine our mad pilgrim's baggage and see if we can't find
out what it was that made him think, when he arrived in the revolutionary heaven, that it was hell for "us poets." He got the stuff
where we all got ours, so it's probably uniform and familiar to our
Western culture. In one bag there are Justice and Democracy, in
another there are the Truth and Right and Loyalty, Heroes and some
Romance. The Soviet Russians have some truck like that, but it is
mostly revolutionized or hand-made. Our idea of Justice is that it is
something rare and precious to be done to great men, like Grant or
Trotsky, who earned it by service to the nation. But our loyal fellow
travelers were going into a strange country where the people have a
funny, un-Western complex to the effect that Justice is to be done,
first, to the prosaic, anonymous mob that matters more than Grant
or Trotsky. In terms of Western baggage, we like, as a matter of
justice, to make our great General Grant a bum President. And that's
democracy, too. The rude Russians, being scared and new to democracy, seem to mix it up with a united front. They think that, no
matter what happens to General Trotsky, the important thing for
them is to hang together and not permit any mere heroes splitting
them up. In our baggage is a sort of slogan: "First, be sure you're
right, then go ahead." In Russia, where our conscientious pilgrim
went, they prefer to go ahead and trust to getting right on the way.
Very confusing. But, thinking this way about the Right and Justice,
the Russian democracy avoids that idiocy of ours known as the Third
Party; and, so far also, the Second Party. They really act, that immense mass of people, upon the scientific perception that whether
it's with Stalin or Trotsky, they must all follow one leader, one
party, one plan. Even if they admire Trotsky and hate Stalin's guts
(as Eastman confessed he did), they must maintain that solid front.

It seems to an old politician like this reviewer, that there is a scientific suggestion in that, not a point to stab Stalin with. If only our workers would banish their leaders, labor, political and financial, when they see that they are getting justice, power and wealth for themselves!

There are lots of flies on Russia. It's lousy. The Russians are covered with these pests, as we Westerners are eaten up by millionaires. And there is danger that they will get used to their lice as we are used to and patient with ours. They need fly-swatters over there, but though we mass-produce these handy weapons, we haven't many swatters of our own flies.

Fine old liberals like Max Eastman might better go to Russia to learn what the Russians can teach us, to the end that we may get out of our uniforms. We have to learn, for example, to see them and see, too, that art is a weapon. There is no perception in this book that artists in Egypt, Greece, Rome, in middle-age Europe and in the United States today, had to and did put uniforms on their art; and that they kept them on till the artists themselves came to like and hardly to notice it. In Hollywood, where a great new art is being molded to fit the purposes of our civilization, the friction throws off hundreds of stories more ridiculous and tyrannical than Max Eastman's citations from Russia. And Stalin did cast out the tyrants there; he did it, too, before our author had finished his exposure. That may have been annoying to the muckraker. But think how long it took us to correct our Anthony Comstocks and our Sumners. The artists in Russia, like everybody else, had to be in the service of a new and universally hopeful civilization, and it seems to me, a scientific reporter, that they are sacrificing (if they are) the writers and the painters and the musicians and the screen makers to the audience, to the "mob," to the democracy, just as they did Justice, Loyalty and Truth. Lest, for example, some capitalist writer might write beautifully a mean book to get some hateful guy's goat.

Maybe the audience is the thing.

The Purges

The burst of political terror following Kirov's assassination proved to be only the prelude for a spectacular wave of purges which eventually engulfed almost the entire Party leadership (including all members of Lenin's Politburo except Stalin) and which swept through the ranks of the army, trade-unions, and the general public.

During 1936–38, the purges acquired a terrific momentum. Zinoviev and Kamenev had already been convicted and imprisoned for treason, but in mid-1936 they and a group of their followers were put on trial again, this time accused of plotting with Trotsky and Fascist governments to overthrow Stalin's regime. In this first public "purge trial," they confessed openly to most of the charges; 16 of the accused were then executed. A second public trial, this one of Karl Radek and other Old Bolshevik leaders in January, 1937, produced similar confessions and 13 more executions.

The trials coincided with a growing turbulence on the international scene. Hitler's Germany and Mussolini's Italy were menacing Europe with aggressive Fascist designs. Spain erupted in a civil war which, after Communist and Fascist intervention, increasingly resembled a rehearsal for world war. Meanwhile, France and England confronted the Fascist powers with diplomatic appeasement while the United States remained aloof. The Soviet Union, by contrast, sponsored in 1935 the policy of a Popular Front among Communist, socialist, and "bourgeois" groups against Fascism. In response, American radicals and liberals lauded Russia as the bulwark of Western democracy.

As the purges spread through the Old Bolshevik ranks during the winter of 1936–37, an editorial in The Nation *and Suzanne La Follette's reply in the letter columns of its next issue reveal the consternation among American liberals. Miss La Follette soon was serving as secretary to the controversial "Commission of Inquiry." Under the chairmanship of the philosopher John Dewey and with a staff of anti-Communist intellectuals, the Commission investigated the Soviet charges made at the trials, cross-examined Trotsky in his Mexican refuge, and finally published a report condemning the trials as "frame-ups" and proclaiming Trotsky not guilty. The formation of the Commission accentuated the factional friction within the Left, as can be seen in the manifesto published by* Soviet Russia Today, *an official Soviet organ in the United States.*

25   LIBERAL PERSPECTIVE *

It is possible that it will be another hundred years before all the actual facts about the recent Soviet trials are known. That is true of any complex event that involves clashes of national policy and the

* "Behind the Soviet Trials," *Nation*, Vol. CXLIV (February 6, 1937), pp. 143-45.

ambitions of individuals. Meanwhile it is the task of progressives all over the world to appraise, without any political or emotional commitments, the meaning and implications of what has happened in Russia, to separate legal procedures from political realities and both from matters of faith. Russia is the laboratory in which the success of a workers' state is being tested. And when there is an explosion in the laboratory, the whole world watches the results.

The foremost question in the recent war of the pamphlets has turned on how authentic the confessions are and how fair the judicial procedure. The other big question is the relation of the trials to the struggle for power going on in Russia. Both questions must be viewed in the context of Soviet law and revolutionary history.

Soviet public law differs from ours in several essential respects. In a regime of Socialist construction such offenses as sabotage and wrecking, which in other regimes would be classed merely as property crimes, are considered crimes against the state. Moreover, Soviet judicial procedure is patterned more on the Continental model than on the Anglo American. A man is held for a political crime after an initial investigation by the Department of State Security. There follows an elaborate examination by the State Prosecutor, witnesses being called and a verbatim report of the evidence taken down. All this is secret. Finally comes the trial itself, in which the defendant is given the right of counsel (whatever may be its value in the hostile atmosphere of the regime) and of utterance, and in which he has a chance to deny or withdraw confessions or testimony given in the preliminary examination. Like other Continental trials, the Soviet trial is informal, both prosecutor and defendant being allowed to make speeches which we should consider as belonging on the hustings rather than in a courtroom. The tribunal is the Supreme Court of the U.S.S.R. and from it no appeal lies. Death penalties are provided for a whole series of political and economic crimes against the state. Nor is there anything unusual, even outside Russia, in basing a conviction upon confessions. In both English and American law all that is needed to prove treason is two witnesses to the overt act or confession in open court. The heart of the difference between Soviet and Anglo-American law lies rather in the meaning assigned to "open court." With us the trial is the thing itself, with the burden of proof resting upon the prosecution; with the Soviets it is the final stage in a series of investigations, and the defendant's safeguards lie not in the sifting of every scrap of testimony and documentary evidence but in his chance to challenge or repudiate any testimony. According to Soviet law, the government is under no obligation to publish documentary evidence, and seems in these cases to have lived up to its own judicial procedures. But the prosecution's failure to produce and publish such evidence has profoundly disturbed everyone brought up in the Anglo-Saxon concept of due process.

The first reaction of liberals to the trials was one of sheer incredulity. Surely the thing was not possible! Given crimes so monstrous, how explain the fulness, even the fulsomeness of the confessions? To the credit of most liberals, they did not place much stock in the theories advanced by the Hearst papers, the *American Mercury,* and their close runner-up, the now reactionary *Time*—theories of the use of torture or of some strange and hypnotic "confession gas." The first trial had a bad press, both in England and America. If the second has had a markedly better press—and we believe it has — one reason is that the incredulity has decreased before the relentless piling up of the testimony. Another reason is that the defendants in the second trial, especially Radek, Piatakov, and Serebriakov, were men of more stubborn strength and greater integrity than those of the first trial, and their confessions were therefore more impressive. Finally, the suspicion that the confessions might in the first trial have been extorted by a promise of freedom was weakened when the executions were carried out and when it became clear that the defendants in the second trial made their confessions while facing what they believed to be certain death. It would have been possible for Radek to say a few words of repudiation in open court in the presence of foreign correspondents and the diplomatic corps, and with those words to electrify the whole world. That he did not do so carries considerable conviction.

This leads us from the realm of judicial proccdurc to that of polical reality. It must be clear that the two recent trials do not stand alone. They are best viewed as rounding out (of course there will be other trials soon, but they will be sequels to the last two) a chain of judicial prosecutions of political offenses that stretches back over the last fifteen years. . . . But they differ from those that have preceded in that the defendants have been "Old Bolsheviks" who served with Lenin and occupy an important place in the calendar of revolutionary heroes.

This whole sequence of sabotage and conspiracy on the one hand and ruthless judicial prosecution on the other is best explained in terms of the struggle for power that has been an inevitable part of the consolidation of the revolutionary regime—a struggle that has involved both men and ideas. To understand this struggle it must be remembered that most of the defendants in the last two trials were, along with Lenin and Stalin, the leaders of the October revolution. It was difficult for these men, as Stalin moved into power, to take subordinate positions to one whom they considered their intellectual inferior. One must understand the bitterness of men who were once giants in the revolution and who now felt that their opinions were ignored and their talents wasted in minor administrative posts. One must understand also the bitterness of Stalin and his following, who believed that these men would stop at nothing to displace them from power. One must remember the long sequence of secret maneuvers, arrests, exile, repentance, and pardon in the cases of Zinoviev, Kamenev, and several of the others. And one must see these personal conflicts and hatreds, finally, in the context of a struggle between two theories of revolution—between the belief that the social revolution all over the world must be put ahead of everything else, and the belief that the best contribution to the revolutionary cause was the defense at all costs of the hard-won Socialist gains in Soviet Russia. This struggle was exacerbated by events in Germany and China, and it came to its highest pitch in the belief of the anti-Stalin group (now seen to be mistaken) that Russia would leave the Spanish masses to their fate.

The part of the charges most difficult of belief is the part that has to do with conspiracy with fascist powers. Here one can only suspend judgment. That the opposition group, seeing the economic gains that the Stalin regime had achieved, seeing also the massive administrative machine and the fabulously strong army that it had built up, and realizing that it had intrenched itself in the opinion of the masses—that in the light of this the group should have turned to terrorism and conspiracy is quite plausible. It is less credible that they should have gone so far as to negotiate with hostile foreign powers, although it may be made to fit into the same pattern. For it has been part of the creed of world revolution that national boundaries are less important than revolutionary gains. . . .

From the side of the Soviet government it is probable that the trials have been not only judicial prosecutions but also publicity exhibits. In the present position of Soviet Russia, threatened as it is by war, the health of the state consists in complete unity, and the discrediting of "Trotskyism" by connecting it with terrorism, sabotage, and fascist conspiracies may have seemed an effective way of removing the last vestige of opposition. In foreign affairs the Soviet policy of forming a popular front with the democratic forces and against fascism is threatened by similar opposition. The charges of foreign conspiracy and attempts to restore capitalism in Russia may therefore have been emphasized for their effect upon mass opinion.

A final question remains—whether the whole episode indicates a political weakness inherent in the Soviet system. The passing of a handful of men, however important as revolutionary figures, is of minor importance and in itself cannot touch the inner fabric of the regime. But the trial itself and the conspiracy from which it emerged, even assuming as true the most extreme charges of the government, are both disturbing. The plain fact is that under a proletarian dictatorship men who differ fundamentally from the government cannot express their differences through political action. When a regime makes opposition illegal it sows the seeds of conspiracy; the inevitable result is the growth of plots which find their sequel in ruthless repression and in trials like the one just concluded. This circle can probably be broken only when stability—domestic and international—has existed long enough to allow the realization of the democratic aims embodied in the new Soviet constitution, and by further additions of democratic procedures in ever larger doses in the future. Ultimately in a proletarian dictatorship, as distinguished from a fascist state, no ruling group can remain in power unless it uses its energy and strength for purposes of which the working class approves. That must be the final test of the Soviet system. Meanwhile the sympathetic outside observer must offer the Russian government a measure of that criticism which a legal opposition provides the government of a democracy. He must point out the dangers inherent in a prolonged dictatorship, while refusing to use the trial as the enemies of the Soviet Union are using it—as a curtain which they draw down upon Russia's positive achievements in building a collective economy and a culture.

26 LIBERAL DISSENT*

New York, February 5

Dear Sirs:

Your editorial on the latest Moscow trial strikes me as an interesting study in the hypnotic effect of revolution on decent people. If the trial had taken place in Germany, *The Nation* would surely have

*Suzanne La Follette [letter to the editor], *Nation,* Vol. CXLIV (February 13, 1937), p. 196.

repudiated it at once, without indulging in any rationalization about the difference between Nazi and Anglo-Saxon concepts of justice. But because this thing happened in the Soviet Union, *The Nation* adopts an attitude of Olympian impartiality, and proceeds by implication to indorse or at least condone the whole questionable procedure. Why? I assume because it is afraid that any genuine criticism of the Stalinist regime may be construed as an attack upon the Soviet Union and the October Revolution—as if a *Nation* editorial could hurt Niagara Falls!

I shall not be surprised if within ten years *The Nation's* left-handed indorsement of Stalin's liquidation of the October Revolution is something that its editors would prefer to forget. For it may just possibly be that the true friends of the Soviet Union are the people who either repudiate these recurrent "blood-purges" or at least really "suspend judgment," and not those who accept the Stalinist justification with or without a protective show of pseudo-liberal hocus-pocus. If liberal journalism has any function at present it is that of clear analysis and fair judgment. Your editorial never once strikes below the surface of the political situation of which the trials are symptomatic, and in dealing with the surface it is either naive or disingenuous.

 Suzanne La Follette

27 A PLEA FOR LIBERAL UNITY*

The Open Letter reprinted below speaks for itself. Its specific and immediate purpose was, of course, to show those liberals who had joined the American Committee for the Defense of Leon Trotsky the implications and effects of their association. But in addition I am sure that the signatories also wished to take the opportunity of going on record as reaffirming their faith in the Soviet Union, their confidence in the Soviet Government, and their friendship for the Soviet people.

These are critical times. In Spain an international war, with the Fascists as the aggressors, is being openly waged. In the rest of Europe and in large sections of Asia there exists a state of near-war with all sorts of underground plottings and conspiracies as the order of the day. Again, the Fascist and the semi-Fascist governments are the aggressors. The chief aim of their schemes is the smashing of the Soviet Union, where for the first time in history a planned socialist society has been established. The stakes are indeed high. And the enemies of Soviet Russia will literally stop at nothing to achieve their ends.

---

* "An Open Letter to American Liberals," *Soviet Russia Today*, Vol. VI (March, 1937), pp. 14–15.

Thus, not since its earliest years has the U.S.S.R. so needed the support of its friends wheresoever they may be. And it was to help rally all genuine friends of the Soviet Union in America that this Open Letter was written.

Corliss Lamont

We wish to address ourselves to liberals who may be approached by the American Committee for the Defense of Leon Trotsky, an organization which, we believe, is attempting to enlist their support for partisan political purposes under the guise of defense of certain principles of civil liberties. Especially do we address those members of the committee whose names have been identified in the minds of the American public with truly liberal and progressive ideas, and who have always been counted among those who believe that the Soviet Union should be permitted to work out its problems without interference from the outside world. We hold it of great importance that such members should make their position clear at the present time.

A number of persons joined the Trotsky defense committee for the purpose of defending the right of asylum for Trotsky and to provide him with "the fullest opportunity to state his case." Since Trotsky is now safely domiciled in Mexico, the right of asylum is no longer an issue. The Mexican Government and the American press have certainly allowed him full freedom of expression in his own defense.

Under these circumstances it is proper to inquire into the nature of the further activities of the committee, since we believe it likely that these were not endorsed by its liberal members. Its publications have included not only violent attacks on the Moscow trials, but bitter denunciations of the Soviet Government. Speakers at meetings sponsored by the committee have not merely defended Trotsky and his theories, but have gone so far in their attacks on the Soviet regime as to advocate armed uprising. One of the announced purposes of the committee is the organization of "a complete and impartial investigation of the Moscow trials." The thirty-three defendants in the trials under attack all confessed fully the crimes of high treason of which they were convicted. Impartial observers and newspaper correspondents present at the trials have reported that the trials were properly conducted and the accused fairly and judicially treated. The committee has offered no shred of evidence to the contrary. The demand for an investigation of trials carried on under the legally constituted judicial system of the Soviet Government can only be interpreted as political intervention in the internal affairs of the Soviet Union with hostile intent. . . .

We believe that it is imperative, in the interest of separating liberal ideas from active hostility against the Soviet Union, that liberal members of the committee, who presumably have no hostile intent against that nation but whose names are being used to further these hostile purposes, should clarify their position on the following questions:

1. Did you join the committee out of interest in Trotskyism or wholly in defense of the right of asylum and free speech? If the latter is true, do not the present activities of the committee indicate that the alignment of liberals with enemies of the Soviet Union and defenders of the political principles of Trotsky can only result in confusion and the distortion of true liberalism?

2. Are you willing to ally yourselves, even incidentally, with the internal political movement which has opposed the progressive movement undertaken by the Soviet Union under the five-year plan and the Soviet foreign policy of peace and international understanding and other achievements which have commanded the respect of liberals throughout the world?

3. In uniting with avowed Trotskyists in this committee have you taken account of the effect of its activities in lending support to the fascist forces which are attacking democracy in Spain and throughout the world? Do you not agree with us that there is also a genuine menace to real democracy in the fact that the campaign to defend Trotsky is being supported by the reactionary press and by the very elements which attack the labor movement and freedom of speech in this country?

4. Should not a country recognized as engaged in improving conditions for all its people, whether or not one agrees with all the means whereby this is brought about, be permitted to decide for itself what measures of protection are necessary against treasonable plots to assassinate and overthrow its leadership and involve it in war with foreign powers?

We ask you to clarify these points not merely because we believe that the Soviet Union needs the support of liberals at this moment when the forces of fascism, led by Hitler, threaten to engulf Europe. We believe that it is important for the progressive forces in this country that you make your position clear. The reactionary sections of the press and public have been precisely the ones to seize most eagerly on the anti-Soviet attacks of Trotsky and his followers to further their own aims. We feel sure that you do not wish to be counted an ally of these forces.

Signed by:

John C. Ackley, *College of the City of New York*

Newton Arvin, *Professor of English, Smith College*

Heywood Broun, *President of the American Newspaper Guild*

Edwin Berry Burgum, *Professor of English, New York University*

Allan Campbell, *actor*

Haakon Chevalier, *Professor of French, University of California*

Ethel Clyde

Humphrey Cobb, *author*

Gifford Cochran, *attorney*

Malcolm Cowley, *Literary Editor, "The New Republic"*

Addison T. Cutler, *Department of Economics, Columbia University*

Jerome Davis, *Yale University Divinity School*

Dorothy Douglas, *Professor of Economics, Smith College*

Theodore Dreiser, *novelist*

Mary Dublin, *Sarah Lawrence College*

Guy Endore, *author*

Mildred Fairchild, *Professor of Economics, Bryn Mawr College*

Louis Fischer, *author and foreign correspondent of "The Nation"*

Robert Gessner, *author and poet*

B. Z. Goldberg, *columnist, Jewish Day*

Alphonse Goldschmidt, *Director of Social Economic Laboratory*

Wyllystine Goodsell, *Professor of Education, Columbia University (Retired 1936)*

Lillian Hellman, *dramatist and author*

Granville Hicks, *literary critic*

Arthur Kallet, *Technical Director, Consumers' Union, author "100,-000 Guinea Pigs"*

Vladimir Kazakevich, *economist, Columbia University*

Rockwell Kent, *artist*

Paul Kern, *New York Civil Service Commission*

Dr. John A. Kingsbury, *Director National Tuberculosis Ass'n.*

Mary Van Kleeck, *Director of Industrial Studies, Russell Sage Foundation*

Dr. Corliss Lamont, *author and lecturer*

Ring Lardner, Jr., *author*

Max Lerner, *Editor, "The Nation"*

Robert Morss Lovett, *Editor, "The New Republic"*

Katherine Lumpkin, *economist, Smith College*

Robert S. Lynd, *Columbia University, author of "Middletown"*

William Malisoff, *Editor, "Philosophy of Science"*

William P. Mangold, *Contributing Editor, "The New Republic"*

Anita Marburg, *Sarah Lawrence College*

Elizabeth Dublin Marshall

George Marshall, *writer and research worker*

Clifford T. McAvoy, *C.C.N.Y.*

John McAlpin Millen

Lewis Milestone, *motion picture director*

V. J. McGill, *Professor of Philosophy, Hunter College*

Carey McWilliams, *writer*

Herbert A. Miller, *Professor of Economics, Bryn Mawr College*

Loren Miller, *author*

Edwin Mims, Jr., *Harvard University*

M. Y. Munson, *Department of History, Columbia University*

Dudley Nicholls, *author*

Samuel Ornitz, *author*

Dorothy Parker, *writer*

Walter N. Polakov, *engineer and author*

D. W. Prall, *Professor of Aesthetics, Harvard University*

Samson Raphaelson, *dramatist*

Col. Raymond Robins, *former head of American Red Cross in Russia*

Henry Roth, *novelist*

Margaret Schlauch, *Professor of Linguistics, New York University*

William Seagle, *legal expert and author*

Howard Selsam, *Professor of Philosophy, Brooklyn College*

Arnold Shukutoff, *C.C.N.Y.*

Dr. Henry E. Sigerist, *Johns Hopkins University*

Irina Skariatina, *author*

Bernard Smith, *Literary Editor, Alfred A. Knopf*

Dr. Tredwell Smith, *educator*

Robert K. Speer, *New York University*

Rev. William B. Spofford, *Executive Secretary of Church League for Industrial Democracy*

Viola Brothers Shore, *scenarist*

Tess Slesinger, *novelist*

Bernhard J. Stern, *Columbia University*

Donald Ogden Stewart, *author and actor*

Maxwell Stewart, *Editor, "The Nation"*

Anna Louise Strong, *author and foreign correspondent*

Paul M. Sweezy, *Instructor of Economics, Harvard University*

Lillian D. Wald, *leading social worker*

Mark Waldman, *C.C.N.Y.*

Eda Lou Walton, *poet and critic*

Lynd Ward, *artist*

Clara Weatherwax, *novelist*

Max Weber, *painter*

Louis Weisner, *Mathematician, Hunter College*

Nathaniel West, *writer*

David McElvy White

James Waterman Wise, *editor and author*

Art Young, *artist*

William Zorach, *artist*

Leane Zugsmith, *author*

The Nazi-Soviet Pact

When the purges finally subsided at the close of 1938, an estimated eight million Russians had been arrested, and Stalin had established an unshakable dictatorship. But by then the purge trials no longer obsessed the American Left with such force; that obsession had been displaced by another—the specter of a second world war.

Hitler's annexation of Austria, followed by his demands for the predominantly German-inhabited areas of Czechoslovakia, inflamed international tensions to an explosive pitch. The Soviet Union called upon France and England to defend the Czechs with force. But late in September of 1938, Premier Edouard Daladier and Prime Minister Neville Chamberlain conferred with Hitler and Mussolini at Munich,

*excluding Soviet representatives. The conference resulted in British
and French concession to the partial dismemberment of Czechoslovakia. Six months later, Hitler seized the rest of the country.*

*During the spring and summer of 1939, Britain and France nego-
tiated with the USSR on the terms of an alliance against further
German expansion. But the Anglo-French representatives refused to
accept the Soviet insistence on stationing troops in Poland and the
Baltic countries. Having guaranteed to defend Poland against Hitler,
the English would not consent to what they regarded as disguised
Polish annexation by Stalin. The futile negotiations came to an
abrupt end on August 23, when Germany and Russia astounded the
world by signing a treaty of mutual nonaggression and neutrality.*

*News of the Nazi-Soviet Pact exploded with incredible impact
upon the American left wing. By a process of "triangulation," the
following three selections survey the damage. A letter by numerous
intellectuals, praising the USSR as a bulwark of peace and democracy, outlines the position of Soviet defenders on the eve of the Pact;
ironically, the letter was published in* The Nation *only after the
treaty was announced. The liberals' reactions to the unexpected
event are discussed first by James Wechsler, once a Communist youth
leader, and then by a writer in the Communist* New Masses.

28   SUPPORT PRIOR TO THE PACT*

New York, August 10

Dear Sirs:

One of the gravest problems confronting all those engaged in the
struggle for democracy and peace, whether they be liberals, progressives, trade unionists, or others, is how to unite their various forces
so as to achieve victory for their common goals. The fascists and
their allies are well aware that democracy will win if its supporters
are united. Accordingly, they are intent on destroying such unity at
all costs.

On the international scene the fascists and their friends have tried
to prevent a united anti-aggression front by sowing suspicion between
the Soviet Union and other nations interested in maintaining peace.

---

* "To All Active Supporters of Democracy and Peace," *Nation*, Vol. CXLIX (August 26,
1939), p. 228.

Rochester Times-Union

Rising over the Horizon

On the domestic scene the reactionaries are attempting to split the democratic front by similar tactics. Realizing that here in America they cannot get far with a definitely pro-fascist appeal, they strive to pervert American anti-fascist sentiment to their own ends. With the aim of turning anti-fascist feeling against the Soviet Union they have encouraged the fantastic falsehood that the U.S.S.R. and the totalitarian states are basically alike. By this strategy they hope to create dissension among the progressive forces whose united strength is a first necessity for the defeat of fascism.

Some sincere American liberals have fallen into this trap and unwittingly aided a cause to which they are essentially opposed. Thus, a number of them carelessly lent their signatures to the recent manifesto issued by the so-called Committee for Cultural Freedom. This manifesto denounces in vague, undefined terms all forms of "dictatorship" and asserts that the fascist states and Soviet Russia equally menace American institutions and the democratic way of life.

While we prefer to dwell on facts rather than personalities, we feel it is necessary to point out that among the signers of this manifesto are individuals who have for years had as their chief political objective the maligning of the Soviet people and their government. . . .

A number of other committees have been formed which give lip-service to democracy and peace while actually attacking the Soviet Union and aiding reaction. . . .

The undersigned do not represent any committee or organization, nor do they propose to form one. Our object is to point out the real purpose behind all these attempts to bracket the Soviet Union with the fascist states, and to make it clear that Soviet and fascist policies are diametrically opposed. To this end we should like to stress ten basic points in which Soviet socialism differs from totalitarian fascism.

1. The Soviet Union continues as always to be a bulwark against war and aggression, and works unceasingly for a peaceful international order.

2. It has eliminated racial and national prejudice within its borders, freed the minority peoples enslaved under the czars, stimulated the culture and economic welfare of these peoples, and made the expression of anti-Semitism or any racial animosity a criminal offense.

3. It has socialized the means of production and distribution through the public ownership of industry and the collectivization of agriculture.

4. It has established nation-wide socialist planning, resulting in increasingly higher living standards and the abolition of unemployment.

5. It has built the trade unions, in which almost 24,000,000 workers are organized, into the very fabric of its society.

6. The Soviet Union has emancipated woman and the family, and has developed an advanced system of child care.

7. From the viewpoint of cultural freedom, the difference between the Soviet Union and the fascist countries is most striking. The Soviet Union has effected one of the most far-reaching cultural and educational advances in all history and among a population which at the start was almost three-fourths illiterate. Those writers and thinkers whose books have been burned by the Nazis are published in the Soviet Union. The best literature from Homer to Thomas Mann, the best thought from Aristotle to Lenin, are available to the masses of the Soviet people. . . .

8. It has replaced the myths and superstitions of old Russia with the truths and techniques of experimental science, extending scientific procedures to every field, from economics to public health.

9. The Soviet Union considers political dictatorship a transitional form and has shown a steadily expanding democracy in every sphere. Its epoch-making new constitution guarantees Soviet citizens universal suffrage, civil liberties, the right to employment, to leisure, to free education, to free medical care, to material security in sickness and old age, to equality of the sexes in all fields of activity, and to equality of all races and nationalities.

10. In relation to Russia's past, the country has been advancing rapidly along the road of material and cultural progress in ways that the American people can understand and appreciate.

The Soviet Union has an economic system different from our own. But Soviet aims and achievements make it clear that there exists a sound and permanent basis in mutual ideals for cooperation between the U.S.A. and the U.S.S.R. in behalf of world peace and the security and freedom of all nations.

Jay Allen	William Gropper
Marc Blitzstein	Thomas H. Harris
Millen Brand	Dashiell Hammett
Robert A. Brady	Granville Hicks
Robert M. Coates	Matthew Josephson
Kyle Crichton	George Kaufman
Kenneth Fearing	Rockwell Kent
Irving Fineman	Arthur Kober
Waldo Frank	Alfred Kreymborg
Wanda Gag	Paul De Kruif

Corliss Lamont
Emil Lengyel
Halford E. Luccock
Max Lerner
Robert Morss Lovett
George Marshall
Aline MacMahon
Harvey O'Connor
Clifford Odets
Shaemus O'Sheel
S. J. Perelman
Walter Rautenstrauch

Raymond Robins
Frederick L. Schuman
Vincent Sheean
A. E. Steig
Donald Ogden Stewart
Maxwell S. Stewart
I. F. Stone
Louis Untermeyer
James Thurber
Mary Van Kleeck
Harry F. Ward
William Carlos Williams

[We regret that we are able to print only this partial list of signatures.
More than 400 names were signed to the letter. . . .
Editors *The Nation.]*

29   THE HOMELESS RADICALS*

For two decades American radicals have participated vicariously in the triumphs and retreats of the Soviet regime. Events in Moscow have molded their thinking, overshadowed native politics, conditioned their emotional level. The ten days of October that John Reed chronicled were to influence American radical thought for a generation; and in August, 1939, the ten days that elapsed between Berlin's announcement and Moscow's ratification of the German-Russian pact seemed equally momentous. Certainly not since the advent of Hitler had there been an equivalent period of tension, so deep a premonition of change. A month later one can still only hint at the possible repercussions among those who, for better or worse, had been wedded to the fortunes of the Russian Revolution.

This article, written in the immediate chaotic aftermath of the event, aims to give an outline of what representative radicals and liberals were thinking in this period of upheaval. There was, I believe, wide agreement that final judgments must be suspended and even tentative theories held subject to change without notice. One can only reproduce the immediate picture and suggest the eventualities which would prove decisive. Put simply: if the pact is the forerunner of a full-fledged military alliance against the West, its effect

* James Wechsler, "Stalin and Union Square," *Nation,* Vol. CXLIX (September 30, 1939), pp. 342–45.

in American leftist circles will be overwhelming. If no such sweeping and permanent accord emerges, there is likely to be a period of prolonged ferment in which new alignments will be indefinitely delayed.

The major concomitant of the line of the "democratic front" adopted by the Comintern in 1935 was the creation of a multitude of non-Communist groups. They carried the banners of anti-fascist unity among "men of good-will"; they preached collective security against fascist aggression. . . . Few voices were raised against Communist participation in these groups because, by and large, Communist policy from 1935 to 1939 harmonized with the position of large numbers of independent progressives for whom the growth of fascism was the central fact of political life. Then on August 21 a European dispatch suddenly shattered the framework within which this unity had flourished.

At once there were several important defections from the company of fellow-travelers. Turmoil was perceptible in bodies like the League for Peace and Democracy. It was evident that the stir would be most pronounced in those groups where liberal, middle-class, intellectual elements predominated. Undoubtedly the party will minimize such defections in terms of those adjectives. But certainly they define the circles in which the Communists have made their most impressive inroads during the last four years. The names of the casualties are less important than the fact that most of them had ardently identified themselves with popular-front objectives. . . .

Such developments are undoubtedly manifestations of a far-flung trend. But they do not constitute the whole story. There is probably an equal body of opinion still unprepared to render a final verdict; its chief characteristic is bewilderment. While almost universal dismay is felt over the timing of the pact, there is considerable reluctance to believe that it foreshadows an ideological alliance or that the primary guilt is Stalin's rather than Chamberlain's. And because this is true, the full fury of left resentment at the pact was not unleashed on Moscow. A considerable disposition still exists, moreover, to hope for a turn as swift as those which have already occurred. Among those most distraught by such events as the Moscow trials, the most pessimistic views are heard; among those less disposed to question earlier developments, there is less haste in rendering judgment; and among the most permanently devout fellow-travelers, persons like Corliss Lamont, whose faith in Soviet policy has never wavered, one finds a quick adjustment to what is cryptically called "a new situation.". . .

These shadings of opinion could be enumerated indefinitely, but one reaction is almost universal among popular-front intellectuals. It is prompted less by the actions of the Soviet Union than by the utterances of the American Communist Party, the succession of ambiguous, frequently conflicting, but no less dogmatic statements which streamed out of party headquarters in the days after the signing of the pact. The *Daily Worker's* twenty-four-hour silence was at worst pitiable; it assumed an almost dignified aspect in contrast with ensuing somersaults. There was, first of all, Earl Browder's prophecy that the pact would contain an escape clause; it didn't. There was the assurance voiced by Israel Amter in the pre-war hours that if Poland really fought, the U.S.S.R. would come to its aid. There was the fervid plea for help to Poland carried by the *Daily Worker;* a fortnight later the same paper rejoiced at the political death of Poland's "semi-fascist clique." And throughout this period there was the slow emergence of a new foreign policy in the editorials of the Communist press, an evolution never accompanied by recognition of earlier errors. Each day, it appeared, the party was ruthlessly advancing to a position which the next day's events compelled it to abandon. To those asking for leadership it offered only the most desperate and unpersuasive rationalizations. And it offered them with neither humility nor reticence.

I found, in conversation with a host of individuals heretofore sympathetic to the party, that this tragic blundering had left a deep scar. They were almost unanimous in feeling that the party had been reduced to the role of a social secretary for Moscow, sending out apologies for its employer's antics without any comprehension of what they meant. This reaction was not a crude complaint against a "Moscow gold arrangement" for services rendered; it was a reaction against the lack of independence, self-reliance, and native reorientation allegedly revealed by the performance. Fundamentally it expressed revulsion against an institution in which intellectual consistency appeared less important than maintaining the doctrine of Soviet infallibility. . . .

In the light of these altered policies many liberals and radicals see only the bleakest future for the "united-front organizations" in which the Communists have figured so prominently. Can these organizations survive without Communist inspiration? Conversely, can they survive if the Communists seek to impose their newly acquired policies on them? I have heard that within the League for Peace and

Democracy there is a 40 per cent bloc critical of Russian policy, the remaining being either neutral or sympathetic. On what platform, if any, can these divergent views be united? Will there be a shift toward the isolationism now manifest in Communist policy? Will the drive for repeal of the embargo be pressed as vigorously as it would have been before the Communist reorientation? Will the Communists slowly retire again to the position of relative obscurity which they held before the new line was adopted? And if they do, will the organizations which they helped to create survive their departure?

The deepening uncertainty has, momentarily at least, produced a new kind of refugee—the homeless radical. In the past he has been identified with efforts in which the Communist Party played a vital role. He has belonged to groups and leagues and committees which were pro-Soviet, anti-fascist, and dedicated in an immediate sense to the protection of bourgeois democracy. He may have been socialist in ultimate conviction, or committed to nothing more drastic than reforms within the framework of capitalistic democracy. He is now confronted with the necessity of evaluating his own position, rediscovering some organizational ties, or fleeing into a lonely isolation. Where does he go from here?

I have already encountered tentative groping toward a new alignment. Its most likely form would be a loose, flexible body comparable to the "New Beginnings" group which emerged in post-Hitler Germany, a group socialist in ultimate objective but committed to no orthodox doctrine or to any International, and unwilling to assume the shape and functions of a political party until its strength has been established. It would strive to revitalize native currents in American radicalism, formulate a declaration of American radical independence, and shape a program for the unorganized American left as the war develops. Its most immediate goals would be the defense of civil liberties, especially as they are threatened by "emergency decrees," and protection of the social gains achieved under the New Deal. Neither the form nor the content of such a grouping is any clearer than I have indicated, nor has its organization advanced beyond the discussion stage. . . .

If the ranks of those who had allied themselves with "democratic front" groups without accepting the credo of the party have been depleted, no comparable movement is evident within the party itself. Tumultuous debates at unit meetings have been followed by threatened resignations and these in turn by reconversions, but by and large the ranks have remained firm, even as the line wavered. There is no simple explanation for this phenomenon. It is deeply rooted in the habits of mind and the attitude toward society that pervade the Communist ranks. The cardinal factor, most observers agree, is the survival of the "faith." And the major article of this faith is the incorruptibility of the U.S.S.R. For two decades Communist policy throughout the world has veered sharply, often in opposing directions; but loyalty to the Soviet Union has remained fixed.

But this is not the only explanation of the party's solidity. While the Communists since 1935 have abandoned a good many of their most sectarian habits, they have retained a half-veiled suspicion and distrust of the world beyond the party. It was not a "respectable" party even when its position conformed most closely to that of the moderately respectable New Deal. Then suddenly, with the signing of the pact, the peril of its own isolation loomed again. Now was the time for all good men to come to the aid of the party. They did.

Shortly after the invasion of Poland a mass-meeting was staged in Madison Square Garden. Beforehand there was considerable speculation: would the Garden be half empty, would the meeting be listless, would there be large-scale heckling? In fact the Garden was jammed, the crowd almost frenzied in its enthusiasm, dissenters nowhere in evidence. Not that ideological clarity had been miraculously restored. The crowd appeared at times uncertain as to whether boos or cheers were called for in the light of the new policy. . . . The thing that stood out in the meeting was the almost desperate huddling together of people confronted by a monumental world crisis, taking refuge in a reaffirmation of their own solidarity. One felt that what was said from the speakers' platform was less important to the audience than the reassuring knowledge that 20,000 people agreed with it.

There is a final factor which explains the ease with which at least a section of the party has adjusted itself to the new line. It must be remembered that even in the era of the popular front there were many "old Bolsheviks" within the party who maintained a cynical reticence while outwardly embracing capitalist democracy. The party never developed any systematic elaboration of a democratic credo. To many of its adherents, even amid the most rhapsodic devotion to the New Deal, the dictatorship of the proletariat remained a far more glowing emblem.

But in some circles, within the party as well as outside, neither official rationalizations nor the appearance of stability in a crisis, both of which the party offers, have sufficed. Already it has been reported that Granville Hicks has resigned from the party and is publishing a statement of the reasons for his withdrawal in the *New Republic*. Robert Forsythe's name has been removed, at his request, from the masthead of the *New Masses*, Richard Rovere, one of the *New Masses'* younger editors, has also withdrawn. . . . But the bulk of party writers is likely to remain devoted, at least pending some even more spectacular development. The most primitive interpretation of this fealty is that they have a "vested interest" in the party's existence. In a sense they have; but it is above all an emotional investment. The same condition prevails in the higher realms of the party leadership, from which no reports of defection have emanated.

A Communist leader cannot easily find another political foothold; no other left groups are clamoring for his services, and an effective revolt within the party cannot be readily engineered. Under these conditions men seldom resolve their doubts; they steel themselves against having them. It is still premature to say that no split may ultimately evolve out of the present ferment. But in both its ideological tenacity and its organizational structure the Communist Party is singularly well equipped to avert that development. . . .

While the pro-popular-front liberals grope for their bearings and the bulk of Communist Party members remain fixed in their devotion, the other left parties have tried, not too effectually, to strengthen their ranks. In this camp the three outstanding groups are the Socialist Party, led by Norman Thomas, the Independent Labor League, led by Jay Lovestone, and the Socialist Workers' Party, following Leon Trotsky. Typical of the smaller groups is the League for a Revolutionary Workers' Party. All these organizations have been consistently and fiercely "anti-Stalinist"; all of them have assumed the corrupt nature of the Soviet regime and now interpret the Russo-German pact as a vindication of their Cassandra-like warnings. Their utterances since the pact reflect relief at the fulfilment of their prophecies. Not that joy is unconfined; it would be inaccurate to suggest that they are unaware of the darkness of the world scene. The pact's effect on their policies, however, is far less striking than its effect on the Communist Party. Before the pact they insisted that the coming war was a struggle between rival imperialisms, and they still say so. To that extent, paradoxically enough, their position roughly coincides with the new program of the Communist Party. But the heritage of factional strife, even among these anti-Stalinist groups, is so bitter that no unity has been achieved; and their broad agreement with the Communist position on war is unlikely to obscure the more passionate discord over Russia's role. Meanwhile, the Social Democratic Federation, through its organ, the *New Leader,* remains virtually alone among organized groups in advancing the position that Hitlerism must be smashed, that this war is an anti-fascist war, and that if American military intervention is necessary, it should be forthcoming.

The central fact is that these are moments of transition among radical and liberal forces. If the issue of Russian policy has once more troubled and divided them, it must now be seen in the context of the greater issue of the war itself. . . . The darkest aspect of the present period is the confusion which has gripped so large a section of the left and the internal warfare which destroys its efforts. Its immediate survival may be threatened by an onrush of repressive legislation in Washington. Its ultimate direction may still be determined by the future course of Russian policy.

30 VINDICATION PREDICTED*

Every year or so the diplomatic relations between the Soviet Union and its liberal sympathizers in the capitalist democracies are ruptured by what seems to the latter a political bombshell. In retrospect the "bombshells" have proved to be neither unexpected political phenomena nor startling violations of fundamental Soviet principles and practice. But to many liberals, whose historical horizon is bounded by what they can remember of the past fortnight's newspaper reading, these developments are undoubtedly startling and upsetting. They start scurrying belligerently to the nearest Communist for an explanation, and their axiom is that the Soviet Union is guilty until it is proved innocent. . . .

Just now our liberal friends are stunned by a new "bombshell," the Soviet-German Non-Aggression Pact. History, which has always vindicated the Soviet Union's policy, will repeat itself. A few months from now, perhaps a few weeks from now, many of our friends will feel very guilty about their lack of intelligence if not about their lack of confidence. In the meantime let me prescribe a review of recent diplomatic history as a sedative for their nerves.

---

*Alter Brody, "Liberals and the Pact," *New Masses,* Vol. XXXII (September 5, 1939), pp. 13–14.

WHAT HAPPENED AT MUNICH

The Soviet Union has scored a number of impressive diplomatic triumphs in the course of its existence but it would be idle to claim that it has not suffered some serious defeats. The proposed four-power Munich pact was the worst of them. To appraise realistically the present Soviet-German Non-Aggression Pact, it is necessary to grasp the full implications of what happened at Munich and *why* it happened.

Most people speak glibly of the "Munich betrayal" but on analysis it will be found that they have only a hazy idea of what was betrayed. Chamberlain did not fly to Godesberg and Berchtesgaden just to inform Hitler that Britain would not defend Czechoslovakia. The British ambassador at Berlin could easily have taken care of such a diplomatic errand and saved a very old man several arduous airplane trips. But Chamberlain did not fly to Godesberg and Berchtesgaden just to arrange for the betrayal and partition of Czechoslovakia. *He flew there to connive for the betrayal and partition of the Soviet Union.* Before Munich, only a few astute political analysts like Prof. Frederick L. Schuman (in a series of articles in the *New Republic*) were able to penetrate the tory designs. After Munich the whole world was taken into the secret—simply because the tories were so cocksure about the success of their plot that they crowed aloud about it in the world press. "Peace" was assured, they chortled as they handed Czechoslovakia, the gateway to the East, to Hitler. "On to the Ukraine!" was the jubilant cry of the London and Paris press. "There would be no war in Europe," Ambassador Kennedy joyfully assured President Roosevelt—because Hitler would be busy attacking the Soviet Union. In that October week, Chamberlain and Daladier stumbled over themselves in their haste to conclude non-aggression pacts with Germany, *though France was still bound to the Soviet Union in a defensive military alliance aimed to preserve peace in Europe. . . .*

WHY IT HAPPENED

This is what happened at Munich. It is now fruitful to consider one of the reasons *why* it happened. Specifically, how was it that despite Soviet diplomacy a diplomatic situation could develop in Europe which made it possible for the Soviet Union to be so isolated diplomatically that all the powers of Europe could unite in a pact to destroy it, even though it was well known that it harbored no aggressive designs against any one of them? The explanation for the Soviet diplomatic impotence at Munich lies in the inherent disadvantage which Soviet diplomacy labors under. This diplomatic "handicap" lies in the public knowledge that the Soviet foreign policy is immovably anchored to the fact that the USSR is the world's only proletarian state and the only country whose inner economic contradictions have been resolved by socialism. As the world's only proletarian state it can never enter into a military alliance with the chief enemy of the proletariat. As the only country that has resolved its economic contradictions by socialism it has no need for war as an instrument of imperialist expansion and therefore can never enter into any aggressive alliance either with the fascist powers or with the capitalist powers.

As a result, the Soviet Union, alone among world powers, comes to the international diplomatic card table with its cards up. Now the essence of the diplomatic game is to keep your opponents and even your partners guessing—as Anglo-French, Italo-German, and German-Japanese relations abundantly testify. Contrary to the propaganda which seeks to portray Soviet diplomacy as mysterious and unpredictable, Soviet diplomacy suffers from being altogether too predictable. Despite the flood of lies that were and are being poured out on the subject, Chamberlain, Daladier, Hitler, and Mussolini have always known for certain that there is a gulf between the world's only socialist state and the world's fascist states which can never be bridged to the extent of a military alliance. Hence the Soviet Union's liberty of action is severely limited in any diplomatic conference, for its position can be gauged in advance. . . .

Even if Soviet diplomats had been naive enough to forget the lesson of Munich, Chamberlain has since done his best to keep them reminded. When the Polish crisis broke in April, Chamberlain rushed in to "guarantee" Poland, completely ignoring the existence of "isolated" Russia. Now that the Soviet-German Non-Aggression Pact has been signed it is suddenly discovered by our press that the British guarantee is worthless without Soviet aid. If so, what motivated Chamberlain in making a guarantee that he must have known was worthless? Such a guarantee could not protect the integrity of Poland but it *could* light the flames of war in the East, and Chamberlain's old eyes are always hopefully turned toward the East.

Exposed and prodded by the Opposition in Parliament, Chamberlain finally made a gesture of inviting the Soviet Union to join an anti-aggression front. But it became evident very early that it was only a gesture—a gesture to gain time for another Munich. Weeks and months passed in "bickerings" over points that should have been taken for granted as the only possible bases of a genuine anti-aggression front—the British ingeniously maintaining at first that the Soviet Union should be obligated to come to the aid of Britain and France but not vice versa. In the meantime, while the negotiations (conducted by a senior Foreign Office clerk) proceeded, Chamberlain was brazenly dickering with Hitler for another Munich. Every other week a new Munich trial balloon made the headlines. But, as I remember, there were no horrified editorial gasps such as have greeted the news of the Soviet-German Non-Aggression Pact. Perhaps it is the capitalist press' subtle way of paying a compliment to the Soviet Union, to judge it by a higher code of ethics than England or France. But the Soviet Union has a more important mission in the world than fishing for the compliments of the capitalist press. It is interested in safeguarding itself and the future of democracy and of world socialism against the danger of another four power pact such as Chamberlain brewed out of the remains of Czechoslovakia. That is the A B C of the Soviet-German Non-Aggression Pact. If England and France are still interested in stopping fascist aggression, the front door of the Soviet Union is still open. But if their object is to engage the Soviet Union in diplomatic "conversations" while their accomplices break in at the back door, they will find that the back door has been securely locked.

THE REAL CHOICE

The fallacy underlying liberal confusion on the Soviet-German Non-Aggression Pact is the idea, carefully fostered by British propaganda, that the Soviet Union was choosing between a democratic front against fascist aggression and a Soviet-German Non-Aggression Pact, when it signed the latter. Nothing could be further from the truth. The tactics of Anglo-French diplomacy during the protracted Anglo-French-Russian negotiations, brought home to Moscow the fact that the choice was fast narrowing down to the kind of exposed isolation into which Chamberlain maneuvered the Soviet Union after Munich, and a Soviet-German Non-Aggression Pact. One fact stood out alarmingly. If Chamberlain was plotting another Munich with Poland in the role of Czechoslovakia, the Soviet Union could not afford to follow a policy of embattled isolation such as it followed when Czechoslovakia turned down its last-minute offer of single-handed intervention. Poland was too dangerously close for such a policy. . . .

Nor could the Russians ignore Nazi penetration of the Baltic countries within gunshot of Leningrad, as the British blithely recommended. An isolated Russia would be unable to intervene unless war actually reached its borders. As co-signer of the Soviet-German Non-Aggression Pact the Soviet Union has no doubt made sure of safeguarding its interests against such an eventuality.

The Soviet-German Non-Aggression Pact is a burglary insurance policy which Soviet diplomacy has been forced to take out against the threat of another and more dangerous Munich. Burglary insurance is no substitute for a vigorous drive to stamp out crime—but when so many convicted diplomatic criminals are on the police force, aiding and abetting crime, it is an indispensable precaution.

However, there is the likelihood that by thus taking the profit out of another Munich the Soviet Union may yet save Poland from betrayal by its ardent allies. For the only possible value of a Polish Munich—as of a Czech Munich—to Chamberlain and Daladier is the creation of a four power pact to dismember the Soviet Union. By insuring itself against such a plot the Soviet Union may be insuring Poland against a Chamberlain-Daladier sell out. If Poland cares to make this insurance absolute it must make up its mind quickly as to whether it prefers the presence of the Red Army as an ally to occupation by the Reichwehr.

Finland Invaded

The Nazi-Soviet Pact formed the prelude to German invasion of Poland nine days later, which in turn provoked declarations of war by France and England. It also formed the basis, according to secret clauses, for Soviet troops to enter Poland, to establish military bases in Estonia, Latvia, and Lithuania, and finally in November to invade Finland. By the end of 1939 no one could doubt that World War II was underway.

The Russian invasion of Finland provoked the following editorial assessment from The New Republic, *which had been a faithful supporter of the Soviet Revolution almost from the first of those ten days that shook the world 22 years earlier.*

31 STALIN SPREADS THE WAR*

There never has been a clearer case of calculated and unprovoked aggression by a large power against a small neighbor than the invasion of Finland by the Soviet Union. There never has been one more universally denounced by persons of all classes and of all shades of belief, the world around. So far as we know, the only exceptions are those members of the Communist Party and others—like the Nazis—who believe, or pretend to believe, the palpable absurdity that the Finns themselves were the aggressors and intended to provoke the conflict. The only comparable case in recent history is the violent absorption of Czecho-Slovakia by Hitler. But even here, the aggressor had better excuses because there actually were German minorities and a native government could be found that would bow to Hitler's will.

A review of the events immediately preceding the outbreak of the new war will make the denunciation clear. The Soviet Union demanded the cession of certain islands in the Gulf of Finland and a lease of territory on the Hangoe peninsula, all of which it intended to use as naval bases. It demanded a strip of land near Leningrad, to push the frontier farther from that important city. It demanded part of Finland's Arctic seacoast. It demanded a demilitaiization of the Russo-Finnish frontier. In exchange it offered a strip of land in Karelia which historically had been inhabited by Finns. Finland negotiated about these demands, conceding some of them but refusing others. . . . They did not wish to render themselves defenseless or to be drawn willy-nilly into the Russian sphere of influence as the Baltic states had been. Here the controversy rested for awhile, although negotiations were not permanently broken off. The Russian press attacked Finland savagely, and the Finns, thoroughly alarmed, mobilized. Soviet troops were also concentrated on the frontier.

The final crisis occupied just four days. . . . Sunday, [November 26] at midnight the official Soviet radio alleged that Finnish artillery had fired on Russian troops. The government in consequence demanded the immediate withdrawal of the Finnish army. On Monday, Finland replied at once to the note, denying the firing and saying that artillery fire had been observed on the Russian side of the border. It offered, however, to negotiate for a withdrawal of troops

* "Stalin Spreads the War," *New Republic*, Vol. CI (December 13, 1939), pp. 218–19. Reprinted by permission of The New Republic, copyright 1939, Harrison-Blaine of New Jersey, Inc.

Talburt, New York World-Telegram

Peace!

from both sides of the frontier, and suggested an investigation of the alleged incident by a joint commission. The reply of Molotov on Tuesday was to reject these proposals, to accuse the Finns of menacing Russia, and, in the same breath, to denounce the non-aggression treaty with Finland which had until 1945 to run. Meanwhile, the Soviet press and radio centered their broadsides on Finland, threatening her with the fate of Poland, while numerous factory meetings passed incendiary resolutions. Finland sent another note. Before its delivery, Molotov spoke over the radio Wednesday at midnight, breaking off diplomatic relations on the ground that Finland was hostile toward the Soviet Union and had rejected friendly overtures. It was on the next day that Soviet planes bombed Helsinki, killing many civilians, while the Soviet army and navy attacked in force. The Russian radio and press did not tell the people of the existence of war for sixteen hours after it had started, and then presented it as a Finnish invasion which was thrust back.

The Finns, at a secret meeting of Parliament, voted confidence in their government, but the Cabinet resigned and a new one was formed representative of all the elements in the population. This promptly began an attempt to reopen negotiations. Meanwhile, however, Russia announced the establishment of a "Finnish People's Government" on a small piece of marshland taken from Finland; its Premier was a Finn who had been in Russia for twenty years and was in charge of Scandinavian relations for the Comintern. Russia promptly made an agreement with this "government" embodying all the concessions she wanted. . . .

Even though we should make the monstrous admission that the facts are as Soviet government propaganda states them, still its action could not make sense. A Russian government afraid of Finnish invasion would have accepted Finland's offer for a mutual withdrawal of troops from the frontier and for a joint investigation of the border incident. So would a Russian government which feared that Finland was seeking a chance to foment a war in which Britain could take part. A reasonable settlement of the outstanding dispute—which Finland certainly gave signs of being willing to make—would have been the indicated course in this event. And, if the Finnish people had been oppressed and were looking for a way of throwing off the yoke of their masters, air bombings and a *Blitzkrieg* on land and sea would not have been the way to induce them to accept their liberators.

Indeed, it is the very assumption that there is some justification for the Soviet government's fear of future attack by the great capitalist powers that underlines the criminal folly of what Stalin has done in Finland. There are, all through the world, powerful forces that would like nothing so well as to turn this war into a holy crusade against Bolshevism. They exist in Germany, in Italy and the Vatican, in France, in Japan and, by no means least, in Great Britain and the United States. The plea of these forces is that the Western nations—including Germany—should cease their civil war and unite to oppose the Asiatic menace. Even publicists like Walter Lippmann and Dorothy Thompson have talked like this at times; it is the secret hope of every Tory in the world. So far, the drift in this direction has been held in check by the comparative self-restraint of Stalin's action. In Poland, he only took territory that had previously been granted to Russia by the "Curzon line" and that was inhabited by peoples akin to those already in the Soviet Union. The former government of Poland, moreover, had been incompetent and dictatorial; while the territories in question would probably have been overrun by the Nazis if the Red Army had not moved in. In the Baltic states, the somewhat precarious existing governments had had to yield nothing except military bases. Those whose enmity was directed mainly against Hitlerism kept cherishing the hope that in the end the Soviet Union would act as an offset to the Reich and would be satisfied with strengthening its own position.

The *New Republic* in the past has pointed out that Stalin's action had been immensely successful in terms of power politics but that a final judgment on his shrewdness would have to be reserved, for it was possible that he would overplay his hand. This he has done, in a most blatant and obvious way, in Finland. By a brutal assault on a well governed, intelligent nation that had won the admiration of the world for its sturdy and progressive culture, the Soviet Union has unleashed the dogs of hate that were already straining to tear it to pieces. It has made defense of its action impossible on the part of those who were friendly or were willing to reserve judgment. It has provided a strong moral case for those who wish to destroy communism and all its works. It has diverted against itself much of the hostility that had hitherto been concentrated on its greatest and nearest political enemy. This is a disaster, not only for Finland but also and more certainly for world communism and the Soviet state itself.

IV

THE STRANGE ALLIANCE
1941-1945
the question of world power

A Common Enemy

After the Nazi-Soviet Pact and the invasion of Finland, American antipathy toward the USSR was stronger than at any time since Lenin's first year in power. In many ways 1939 repeated 1918: the Russians reached a separate understanding with the Germans, thereby leaving the Western democracies to fight the world war without the advantage of a second front on Germany's east. This time the Americans were not yet in the war, but they reacted as vehemently as they had after the Brest-Litovsk treaty. When a Fortune *public opinion poll early in 1940 asked "Which nation do you regard as the worst influence in Europe?" the responses made a strikingly lopsided list:*

Germany	*55.3%*
Russia	*34.2*
England	*1.8*
Italy	*1.2*
France	*0.3*
Don't Know	*12.9*

The Soviet Union resumed its role as an American villain. The USSR's neutrality pact with Japan, signed in the spring of 1941, further tainted the Soviet image. But history did not repeat itself exactly. In 1918 the United States and the Allies had sent troops into Russia; in June of 1941 Russia was again invaded, but this time by German troops. As the Nazis pushed brutally into the Soviet heartland and as the Russians defended themselves desperately and valiantly, American feelings changed with remarkable speed. The "treacherous Reds" became the "brave Russians." In the summer, President Roosevelt sent Harry Hopkins as his personal emissary to meet with Stalin, a gesture which signified the newly cordial United States policy and which was soon followed by a lend-lease credit of one billion dollars.

By 1942, after American entry into the war, this relationship of expediency had matured into an expedient alliance. Communist Russia joined forces with the United States and Britain against a common enemy in Europe (and promised in 1943 to do the same against the Japanese, once Germany was defeated). But alliance hardly meant agreement. Already Stalin was putting pressure on his Anglo-American partners to expand the delivery of military supplies, to relieve the Russian armies by setting up a second front in Western Europe, and to recognize Russian annexation of the Baltic States which the Red Army had occupied after the Nazi-Soviet Pact. The latter issue was ultimately the most troubling, because it violated American commitments to the principles of national self-determination and personal freedom—principles to which Roosevelt and Churchill had just pledged themselves in the Atlantic Charter.

During the first year after Pearl Harbor, however, ideological friction was minimal; the question of military victory remained all too open. To the general American public, that question was foremost, and hence the heroism of the Russian people mattered more than the diplomacy of the Kremlin leaders.

Joseph E. Davies' memoir of his experiences as American Ambassador to the USSR during 1937-38, entitled Mission to Moscow, *achieved phenomenal success. As a best-seller in 1942 and then as a Hollywood film, it measured not only Americans' interest in Russia, but their receptivity to Davies' friendly view of the Soviets. The following selection is the excerpt which appeared in* The Reader's Digest.

32 WHAT WE DIDN'T KNOW ABOUT RUSSIA*

When Hitler suddenly attacked the Soviet Union last June, I made the statement that the Red Army's resistance would amaze the world.

*Joseph E. Davies, "What We Didn't Know About Russia," *Reader's Digest,* Vol. XL (March, 1942), pp. 45-50. Based on *Mission to Moscow,* copyright, 1941, by Joseph E. Davies. Reprinted by permission of Simon & Schuster, Inc. Reprinted here with permission from the March 1942 *Reader's Digest.* Copyright 1942 by The Reader's Digest Assn., Inc.

I added that even if Hitler took a substantial portion of the Ukraine his troubles would just begin. This view ran counter to the opinions of many military experts and other supposedly well-informed people, some of whom thought the Germans could take Moscow in three weeks. But it was based on what I had seen for myself in Russia.

I saw the impressive manpower of the Red Army in 1937 and 1938. Even then Russia had more than 15,000,000 trained men. These men had begun their training at the age of six in their youth organizations. As they grew older it included intensive physical exercises, military drill, marksmanship, parachute-jumping, glider practice. About 1,500,000 of these superb physical specimens were called to the colors each year. By the time Hitler launched his attack the Russians must have had close to 18,000,000 excellently trained officers and men available.

As long ago as 1938 the Red Army, I was reliably informed, had 4,000 tanks. On Red Army Day that year I saw 480—some of enormous size—race across Red Square. Military experts commented later that the performance had revealed few if any breakdowns or weaknesses.

A still more feverish program of all-out arming followed the Munich Conference of September 1938. During 1938, 1939 and 1940, Soviet defense expenditures averaged six billion dollars annually— almost as much as the United States raised by federal taxation in each of those years.

The Soviet Union put much of its defense spending into new plants, many of them in the Ural Mountains. Foundries and tractor plants were also converted to war uses. Naturally, it took time for the new or converted plants to start production, but in some instances this delay proved a blessing. The Germans, for example, froze their Messerschmitt plane designs in 1939 to achieve mass production. The Russians, starting later, were able to incorporate improvements. Last September, in Washington, I talked with a group of outstanding Russian fliers, fresh from the fighting front. They told me the newest Russian fighter planes were better than either Messerschmitts or Spitfires. The newest Russian bombers had better steel armor than German bombers, and could fly so high and fast that they needed no pursuit planes for protection.

Almost certainly the Russians can hold off the Germans throughout 1942. But Germany cannot be defeated by defensive tactics only. Russian troops must carry their counter-offensive of this winter right up to the German frontiers in the spring and summer. And to stage such a counter-offensive, they will need tanks, planes, guns and ammunition from the outside world. The Germans have occupied many important Russian industrial centers, and the industries of the Ural regions alone may not be able to sustain a prolonged offensive.

To one familiar with Russia's resources and industrial power, and above all Russia's people, Hitler's assault on the U.S.S.R. seemed foolhardy. The Soviet Union, embracing one sixth of the earth's surface, contains close to one tenth of the world's population—170,000,000 people. The Russian people have always lived hard lives; they have endured the same conditions as our own pioneer ancestors, and have developed many of the same virtues. Their country has immense agricultural resources and is largely self-sufficient in almost all the strategic raw materials—notably oil. Prior to Hitler's attack, the Soviet Union stood second only to the United States in the production of tractors, harvester combines, motor trucks, freight cars and locomotives; only Germany and the United States produced more steel; only Germany, Britain and the United States produced more coal.

A strong central state power, animated by a crusading zeal, has made possible Russia's industrial achievements of the past 20 years. And while the Stalin regime professes devotion to Communism it has moved constantly toward the Right in its economic policies. The state still owns all the means of production, and has not restored the profit system as we know it, but at least it has given the individual increased incentive to do better work. The so-called Stakhanov system established, in effect, the piecework system of wages: workers receive pay and other privileges in proportion to their individual output. And the Soviet Union rewards efficient factory managers and officials in terms of better houses, better hospitalization, better schools for their children, special transportation and vacation privileges.

The Soviet Union is a one-party state, and this party contains less than 3,000,000 members. It is dominated by one man—Joseph Stalin. A Central Committee of approximately 100 members governs the Communist Party; the *Politbureau* of 11 members runs the Party and the government; the *Politbureau* executes the will of Stalin. Any opposition is liquidated at once. Yet the devotion with which Russians have defended their homes, the unity they have achieved in fighting the Germans leave little doubt that the Stalin regime commands widespread confidence. What is the secret of Stalin's success?

The answer lies, in large measure, in the youth and vigor of Soviet leaders and the natural wealth of their country. Stalin himself, President Kalinin, Foreign Minister Molotov, War Commissar Voroshilov and Ambassador Litvinov are the only outstanding survivors of the Lenin-Trotsky period of 20 years ago. All the rest of Russia's present leaders are aggressive, able members of a younger generation. Those I met impressed me as strong and competent men.

Stalin, although he has utterly eliminated all competitors, is the "easy boss" type—quiet, self-effacing, personally kindly. Like all the other Soviet leaders, Stalin works hard, lives simply, and administers his job with complete honesty. It is generally admitted that no graft exists in high places in Moscow.

I witnessed two sets of trials in the famous series of purges. Nearly all newspapermen and diplomats in Moscow agreed that the defendants had conspired against the regime, but one feature of the trials most of us missed. Surveying the translated record of the proceedings I saw that the defendants had admitted engaging in every form of what we now know as "fifth column" activity. When, therefore, I was asked at the time Hitler attacked Russia, "What about fifth columnists in Russia?" I replied, off the anvil, "There aren't any—they shot them."

Despite the present value of that elimination, the purges brought home to me the price of dictatorial control. Because no outlet for legal opposition exists, all opposition becomes illegal. Those who disagree with government policy have only two choices: either they must take it and like it, or they find themselves ultimately conspiring against the state. The purges also created an atmosphere in which certain individuals could—and did—try to settle personal scores by snooping and informing on people they disliked. Undoubtedly innocent people were liquidated. Conceding to the Soviet leaders, as I do, all the idealism and integrity in the world, I remain convinced that dictatorship of any kind can never be worth the price society must pay.

To say this is not to say that the Communist and the Nazi dictatorships are like two peas in a pod. Russian Communists justify the Stalin regime on the ground that it is a temporary expedient until the people can rule themselves under a system in which the individual rather than the state shall be supreme. The Nazis, on the other hand, glorify dictatorship as such and deliberately seek to extend state power at the expense of the individual. Nazis do not apologize for Hitler's supreme authority; they glory in it.

The Nazi-Soviet Pact led many Americans to suspect there is something mysterious, even tricky, about Soviet diplomacy. An examination of the record will clear up misunderstanding on this score. While the United States was selling scrap iron and oil to Japan, Russia

steadfastly aided China. While the British preached "nonintervention" in Spain, the Soviets sent men and munitions to the Loyalists.
And what distinguished the Soviet government from all other governments before the war was its open, official recognition of the German menace. Stalin frankly expounded to me his views on the world
situation in June 1938. I summed up his statement in a dispatch to
Secretary of State Hull:

"He said the outlook for European peace was very bad. He added
that the Chamberlain government in England was determined upon
a policy of making Germany strong, thus placing France in a position
of increasing dependence upon England; also with the purpose of
ultimately making Germany strong against Russia. He stated that in
his opinion Chamberlain did not represent the English people and
that he would probably fall because the fascist dictators would drive
too hard a bargain."

The exclusion of the Soviet Union from the Munich Conference
rankled. In March 1939, after Hitler broke the Munich Agreement by
occupying Prague, Stalin warned that the Soviet Union could not be
expected to pull other nations' chestnuts out of the fire. On May 30,
Molotov, then Foreign Commissar, repeated the warning and again
called for an immediate mutual assistance pact. But the British and
French ignored both the Russian threat and the Russian offer. Convinced that no effective general agreement could be made with Britain and France under Chamberlain and Daladier, the Russian leaders
made the best of a bad situation and signed their nonaggression pact
with Hitler. The facts do not justify the British, the French, or anyone else in accusing the Russians of double-dealing.

The actions and statements of Soviet leaders soon showed that
they had no faith in Hitler's pledge of nonaggression, that there was
no "unholy alliance" between Hitler and Stalin. In occupying the
Baltic states and Bessarabia, and in attacking Finland, the Soviets
were protecting themselves against prospective German invasion.
During the Battle of Britain, Soviet military publications praised the
RAF. Just before the German attack on Yugoslavia, the Soviet Union
signed a treaty of friendship and nonaggression with that country.
The Soviet Foreign Office warned the Bulgarians against permitting
German troops to enter their country.

Today only one consideration would move Stalin to make peace
with Hitler. That would be the conviction that further resistance is
hopeless; that Britain and the United States cannot or will not deliver the goods to enable the Russian effort to continue. If therefore,

we would eliminate the possibility of a separate Russo-German peace, we must provide the material Russia needs.

Now that the United States and the U.S.S.R. find themselves at war against a common enemy, what sort of relations can we expect between the two countries? The traditional relationship between the American and Russian peoples has been one of friendship and good will. As continental powers we have no clashing interests abroad. We both stand to gain from peace, to lose from war. We have no territorial ambitions, no vast overseas commitments. And there is also a positive bond. American engineers have already played an important part in building the new Russia; they can play a bigger part in building and rebuilding postwar Russia. We have always depended on Russia for some of our manganese, chrome, potash and mercury; Russia has imported copper from the United States, and in the postwar period will certainly increase its purchases of plant equipment and industrial goods.

Two questions about Russia probably vex most Americans. First, what about Communist Party activity here in the United States? Second, why hasn't Russia attacked Japan?

Those who fear Russian Communism here in America grossly underrate the strength of their own country and its institutions. Not only have I every confidence in the superiority of our form of government to any other in this world; I am equally confident that it can best continue to assert its superiority by letting the advocates of other systems speak their minds and organize openly. That opportunity has been accorded to Communists—and to many other minority groups—and the Communist Party has never attracted more than 100,000 of our 130,000,000 inhabitants at any one time. Given a fair field and no favor, democracy wins hands down.

Moreover, in the Roosevelt-Litvinov agreements that accompanied American diplomatic recognition of the Soviet Union in 1933, the Soviet government pledged itself not to interfere in the domestic affairs of the United States. At the same time it promised to guarantee religious freedom to American citizens in the U.S.S.R. I know from personal observation that the latter pledge was kept, and I am convinced from the Soviet government's consistent record of straight dealing that the former was also strictly observed.

Of course we must expect, in spite of this agreement, that individuals who purport to represent the Soviet Union will overreach themselves. All political movements attract to themselves certain followers who are playing their own game.

Would not Russian self-interest dictate a policy of strict noninterference in American affairs? Stalin is a realist. He knows how most Americans feel about Communism. He knows it is to his interest to have the coöperation of a strong America—as it is to our interest to have the coöperation of a strong Russia.

It may be objected that after the war the Party Line will undergo still another change. But the more coöperation we have between the U.S.A. and the U.S.S.R. now in the fight against Hitler, the stronger we shall be to meet any future dangers that may arise. And after all, with such mighty issues at stake in this war, the Communist danger in America seems almost the least of our worries right now.

As for the failure of the Russians to bomb Tokyo the minute the Japanese bombed Pearl Harbor, we should remember that the Red Army is the only fighting force that has traded blow for blow with the Germans and made them retreat. To do it, many of Russia's Far Eastern troops had to be brought to the European front. Russian air attacks on Japanese cities would lead at once to a Japanese invasion of Siberia. It would be a poor exchange to swap the initiative Russia has developed against Hitler for a dubious advantage against Japan.

These questions of Communism in America and Russian aid against Japan go back to two fundamental aspects of this war. We cannot hope to win unless we have complete faith in our own institutions and full confidence in our allies. To worry about Russian Communism in America is to give way to defeatism before we have even begun to fight. And to expect the Russians to carry the fight to Japan after they have given Hitler his first real setback is to demand that other nations do all the bleeding, fighting and dying. Every one of us is in this war up to his ears. President Roosevelt has warned us to expect bad news at first, but he has set a course that will lead to victory. Our immediate task is to hold our faith—in ourselves and in those fighting beside us. The record the Russians have written on the scorched earth of their own land should fortify our confidence in our friends and in our cause.

The First Doubts

As the military course of the war changed, so did Moscow-Washington relations and American attitudes toward the Soviet Union. By the beginning of 1943 the tide of battle had turned in both Europe and Asia. The Allies could at last be fairly confident of eventual victory. But as warmaking evolved into peacemaking, frictions within the Alliance intensified. In a series of conferences during 1943–45, Stalin, Roosevelt, and Churchill discussed the kind of political settlement which would accompany victory; they uncovered as many profound disagreements as they produced optimistic but tenuous compromises.

The primary question centered on Eastern Europe. After two German invasions within less than 30 years, the Soviets desperately wanted a buffer zone on their western border. But the British and American governments were suspicious, fearing that the issue of Russia's national security was a mask for Communist expansionism. The long controversy over Poland's future became, in effect, a test of Western-Soviet relations.

After the Nazi-Soviet partition of their country in 1939, a group of Poles fled to London where they set up a government in exile. When the USSR joined the war against Germany, these Poles opened diplomatic relations with Moscow and began a tireless but fruitless argument about the Polish-Russian border. They insisted on the frontier drawn in 1921 after Polish defeat of the Bolsheviks; Stalin insisted on the frontier of 1941 as it was drawn after partition and prior to Germany's attack on Russia. One third of Poland lay between the two lines. The Polish government-in-exile meanwhile pleaded their case with Churchill and Roosevelt, both of whom expressed sympathy but also hesitated to antagonize their Soviet ally.

The USSR soon began to settle the dispute in its own way and on its own terms. When the Germans announced the discovery of the graves of 8,000 Polish officers at Katyn, allegedly murdered while Russian prisoners in 1940, the London Poles demanded an investigation by the Red Cross. Stalin angrily broke off diplomatic relations with the government-in-exile. By mid-1944, as Russian armies moved into Poland, the Soviet government had organized a Communist junta (called the "Lublin Committee") as a rival authority to the London Poles. The frontier dispute thus became secondary to the more momentous issue of who would rule postwar Poland. Much was at stake in the outcome of that issue: the American principle of national self-determination; the continuance of Soviet-American cooperation; and the balance of power in Europe after the war.

By this time the American public was well aware of the tension among the Allies and increasingly apprehensive of the Soviet Union. The image of the "brave Russians" was undergoing a transformation.

According to Elmo Roper's opinion poll for Fortune *in the spring of 1943, more than 80 percent of the American people thought "we should try to work with Russia as an equal partner in fighting the war and in working out the peace." But at the same time, only 30 percent expected that the USSR would want the same kind of peace as the United States; almost one out of two persons expected the Soviets to make unacceptable demands. Lastly, 40.5 percent of those polled thought that "Russia will try to bring about Communist governments in other European countries." Clearly, comradeship was competing with suspicion.*

The following two selections mark the growing American awareness of the problems in Eastern Europe. The New York Times *editorial, written in the middle of the war, balanced doubts and reassurance concerning Soviet intentions. A year later, when the question of postwar territorial settlements had come more fully into the open,* The New Republic *presented a vigorous example of the liberals' case. (The same journal's editorial on the invasion of Finland in 1940 forms an interesting contrast.)*

33 RUSSIA AND THE WEST*

Swiftly, inexorably, the Russian armies continue to drive toward the west. One supposedly impregnable Nazi stronghold after another falls before their assault, and the heroic defense of Stalingrad is being matched by the gallant conquest of Kursk, of Belgorod, of many other places, to which the Nazi keypoints of Rostov and Kharkov will soon be joined. They are names which sound the knell of Nazi ambitions and foreshadow the collapse of that "New Order" which Hitler started to impose on the world.

But as the Red Armies plunge forward, they are also raising many questions in many minds as to what other order they have written on their banners, and the greater the Russian victories grow the more insistent these questions become. They are raised in private conversations, in the press, over the radio and in Congress. And these questions carry the danger that they will provide a fertile ground for the latest Nazi propaganda with which Hitler hopes to escape the consequences of defeat—the propaganda which raises the bogy of a Bol-

* "Russia and the West," *New York Times,* February 14, 1943. Copyright 1943 by The New York Times Company. Reprinted by permission.

shevist domination of Europe in an effort to scare the world, divide the United Nations and therewith pave the way for a compromise peace.

Under these circumstances it would do more harm than good to ignore them. For the hush-hush policy advocated by some merely breeds more suspicions and the kowtows to Russia advocated by others merely create a political vacuum into which Russia might be compelled to step at the cost of increased alarm at home and abroad. The best answer to the Nazi propaganda is a frank discussion of the problem.

The fears and suspicions about Russia are based primarily on two considerations. The first is that Russia will use Communist groups in other countries as instruments of ideological conquest. And the second fear is that the power which has the greatest share in victory will also dictate the peace, and that Russia, having the power, will also use it for conquest, or at least for gaining "strategic frontiers." In this connection we cannot fail to note the Washington dispatches yesterday, reporting that the Soviet Embassy is circulating an English translation of an editorial from *Pravda,* asserting an emphatic claim to Bessarabia, Estonia, Latvia and Lithuania, on the ground that they are legally a part of Russia. This is a claim that our Government has not recognized.

Against these considerations, however, stand others to which it is necessary to call attention, for the benefit of Europe and of the United Nations, including Russia herself. These considerations are based on the binding engagements, pledges and ideals with which Russia has been waging a war of life or death on the political and propagandistic front. Here the record is clear, and that record embodied in pronouncements by Stalin and Molotov, in international treaties and agreements, shows:

1. That Russia has obligated herself to conduct this war as a joint war of all the United Nations against Nazi-Fascist aggression and to eschew any aggression of her own.

2. That Russia has accepted the principles of the Atlantic Charter, which provides, among other things, "no aggrandizement, territorial or other; no territorial changes that do not accord with the freely expressed wishes of the peoples concerned; respect for the right of all peoples to choose the form of government under which they will live; restoration of the sovereign rights and self-government to those who have been forcibly deprived of them."

Binding Russian engagements to observe these principles were laid down in both the Anglo-Russian Mutual Assistance Agreement of May 26, 1942, and in the War Aid Pact between Russia and the United States of June 11, 1942, and it was on the basis of such acceptances that both America and Great Britain agreed to extend material and other aid to Russia — aid which she solicited, aid for which Stalin expressed public gratitude, and aid which helped to make the Russian victories possible.

In these circumstances it seems clear that further and more explicit agreements are necessary in order to give concrete meaning to the Atlantic Charter and to erect a common defense system for the future. In this connection it would be of great immediate value if the Congress of the United States were now to adopt some resolution pledging this country formally to acceptance of joint responsibility for the maintenance of peace in the postwar world. The passage of such a resolution at this time would help to quiet fears abroad that, when the war is over, the United States will return to its old ways of isolation—leaving its present Allies no realistic alternative except to look to their own defenses and strategic frontiers at the expense of principles.

34   RUSSIA'S SPHERE OF INFLUENCE*

Aside from the objection of nationalist and other special interests to the attitude of the Soviet Union in eastern Europe, the major criticism has been that its insistence on unilateral decision, however justified its demands may be, cuts across the international coöperation which, it had been thought, had been established as a basis of future peace. According to this criticism, Soviet foreign policy is returning to the old practice of mapping out and protecting "spheres of influence." This was essentially an imperialist policy, and is diametrically opposed to the international equality and the universal consent which will be necessary if the United Nations or any successor is to be more than a name.

It is pointed out that Soviet delegates have been invited on terms of equality to join agencies dealing with Italy and with Europe as a whole; neither Britain nor the United States has sought to reserve these areas as special concerns of their own. Yet when it comes to

* "Russia's Sphere of Influence," *New Republic,* Vol. CX (February 21, 1944), pp. 230–31. Reprinted by permission of The New Republic, copyright 1944, Harrison-Blaine of New Jersey, Inc.

Czecho-Slovakia, Poland, the Baltic states and presumably Finland or
Rumania, the Soviet government seems to be following lines determined solely by itself, without bothering first to consult anyone else.
If this is to be the practice, it is argued, then Britain may be expected
to create her own sphere of influence in western Europe, the United
States to establish one in the Western Hemisphere and China one in
Asia. The world will be in effect carved up among competitive empires, the war danger will be heightened, and no room will be left for
democratic international organization.

This argument, logical as it sounds, seems to us a fabric of flimsy
semantics. A name that has accumulated bad associations in the past
is arbitrarily applied to what Russia is doing in the neighborhood of
her western boundary, and is by implication extended to the expression by any nation anywhere of any kind of special interest. It is
also assumed that any action regarding the future international set-up
which may be taken by one nation without consulting the rest is
entirely incompatible with international government. This sort of
thinking seems to us artificial in the extreme.

What is really meant by a "sphere of influence" and why is it
incompatible with a democratic internationalism? In the old diplomatic terminology, it referred as a rule to a territory which was being
developed and exploited by capital from a great power which claimed
exclusive right to the sphere. Financial or commercial interests from
competing powers were kept out. Political and military dominance,
open or subtly concealed, usually followed the economic penetration. The territory might be near the great power concerned, or on
the other side of the world. No thought of the wishes or welfare
of the native population was usually involved, except as a defense
against criticism. The sphere of influence was a sort of unlegalized
colonial possession. It was the forerunner of the kind of treatment
which the Nazi regime has attempted to apply to Europe itself, which
Japan has tried to set up in Asia and the Pacific, and which both
suggested, for purposes of propaganda, that the United States was
seeking to establish in the Western Hemisphere.

If this were what the Soviet Union was attempting to do in eastern
Europe, the criticism would be justified. Whenever Russia takes any
action, if she does so, which merits this description, *The New Republic* will be among the first to object. But as we understand the situation, the term is hardly applicable, in its old meaning.

Two considerations have mainly governed Soviet policy in this
area. First, it is asserted that certain fairly well defined and bordering

strips of territory either have joined or must become a part of the Soviet Union, not as colonial possessions but as integral parts of the Union. These are, reading from south to north, Bessarabia, which Rumania took by force of arms, those parts of the Ukraine and White Russia which were seized by Poland in 1920, the three Baltic States which were separated from Russia after the last war, and Finnish Karelia. The reasons are partly historical, partly strategic and partly dependent on the nature and interests of the populations. They are in general similar to the claim of France to Alsace-Lorraine in 1919, or that of the United States to Texas and California in the middle of the nineteenth century.

Second, the Soviet government insists that those neighbors to the west which are independent must have democratic governments willing to remain on terms of friendship with the USSR. This aim has been expressed positively by the treaty with Czecho-Slovakia, and negatively by the refusal to negotiate with the Polish government in London or the Yugoslav Government-in-Exile associated with Mihailovich. From the case of Czecho-Slovakia it is obvious that this does not imply any demand on the part of the Soviet Union that the governments in question be communist-dominated, or even socialist in character, or that the countries in question surrender their independence or grant Russia any special economic favors. It is merely an insistence that they do not offer breeding grounds for intrigue against the Soviet Union, and that in any future war they will be on the same side.

If this can justly be called a sphere of influence, then the words are being used in a sense that do not suggest their association with nineteenth-century imperialism. They mean rather something much more like the "good-neighbor" policy of the United States in Latin America. We support a friendly government in Mexico, and have been at some pains to see that other American nations join us in opposing German and Japanese aggression. We now refuse to recognize what we believe to be a pro-Axis government in Bolivia. Canada is in something like the same relationship to us that Czecho-Slovakia bears to Russia. We have not thought it necessary to consult our allies in formulating these policies and in making the treaties or taking the other diplomatic decisions which express them. It never occurs to us that they need prevent us from sincerely taking a full part in democratic international organization in the future.

The Monroe Doctrine, as understood in past years by our Latin American neighbors, was much more like the old sphere of influence of the objectionable type. Literally, it was merely a unilateral warning that European nations must not add to their territory on this side of the Atlantic. In this sense it still stands. Those whom it was supposed to protect disliked it, however, not because they had any wish to be conquered by European imperialists, but because, first, they did not participate in it, and second, they understood that it offered no protection against United States Marines or economic imperialism. Since then it has been mutualized, and this country has been scrupulous in not demanding exclusive privileges. If we had recently suffered invasion by Japan or Germany through Mexico, and now demanded no more in the way of coöperative neighboring governments than Russia is demanding, we should be at a loss to understand why any of our allies should complain. Especially so if the invasion had cost us millions of lives, untold suffering and the temporary loss of the richest part of our country.

The special interest of the United States in the affairs of the Western continents does not mean that it regards other nations in them as satellites, or that nations of other continents cannot buy from, sell to or invest in these nations on the same terms. It does not mean that the American nations cannot be fully participating members in an international organization of worldwide scope. Neither, we believe, does the kind of sphere of influence which Russia is seeking in the Balkans, Czecho-Slovakia, Poland or Finland mean any of those things. The United States would not, however, be content to rely solely upon any world league which is as yet in an embryo stage to protect itself and its neighbors against possible enemies. It is scarcely unreasonable for the Soviet Union to adopt a similar attitude.

It is of course possible that these judgments as to the motives and aims of the Soviet Union are mistaken. Perhaps its rulers are following some hidden and Machiavellian course which we do not understand. But no development so far indicates that this is so. That issue would have to be faced if Russia tried to annex all of Finland or Rumania, or denied an independent existence to Poland, or made imperialistic demands on the Scandinavian nations or Turkey. Meanwhile it must be remembered that the judgment here registered does not rest on any such fatuous supposition as that the Soviet government is moved by altruistic idealism in international affairs, or indeed by anything but intelligent self-interest. Is it not a fact, however, that its interest does not demand large acquisitions of territory and exploitation of foreign populations? Is it not a fact that interest is overwhelmingly concerned with one aim alone—immunity from attack and a chance for internal reconstruction and development? This has been the case now for many years, and it is reasonable to suppose that it will continue to be the case for many years more.

On the Eve of Cold War

Between the summer of 1944 and the defeat of Germany and Japan in 1945, Soviet intentions become more and more apparent to Anglo-American leaders and, somewhat less clearly, to the American public. The fate of Poland continued to serve as a dramatic symbol. As the Red Army neared the outskirts of Warsaw in July of 1944, the Warsaw underground (composed of supporters of the government-in-exile but nevertheless trusting the Soviets) saw an opportunity to rise up against their Nazi oppressors. As soon as the rebellion began, the Soviet troops stopped; for two months they stood idle, twelve miles from the center of Warsaw, as the Germans methodically suppressed the uprising. Meanwhile, Stalin effectively prevented Allied intervention by refusing to let American and British planes land on Soviet-controlled airfields after flying supplies to Warsaw. Churchill begged Roosevelt to join him in a protest to Stalin, but the American President again feared antagonizing the Russian Premier. By October the opponents of Moscow-controlled forces inside Poland were few and powerless; by the end of the year, the USSR officially recognized the Lublin Committee as the legitimate Polish government.

The last conference of the Big Three took place at Yalta in February, 1945. Their decisions were made amid three circumstances advantageous to Stalin. First of all, Churchill had visited "Uncle Joe" in Moscow during the previous autumn in hopes of reconciling the Poles and Russians. Although he failed on this point, Churchill succeeded in obtaining accord with Stalin on the future of southeastern Europe. The Prime Minister proposed an arithmetic formula: in Rumania, the Soviets would have a "90–10" preponderance; in Bulgaria, "75–25"; in Yugoslavia and Hungary, influence would be divided "50–50" with the West; in Greece, the balance would be "90–10" in the Western favor. Stalin quickly accepted this pattern for postwar spheres of influence. When the question of Eastern Europe was raised at Yalta, therefore, it was really already half-answered.

Secondly, the Red Army's occupation of most of Eastern and Central Europe ensured Soviet control of these countries after the war. The wording of the Yalta agreement on Poland, for example, ostensibly guaranteed free elections, but actually conceded control to the Communists. The Declaration on Liberated Europe promised the same insubstantial guarantee for the other nations on Russia's western flank.

Thirdly, Roosevelt still avoided any showdown with Stalin, in general because he continued to hope that a trustful policy would encourage trust in return, but specifically because he wanted two commitments from Stalin: Soviet entry into the war against Japan, and Soviet participation in the postwar United Nations. For these two goals—one apparently vital to victory, the other apparently vital to peace—Roosevelt was willing to be lenient on the European territorial settlements. He won Stalin's consent on both counts, but only after permitting Soviet acquisition of certain Japanese possessions, special rights in Manchuria, and separate United Nations seats for the Ukraine and Belorussia.

In April, 1945, Roosevelt died. His successor, Harry S. Truman, quickly demonstrated that he would have a tougher Soviet policy. At the Potsdam Conference in July, Truman and Stalin entered into several sharp exchanges about Soviet actions in Eastern Europe. But words could no longer change the situation which had developed. It was almost a year later that Churchill described the "iron curtain" which had fallen across Europe, but the outlines of that metaphorical division were already becoming visible when Germany surrendered. The Potsdam Conference produced several important decisions: on the Soviet declaration of war against Japan, on the disposition of Japanese possessions, and on the postwar treatment of Germany. But the mold of future Soviet-American relations had been cast. As the Second World War ended, the Cold War began.

The following editorial in Life magazine, published during the Potsdam Conference, dealt not only with the specific issues on the agenda, but also with the broad outlines of Soviet-American relations. Meanwhile, an opinion poll by Elmo Roper produced a revealing survey of popular American feelings toward Soviet Russia 18 years after the Bolshevik Revolution and on the eve of the Cold War.

35 SEMANTICS AND PROPAGANDA*

When Harry S. Truman became President those who had known him a long time pointed out that he was, if not anti-British, at least

* "America and Russia," *Life*, Vol. XIX (July 30, 1945), p. 20. *Life* Magazine copyright 1945, Time, Inc.

skeptical of some of the purposes of the British Foreign Office. Later, when he figuratively rapped Molotov over the knuckles on a matter of protocol, it became clear that he meant to be just as firm with the Russians as he intended to be with the Empire. And at Kansas City, in a speech that got only perfunctory attention from the press, Truman sounded his distinctively American note again: the U.S. intended to offer leadership in world affairs.

It cannot be said, then, that our President is sitting down at Potsdam for his talks with Churchill and Stalin in a weak or indecisive frame of mind. He is certainly in a stronger position than Churchill, whose authority is at the mercy of this week's British election returns. But inasmuch as all the important problems of the Potsdam conference involve the large and confusing major problem of an expansion-minded Russia, it would be surprising if Truman were absolutely sure of his direction. The average American doesn't quite know how to take Russia, and Truman is very much the average American.

NO WAR WITH RUSSIA

Russia is the No. 1 problem for America because it is the only country in the world with the dynamic power to challenge our own conceptions of truth, justice and the good life. If there is one thing most Americans are agreed on, it is that they don't want to meet the Russian challenge by resorting to war. From the New York *Daily News,* whose slogan of "No Fight Russia" is based on purely isolationist grounds, to the businessmen who hope to make money by selling goods to the Soviet on long-term credits, the feeling of "we must have peace" is practically universal. But most Americans wish also to protect democratic standards throughout the world as they understand them in the light of their own traditions. They don't like to see Russian institutions, Russian standards of "democracy" and "freedom of the press" spreading into the power vacuums of Eastern Europe. Nor do they like to contemplate the fact that the Japanese war may end with Russian-sponsored "peoples' governments" in Manchuria, Korea, and even in Chinese provinces reaching south to the Yellow River.

Since the "no fight Russia" mood is as deep as it is widespread, Americans have practically served notice that they will not appeal to the ultimate sanction of force to make their wishes for free governments prevail in Poland, Hungary, Rumania, Yugoslavia or Bulgaria. There are other sanctions, however, beside that of naked force.

One of these sanctions is the power of persuasion. Americans are willing enough to try persuasion, but here they run into something pretty baffling. When they try to base their case on an appeal to the superiority of democratic principles, they discover that the Russians have stolen their language; the Russians use democratic concepts to cover totalitarian practices. Thus the Soviet state is both a dictatorship and a "democracy." In an article on "Democracy" in *War and the Working Class,* a Soviet writer, A. Sokolov, explains there are different types of democracy, that of England and America—and that which the Soviet Union hopes to see prevail in countries contiguous to its borders.

In this battle of the definitions, this war of semantics, the Russians have practically everything rigged in their favor. In virtually all capitalist lands the Russians have their own Communist political organizations. Beyond the party are the peripheral organizations, the bewildering profusion of leagues, institutes, caucuses within unions, cells in other political parties, magazines that are subsidized by Russophiles, schools for Marxist studies and whatnot. The "fellow traveler" is everywhere, in Hollywood, on college faculties, in government bureaus, in publishing companies, in radio offices, even on the editorial staffs of eminently capitalist journals. Since a free competition in ideas is desirable, democrats must be satisfied with the privilege of calling Communists and Communist sympathizers by their right names; they cannot ask for suppression or proscription of the fellow traveler.

But Americans can't use the same technique of persuasion inside of Russia or countries dominated by Russia that the Russians use within our borders as a matter of casual right. If the power of persuasion were to be equalized as between Russia and the U.S., there would be a *Daily Capitalist* in Moscow, an Adam Smith Institute, a Jeffersonian Party headed by a young democratic capitalist sympathizer from Irkutsk, U.S. sympathizers in key spots on Soviet publications, and if anyone were to publish a book making snide remarks about the operations of capitalism in the U.S. there would be a local organization known as the Soviet Friends of the American Republic to drum up 15 prominent writers' signatures against it.

THE HELPLESS FEELING

The foregoing farce comedy may serve to highlight the reason why most Americans feel helpless about competing with the Soviet Union

in the propaganda field. This feeling of helplessness has been compounded since V-E Day by the fact that, whereas Communists can
both talk philosophy and practice politics and journalism in the parts
of Europe we have liberated or conquered, our men haven't equivalent privileges in Soviet-dominated nations east of the Elbe and the
Adriatic.

The feeling of bafflement that haunts an American who wishes to
push the case for his way of life in competition with the Russian has
a psychological issue in fear. This fear, in some people, begets truculence and a demand to "let's fight 'em now while we have an army
on the spot." In other people the fear begets a masochistic "for-
Gawd's-sake-don't-offend Joe" attitude that sounds curiously like the
one the appeasers had toward Hitler. Neither of the fear-born states
of mind can result in good U.S. policy, for they are not conducive to
an accurate appraisal of what the Marxists call "the objective situation." But what is the proper U.S. policy vis-à-vis Russia, and how
shall we recognize it? If we can't get into Poland, for example, to
make a stab at upholding our type of democracy in Eastern Europe,
then how can we have any positive policy at all?

POLICY FOR THE U.S.

The answers to these questions are not easy. But since President
Truman's assertion of world leadership requires that answers be
forthcoming, Americans must begin to pull their thoughts together
on the subject. Obviously we aren't going to fight Stalin for Poland.
But if we must allow Russian dynamism to move into power vacuums in Eastern Europe, it should not be construed by Stalin as a
"Munich" invitation to move anywhere. Americans wish to live in a
world of undominated governments, and in the past they have fought
when the line of a dominated world moved too close toward them.

If the Russians are pursuing the politics of the *cordon sanitaire* in
reverse out of fear of possible capitalist encirclement in the future,
we have an opportunity to remove that fear by a counter-policy of
good deeds, using our position to act as "honest broker" to persuade traditionally imperialist countries to relax their grip—in India,
in the Near East, in the East Indies, in China. The Russian demand
for trade recognition in Latin America might also engage our attention. A positive U.S. policy in such matters might be the *quid pro
quo* that would buy us consideration for our ideas on democracy in
Poland and Yugoslavia.

These are questions for argument and exploration. But beyond argument is the fact that U.S. diplomacy has one strong card to play, and that is the economic. The U.S. is the most productive country the world has ever seen, and our economic power of persuasion can be used to generate its own propaganda. Loans, the promise of credits, outright gifts—these can be closely tied to the diplomacy of spreading our own principles of freedom. Certainly they should not be granted to those who use them against us.

36 A SURVEY OF OPINION ON RUSSIA*

About 200 books concerned with Russia have been published in the U.S. since the beginning of 1943. Of all U.S. newspaper editorials concerned with foreign relations in the first half of 1945, more than 20 per cent dealt directly with Russia, a considerably higher percentage dealt indirectly. Although correspondents in Moscow have been curtailed in getting and sending news, particularly political news, a vast quantity of writing about and discussion of Russia has poured through the U.S. public mind. Perhaps no one question—except possibly the question of Russian opinion on the U.S.—has more significance to the world today than U.S. opinion on Russia.

What over-all impression has the U.S. received? In the present report *Fortune's* editors attempt an answer, viz, the U.S. attitude toward Russia is friendly but tough. Russia is not regarded as a child to be humored but as a nation of grown men and women, a nation that understands the simple rules of give and take. The friendship proffered is not uncritical. It is sturdy, stout, take-it-or-leave-it. Probably it is very close, if the behavior of the Russian Government is a guide, to the Russians' attitude toward the U.S.

The detail of the report underscores a point *Fortune's* Survey editors have made repeatedly in recent years—the close relation between opinion and information. The well-informed express a strikingly more balanced and discriminating opinion on Russia than do the uninformed. And the report contains a few surprises, notably these: businessmen are far more favorable to Russia than are the "poor and oppressed"; the U.S. press, although constantly harried by the Russian press, is on balance a booster of Russia. The U.S. is

* "U.S. Opinion on Russia," *Fortune*, Vol. XXXII (September, 1945), pp. 233–38. Reprinted by permission from *Fortune* Magazine, September, 1945; copyright 1945 Time, Inc.

clearly ready to go at least halfway toward active friendly relations with Russia. The rest is up to Russia.

1. SURVEY ON RUSSIA

In the mind of the U.S. public, there is little doubt of the importance of friendly relations with Russia. The following attitude scale shows the Russophobes in a minority of less than 10 per cent, those cool toward Russia a mere 11 per cent—both together about balanced by those who say it is important to keep on friendly terms with Russia. But most significantly, the scale shows that the largest segment of the public wants to put a stop-loss order on its endorsement of Russia's importance. Success or failure of the relationship is looked on as a joint responsibility of the two countries.

With which one of these four statements do you come closest to agreeing?

It is going to be very important to keep on friendly terms with Russia after the war, and we should make every possible effort to do so	22.7%
It is important for the U.S. to be on friendly terms with Russia after the war, but not so important that we should make too many concessions to her	49.2
If Russia wants to keep on friendly terms with us after the war, we shouldn't discourage her, but there is no reason why we should make any special effort to be friendly	11.3
We shall be better off if we have just as little as possible to do with Russia after the war	9.3
Don't know	7.5

Hopes for success are down a little from last January and "don't know" answers have increased, probably because of V-E strains, but hope still predominates.

Thinking back for a moment to our relations with Russia a few years before the war, do you think we will get along better with Russia in the future than we did in the past, not so well, or about the same?

	January	This survey
Better	48.3%	42.4%
Not so well	22.0	19.1
About the same	20.1	23.5
Don't know	9.6	15.0

Russian Motives—the U.S. View

What does the U.S. public deduce as Russia's purpose? The first question exploring this area brought an almost exact standoff:

Would you describe Russia as a peace-loving nation, willing to fight only if she thinks she has to defend herself—or as an aggressive nation that would start a war to get something she wants?

Peace-loving	38.6%
Aggressive	37.8
Both (volunteered)	8.4
Don't know	15.2

Although the Russian attitude toward the world thus seems to puzzle Americans, there is little feeling that the Russian people are definitely hostile to the U.S. Yet only a bare majority feel sure of Russian friendliness:

Do you feel that most of the common people in Russia are now pretty friendly toward the U.S., or not so friendly, or that most of them don't have any feeling one way or the other?

Friendly toward U.S.	52.7%
Not so friendly	7.0
Not one way or other	22.0
Don't know	18.3

A good part of the U.S. public apparently assumes friendship on the part of the Russians because it has a clear conscience—whether justified or not—on its own behavior toward Russia. Asked if the U.S. had done anything since the last war that may have given the Russians reason to doubt our friendship, 73.7 per cent answered that there was nothing they could think of. Among those who could think of unfriendly acts, mention was made most frequently of the failure of the U.S. to recognize the Russian Government.

Russian interest in the countries close to her is appraised by the U.S. public, perhaps correctly, in military and political terms. As follows:

Which one of these do you think is the most important reason behind Russia's interest in the countries lying along her borders?

She wants to spread communism	25.6%
She needs things they can produce	16.4
She wants to be able to count on them in case of attack	29.4
She wants to improve conditions for people in those countries	8.7
Don't know	19.9

Military security is seen as paramount, political security as a close second. Whatever ominous implications there may be in Russia's policy on her Manchurian border, either the public is ignorant of the situation, which is quite likely, or else does not consider it nearly so important as shortening the Japanese war. Asked if they would like to see Russia join us in the war against Japan or would rather she stayed out, 71.4 per cent of the people wanted Russia in, only 18.5 per cent wanted her to stay out. The compelling reason probably lies in public feeling about the toughness of the Japanese war. Only 26.9 per cent of the people think Japan will give up before she is beaten as Germany was; 62.2 per cent think Japan will fight on.

Good Russian Points and Bad

The public was asked to volunteer its own ideas about Russia's good points and bad points. Forty-three per cent could think of no particular good points, 33 per cent could think of no particular bad points. Those who answered scattered their replies over a wide range. On the asset side the Russian military performance was mentioned most frequently, but it was closely followed by approval of the re-distribution of wealth, of equality, and of economic security. Russian educational opportunities were frequently mentioned, as well as advances in industrial production. When personal characteristics were considered, Russian patriotism, courage, and industriousness came in for praise.

Foremost among the bad points Americans see in Russia is communism, followed by Russian hostility to religion and various aspects of Russia's dictatorial government and lack of personal freedom. A number of Americans believe that Russia's foreign policy is purely selfish and acquisitive. Objections to Russia, however, concentrated on matters of government and policy—only 1.8 per cent had any hard words to say about the Russian people.

When asked more specific questions about Russian policies, the people continued to show high proportions who had no information or opinion. For instance:

Which of these things have you liked about Russia, and which haven't you liked so well?

	Liked	Liked part	Not liked	Don't know
The way she handles her diplomatic relations with this country	18.0%	8.5%	42.6%	30.9%
The way she handles her military campaigns	66.9	3.0	4.2	25.9
The way she handles our news correspondents	8.5	3.5	39.7	48.3
The way she handles justice and the legal rights of her own people	16.1	2.5	24.1	57.3

Comments made by those expressing an opinion on the last of these questions repeated the feeling that Russians have little in the way of personal rights. Those who said they like Russian justice were frequently at a loss to say why.

Most of the U.S. people have acquired the belief that the Russian Government considers itself to be above the source of law.

Do you think the Russian Government pays a lot of attention to what the Russian people (and people in the rest of the world) think, or that it decides what it is going to do without taking what they think much into account?

	The Russian people	People in the rest of the world
Pays attention to them	16.0%	16.0%
Decides without them	64.8	67.6
Don't know	19.2	16.4

Thus public opinion, the balance wheel of American politics, is believed to have little weight in Russian policy making.

When the people were asked to compare Russia and the U.S. on a number of points, only very small minorities gave Russia the advantage. Asked "which country gives its people as a whole a better chance to get ahead," 86.1 per cent named the U.S., only 2.3 per cent named Russia. Seventy per cent think that the U.S. also gives its people as a whole a better sense of economic security, and 75 per cent think the U.S. has a better setup for encouraging good new inventions. And U.S. eminence in these and other respects is not believed to be threatened—65.5 per cent think that the U.S. will be more important than Russia in world affairs twenty-five years from now. Only 6.3 per cent think that Russia will then be more important; only 11.5 per cent think the two nations will be of about the same importance. Her military accomplishments alone bring Russia abreast of the U.S. in U.S. opinion. Asked whether Germany could have been defeated this year if Russia had not been in the war, 84 per cent said "No." But even fewer believed that Russia and Britain could have done it alone—92 per cent thought Germany could not have been defeated this year if the U.S. had not been in the war.

V

THE COLD WAR
1946-1952
the question of containment

Policies and Predictions

At the end of the Second World War, almost 40 percent of the American public characterized the USSR as "peace-loving" while virtually the same proportion labeled her "aggressive." By August, 1946, opinion had changed significantly. According to national polls, seven out of ten Americans disapproved of Soviet foreign policy, while only 7 percent approved. Between 50 and 60 percent of those interviewed by two opinion-research agencies believed that Russia was trying to make herself the ruling power of the world.

Expectations of Soviet-American friendship were dwindling. The Yalta and Potsdam agreements on Eastern Europe were followed by the creation of Communist dictatorships in Poland, Yugoslavia, Rumania, Hungary, Bulgaria, and Albania. The status of Germany exacerbated Soviet-American relations even more. The defeated nation had been divided into four occupied zones, eventually to be reunited politically and meanwhile to be treated as a single economic unit. But Russia and the other Allied Powers clashed over policies. Anxious to rebuild their war-torn country, the Soviets were intent on obtaining what they considered their due amount of German reparations (an issue which had bitterly divided Stalin and Truman at the Potsdam Conference). The United States and Great Britain, however, were more concerned about rehabilitating Germany.

166

During 1946, Soviet and Anglo-American officials traded charges of violations of the Potsdam reparations agreements. Any hope of a concerted East-West policy for Germany evaporated.

In February, 1946, Stalin spoke of an irreconcilable conflict between Communism and capitalism. A month later, Churchill spoke of an "iron curtain" across Europe. Amid the growing split between the two great powers of the world, Americans sought to establish a perspective—a policy—toward the Soviet Union. That task was not easy. Postwar events had been too sudden, and hopes of international peace and friendship too strong, for reassessment to take place quickly and with consensus. But by the end of 1947 the transition was complete. The "strange alliance" had given way to a policy of "containment."

The following three selections trace the evolution of that reassessment. Late in 1946 a public controversy developed between Secretary of Commerce Henry A. Wallace and President Truman about American policy toward Russia; it ended abruptly with Wallace's dismissal from the Cabinet. The first selection reprints excerpts from Wallace's speech in New York City on September 12, at a rally sponsored by three liberal groups, followed by the statements issued by the Secretary and the President.

The second selection reprints the celebrated and influential article by "X" in Foreign Affairs. The author was soon known to be George F. Kennan, a State Department expert on Soviet affairs and former Counselor in Moscow. The third selection includes excerpts from a probing critique of the "containment" theory by Walter Lippmann, whose newspaper columns, lectures, and books have won him a prestigious place among American political commentators.

37   PEACE–AND HOW TO GET PEACE*

Tonight I want to talk about peace—and how to get peace. Never have the common people of all lands so longed for peace. Yet, never in a time of comparative peace have they feared war so much.

Up till now peace has been negative and unexciting. War has been positive and exciting. Far too often, hatred and fear, intolerance and deceit have had the upper hand over love and confidence, trust and

*Speech by Secretary of Commerce Henry A. Wallace at a Madison Square Garden rally on September 12, 1946.

joy. Far too often, the law of nations has been the law of the jungle; and the constructive spiritual forces of the Lord have bowed to the destructive forces of Satan.

During the past year or so, the significance of peace has been increased immeasurably by the atom bomb, guided missiles and airplanes which soon will travel as fast as sound. Make no mistake about it—another war would hurt the United States many times as much as the last war. We cannot rest in the assurance that we invented the atom bomb—and therefore that this agent of destruction will work best for us. He who trusts in the atom bomb will sooner or later perish by the atom bomb—or something worse.

I say this as one who steadfastly backed preparedness throughout the '30s. We have no use for namby-pamby pacifism. But we must realize that modern inventions have now made peace the most exciting thing in the world—and we should be willing to pay a just price for peace. If modern war can cost us $400,000,000,000, we should be willing and happy to pay much more for peace. But certainly, the cost of peace is to be measured not in dollars, but in the hearts and minds of men.

The price of peace—for us and for every nation in the world—is the price of giving up prejudice, hatred, fear and ignorance. . . .

I plead for an America vigorously dedicated to peace—just as I plead for opportunities for the next generation throughout the world to enjoy the abundance which now, more than ever before, is the birthright of man.

To achieve lasting peace, we must study in detail just how the Russian character was formed—by invasions of Tartars, Mongols, Germans, Poles, Swedes, and French; by the czarist rule based on ignorance, fear and force; by the intervention of the British, French and Americans in Russian affairs from 1919 to 1921; by the geography of the huge Russian land mass situated strategically between Europe and Asia; and by the vitality received from the rich Russian soil and the strenuous Russian climate. Add to all this the tremendous emotional power which Marxism and Leninism gives to the Russian leaders—and then we can realize that we are reckoning with a force which cannot be handled successfully by a "get tough with Russia" policy. "Getting tough" never bought anything real and lasting—whether for schoolyard bullies or businessmen or world powers. The tougher we get, the tougher the Russians will get.

Throughout the world there are numerous reactionary elements which had hoped for Axis victory—and now profess great friendship for the United States. Yet, these enemies of yesterday and false friends of today continually try to provoke war between the United States and Russia. They have no real love of the United States. They only long for the day when the United States and Russia will destroy each other.

We must not let our Russian policy be guided or influenced by those inside or outside the United States who want war with Russia. This does not mean appeasement.

We most earnestly want peace with Russia — but we want to be met halfway. We want co-operation. And I believe that we can get co-operation once Russia understands that our primary objective is neither saving the British Empire nor purchasing oil in the Near East with the lives of American soldiers. We cannot allow national oil rivalries to force us into war. All of the nations producing oil, whether inside or outside of their own boundaries, must fulfill the provisions of the United Nations Charter and encourage the development of world petroleum reserves so as to make the maximum amount of oil available to all nations of the world on an equitable peaceful basis— and not on the basis of fighting the next war.

For her part, Russia can retain our respect by co-operating with the United Nations in a spirit of open-minded and flexible give and take.

The real peace treaty we now need is between the United States and Russia. On our part, we should recognize that we have no more business in the *political* affairs of Eastern Europe than Russia has in the *political* affairs of Latin America, Western Europe and the United States. We may not like what Russia does in Eastern Europe. Her type of land reform, industrial expropriation, and suppression of basic liberties offends the great majority of the people of the United States. But whether we like it or not, the Russians will try to socialize their sphere of influence just as we try to democratize our sphere of influence. This applies also to Germany and Japan. We are striving to democratize Japan and our area of control in Germany, while Russia strives to socialize Eastern Germany.

As for Germany, we all must recognize that an equitable settlement, based on a unified German nation, is absolutely essential to any lasting European settlement. This means that Russia must be assured that never again can German industry be converted into military might to be used against her—and Britain, Western Europe and the United States must be certain that Russia's Germany policy will not become a tool of Russian design against Western Europe.

The Russians have no more business in stirring up native Communists to political activity in Western Europe, Latin America and the United States than we have in interfering in the politics of Eastern Europe and Russia. We know what Russia is up to in Eastern Europe, for example, and Russia knows what we are up to. We cannot permit the door to be closed against our trade in Eastern Europe any more than we can in China. But at the same time we have to recognize that the Balkans are closer to Russia than to us—and that Russia cannot permit either England or the United States to dominate the politics of that area.

China is a special case, and, although she holds the longest frontier in the world with Russia, the interests of world peace demand that China remain free from any sphere of influence, either politically or economically. We insist that the door to trade and economic development opportunities be left wide open in China as in all the world. However, the open door to trade and opportunities for economic development in China are meaningless unless there is a unified and peaceful China—built on the co-operation of the various groups in that country and based on a hands-off policy of the outside powers.

We are still arming to the hilt. Our excessive expenses for military purposes are the chief cause of our unbalanced budget. If taxes are to be lightened we must have the basis of a real peace with Russia—a peace that cannot be broken by extremist propagandists. We do not want our course determined for us by master minds operating out of London, Moscow or Nanking.

Russian ideas of social-economic justice are going to govern nearly a third of the world. Our ideas of free-enterprise democracy will govern much of the rest. The two ideas will endeavor to prove which can deliver the most satisfaction to the common man in their respective areas of political dominance. But by mutual agreement, this competition should be put on a friendly basis and the Russians should stop conniving against us in certain areas of the world, just as we should stop scheming against them in other parts of the world. Let the results of the two systems speak for themselves.

Meanwhile, the Russians should stop teaching that their form of communism must, by force if necessary, ultimately triumph over democratic capitalism — while we should close our ears to those among us who would have us believe that Russian communism and our free-enterprise system cannot live, one with another, in a profitable and productive peace.

Under friendly, peaceful competition the Russian world and the

American world will gradually become more alike. The Russians will be forced to grant more and more of the personal freedoms; and we shall become more and more absorbed with the problems of social-economic justice.

Russia must be convinced that we are not planning for war against her, and we must be certain that Russia is not carrying on territorial expansion or world domination through native Communists faithfully following every twist and turn in the Moscow party line. But in this competition, we must insist on an open door for trade throughout the world. There will always be an ideological conflict—but that is no reason why diplomats cannot work out a basis for both systems to live safely in the world side by side.

Once the fears of Russia and the United States Senate have been allayed by practical regional political reservations, I am sure that concern over the veto power would be greatly diminished. Then the United Nations would have a really great power in those areas which are truly international and not regional. In the world-wide, as distinguished from the regional, field, the armed might of the United Nations should be so great as to make opposition useless. Only the United Nations should have atomic bombs, and its military establishment should give special emphasis to air power. It should have control of the strategically located air bases with which the United States and Britain have encircled the world. And not only should individual nations be prohibited from manufacturing atomic bombs, guided missiles and military aircraft for bombing purposes, but no nation should be allowed to spend on its military establishment more than perhaps 15 per cent of its budget.

Practically and immediately, we must recognize that we are not yet ready for world federation. Realistically, the most we can hope for now is a safe reduction in military expense and a long period of peace based on mutual trust between the Big Three.

During this period, every effort should be made to develop as rapidly as possible a body of international law based on moral principles and not on the Machiavellian principles of deceit, force and distrust—which, if continued, will lead the modern world to rapid disintegration.

In brief, as I see it today, the world order is bankrupt—and the United States, Russia and England are the receivers. These are the hard facts of power politics on which we have to build a functioning, powerful United Nations and a body of international law. And as we build, we must develop fully the doctrine of the rights of small peoples as contained in the United Nations Charter. This law should ideally apply as much to Indonesians and Greeks as to Bulgarians and Poles—but practically, the application may be delayed until both British and Russians discover the futility of their methods.

In the full development of the rights of small nations, the British and Russians can learn a lesson from the Good Neighbor policy of Franklin Roosevelt. For under Roosevelt, we in the Western Hemisphere built a workable system of regional internationalism that fully protected the sovereign rights of every nation—a system of multilateral action that immeasurably strengthened the whole or world order.

In the United States an informed public opinion will be all-powerful. Our people are peace-minded. But they often express themselves too late—for events today move much faster than public opinion. The people here, as everywhere in the world, must be convinced that another war is not inevitable, and through mass meetings such as this, and through persistent pamphleteering, the people can be organized for peace—even though a large segment of our press is propagandizing our people for war in the hope of scaring Russia. And we who look on this war-with-Russia talk as criminal foolishness must carry our message direct to the people — even though we may be called Communists because we dare to speak out.

I believe that peace—the kind of peace I have outlined tonight—is the basic issue, both in the congressional campaign this fall and right on through the presidential election in 1948. How we meet this issue will determine whether we live not in "one world" or "two worlds"— but whether we live at all.

STATEMENT OF THE PRESIDENT

Sept. 14, 1946

There has been a natural misunderstanding regarding the answer I made to a question asked at the press conference on Thursday, September twelfth, with reference to the speech of the Secretary of Commerce delivered in New York later that day. The question was answered extemporaneously, and my answer did not convey the thought that I intended it to convey.

It was my intention to express the thought that I approved the right of the Secretary of Commerce to deliver the speech. I did not intend to indicate that I approved the speech as constituting a statement of the foreign policy of this country.

There has been no change in the established foreign policy of our

Government. There will be no significant change in that policy without discussion and conference among the President, the Secretary of State and congressional leaders.

STATEMENT OF MR. WALLACE

Sept. 16, 1946

Secretary of Commerce Henry A. Wallace, today issued this statement:

I stand upon my New York speech.

It was interesting to find that both the extreme right and the extreme left disagreed with the views I expressed.

Feeling as I do, however, that most Americans are concerned about, and willing to work for peace, I intended to continue my efforts for a just and lasting peace and I shall, within the near future, speak on this subject again.

MR. WALLACE'S STATEMENT AFTER CONFERRING WITH PRESIDENT TRUMAN, SEPTEMBER 18

The President and the Secretary of Commerce have just had a detailed and friendly discussion, after which the Secretary of Commerce reached the conclusion that he is to make no public statements or speeches until the foreign ministers' conference at Paris is over.

38 THE SOURCES OF SOVIET CONDUCT*

The political personality of Soviet power as we know it today is the product of ideology and circumstances: ideology inherited by the present Soviet leaders from the movement in which they had their political origin, and circumstances of the power which they now have exercised for nearly three decades in Russia. There can be few tasks of psychological analysis more difficult than to try to trace the interaction of these two forces and the relative rôle of each in the determination of official Soviet conduct. Yet the attempt must be made if that conduct is to be understood and effectively countered.

---

* "X" (George F. Kennan), "The Sources of Soviet Conduct," *Foreign Affairs,* Vol. XXV (July, 1947), pp. 566–82. Reprinted by special permission from *Foreign Affairs,* July, 1947. Copyright by the Council on Foreign Relations, Inc., New York.

It is difficult to summarize the set of ideological concepts with which the Soviet leaders came into power. Marxian ideology, in its Russian-Communist projection, has always been in process of subtle evolution. The materials on which it bases itself are extensive and complex. But the outstanding features of Communist thought as it existed in 1916 may perhaps be summarized as follows: (*a*) that the central factor in the life of man, the factor which determines the character of public life and the "physiognomy of society," is the system by which material goods are produced and exchanged; (*b*) that the capitalist system of production is a nefarious one which inevitably leads to the exploitation of the working class by the capital-owning class and is incapable of developing adequately the economic resources of society or of distributing fairly the material goods produced by human labor; (*c*) that capitalism contains the seeds of its own destruction and must, in view of the inability of the capital-owning class to adjust itself to economic change, result eventually and inescapably in a revolutionary transfer of power to the working class; and (*d*) that imperialism, the final phase of capitalism, leads directly to war and revolution.

The rest may be outlined in Lenin's own words: "Unevenness of economic and political development is the inflexible law of capitalism. It follows from this that the victory of Socialism may come originally in a few capitalist countries or even in a single capitalist country. The victorious proletariat of that country, having expropriated the capitalist and having organized Socialist production at home, would rise against the remaining capitalist world, drawing to itself in the process the oppressed classes of other countries."[1] It must be noted that there was no assumption that capitalism would perish without proletarian revolution. A final push was needed from a revolutionary proletariat movement in order to tip over the tottering structure. But it was regarded as inevitable that sooner or later that push be given.

For 50 years prior to the outbreak of the Revolution, this pattern of thought had exercised great fascination for the members of the Russian revolutionary movement. Frustrated, discontented, hopeless of finding self-expression—or too impatient to seek it—in the confining limits of the Tsarist political system, yet lacking wide popular support for their choice of bloody revolution as a means of social betterment, these revolutionists found in Marxist theory a highly

---

[1] "Concerning the Slogans of the United States of Europe," August 1915. Official Soviet edition of Lenin's works.

convenient rationalization for their own instinctive desires. It afforded pseudo-scientific justification for their impatience, for their categoric denial of all value in the Tsarist system, for their yearning for power and revenge and for their inclination to cut corners in the pursuit of it. It is therefore no wonder that they had come to believe implicitly in the truth and soundness of the Marxian-Leninist teachings, so congenial to their own impulses and emotions. Their sincerity need not be impugned. This is a phenomenon as old as human nature itself. It has never been more aptly described than by Edward Gibbon, who wrote in "The Decline and Fall of the Roman Empire": "From enthusiasm to imposture the step is perilous and slippery; the demon of Socrates affords a memorable instance how a wise man may deceive himself, how a good man may deceive others, how the conscience may slumber in a mixed and middle state between self-illusion and voluntary fraud." And it was with this set of conceptions that the members of the Bolshevik Party entered into power.

Now it must be noted that through all the years of preparation for revolution, the attention of these men, as indeed of Marx himself, had been centered less on the future form which Socialism[2] would take than on the necessary overthrow of rival power which, in their view, had to precede the introduction of Socialism. Their views, therefore, on the positive program to be put into effect, once power was attained, were for the most part nebulous, visionary and impractical. Beyond the nationalization of industry and the expropriation of large private capital holdings there was no agreed program. The treatment of the peasantry, which according to the Marxist formulation was not of the proletariat, had always been a vague spot in the pattern of Communist thought; and it remained an object of controversy and vacillation for the first ten years of Communist power.

The circumstances of the immediate post-revolution period—the existence in Russia of civil war and foreign intervention, together with the obvious fact that the Communists represented only a tiny minority of the Russian people—made the establishment of dictatorial power a necessity. The experiment with "war Communism" and the abrupt attempt to eliminate private production and trade had unfortunate economic consequences and caused further bitterness against the new revolutionary régime. While the temporary relaxation of the effort to communize Russia, represented by the New Economic Policy, alleviated some of this economic distress and there-

[2]Here and elsewhere in this paper "Socialism" refers to Marxist or Leninist Communism, not to liberal Socialism of the Second International variety.

by served its purpose, it also made it evident that the "capitalistic sector of society" was still prepared to profit at once from any relaxation of governmental pressure, and would, if permitted to continue to exist, always constitute a powerful opposing element to the Soviet régime and a serious rival for influence in the country. Somewhat the same situation prevailed with respect to the individual peasant who, in his own small way, was also a private producer.

Lenin, had he lived, might have proved a great enough man to reconcile these conflicting forces to the ultimate benefit of Russian society, though this is questionable. But be that as it may, Stalin, and those whom he led in the struggle for succession to Lenin's position of leadership, were not the men to tolerate rival political forces in the sphere of power which they coveted. Their sense of insecurity was too great. Their particular brand of fanaticism, unmodified by any of the Anglo-Saxon traditions of compromise, was too fierce and too jealous to envisage any permanent sharing of power. From the Russian-Asiatic world out of which they had emerged they carried with them a skepticism as to the possibilities of permanent and peaceful coexistence of rival forces. Easily persuaded of their own doctrinaire "rightness," they insisted on the submission or destruction of all competing power. Outside of the Communist Party, Russian society was to have no rigidity. There were to be no forms of collective human activity or association which would not be dominated by the Party. No other force in Russian society was to be permitted to achieve vitality or integrity. Only the Party was to have structure. All else was to be an amorphous mass.

And within the Party the same principle was to apply. The mass of Party members might go through the motions of election, deliberation, decision and action; but in these motions they were to be animated not by their own individual wills but by the awesome breath of the Party leadership and the overbrooding presence of "the word."

Let it be stressed again that subjectively these men probably did not seek absolutism for its own sake. They doubtless believed—and found it easy to believe—that they alone knew what was good for society and that they would accomplish that good once their power was secure and unchallengeable. But in seeking that security of their own rule they were prepared to recognize no restrictions, either of God or man, on the character of their methods. And until such time as that security might be achieved, they placed far down on their scale of operational priorities the comforts and happiness of the peoples entrusted to their care.

Now the outstanding circumstance concerning the Soviet régime is that down to the present day this process of political consolidation has never been completed and the men in the Kremlin have continued to be predominantly absorbed with the struggle to secure and make absolute the power which they seized in November 1917. They have endeavored to secure it primarily against forces at home, within Soviet society itself. But they have also endeavored to secure it against the outside world. For ideology, as we have seen, taught them that the outside world was hostile and that it was their duty eventually to overthrow the political forces beyond their borders. The powerful hands of Russian history and tradition reached up to sustain them in this feeling. Finally, their own aggressive intransigence with respect to the outside world began to find its own reaction; and they were soon forced, to use another Gibbonesque phrase, "to chastise the contumacy" which they themselves had provoked. It is an undeniable privilege of every man to prove himself right in the thesis that the world is his enemy; for if he reiterates it frequently enough and makes it the background of his conduct he is bound eventually to be right.

Now it lies in the nature of the mental world of the Soviet leaders, as well as in the character of their ideology, that no opposition to them can be officially recognized as having any merit or justification whatsoever. Such opposition can flow, in theory, only from the hostile and incorrigible forces of dying capitalism. As long as remnants of capitalism were officially recognized as existing in Russia, it was possible to place on them, as an internal element, part of the blame for the maintenance of a dictatorial form of society. But as these remnants were liquidated, little by little, this justification fell away; and when it was indicated officially that they had been finally destroyed, it disappeared altogether. And this fact created one of the most basic of the compulsions which came to act upon the Soviet régime: since capitalism no longer existed in Russia and since it could not be admitted that there could be serious or widespread opposition to the Kremlin springing spontaneously from the liberated masses under its authority, it became necessary to justify the retention of the dictatorship by stressing the menace of capitalism abroad.

This began at an early date. In 1924 Stalin specifically defended the retention of the "organs of suppression," meaning, among others, the army and the secret police, on the ground that "as long as there is a capitalist encirclement there will be danger of intervention with all the consequences that flow from that danger." In accordance with that theory, and from that time on, all internal opposition forces in

Russia have consistently been portrayed as the agents of foreign forces of reaction antagonistic to Soviet power.

By the same token, tremendous emphasis has been placed on the original Communist thesis of a basic antagonism between the capitalist and Socialist worlds. It is clear, from many indications, that this emphasis is not founded in reality. The real facts concerning it have been confused by the existence abroad of genuine resentment provoked by Soviet philosophy and tactics and occasionally by the existence of great centers of military power, notably the Nazi régime in Germany and the Japanese Government of the late 1930's, which did indeed have aggressive designs against the Soviet Union. But there is ample evidence that the stress laid in Moscow on the menace confronting Soviet society from the world outside its borders is founded not in the realities of foreign antagonism but in the necessity of explaining away the maintenance of dictatorial authority at home.

Now the maintenance of this pattern of Soviet power, namely, the pursuit of unlimited authority domestically, accompanied by the cultivation of the semi-myth of implacable foreign hostility, has gone far to shape the actual machinery of Soviet power as we know it today. Internal organs of administration which did not serve this purpose withered on the vine. Organs which did serve this purpose became vastly swollen. The security of Soviet power came to rest on the iron discipline of the Party, on the severity and ubiquity of the secret police, and on the uncompromising economic monopolism of the state. The "organs of suppression," in which the Soviet leaders had sought security from rival forces, became in large measure the masters of those whom they were designed to serve. Today the major part of the structure of Soviet power is committed to the perfection of the dictatorship and to the maintenance of the concept of Russia as in a state of siege, with the enemy lowering beyond the walls. And the millions of human beings who form that part of the structure of power must defend at all costs this concept of Russia's position, for without it they are themselves superfluous.

As things stand today, the rulers can no longer dream of parting with these organs of suppression. The quest for absolute power, pursued now for nearly three decades with a ruthlessness unparalleled (in scope at least) in modern times, has again produced internally, as it did externally, its own reaction. The excesses of the police apparatus have fanned the potential opposition to the régime into something far greater and more dangerous than it could have been before those excesses began.

But least of all can the rulers dispense with the fiction by which the maintenance of dictatorial power has been defended. For this fiction has been canonized in Soviet philosophy by the excesses already committed in its name; and it is now anchored in the Soviet structure of thought by bonds far greater than those of mere ideology.

II

So much for the historical background. What does it spell in terms of the political personality of Soviet power as we know it today?

Of the original ideology, nothing has been officially junked. Belief is maintained in the basic badness of capitalism, in the inevitability of its destruction, in the obligation of the proletariat to assist in that destruction and to take power into its own hands. But stress has come to be laid primarily on those concepts which relate most specifically to the Soviet régime itself: to its position as the sole truly Socialist régime in a dark and misguided world, and to the relationships of power within it.

The first of these concepts is that of the innate antagonism between capitalism and Socialism. We have seen how deeply that concept has become imbedded in foundations of Soviet power. It has profound implications for Russia's conduct as a member of international society. It means that there can never be on Moscow's side any sincere assumption of a community of aims between the Soviet Union and powers which are regarded as capitalist. It must invariably be assumed in Moscow that the aims of the capitalist world are antagonistic to the Soviet régime, and therefore to the interests of the peoples it controls. If the Soviet Government occasionally sets its signature to documents which would indicate the contrary, this is to be regarded as a tactical manœuvre permissible in dealing with the enemy (who is without honor) and should be taken in the spirit of *caveat emptor.* Basically, the antagonism remains. It is postulated. And from it flow many of the phenomena which we find disturbing in the Kremlin's conduct of foreign policy: the secretiveness, the lack of frankness, the duplicity, the wary suspiciousness, and the basic unfriendliness of purpose. These phenomena are there to stay, for the foreseeable future. There can be variations of degree and of emphasis. When there is something the Russians want from us, one or the other of these features of their policy may be thrust temporarily into the background; and when that happens there will always be Americans who will leap forward with gleeful announcements that "the Russians have changed," and some who will even try to take credit for having brought about such "changes." But we should not be misled by tactical manœuvres. These characteristics of Soviet policy, like the postulate from which they flow, are basic to the internal nature of Soviet power, and will be with us, whether in the foreground or the background, until the internal nature of Soviet power is changed.

This means that we are going to continue for a long time to find the Russians difficult to deal with. It does not mean that they should be considered as embarked upon a do-or-die program to overthrow our society by a given date. The theory of the inevitability of the eventual fall of capitalism has the fortunate connotation that there is no hurry about it. The forces of progress can take their time in preparing the final *coup de grâce*. Meanwhile, what is vital is that the "Socialist fatherland" – that oasis of power which has been already won for Socialism in the person of the Soviet Union – should be cherished and defended by all good Communists at home and abroad, its fortunes promoted, its enemies badgered and confounded. The promotion of premature, "adventuristic" revolutionary projects abroad which might embarrass Soviet power in any way would be an inexcusable, even a counter-revolutionary act. The cause of Socialism is the support and promotion of Soviet power, as defined in Moscow.

This brings us to the second of the concepts important to contemporary Soviet outlook. That is the infallibility of the Kremlin. The Soviet concept of power, which permits no focal points of organization outside the Party itself, requires that the Party leadership remain in theory the sole repository of truth. For if truth were to be found elsewhere, there would be justification for its expression in organized activity. But it is precisely that which the Kremlin cannot and will not permit.

The leadership of the Communist Party is therefore always right, and has been always right ever since in 1929 Stalin formalized his personal power by announcing that decisions of the Politburo were being taken unanimously.

On the principle of infallibility there rests the iron discipline of the Communist Party. In fact, the two concepts are mutually self-supporting. Perfect discipline requires recognition of infallibility. Infallibility requires the observance of discipline. And the two together go far to determine the behaviorism of the entire Soviet apparatus of power. But their effect cannot be understood unless a third factor be taken into account: namely, the fact that the leadership is at liberty to put forward for tactical purposes any particular thesis which it finds useful to the cause at any particular moment and to require the faithful and unquestioning acceptance of that thesis by the members of the movement as a whole. This means that truth is not a constant but is actually created, for all intents and purposes, by the Soviet leaders themselves. It may vary from week to week, from month to month. It is nothing absolute and immutable — nothing which flows from objective reality. It is only the most recent manifestation of the wisdom of those in whom the ultimate wisdom is supposed to reside, because they represent the logic of history. The accumulative effect of these factors is to give to the whole subordinate apparatus of Soviet power an unshakeable stubbornness and steadfastness in its orientation. This orientation can be changed at will by the Kremlin but by no other power. Once a given party line has been laid down on a given issue of current policy, the whole Soviet governmental machine, including the mechanism of diplomacy, moves inexorably along the prescribed path, like a persistent toy automobile wound up and headed in a given direction, stopping only when it meets with some unanswerable force. The individuals who are the components of this machine are unamenable to argument or reason which comes to them from outside sources. Their whole training has taught them to mistrust and discount the glib persuasiveness of the outside world. Like the white dog before the phonograph, they hear only the "master's voice." And if they are to be called off from the purposes last dictated to them, it is the master who must call them off. Thus the foreign representative cannot hope that his words will make any impression on them. The most that he can hope is that they will be transmitted to those at the top, who are capable of changing the party line. But even those are not likely to be swayed by any normal logic in the words of the bourgeois representative. Since there can be no appeal to common purposes, there can be no appeal to common mental approaches. For this reason, facts speak louder than words to the ears of the Kremlin; and words carry the greatest weight when they have the ring of reflecting, or being backed up by, facts of unchallengeable validity.

But we have seen that the Kremlin is under no ideological compulsion to accomplish its purposes in a hurry. Like the Church, it is dealing in ideological concepts which are of long-term validity, and it can afford to be patient. It has no right to risk the existing achievements of the revolution for the sake of vain baubles of the future. The very teachings of Lenin himself require great caution and flexibility in the pursuit of Communist purposes. Again, these precepts are fortified by the lessons of Russian history: of centuries of obscure battles between nomadic forces over the stretches of a vast unfortified plain. Here caution, circumspection, flexibility and deception are the valuable qualities; and their value finds natural appreciation in the Russian or the oriental mind. Thus the Kremlin has no compunction about retreating in the face of superior force. And being under the compulsion of no timetable, it does not get panicky under the necessity for such retreat. Its political action is a fluid stream which moves constantly, wherever it is permitted to move, toward a given goal. Its main concern is to make sure that it has filled every nook and cranny available to it in the basin of world power. But if it finds unassailable barriers in its path, it accepts these philosophically and accommodates itself to them. The main thing is that there should always be pressure, unceasing constant pressure, toward the desired goal. There is no trace of any feeling in Soviet psychology that that goal must be reached at any given time.

These considerations make Soviet diplomacy at once easier and more difficult to deal with than the diplomacy of individual aggressive leaders like Napoleon and Hitler. On the one hand it is more sensitive to contrary force, more ready to yield on individual sectors of the diplomatic front when that force is felt to be too strong, and thus more rational in the logic and rhetoric of power. On the other hand it cannot be easily defeated or discouraged by a single victory on the part of its opponents. And the patient persistence by which it is animated means that it can be effectively countered not by sporadic acts which represent the momentary whims of democratic opinion but only by intelligent long-range policies on the part of Russia's adversaries—policies no less steady in their purpose, and no less variegated and resourceful in their application, than those of the Soviet Union itself.

In these circumstances it is clear that the main element of any United States policy toward the Soviet Union must be that of a long-term, patient but firm and vigilant containment of Russian expansive tendencies. It is important to note, however, that such a policy has nothing to do with outward histrionics: with threats or blustering or superfluous gestures of outward "toughness." While the Kremlin is basically flexible in its reaction to political realities, it is by no means unamenable to considerations of prestige. Like almost any other government, it can be placed by tactless and threatening gestures in a position where it cannot afford to yield even though this might be dictated by its sense of realism. The Russian leaders are keen judges of human psychology, and as such they are highly conscious that loss of temper and of self-control is never a source of strength in political affairs. They are quick to exploit such evidences of weakness. For these reasons, it is a *sine qua non* of successful dealing with Russia that the foreign government in question should remain at all times cool and collected and that its demands on Russian policy should be put forward in such a manner as to leave the way open for a compliance not too detrimental to Russian prestige.

III

In the light of the above, it will be clearly seen that the Soviet pressure against the free institutions of the western world is something that can be contained by the adroit and vigilant application of counter-force at a series of constantly shifting geographical and political points, corresponding to the shifts and manœuvres of Soviet policy, but which cannot be charmed or talked out of existence. The Russians look forward to a duel of infinite duration, and they see that already they have scored great successes. It must be borne in mind that there was a time when the Communist Party represented far more of a minority in the sphere of Russian national life than Soviet power today represents in the world community.

But if ideology convinces the rulers of Russia that truth is on their side and that they can therefore afford to wait, those of us on whom that ideology has no claim are free to examine objectively the validity of that premise. The Soviet thesis not only implies complete lack of control by the west over its own economic destiny, it likewise assumes Russian unity, discipline and patience over an infinite period. Let us bring this apocalyptic vision down to earth, and suppose that the western world finds the strength and resourcefulness to contain Soviet power over a period of ten to fifteen years. What does that spell for Russia itself?

The Soviet leaders, taking advantage of the contributions of modern technique to the arts of despotism, have solved the question of obedience within the confines of their power. Few challenge their authority; and even those who do are unable to make that challenge valid as against the organs of suppression of the state.

The Kremlin has also proved able to accomplish its purpose of building up in Russia, regardless of the interests of the inhabitants, an industrial foundation of heavy metallurgy, which is, to be sure, not yet complete but which is nevertheless continuing to grow and is approaching those of the other major industrial countries. All of this, however, both the maintenance of internal political security and the building of heavy industry, has been carried out at a terrible cost in human life and in human hopes and energies. It has necessitated the use of forced labor on a scale unprecedented in modern times under conditions of peace. It has involved the neglect or abuse of other phases of Soviet economic life, particularly agriculture, consumers' goods production, housing and transportation.

To all that, the war has added its tremendous toll of destruction, death and human exhaustion. In consequence of this, we have in Russia today a population which is physically and spiritually tired. The mass of the people are disillusioned, skeptical and no longer as accessible as they once were to the magical attraction which Soviet power still radiates to its followers abroad. The avidity with which people seized upon the slight respite accorded to the Church for tactical reasons during the war was eloquent testimony to the fact that their capacity for faith and devotion found little expression in the purposes of the régime.

In these circumstances, there are limits to the physical and nervous strength of people themselves. These limits are absolute ones, and are binding even for the cruelest dictatorship, because beyond them people cannot be driven. The forced labor camps and the other agencies of constraint provide temporary means of compelling people to work longer hours than their own volition or mere economic pressure would dictate; but if people survive them at all they become old before their time and must be considered as human casualties to the demands of dictatorship. In either case their best powers are no longer available to society and can no longer be enlisted in the service of the state.

Here only the younger generation can help. The younger generation, despite all vicissitudes and sufferings, is numerous and vigorous; and the Russians are a talented people. But it still remains to be seen what will be the effects on mature performance of the abnormal emotional strains of childhood which Soviet dictatorship created and which were enormously increased by the war. Such things as normal security and placidity of home environment have practically ceased to exist in the Soviet Union outside of the most remote farms and villages. And observers are not yet sure whether that is not going to leave its mark on the over-all capacity of the generation now coming into maturity.

In addition to this, we have the fact that Soviet economic development, while it can list certain formidable achievements, has been precariously spotty and uneven. Russian Communists who speak of the "uneven development of capitalism" should blush at the contemplation of their own national economy. Here certain branches of economic life, such as the metallurgical and machine industries, have been pushed out of all proportion to other sectors of economy. Here is a nation striving to become in a short period one of the great industrial nations of the world while it still has no highway network worthy of the name and only a relatively primitive network of railways. Much has been done to increase efficiency of labor and to teach primitive peasants something about the operation of machines. But maintenance is still a crying deficiency of all Soviet economy. Construction is hasty and poor in quality. Depreciation must be enormous. And in vast sectors of economic life it has not yet been possible to instill into labor anything like that general culture of production and technical self-respect which characterizes the skilled worker of the west.

It is difficult to see how these deficiencies can be corrected at an early date by a tired and dispirited population working largely under the shadow of fear and compulsion. And as long as they are not overcome, Russia will remain economically a vulnerable, and in a certain sense an impotent, nation, capable of exporting its enthusiasms and of radiating the strange charm of its primitive political vitality but unable to back up those articles of export by the real evidences of material power and prosperity.

Meanwhile, a great uncertainty hangs over the political life of the Soviet Union. That is the uncertainty involved in the transfer of power from one individual or group of individuals to others.

This is, of course, outstandingly the problem of the personal position of Stalin. We must remember that his succession to Lenin's pinnacle of preëminence in the Communist movement was the only such transfer of individual authority which the Soviet Union has experienced. That transfer took 12 years to consolidate. It cost the lives of millions of people and shook the state to its foundations. The attendant tremors were felt all through the international revolutionary movement, to the disadvantage of the Kremlin itself.

It is always possible that another transfer of preëminent power may take place quietly and inconspicuously, with no repercussions anywhere. But again, it is possible that the questions involved may unleash, to use some of Lenin's words, one of those "incredibly swift transitions" from "delicate deceit" to "wild violence" which characterize Russian history, and may shake Soviet power to its foundations.

But this is not only a question of Stalin himself. There has been, since 1938, a dangerous congealment of political life in the higher circles of Soviet power. The All-Union Congress of Soviets, in theory the supreme body of the Party, is supposed to meet not less often than once in three years. It will soon be eight full years since its last meeting. During this period membership in the Party has numerically doubled. Party mortality during the war was enormous; and today well over half of the Party members are persons who have entered since the last Party congress was held. Meanwhile, the same small group of men has carried on at the top through an amazing series of national vicissitudes. Surely there is some reason why the experiences of the war brought basic political changes to every one of the great governments of the west. Surely the causes of that phenomenon are basic enough to be present somewhere in the obscurity of Soviet political life, as well. And yet no recognition has been given to these causes in Russia.

It must be surmised from this that even within so highly disciplined an organization as the Communist Party there must be a growing divergence in age, outlook and interest between the great mass of Party members, only so recently recruited into the movement, and the little self-perpetuating clique of men at the top, whom most of these Party members have never met, with whom they have never conversed, and with whom they can have no political intimacy.

Who can say whether, in these circumstances, the eventual rejuvenation of the higher spheres of authority (which can only be a matter of time) can take place smoothly and peacefully, or whether rivals in the quest for higher power will not eventually reach down into these politically immature and inexperienced masses in order to find support for their respective claims? If this were ever to happen, strange consequences could flow for the Communist Party: for the membership at large has been exercised only in the practices of iron discipline and obedience and not in the arts of compromise and accommodation. And if disunity were ever to seize and paralyze the Party, the chaos and weakness of Russian society would be revealed in forms beyond description. For we have seen that Soviet power is only a crust concealing an amorphous mass of human beings among whom no independent organizational structure is tolerated. In Russia there is not even such a thing as local government. The present generation of Russians have never known spontaneity of collective action.

If, consequently, anything were ever to occur to disrupt the unity and efficacy of the Party as a political instrument, Soviet Russia might be changed overnight from one of the strongest to one of the weakest and most pitiable of national societies.

Thus the future of Soviet power may not be by any means as secure as Russian capacity for self-delusion would make it appear to the men in the Kremlin. That they can keep power themselves, they have demonstrated. That they can quietly and easily turn it over to others remains to be proved. Meanwhile, the hardships of their rule and the vicissitudes of international life have taken a heavy toll of the strength and hopes of the great people on whom their power rests. It is curious to note that the ideological power of Soviet authority is strongest today in areas beyond the frontiers of Russia, beyond the reach of its police power. This phenomenon brings to mind a comparison used by Thomas Mann in his great novel "Buddenbrooks." Observing that human institutions often show the greatest outward brilliance at a moment when inner decay is in reality farthest advanced, he compared the Buddenbrook family, in the days of its greatest glamour, to one of those stars whose light shines most brightly on this world when in reality it has long since ceased to exist. And who can say with assurance that the strong light still cast by the Kremlin on the dissatisfied peoples of the western world is not the powerful afterglow of a constellation which is in actuality on the wane? This cannot be proved. And it cannot be disproved. But the possibility remains (and in the opinion of this writer it is a strong one) that Soviet power, like the capitalist world of its conception, bears within it the seeds of its own decay, and that the sprouting of these seeds is well advanced.

IV

It is clear that the United States cannot expect in the foreseeable future to enjoy political intimacy with the Soviet régime. It must continue to regard the Soviet Union as a rival, not a partner, in the political arena. It must continue to expect that Soviet policies will reflect no abstract love of peace and stability, no real faith in the possibility of a permanent happy coexistence of the Socialist and capitalist worlds, but rather a cautious, persistent pressure toward the disruption and weakening of all rival influence and rival power.

Balanced against this are the facts that Russia, as opposed to the western world in general, is still by far the weaker party, that Soviet policy is highly flexible, and that Soviet society may well contain deficiencies which will eventually weaken its own total potential. This would of itself warrant the United States entering with reasonable confidence upon a policy of firm containment, designed to confront the Russians with unalterable counter-force at every point where they show signs of encroaching upon the interests of a peaceful and stable world.

But in actuality the possibilities for American policy are by no means limited to holding the line and hoping for the best. It is entirely possible for the United States to influence by its actions the internal developments, both within Russia and throughout the international Communist movement, by which Russian policy is largely determined. This is not only a question of the modest measure of informational activity which this government can conduct in the Soviet Union and elsewhere, although that, too, is important. It is rather a question of the degree to which the United States can create among the peoples of the world generally the impression of a country which knows what it wants, which is coping successfully with the problems of its internal life and with the responsibilities of a World Power, and which has a spiritual vitality capable of holding its own among the major ideological currents of the time. To the extent that such an impression can be created and maintained, the aims of Russian Communism must appear sterile and quixotic, the hopes and enthusiasm of Moscow's supporters must wane, and added strain must be imposed on the Kremlin's foreign policies. For the palsied decrepitude of the capitalist world is the keystone of Communist philosophy. Even the failure of the United States to experience the early economic depression which the ravens of the Red Square have been predicting with such complacent confidence since hostilities ceased would have deep and important repercussions throughout the Communist world.

By the same token, exhibitions of indecision, disunity and internal disintegration within this country have an exhilarating effect on the whole Communist movement. At each evidence of these tendencies, a thrill of hope and excitement goes through the Communist world; a new jauntiness can be noted in the Moscow tread; new groups of foreign supporters climb on to what they can only view as the band wagon of international politics; and Russian pressure increases all along the line in international affairs.

It would be an exaggeration to say that American behavior unassisted and alone could exercise a power of life and death over the

Communist movement and bring about the early fall of Soviet power in Russia. But the United States has it in its power to increase enormously the strains under which Soviet policy must operate, to force upon the Kremlin a far greater degree of moderation and circumspection than it has had to observe in recent years, and in this way to promote tendencies which must eventually find their outlet in either the break-up or the gradual mellowing of Soviet power. For no mystical, Messianic movement—and particularly not that of the Kremlin—can face frustration indefinitely without eventually adjust-itself in one way or another to the logic of that state of affairs.

Thus the decision will really fall in large measure in this country itself. The issue of Soviet-American relations is in essence a test of the over-all worth of the United States as a nation among nations. To avoid destruction the United States need only measure up to its own best traditions and prove itself worthy of preservation as a great nation.

Surely, there was never a fairer test of national quality than this. In the light of these circumstances, the thoughtful observer of Russian-American relations will find no cause for complaint in the Kremlin's challenge to American society. He will rather experience a certain gratitude to a Providence which, by providing the American people with this implacable challenge, has made their entire security as a nation dependent on their pulling themselves together and accepting the responsibilities of moral and political leadership that history plainly intended them to bear.

39   THE BALANCE OF POWER*

The policy of containment, which Mr. X recommends, demands the employment of American economic, political, and in the last analysis, American military power at "sectors" in the interior of Europe and Asia. This requires, as I have pointed out, ground forces, that is to say reserves of infantry, which we do not possess.

The United States cannot by its own military power contain the expansive pressure of the Russians "at every point where they show signs of encroaching." The United States cannot have ready "unalterable counterforce" consisting of American troops. Therefore, the

*Walter Lippmann, *The Cold War* (New York: Harper & Bros., 1947), pp. 21–28, 30–31, 33–36, 38–39, 43–51, 60–62.

counterforces which Mr. X requires have to be composed of Chinese, Afghans, Iranians, Turks, Kurds, Arabs, Greeks, Italians, Austrians, of anti-Soviet Poles, Czechoslovaks, Bulgars, Yugoslavs, Albanians, Hungarians, Finns and Germans.

The policy can be implemented only by recruiting, subsidizing and supporting a heterogeneous array of satellites, clients, dependents and puppets. The instrument of the policy of containment is therefore a coalition of disorganized, disunited, feeble or disorderly nations, tribes and factions around the perimeter of the Soviet Union.

To organize a coalition among powerful modern states is, even in time of war and under dire necessity, an enormously difficult thing to do well. To organize a coalition of disunited, feeble and immature states, and to hold it together for a prolonged diplomatic siege, which might last for ten or fifteen years, is, I submit, impossibly difficult.

It would require, however much the real name for it were disavowed, continual and complicated intervention by the United States in the affairs of all the members of the coalition which we were proposing to organize, to protect, to lead and to use. Our diplomatic agents abroad would have to have an almost unerring capacity to judge correctly and quickly which men and which parties were reliable containers. Here at home Congress and the people would have to stand ready to back their judgments as to who should be nominated, who should be subsidized, who should be whitewashed, who should be seen through rose-colored spectacles, who should be made our clients and our allies.

Mr. X offers us the prospect of maintaining such a coalition indefinitely until—eventually—the Soviet power breaks up or mellows because it has been frustrated. It is not a good prospect. Even if we assume, which we ought not, that our diplomatic agents will know how to intervene shrewdly and skillfully all over Asia, the Middle East, and Europe, and even if we assume, which the Department of State cannot, that the American people will back them with a drawing account of blank checks both in money and in military power, still it is not a good prospect. For we must not forget that the Soviet Union, against which this coalition will be directed, will resist and react.

In the complicated contest over this great heterogeneous array of unstable states, the odds are heavily in favor of the Soviets. For if we are to succeed, we must organize our satellites as unified, orderly and reasonably contented nations. The Russians can defeat us by disorganizing states that are already disorganized, by disuniting peoples that are torn with civil strife, and by inciting their discontent which is already very great.

As a matter of fact this borderland in Europe and Asia around the perimeter of the Soviet Union is not a place where Mr. X's "unassailable barriers" can be erected. Satellite states and puppet governments are not good material out of which to construct unassailable barriers. A diplomatic war conducted as this policy demands, that is to say conducted indirectly, means that we must stake our own security and the peace of the world upon satellites, puppets, clients, agents about whom we can know very little. Frequently they will act for their own reasons, and on their own judgments, presenting us with accomplished facts that we did not intend, and with crises for which we are unready. The "unassailable barriers" will present us with an unending series of insoluble dilemmas. We shall have either to disown our puppets, which would be tantamount to appeasement and defeat and the loss of face, or must support them at an incalculable cost on an unintended, unforeseen and perhaps undesirable issue.

There is still greater disadvantage in a policy which seeks to "contain" the Soviet Union by attempting to make "unassailable barriers" out of the surrounding border states. They are admittedly weak. Now a weak ally is not an asset. It is a liability. It requires the diversion of power, money, and prestige to support it and to maintain it. These weak states are vulnerable. Yet the effort to defend them brings us no nearer to a decision or to a settlement of the main conflict. Worst of all, the effort to develop such an unnatural alliance of backward states must alienate the natural allies of the United States.

The natural allies of the United States are the nations of the Atlantic community: that is to say, the nations of western Europe and of the Americas. The Atlantic Ocean and the Mediterranean Sea, which is an arm of the Atlantic Ocean, unite them in a common strategic, economic and cultural system. The chief components of the Atlantic community are the British Commonwealth of nations, the Latin states on both sides of the Atlantic, the Low Countries and Switzerland, Scandinavia and the United States.

The boundaries of the Atlantic community are not sharp and distinct, particularly in the case of the Germans and the western Slavs and the dependencies and the colonies of western Europe. But the nucleus of the Atlantic community is distinct and unmistakable, and among the nations that are indisputably members of the Atlantic community there exists a vital connection founded upon their military and political geography, the common traditions of western

Christendom, and their economic, political, legal, and moral institutions which, with all their variations and differences, have a common origin and have been shaped by much the same historic experience.

Now the policy of containment, as described by Mr. X, is an attempt to organize an anti-Soviet alliance composed in the first instance of peoples that are either on the shadowy extremity of the Atlantic community, or are altogether outside it. The active proponents of the policy have been concerned immediately with the anti-Soviet parties and factions of eastern Europe, with the Greeks, the Turks, the Iranians, the Arabs and Afghans, and with the Chinese Nationalists.

Instead of concentrating their attention and their efforts upon our old allies of the Atlantic community, the makers and the shapers of the policy of containment have for more than a year been reaching out for new allies on the perimeter of the Soviet Union. This new coalition, as we can see only too clearly in Greece, in Iran, in the Arab states and in China, cannot in fact be made to coalesce. Instead of becoming an unassailable barrier against the Soviet power, this borderland is a seething stew of civil strife.

We have not succeeded in organizing the new and alien coalition of the Russian perimeter, and we have failed to consolidate, as the mounting crisis of western Europe and of Latin America shows, the old and familiar coalition of the Atlantic community. The supporters of the Truman Doctrine[1] attribute the divisions and the paralysis of western Europe to the machinations of the Soviet Union, to its obstruction in the United Nations and in all the various peace conferences, to the propaganda, the infiltration of the communist parties. Perhaps. But their argument, if true, destroys the last reason for thinking that the policy of containment can be made to work successfully.

For the nations of the Atlantic community are not occupied by the Red Army. They cannot be occupied by the Red Army unless the Kremlin is prepared to face a full scale world war, atomic bombs and all the rest. Though impoverished and weakened, the nations of the Atlantic community are incomparably stronger, richer, more united and politically more democratic and mature than any of the nations of the Russian perimeter.

If the Soviet Union is, nevertheless, able to paralyze and disorganize them, then surely it can much more readily paralyze and disorganize the nations of the perimeter. They are already paralyzed and

---

[1] See page 204 below. [Ed.]

disorganized. They have never, in fact, been organized and effective modern states. Yet we are asked to believe that we can organize the perimeter of Russia, though the Russians are so strong and so cunning that we cannot consolidate the Atlantic community.

By concentrating our efforts on a diplomatic war in the borderlands of the Soviet Union, we have neglected—because we do not have unlimited power, resources, influence, and diplomatic brain power—the vital interests of our natural allies in western Europe, notably in reconstructing their economic life and in promoting a German settlement on which they can agree.

The failure of our diplomatic campaign in the borderlands, on which we have staked so much too much, has conjured up the specter of a Third World War. The threat of a Russian-American war, arising out of the conflict in the borderlands, is dissolving the natural alliance of the Atlantic community. For the British, the French, and all the other Europeans see that they are placed between the hammer and the anvil. They realize, even if we do not realize it, that the policy of containment, in the hope that the Soviet power will collapse by frustration, cannot be enforced and cannot be administered successfully, and that it must fail. Either Russia will burst through the barriers which are supposed to contain her, and all of Europe will be at her mercy, or, at some point and at some time, the diplomatic war will become a full scale shooting war. In either event Europe is lost. Either Europe falls under the domination of Russia, or Europe becomes the battlefield of a Russian-American war.

Because the policy of containment offers these intolerable alternatives to our old allies, the real aim of every European nation, including Great Britain, is to extricate itself from the Russian-American conflict. While we have been devoting our energies to lining up and bolstering up the Chinese Nationalists, the Iranians, the Turks, the Greek monarchists and conservatives, the anti-Soviet Hungarians, Rumanians, Poles, the natural alignment of the British, French, Belgians, Dutch, Swiss and Scandinavians has been weakened.

And so in any prudent estimate of our world position, they are no longer to be counted upon as firm members of a coalition led by the United States against the Soviet Union. We must not deceive ourselves by supposing that we stand at the head of a worldwide coalition of democratic states in our conflict with the Soviet Union.

The aim of the leading democratic states of Europe and probably also of the Americas is at best to hold the balance of power between Russia and America, and thus to become mediators of that conflict.

At worst, their aim is to isolate themselves in some kind of neutrality which will spare them the dual catastrophe of being overrun by the Red Army and bombed by the American air forces.

For they cannot have reasonable confidence in what Mr. X says is sufficient ground for reasonable confidence. They cannot rely on his wishful prediction which "cannot be proved" and "cannot be disproved," that the Soviet power will break up or "mellow" when it has been frustrated for ten or fifteen years by unassailable barriers in such inaccessible "individual sectors" as Manchuria, Mongolia, north China, Afghanistan, Iran, Hungary and Rumania.

They remember Mr. Chamberlain's efforts to contain Hitler by a guarantee to Poland. They remember Mr. Hull's effort to contain Japan in China. They know that a policy of containment does not contain, that measures of "counterforce" are doomed to be too late and too little, that a policy of holding the line and hoping for the best means the surrender of the strategic initiative, the dispersion of our forces without prospect of a decision and a settlement, and in the end a war which, once begun, it would be most difficult to conclude. . . .

. . .

We may now ask why the official diagnosis of Soviet conduct, as disclosed by Mr. X's article, has led to such an unworkable policy for dealing with Russia. It is, I believe, because Mr. X has neglected even to mention the fact that the Soviet Union is the successor of the Russian Empire and that Stalin is not only the heir of Marx and of Lenin but of Peter the Great, and the Czars of all the Russias.

For reasons which I do not understand, Mr. X decided not to consider the men in the Kremlin as the rulers of the Russian State and Empire, and has limited his analysis to the interaction of "two forces": "the ideology inherited by the present Soviet leaders from the movement in which they had their political origin" and the "circumstances of the power which they have now exercised for nearly three decades in Russia."

Thus he dwells on the indubitable fact that they believe in the Marxian ideology and that "they have continued to be predominantly absorbed with the struggle to secure and make absolute the power which they seized in November 1917." But with these two observations alone he cannot, and does not, explain the conduct of the Soviet government in this postwar era—that is to say its aims and claims to territory and to the sphere of influence which it dominates. The Soviet government has been run by Marxian revolutionists for thirty years; what has to be explained by a planner of American foreign policy is why in 1945 the Soviet government expanded its frontiers and its orbit, and what was the plan and pattern of its expansion. That can be done only by remembering that the Soviet government is a Russian government and that this Russian government has emerged victorious over Germany and Japan.

Having omitted from his analysis the fact that we are dealing with a victorious Russia—having become exclusively preoccupied with the Marxian ideology, and with the communist revolution—it is no wonder that the outcome of Mr. X's analysis is nothing more definite, concrete and practical than that the Soviets will encroach and expand "at a series of constantly shifting geographical and political points." Mr. X's picture of the Soviet conduct has no pattern. It is amorphous. That is why his conclusions about how we should deal with the Soviets have no pattern, and are also amorphous. . . .

The westward expansion of the Russian frontier and of the Russian sphere of influence, though always a Russian aim, was accomplished when, as, and because the Red Army defeated the German army and advanced to the center of Europe [during 1945–47]. It was the mighty power of the Red Army, not the ideology of Karl Marx, which enabled the Russian government to expand its frontiers. It is the pressure of that army far beyond the new frontiers which makes the will of the Kremlin irresistible within the Russian sphere of influence. It is the threat that the Red Army may advance still farther west—into Italy, into western Germany, into Scandinavia that gives the Kremlin and the native communist parties of western Europe an abnormal and intolerable influence in the affairs of the European continent.

Therefore, the immediate and the decisive problem of our relations with the Soviet Union is whether, when, on what conditions the Red Army can be prevailed upon to evacuate Europe.

I am contending that the American diplomatic effort should be concentrated on the problem created by the armistice—which is on how the continent of Europe can be evacuated by the three non-European armies which are now inside Europe. This is the problem which will have to be solved if the independence of the European nations is to be restored. Without that there is no possibility of a tolerable peace. But if these armies withdraw, there will be a very different balance of power in the world than there is today, and one which cannot easily be upset. For the nations of Europe, separately and in groups, perhaps even in unity, will then, and then only, cease to be the stakes and the pawns of the Russian-American conflict.

The material cause and the reason of the conflict will have been dealt with.

The terms of the problem were defined at Yalta in the winter of 1945. There, with a victory over Germany in sight, Roosevelt, Churchill, and Stalin made a military settlement which fixed the boundaries where the converging armies were to meet, and were to wait while the governments negotiated the terms of peace which would provide for the withdrawal of the armies. The crucial issue in the world today is whether the Yalta military boundary, which was intended to be provisional for the period of the armistice, is to become the political boundary of two hostile coalitions. . . .

. . . [I] f, and only if, we can bring about the withdrawal of the Red Army from the Yalta line to the new frontier of the Soviet Union — and simultaneously, of course, the withdrawal of the British and American armies from continental Europe — can a balance of power be established which can then be maintained. For after the withdrawal, an attempt to return would be an invasion—an open, unmistakable act of military aggression. Against such an aggression, the power of the United States to strike the vital centers of Russia by air and by amphibious assault would stand as the opposing and deterrent force. And until treaties are agreed to which bring about the withdrawal of the Red Army, the power of the United States to strike these vital centers would be built up for the express purpose of giving weight to our policy of ending the military occupation of Europe.

All the other pressures of the Soviet Union at the "constantly shifting geographical and political points," which Mr. X is so concerned about—in the Middle East and in Asia—are, I contend, secondary and subsidiary to the fact that its armed forces are in the heart of Europe. It is to the Red Army in Europe, therefore, and not to ideologies, elections, forms of government, to socialism, to communism, to free enterprise, that a correctly conceived and soundly planned policy should be directed. . . .

Now it may be that the Soviet Union, though committed in principle, will not in fact agree to a settlement which means the evacuation of Europe. If her purpose is the domination of Europe and of a large part of the world, she will never agree. For the military evacuation of continental Europe would not be one of those "tactical maneuvers" against which, quite rightly, Mr. X tells us to be on guard.

It would be a strategic change in the balance of power. For once the Red Army had been withdrawn behind the frontiers of the Soviet Union, it could not re-enter Europe without committing an obvious act of military aggression, which would precipitate a general war. The pressure of the Soviets upon Europe by propaganda and infiltration would continue, but that pressure would no longer be backed up by overwhelming military power throughout eastern Europe and by the threat of military intervention in western Europe. Though Tito's army, and perhaps the Polish army, assuming them to be satellites of Moscow, could exert considerable military pressure locally on the neighboring states, they are not capable of conquering and dominating Europe except as contingents of the Red Army.

If the Kremlin really means to dominate Europe, it will not withdraw its armies which are halfway across Europe. Standing on the Elbe line in the middle of Europe and Austria, and on the vulnerable frontier of Italy, the Kremlin is in a far better position to advance farther west than it can be if it withdraws and stands on its own frontiers. The withdrawal of the army is, therefore, the acid test of Soviet conduct and purpose, incomparably clearer, more definite, more practical than whether or not they observe the Yalta Declaration in countries liberated from the Nazis but still occupied by the Red Army. Verbal agreements like the Yalta Declaration and the Atlantic Charter can be made the subject of endless tactical maneuvering. For agreements of this kind do not change the balance of power. But the evacuation of a continent would change the balance of power.

The Kremlin will understand this, and we must expect it to exact the highest price it can obtain for what would be a deep reduction of its present power and influence in Europe, or, if it means to conquer Europe, to obstruct any settlement which meant that the Russian armies must evacuate Europe.

We shall in either case have clarified the real issue. Instead of seeking "to contain" the Soviet Union all over the Eurasian continent, we shall have the initiative and a definite and concrete objective; at the best we shall know the terms on which the main conflict can be settled; at the worst the Soviet Union will have shown its hand on an issue—the liberation of Europe from non-European armies—where there will be no doubt whatever that our cause is just, and that we are the champions of freedom, and that the great masses of the people of Europe will be with us because we stand for the very thing which only traitors can oppose.

We shall have written off the liabilities of the Truman Doctrine which must in practice mean inexorably an unending intervention in all the countries that are supposed to "contain" the Soviet Union. We shall be acting once more in the great American tradition which is to foster the independence of other countries, not to use other countries as the satellites of our own power, however beneficent, and as the instruments of our own policy, however well meant. Our aim will not be to organize an ideological crusade. It will not be to make Jeffersonian democrats out of the peasants of eastern Europe, the tribal chieftains, the feudal lords, the pashas, and the warlords of the Middle East and Asia, but to settle the war and to restore the independence of the nations of Europe by removing the alien armies—all of them, our own included.

We shall have a diplomatic policy that it would be exceedingly difficult for the cleverest propagandist to misrepresent. For everyone can understand such a policy. Practically everyone will wish us to succeed in it. For alien armies are hateful, however well behaved, just because they represent an alien power and are, therefore, a perpetual reminder that the people on whom they are quartered are not masters of their own destiny.

Alien armies are, however, never well behaved: invariably they become corrupted. Thus we may count confidently upon a mounting popular support if we make it our mission to emancipate the ancient and proud continent of Europe from the military control of non-European powers. We shall be drawing upon the elemental and unifying passion of patriotism in Europe which, when it is aroused, is a much stronger passion than factionalism or any ideology.

. . .

The evacuation of Europe can be accomplished only if we can negotiate, sign, and ratify a treaty of peace for Germany and for Austria to which the Soviet government is a party. For the peace treaties about eastern Europe, which is between Germany and Russia, cannot become effective until there are German and Austrian treaties. The Red Army will remain in eastern Europe as long as it remains in Germany and in Austria.

We must turn then to the problem of Germany, and how that problem is defined if we adhere to the Truman Doctrine and how defined if we adopt the alternative policy for which I have been contending.

In its approach to the German problem, which is crucial in a world settlement, we come upon the most dangerous and destructive consequences of what Mr. X calls a policy of firm containment and what the world knows as the Truman Doctrine. Here, ever since Secretary Byrnes went to Stuttgart in 1946 and addressed the German nation, we have been preparing the ground for a gigantic diplomatic disaster.

For the policy of containment envisages the western zones of Germany as an essential part of the "unassailable barriers" which Mr. X tells us we should erect in the path of the Soviet Union. Thus the German nation must, if the policy is to be made to work, participate in the coalition of the containing nations. That it may be willing to participate, it has been deemed necessary to evoke the sentiment of German "unity," and to cultivate the national patriotism of the Germans even to the point where we have allowed the ideal of the unity of Germany to displace the ideal of the unity of Europe.

The underlying assumption, which is implicit though unavowed, has been that since Germany has lost the eastern provinces to the Russians and to a Russian satellite, Poland, German national feeling will naturally be directed against the Soviet Union. Historical experience and the logic of the situation indicate, I believe, that this is a profound miscalculation. For we are encouraging the Germans to want something—namely, national unity—which we cannot give them except by going to war with Russia. Germany cannot have unity, as all Germans must understand unity, except by recovering the lost provinces of eastern Germany We would have to conquer Russia and Poland in order to restore the eastern provinces to Germany.

But Russia can return them to Germany whenever she decides that an alliance with Germany is a vital Russian interest. This can be done by performing another partition of Poland, an act which the men who signed the Molotov-Ribbentrop pact of 1939 could carry out if they deemed it expedient and necessary. Or if they deemed it inexpedient to partition Poland again, but necessary to enlarge the truncated Reich, they can offer the German nationalists compensation in western Europe and elsewhere for the lost provinces in the east. Just as they gave the Poles the German provinces as compensation for the territory east of the Curzon line, so they could offer Austria to the Germans, perhaps Alsace-Lorraine, perhaps Denmark, perhaps the Netherlands and the mouth of the Rhine.

We do not need to know exactly what the Soviet Union would offer the Germans for an alliance. It is enough to know that in an auction for the support of the Germans the Russians could offer them great prizes, and that we can offer the Germans absolutely nothing—except some help in rising from squalor and misery and prostration to the position of a fifth-rate power living a prosaic and

stunted national existence. The idea that we can foster the sentiment of German unity, and make a truncated Germany economically
strong, can keep her disarmed, and can use her in the anti-Soviet
coalition is like trying to square the circle. Applied to Germany, the
policy of containment is a booby trap, constructed by men who do
not understand the politics of power.

The controlling fact in the German problem is that by the advance
of the Red Army beyond Berlin and because of the annexations
which resulted from it, the Soviet Union has destroyed the unity of
the Reich and has acquired the power to restore the unity of the
Reich. The western nations cannot restore the unity of Germany, and
it is therefore suicidal for them to incite the sentiments of unity, and
to treat the western portion of Germany as a prospective ally in the
operation of the Truman Doctrine. For if Germany is to become
allied on either side of the diplomatic conflict, the precedents of
history and the logic of the situation tell us that when she is strong
enough to be a useful ally to anyone, she will become the ally of
Russia. The more we bring what remains of Germany, after the dismemberment of the east, under the unified control of a German
government, the more profitable and the easier it will be for Berlin
and Moscow to make a deal and become allied. If Hitler and Stalin,
Ribbentrop and Molotov could make a deal, how can we dare to
suppose that a Germany ruled by communists, socialists and nationalists would not make a deal?

And if we carried the policy to its ultimate end, as Mr. Hoover has
asked us to do, and made a separate treaty of peace with western
Germany, we should have made a German-Russian alliance even more
certain. The German government with which we had made peace
would again be a sovereign power: it would have to have at a very
minimum the sovereign right of an independent state to have diplomatic agents abroad and to receive them, and to use the diplomatic
apparatus of codes, couriers, and agents.

Having made a separate treaty of peace with us, the new central
German government would necessarily have to begin negotiations for
separate treaties of peace with its eastern neighbors—with Poland,
Czechoslovakia and with Russia. She would enter these negotiations,
having gotten from us all that she could expect—which would not be
much and not nearly enough to satisfy a German patriot. The negotiations with the east would offer the great prizes and all manner of
temptation. These negotiations would take place with the Red Army
in eastern Europe and in what had been the eastern provinces of

Germany, and as a matter of fact with the Red Army in Berlin. Thus Russia, which alone can offer the German nationalists great inducements, would also be in a military position to compel the German nationalists to enter into a deal.

Once we recognized the consequences of the fact that Germany had been dismembered in her eastern provinces, it would become plain that we could not use western Germany to contain Russia. It would become plain, too, that the unity of Germany could not be restored by the United States. Therefore there can be no German settlement, which is tolerable, by reestablishing the sovereign power of a central German government in a truncated area and dedicated to the unity of Germany. The annexations in the east of Germany demand a radical decentralization of western Germany.

The truncated area will have to be decentralized, not unified, and the German states which are in it will have to take their places within a larger European system and a European economy. Not German unity but European unity, not German self-sufficiency but European self-sufficiency, not a Germany to contain Russia but a Germany neutralized as between Russia and the west, not the Truman Doctrine but the Marshall Plan,[2] purged of the Truman Doctrine, should be the aims of our German policy.

These will be sound aims even if we find it impossible to agree with the Russians on a treaty of peace. For we shall have identified ourselves with a policy which opposes the revival of the German power to threaten her neighbors, not with a policy which would place them in a German-Russian nutcracker, would compel them to choose sides for a Third World War, and would make their territory the battlefield of that world war and of the enormous civil war which it would surely precipitate.

Though we could not conclude an agreement with the Russians, we should be identified with a policy which, if an agreement could be concluded, would mean the evacuation of the continent, and the restoration of Europe to the Europeans. Thus, as the diplomatic struggle continued, we should stand forth ever more clearly as the champions of the vital interest of all the peoples of Europe.

We could then leave it to the Europeans to decide how much they are willing to have paid in reparations, in concessions and trade agreements, and as ransom, in order to get the Russians to withdraw the Red Army. If we were wise, and were more interested in settling the

---

[2] See page 233 below. [Ed.]

war than in making gestures of our disapproval of the Russians and of communism, we should offer to contribute our part to the ransom—if paying ransom will achieve the main objective.

If, nevertheless, the Soviet government will not negotiate an agreement, if the price of a settlement is impossibly high, if the ransom is deliberately set in terms which mean that Russia does not intend to evacuate Europe, the situation will be no more dangerous than it is today. But our energies will be concentrated, not dispersed all over the globe, and the real issues will be much clearer. . . .

. . .

At the root of Mr. X's philosophy about Russian-American relations and underlying all the ideas of the Truman Doctrine there is a disbelief in the possibility of a settlement of the issues raised by this war. Having observed, I believe quite correctly, that we cannot expect "to enjoy political intimacy with the Soviet regime," and that we must "regard the Soviet Union as a rival, not a partner in the political arena," and that "there can be no appeal to common purposes," Mr. X has reached the conclusion that all we can do is to "contain" Russia until Russia changes, ceases to be our rival, and becomes our partner.

The conclusion is, it seems to me, quite unwarranted. The history of diplomacy is the history of relations among rival powers, which did not enjoy political intimacy, and did not respond to appeals to common purposes. Nevertheless, there have been settlements. Some of them did not last very long. Some of them did. For a diplomat to think that rival and unfriendly powers cannot be brought to a settlement is to forget what diplomacy is about. There would be little for diplomats to do if the world consisted of partners, enjoying political intimacy, and responding to common appeals.

The method by which diplomacy deals with a world where there are rival powers is to organize a balance of power which deprives the rivals, however lacking in intimacy and however unresponsive to common appeals, of a good prospect of successful aggression. That is what a diplomat means by the settlement of a conflict among rival powers. He does not mean that they will cease to be rivals. He does not mean that they will all be converted to thinking and wanting the same things. He means that, whatever they think, whatever they want, whatever their ideological purposes, the balance of power is such that they cannot afford to commit aggression.

In our conflict with Russia a policy of settlement—as I have sought to show—would aim to redress the balance of power, which is abnormal and dangerous, because the Red Army has met the British and American armies in the heart of Europe. The division between east and west is at that military boundary line. The meeting of those armies caused the division. No state in eastern Europe can be independent of the Kremlin as long as the Red Army is within it and all around it. No state in western Europe is independent while it is in effect in the rear of this military frontier. The presence of these non-European armies in the continent of Europe perpetuates the division of Europe. The Soviet government has been communist for thirty years. For more than a hundred years all Russian governments have sought to expand over eastern Europe. But only since the Red Army reached the Elbe River have the rulers of Russia been able to realize the ambitions of the Russian Empire and the ideological purposes of communism.

A genuine policy would, therefore, have as its paramount objective a settlement which brought about the evacuation of Europe. That is the settlement which will settle the issue which has arisen out of the war. The communists will continue to be communists. The Russians will continue to be Russians. But if the Red Army is in Russia, and not on the Elbe, the power of the Russian communists and the power of the Russian imperialists to realize their ambitions will have been reduced decisively.

Until a settlement which results in withdrawal is reached, the Red Army at the center of Europe will control eastern Europe and will threaten western Europe. In these circumstances American power must be available, not to "contain" the Russians at scattered points, but to hold the whole Russian military machine in check, and to exert a mounting pressure in support of a diplomatic policy which has as its concrete objective a settlement that means withdrawal.

Then we shall know what we are trying to do. The Russians will know it. Europe will know it. We shall be trying to do a great thing which is simple and necessary: to settle the main actual consequences of this particular war, to put an end to the abnormal situation where Europe, one of the chief centers of civilization, though liberated from the Nazis, is still occupied by its non-European liberators.

We shall be addressing ourselves to an objective to which our own power is suited—be it in diplomacy or in war. We shall be seeking an end that all men can understand, and one which expresses faithfully our oldest and best tradition—to be the friend and the champion of nations seeking independence and an end to the rule of alien powers.

The Truman Doctrine

Even before Kennan published his article on "containment," President Truman was asking Congress to commit the country to just such a policy. The occasion was the notice given to the State Department by British leaders that they could no longer afford to aid the Greek and Turkish governments in repressing Communist insurrections within their borders. In effect, the United States was being asked whether it would assume the onerous role of resisting Communist expansion in a distant part of the world.

Truman chose to accept. In a speech to Congress in March, 1947, he outlined what soon became known as the Truman Doctrine. Specifically, he asked for an appropriation of $400 million because, he said, "it must be the policy of the United States to support free peoples who are resisting attempted subjugation by armed minorities or by outside pressures."

The response, within Congress as well as outside of it, was hardly unanimous. On the verge of a momentous step in foreign policy, Americans debated the wisdom and dangers with intensity, often rancor. But a large majority soon formed in support of the President's proposal. By impressive margins, both houses of Congress approved the appropriation request, while 60 percent of the general public endorsed the decision.

The next set of documents outlines the general positions in the debate over American policy toward Greece and Turkey. The speeches by Congressmen Howard H. Buffett (Rep., Nebraska) and Chet Holifield (Dem., California) illustrate two kinds of criticisms typically levied against the President's proposal. The third speech is by Senator Arthur H. Vandenberg, the noted Michigan Republican whose support of the United Nations, the Truman Doctrine, the Marshall Plan, and the North Atlantic Treaty made him a key figure both in the Senate and in American foreign policy of the postwar years.

40   AMERICA OUT ON A LIMB*

Mr. Buffett: Mr. Speaker, Mr. Truman demands large-scale American intervention in the political, economic, and military affairs of

---

*Howard H. Buffett, *Congressional Record,* 80th Cong., 1st sess. (March 18, 1947), pp. 2215-17.

the Balkans. He tells us other lands must have similar intervention.

This proposal prompts me to repeat a comment by Lord Welby, once Treasury head for England. Shortly before World War I started the British Empire toward liquidation, Lord Welby declared: "We are in the hands of an organization of crooks. They are politicians, generals, manufacturers of armaments, and journalists. All of them are anxious for unlimited expenditure, and go on inventing scares to terrify the public and to terrify Ministers of the Crown."

Probably Mr. Truman's demand does not reflect the kind of scare Lord Welby reported. And so, it may have another origin. Could that origin be that American intervention in Greece has been craftily connived for by the Kremlin, and that Mr. Truman has swallowed the bait?

At the outset, Mr. Speaker, I want to make one fact clear. I am not happy talking about foreign affairs. I would prefer to leave that field to others.

But as an American, I am ashamed and appalled by the recent record of failure in foreign affairs. So I cannot remain silent while new and more ghastly blunders are concocted.

A TRAGIC RECORD OF FAILURE

Truly no one could possibly have handled our foreign affairs much worse than the present administration. It is tragic to have to confess that American blood and treasure was used to deliver into communistic tyranny the lands of Poland, Estonia, Latvia, Lithuania, Czechoslovakia, Yugoslavia, Rumania, Bulgaria, Albania, Hungary, Manchukuo, and large parts of Germany, Austria, Finland, China, Korea, and Japan. But it is true.

Even yet it is hard to believe that 400,000 American boys died for the Atlantic Charter and that instead their sacrifice was used to expand communism over two continents.

Mr. Speaker, it is impossible to assess the enormity of this failure. A man from Mars reviewing it would come to one or the other of two conclusions—either our Government has been in the control of Communists, or it has been in the hands of terribly stupid people completely fooled by the Communists.

As the first conclusion would indicate unlimited treachery and treason, it must be ruled out. Left with the second alternative—that the administration has been terribly stupid and misled—we must consider the present Truman demands in the light of that record.

Lacking only the former head man and some minor characters, the present administration, including its Republican collaborators, is the same assortment of officials that have steered America to the brink of chaos. Surely then we must examine their schemes now with the utmost skepticism.

DOES THE LEOPARD CHANGE ITS SPOTS?

Mr. Speaker, for 14 years the New Deal party brazenly carried water for communism in America and throughout the world. Now we are asked to believe that overnight it has changed into the world-wide champion of anticommunism.

While welcoming administration professions of anticommunism, Congress and the people should remember that the Good Book says, "By their fruits ye shall know them." A management which has committed 14 years of blunders for communism is hardly qualified, because of an almost overnight reformation, to be given a blank check for a crusade against communism.

Mr. Speaker, suppose this intervention proposal fits right into Stalin's plans? If American intervention in the Balkans is what the Communists want, we had better learn that fact now.

Most all Americans are agreed now on the dangers of communism. Some of us have been concerned about communism for a long time. Our warnings and our efforts, such as my amendment to prevent post-war lend-lease from going to Russia and others, were ignored.

But now is not a time for recriminations. It is a time to carefully appraise our position and chart our course. The decision involves unlimited consequences. Our intentions do not matter. The consequences follow automatically.

To get a clear understanding of our present situation, we must go back a long way. When our leaders precipitated us into World War I, they thereby committed us to the one lasting consequence of that war. What was that consequence? The establishment of communism in full control of a powerful government—Russia.

NEW DEAL SPARKS COMMUNIST EXPANSION

Following this initial victory, we did not hear much about communism between 1921 and 1933. But when the New Deal took over in 1933, it was not long until Roosevelt gave communism a tremendous boost by official recognition.

This recognition enabled communism to begin to expand its activities, both in Europe and America. At that time the Communists were secretly promoting World War II. Finally Stalin's deal with Hitler precipitated the conflict.

When Hitler attacked Russia in 1941, Roosevelt immediately pledged the Communists unlimited materials from America, with no questions asked and no pledges made in return. Billions of our resources went to Russia. But Russia's hostility toward us never lessened. Many of our officials knew of this continuing hostility, but kept that fact from our people.

Many strange things happened. America's then No. 1 Communist, Earl Browder, was in the Federal penitentiary for violating our statutes. The New Deal pardoned him. All through the war the New Deal high command, both civilian and military, catered to Russia's every whim and every demand. War materials reportedly went to Russia ahead of the necessities of our own troops.

But she returned less in reverse lend-lease than we received from the Fiji Islands.

The Communists saw that the longer the war lasted the greater would be their victory. Accordingly, they cunningly insisted on the barbaric demand for unconditional surrender to prolong enemy resistance.

REAL WAR TRIUMPH WAS STALIN'S

When hostilities ceased, we had the momentary elation of a great military victory. But the real triumph was Stalin's—achieved with the aid of 400,000 Americans who died believing they were fighting for the Atlantic Charter.

Even after VJ-day, our foreign policy remained perfectly attuned to the wishes of the Kremlin. Using human distress in Europe as the bait, Communists promoted UNRRA, with Uncle Sam paying the bill.

Whatever the intentions were, UNRRA added to Stalin's conquests. Congress had been specifically warned that UNRRA would enable Stalin to extend his mastery over Europe. But the New Deal Congress, aided by the failure of the Republican leadership to explode this scheme, voted almost $3,000,000,000 of the savings of the American people for this arsenal of communism.

Our postwar policy in Germany also carried out the desires of the Kremlin. The Morgenthau plan and the official hate-the-German doctrine were Moscow approved and enabled the Communists to woo the German people. The New Deal party carried out Moscow's order.

NOVEMBER ELECTION FORCES
CHANGE IN STRATEGY

Then last November a titanic ballot-box uprising took place in America. The American people demonstrated overwhelming opposition to a foreign and domestic policy which, knowingly or unwittingly, was following the Communist Party line.

So the conspirators in the Kremlin had to revise their strategy for world conquest. Let us visualize the reaction of the top Communists to our election. Stalin knew that direct handouts from America were over. He also knew that America was entirely too strong to challenge militarily; so what should he do in his unswerving objective of world domination?

Surely, Stalin would determine that he must reverse his tactics here to continue his conquests. Perhaps his mind would recall the famous prediction of Huey Long, who declared that "if fascism ever comes to America, it will come in the name of antifascism."

What better tactic could Stalin now develop than to promote communism in America in the name of anticommunism? This tactic, of course, would require the continual creation of communistic scares outside America.

Likewise, if he were to exhibit traditional Russian cunning, an historical Russian tactic would suggest itself to him. He would recall how Czar Alexander I sucked Napoleon into advancing to Moscow, and how that over-extended position so depleted Napoleon's strength that later he toppled easily at Waterloo.

Then Stalin might smile as he recalled Hitler's 1,500-mile supply line to Stalingrad. He would remember how the devouring logistics of that far-flung position decimated Hitler's military machine. So, Stalin would determine that he must keep America overextended and off balance.

AMERICA "OUT ON LIMB"

That would be the political strategy, just as it always has been a favored Russian tactic. He would needle us and play hit-and-run infiltration wherever America could be sucked in, especially remembering, of course, our continued willingness to aid the outposts of the British Empire.

This strategy would have another especial value to Mr. Stalin. With American attention on an external campaign against communism, his army of stooges in the New Deal could quickly be enrobed in a concealing mantle of anticommunism.

So, besides involving the American people in bankrupting commitments abroad, a communistic drive would divert suspicion and attention from Stalin's agents in the New Deal.

This scheme would make use of the tactics long used by subway pickpockets. Do you remember that trick? It was for one thief to concentrate the victim's attention by frontal shoving and jostling, while the thievery was carried out by the accomplice in the rear. He picked the pocket while the victim's attention was on the disturber in front of him. It is a simple trick, but Mr. Stalin has apparently been dealing with simple minds in Washington.

Mr. Speaker, it appears that the Communists have started this strategy, and that Mr. Truman and his advisers have been taken in. He proposes to send large amounts of military aid to Greece and Turkey. Most certainly we will apparently stabilize the situation there for awhile. Probably the Communists will fold their tents like the Arabs and silently steal away.

Mr. Hoffman: Mr. Speaker, will the gentleman yield?

Mr. Buffett: I yield to the gentleman from Michigan.

Mr. Hoffman: Is the gentleman intimating that the Communists are going to quit?

Mr. Buffett: Oh, no; just wait until the next paragraph.

UNCLE SAM, INTERNATIONAL FIREMAN

Then after we have spread ourselves in Greece and Turkey, and our leaders are patting themselves on the back for their successful firm stand, a new alarm will come in. Communistic outbreaks will be reported serious in another area. We will rush to that alarm. A billion-dollar call will come from Korea. There will be renewed demands from China.

All over the world we would soon be answering alarms like an international fireman, maintaining garrisons, and pouring out our resources. Our position would become more over-extended than Hitler's was at the height of his conquests—if it is not already.

In the meantime, what will have happened at home? Economy plans will have generally gone up in smoke. The futility of then attempting to stop the reckless spenders, aided by the sly inside agents of the Kremlin, would quickly become apparent to all. In the pattern developed through the war years of deficit spending, this administration combination would dress up every spending scheme as vital in their anti-Communist program.

Attempts at economy would again be smeared as reactionary efforts to save dollars at the cost of the lives of American boys. Patriots who try to bring about economy would be branded as Stalin lovers.

The misery of the people, from continued militarism and inflation, would soon become unbearable. As their anguished protests became vocal, the shackles of regimentation and coercion, so lately thrown off, could be refastened in the name of stopping communism at home.

Of course, all this spending over the world will both make certain and hasten a financial collapse in America—an economic Pearl Harbor. That is the ultimate goal of the current Red needling.

INFLATION—COMMUNISM'S SECRET WEAPON

Stalin knows, as Lenin taught him, that the surest way to overturn an existing social order is to debauch the currency. When the President mentioned inflation in Greece, he unconsciously touched on the very condition which Stalin is counting on to give the communists victory in America.

And so, Mr. Speaker, if America is now sucked into a state of undeclared war in Greece and other places, we would seem to be paving the way for world triumph of communism. In World Wars I and II our noble objectives vanished when military victory was won. So it will be again if we take the road to war.

We will again learn too late the truth of William Graham Sumner's words: "When a war is begun, it will run its course and bring its consequences. What the intention was makes no difference."

PARTIAL LIST OF CONSEQUENCES

But, Mr. Speaker, we should consider now what some of the ultimate consequences would be. Here are a few of the probable results:

First. Truth-telling would generally disappear in radio, press, and movie. The totalitarian tactics of smear, censorship, and lying propaganda would overwhelm those who resist. Those Americans who correctly anticipated the communistic victory in World War II were politically crucified and silenced in most cases. The same terrorism will happen again if we are now maneuvered into thinly veiled armed conflict with Russia.

Second. Military conscription would soon be demanded to fill the ranks of garrisons for Palestine and the Near East oil fields.

Third. Laboring people would be in danger of a labor draft like President Truman wanted last May. As inflation mounted, class struggle, which the Communists have never yet been able to create in America, might rapidly develop. Every hidden force of inflation would be adding to the distress of the people—as far-flung military and economic operations exhausted our economy.

Fourth. OPA regimentation and coercion would be reimposed under the old forms or in some new sugar-coated version.

Fifth. GI benefits of World War II, when added to these new foreign hand-outs, would soon be an almost impossible financial load for the budget. Postponement by a moratorium, or serious dilution by inflation, could follow

Sixth. Outstanding war bonds would probably be largely frozen in the hands of their owners.

Seventh. Within a few years our currency would become so diluted by inflation that it would have only a fraction of its 1939 purchasing power.

Eighth. Then the condition having been created here that Mr. Truman described in Greece of "savings wiped out by inflation," the people, beaten and bankrupt, would be ripe for a Communist dictatorship.

Mr. Smith of Ohio: Mr. Speaker, will the gentleman yield?

Mr. Buffett: I yield.

Mr. Smith of Ohio: The gentleman is presenting a problem which we ought to consider very carefully. The gentleman spoke of the likelihood of a communistic dictatorship developing. Does the gentleman agree with me that the dictator might not be an American?

Mr. Buffett: Yes; that is entirely possible.

Mr. Hoffman: Mr. Speaker, will the gentleman yield?

Mr. Buffett: I yield.

Mr. Hoffman: Along the line of what the gentleman from Ohio [Mr. Smith] was saying, we have not had an American foreign policy which originated here for 10 or 12 years.

Mr. Buffett: My remarks take recognition of that possibility.

Mr. Hoffman: As I got it, he, the gentleman from Ohio [Mr. Smith] was suggesting that this dictator might come from abroad. My understanding is that our foreign policy has been coming from abroad through the British Empire for something like 10 years. If I am wrong, I would like to have the gentleman from Ohio correct me.

Mr. Buffett: As these consequences began to unfold, all effective political opposition would end. In fact, passage of this scheme, when added to the humbug Presidential campaigns of 1940 and 1944, might indicate that one-party Government has already been largely accomplished.

The smear terrorism long used by the New Deal would be directed against every patriot who resisted successive moves in this so-called anti-Communist drive.

Mr. Speaker, I appeal to the Members of this House to think long and earnestly before they vote us into a probable Stalin trap—either the immediate one in Greece or later ones which may be skillfully concocted to get us out on a limb everywhere.

PROBABLY POLITICAL EXPEDIENCY HAS TEMPTED ADMINISTRATION

I am afraid the Truman high command has been tempted by the domestic political attractions abounding in this scheme. It seems to enable them at one stroke to apparently cast off their long-ingrained Communist taint and simultaneously shift the blame for 14 years of inflation.

This scheme would lay the inflation headache right in the laps of the Republicans. Truman could then say that the end of OPA, not the foreign hand-outs, brought skyrocketing price levels. The Republicans could not point out that excessive foreign hand-outs caused the inflation, because they would be recorded in favor of that policy. So the Balkan deal seems made to order to revive the New Deal domestically and likewise made to order for Stalin internationally.

Even if it were desirable, America is not strong enough to police the world by military force. If that attempt is made, the blessings of liberty will be replaced by coercion and tyranny at home.

Our Christian ideals cannot be exported to other lands by dollars and guns. Persuasion and example are the methods taught by the Carpenter of Nazareth, and if we believe in Christianity we should try to advance our ideals by His methods.

IMPERIALISM ABROAD AND FREEDOM AT HOME WILL NOT WORK

We cannot practice might and force abroad and retain freedom at home. We cannot talk world cooperation and practice power politics.

If we try to face both ways at once, we will repeat the sad lesson of the Crusades. Ernest Barker summed up that tragedy in these words: "The Crusades may be written down as a failure. They ended not in the occupation of the east by the Christian west, but in the conquest of the west by the Mohammedan east."

Mr. Speaker, is the Truman administration truly trying to stop communism? Then its task begins at home. I suggest the same three-point program that I have long advocated, for a starter:

First. Clean out the Communists and the fellow travelers in our own Government.

Second. Stop giving foreign nations free economic support. End the administration policies that have used America as an arsenal for communism. Encourage genuine relief under nonpolitical auspices.

Third. Stop imitating communism. Communism arose out of the ashes of an economy destroyed by currency inflation and was welcomed by a people saddled with tyrannical bureaucracy. To stop communism we must balance the budget, reduce the debt, and cut taxes.

Mr. Speaker, long ago the admonition was offered "Physician, heal thyself." If the Truman administration is now finally interested in stopping the spread of communism, it will take to heart that specific advice from the Founder of the only effective antidote for communism, the Christian religion.

41   THE UNITED NATIONS WAY*

Mr. Holifield: Mr. Speaker, I have asked for this time today to speak on the subject of the Greco-Turkish aid bill. On March 12 President Truman addressed a joint session of Congress. His address was virtually a public declaration of political war on Russia. On that date the President proposed a radical and startling change in our traditional foreign policy of nonintervention in the internal affairs of other nations.

The consideration of Mr. Truman's proposal does not involve partisan politics. It is a question that concerns every American citizen regardless of political affiliation. The charge of imperialistic warmonger and starry-eyed internationalist will be made against those who support intervention as proposed by Mr. Truman. The charge of

*Chet Holifield, *Congressional Record,* 80th Cong., 1st sess. (April 1, 1947), pp. 2994-96.

isolationist, anti-British, and pro-Russian will be made against those who oppose the Truman proposal.

There is a great body of American people who do not accept any of the hysterical labels I have named. There are in this Congress many Members who refuse to be classified under any of the labels noted. I am among that number. Neither blind party loyalty nor fear of labeling from either the extreme right or the extreme left can deter many of us from viewing with great concern this proposal. A proposal which seeks to change our traditional foreign policy in such an abrupt and drastic manner.

TWO FATEFUL ROADS

Mr. Truman's proposal involves the choice of only two roads, and they might be posted as follows: Nonintervention and intervention. Down the road of nonintervention we see the old mud hole of isolation, with its attendant danger of refusing again to accept our world responsibilities in a rapidly shrinking world. Down the second road, which is posted intervention, we see the dangerous quicksands of imperialistic, unilateral procedures which have preceded every war. Before we make our choice between the two roads which stretch so fatefully before us we want to be sure there is not a third and more desirable road as yet undisclosed by our leaders. Maybe there is a third road which we can find, and maybe that road is named United Nations Way. I will return to this alternative road later.

There are many questions to be asked, and there must be many satisfactory answers given, before some of us can choose either the first road—nonintervention—which beckons the traditional isolationists, the Communists, the pro-Russian fellow travelers, as well as the timid group who draw back from world responsibilities, or before we can choose the second road of unconditional intervention, which lures the twentieth century American imperialists, the hate Russia warmonger, and the confused group who do not realize the meaning of the Truman proposal. . . .

The first question which concerns most of us is the basic one of Why has the United Nations been bypassed? Regardless of the belated excuses and explanations by those who wholeheartedly indorsed the Truman proposal, the fact remains that the original proposal was belligerent in its tone, filled with hot generalities, and fraught with most startling and dangerous implications. It was as dangerous from the standpoint of what it left unsaid as it was for the things it said.

WHY HAS THE UNITED NATIONS BEEN BYPASSED?

The furor of public alarm and opposition to the President's approach to this problem is now forcing tardy explanations, ameliorating excuses, and sycophantic references to "a stopgap emergency program pending United Nations action." Which is, to say the least, suspicious. It betrays a policy of second guessing, which strives to cover up the initial mistake. That the original joint message to Congress justifies the question, "Why has the United Nations been bypassed?" cannot be denied. The reaction from every thoughtful person was immediate and shocking, when they realized that the United Nations was practically ignored. People from every walk of life began to wonder if the United Nations was being classified as a futile and functionless shadow. A careful reading of the part of the President's message which summarily dismisses the United Nations as being too slow and ineffective to merit more than a passing bow, or a careless backhand slap, brought consternation and alarm to many thoughtful people. The harm done throughout the world in crushing the feeble flame of hope which exists in the heart of many war-weary people was incalculable. We realize that the United Nations has not been brought to fruition; we know that many parts of the outline are yet to be filled. We will concede that there is no international police force which can be sent into Greece to maintain civil order in the emergency. We will concede that it might be difficult to aid Greece in a monetary way without special multilateral action such as obtained in the establishment of UNRRA. We will concede that a Russian veto might prevent a unanimous edict of policy by the Security Council delegates. All these concessions we are willing to admit, and they do present great difficulties to prevent emergency action by the United Nations in this hour of crisis.

But because they present great difficulties shall we use these arguments as an excuse for killing the United Nations in its infancy? Shall we use the element of short time between the President's proposal on March 12 and the British evacuation on March 31 as an excuse for weakening an organization which holds the hope of millions throughout the world, the hope of millions who pray for the obtaining of world peace?

Or should this Greco-Turkish problem have been used as an opportunity for revitalizing and developing the United Nations in the direction of its original goal; that is, the formation of a vital, functioning, world organization for the solution of international problems and the assurance of world peace?

WHY SUCH UNSEEMLY HASTE?

Let us consider some pertinent factors involved in the proposal. First, the appeal to act hastily on the grounds of the emergency conditions which would ensue immediately after the abrupt withdrawal of British troops on March 31. I would like to know why the British are being allowed to precipitate such an abrupt crisis. Is it not true that our State Department has known for many months that such action was contemplated? If so, why was the proposed British withdrawal not publicized so that Congress would have an adequate period of time to study and debate the subject of American intervention? If the British notice of withdrawal was necessarily as sudden as we have been led to believe, I would like to know if our State Department protested the abrupt action, and whether they requested the British Government to postpone for 60 or 90 days their withdrawal. This would have been a reasonable request and within the possible bonds of British compliance. It would have given us time to explore multilateral action. Laying aside for a moment the ethical question of the subject of intervention, and assuming that external political, economic, and military aid is necessary for the welfare and protection of the Greek people, assuming also that the United Nations has not been developed to the point where it can function in the Greco-Turkish crisis, we are still confronted with this question, "Is there no alternative to unilateral action of the United States?" The Truman proposal in effect says "No." But many of us are not satisfied with this answer. We do not believe that it is impossible to develop an alternative procedure. A procedure which would not duplicate the unilateral imperialistic solutions which have been the basis of all previous wars. We believe that a procedure could have been and still can be developed which will have the moral and spiritual force of multilateral sanction. A procedure which will comply with the spirit of the Atlantic Charter and the proposed goal of the United Nations.

IS THERE AN OVER-ALL FOREIGN POLICY?

Another very important question which I would like to ask is this, Do we have an over-all European, Middle East, and far eastern foreign policy? The reason I ask this question is obvious. The necessity of considering the Greek problem as part of an over-all European, Middle East, and far eastern problem is so plain that even a fool can see it. The solution of any of the various problems in these areas depends upon its relation to the other problems involved in adjoining areas.

Setting up a new procedure, a unilateral procedure on our part toward Greece, does two very important things. First, it ignores multilateral procedure as envisaged by the United Nations; and, second, it sets a precedent of unilateral procedure for not only ourselves but for every other nation in the world. Once we embark upon this course of unilateral solution of international problems, we have no reason to criticize other nations for doing the same thing. That is why this proposal assumes an importance far beyond the scope of the Greek-Turkish aid proposal.

Our policy of piecemeal, spur-of-the-moment development of foreign policy, without regard to an over-all policy, has proven time and again to be a mistake. In this particular case — the Greek case — we know that the question of internationalization of the Dardanelles is involved, or at least Russian demands for egress and ingress to and from a warm-water port in the Baltic. We know that this is the reason the Turkish military loan is tacked onto the Greek loan. It is to strengthen Turkey in her opposition to Russian demands. The excuse of starvation and maintenance of a quasi monarchist-democratic government, which clothes our Greek intervention with an aura of humanitarianism, has not been advanced to justify the Turkish portion of the appropriation. The reason it has not been advanced is because it is palpably untenable. Turkey is not starving, and by no stretch of the imagination can it be classified as even semidemocratic.

WHOSE CHESTNUTS ARE AT STAKE?

Another related problem, of course, is the oil problem. I say "related," but what I mean is it is one of our most important reasons behind our sudden interest in the Mediterranean. Now, lest some of my anti-British friends say, "We are pulling English chestnuts out of the fire," let me make it very clear that in Iran, Iraq, and in Saudi Arabia, there are other chestnuts besides British chestnuts.

Mr. Speaker, I include in my remarks at this point two tables of statistics, which show whose chestnuts are in the fire.

Table No. 1 shows the daily oil production and the estimated oil reserves in barrel units of the Persian Middle East countries.

It also shows that not only the British chestnuts, but American, Dutch, and French chestnuts are in the fire.

Table No. 2 shows the names of the petroleum-developing com-

TABLE 1

Petroleum Production and Reserves of Persian Gulf Countries by
Nationality of Corporate Ownership
(U.S. 42-Gallon Barrels)

	Daily Production*			Reserves†		
	United States	British-Dutch	French	United States	British-Dutch	French
Iran........	....	420,000	....	....	6,500,000,000	....
Iraq........	24,000	48,000	24,000	1,200,000,000	2,400,000,000	1,200,000,000
Qatar......	....	....	....	250,000,000	500,000,000	250,000,000
Kuwait....	20,000	20,000	....	4,500,000,000	4,500,000,000	....
Saudi Arabia ...	200,000	....	....	5,000,000,000	....	....
Bahrein....	20,000	....	....	300,000,000	....	....
Total..	264,000	488,000	24,000	11,250,000,000	13,900,000,000	1,450,000,000

* Oil and Gas Journal, Dec. 28, 1946, p. 175.

† American Petroleum Interests in Foreign Countries, S. Res. 36, 79th Cong., p. 73.

TABLE 2

Middle East Oil Companies—Ownership by Countries, 1947
(Information Supplied by U.S. Department of State)

Country	Company	Ownership by Nationality
Bahrein	Bahrein Petroleum ... Co., Ltd.	100 percent American owned—50 percent Standard Oil Co. of California and 50 percent Texas Co.
Iran	Anglo-Iranian Oil ..... Co., Ltd.	100 percent British owned.
Iraq.........	Iraq Petroleum .... Co., Ltd.	23.75 percent American owned—Near-East Development Corp., in which Standard Oil Co. of New Jersey and Socony-Vacuum Oil Co. share equally. 23.75 percent French owned—Compagnie Francaise des Petroles. 23.75 percent Anglo-Iranian Oil Co., Ltd., British owned. 23.75 percent Dutch owned – Royal Dutch Shell. 0.5 percent owned by "individuals."
Quawait....	Quawait Oil Co., ... Ltd.	50 percent American owned – Gulf Oil Co.
Saudi .... Arabia	Arabian-American .... Oil Co. (Aramco).	100 percent American owned—50 percent Standard Oil Co. of California and 50 percent Texas Co. A deal is pending for Standard Oil of New Jersey to buy 30 percent and for Socony Oil Co. to buy 10 percent of these holdings.

panies and their ownership, by nationalities, and the respective percentages of ownership involved.

I cannot develop at this time the true significance of these tables of statistics, but I am sure that there is enough information presented in these tables to adequately lay the ghost of "British chestnuts" only.

Let us be frank and admit that the Turkish portion of the loan has two great reasons behind it. First, preservation of the status quo in regard to the Dardanelles, and second, the protection of American, Dutch, French, and British chestnuts in the oil deposits of the Middle East. The subject of oil, therefore, cannot be divorced from our consideration of the Greek-Turkish aid bill and we should openly acknowledge its involvement. . . .

MULTILATERAL SOLUTIONS IMPERATIVE

If we are to embark on a world-leadership program, as befits our position among the society of nations, let us be careful to exercise that leadership to give strength and being to the United Nations. We want to exercise that leadership in the full light of United Nations debate. We want to know when we embark on this venture of world leadership that we have the moral and spiritual force of at least the majority of the United Nations behind us. We do not wish to be in the vulnerable position of using our resources in an imperialistic way. We either move forward in the world of tomorrow, in concert with other nations toward multilateral solutions, or we move backward alone to the unilateral fiascos of the past.

THE RUSSIAN VETO

We have been told that one of the reasons why this matter has not been referred to the United Nations has been because of the certainty of a Russian veto. We want to discuss this point for the moment on the assumption that this prediction of a Russian veto is correct. First, let us remember that the veto provision in the Charter is not wholly chargeable to Russia. The United States was equally insistent that this veto provision be included. So in our criticism of Russia, for the misuse of the veto, let us not forget that she uses the tool which we helped to make.

The veto has been used 12 times by members of the Security Council. It was used twice by the United States and the United

Kingdom voting in unison. It was used once by France and Russia voting together and it was used nine times by Russia alone. Many of us have come to the conclusion that the United Nations cannot be effective as a world organization if the nations comprising the "big five" retain the veto power. Let me point out, however, that we are probably no more ready to renounce the veto than Russia. If we find, however, that important international problems cannot be solved on the basis of complete unanimity, we must admit the futility of depending on the United Nations as now constituted to guarantee or facilitate world peace.

POSSIBLE ALTERNATIVES

What is the alternative? Referring specifically to the Greek problem, I notice that the morning papers report that a distinguished member of the other body proposes to offer amendments which will in effect give supervisory powers over our proposed venture to a procedural vote of the Security Council—not subject to veto—or a majority vote of the General Assembly delegates. This proposal, in my opinion, is a very important move toward multilateral approval. A substitute joint resolution has been offered in the House by my distinguished colleague the gentleman from Minnesota [Mr. Blatnik]. While I am not 100 percent in accord with this proposal, I do believe that it is worthy of very serious study as the main theme of the resolution points away from unilateral action and in the direction of multilateral action.

DEVELOPMENT OF REGIONAL ALLIANCES

Addressing myself to the general problem of international organization, I would suggest that we encourage the formation of an adequate number of regional alliances consisting of as many nations as possible in each area who would be willing to work together on the principles of the United Nations. We have already done this in the Western Hemisphere and it has been approved as consistent with the world organization. The great advantage of the regional alliance would be that action could be taken on a policy or procedure without the paralyzing requirement of unanimity.

It may be necessary for the nations to learn to work together on a regional basis before we can function on the world level. We must admit that human nature has not yet attained that peak of perfection where unanimity is commonly achieved. Those functions of the world organization which are possible, and there are many, should still be encouraged and maintained. Many of these international subdivisions of the United Nations are making remarkable progress, without the participation of the U.S.S.R. I speak of the trusteeship council, the provisional International Civil Aviation Organization, the International Labor Organization, and the Food and Agricultural Organization.

Every possible effort should be made to develop multilateral solutions as international problems arise, first on the regional basis and then on the world level. The principle of collective action must be maintained and unilateral action, such as the Truman proposal, avoided as we would avoid the plague. Like the bubonic plague, it is a virulent and contagious disease and a single case can start an epidemic that means certain death to the United Nations.

There is still time to return to the principles of the Atlantic Charter and the United Nations.

In the first part of my speech, I described the choice between the two fateful roads of "nonintervention" and "unconditional intervention." I described the dangers attending the choice of either. I also suggested that there might be a third road which I called the United Nations way.

THE THIRD ROAD:
"THE UNITED NATIONS WAY"

I believe that the third road is opening up before us. I believe that it can be developed and safeguarded by legislative conditions in the appropriation bills and public commitments on the part of the President, the Secretary of State, and the United Nations delegate. To our delegate on the United Nations, the former distinguished Senator from Vermont, the Honorable Warren Austin, we owe a great debt of gratitude for pointing out the third road, "the United Nations way." The echoes of Mr. Truman's speech of March 12 had hardly ceased before the tide of public criticism began to mount, throughout the length and breadth of the United States. The people who had sacrificed so much in the great war just concluded, the people who saw the League of Nations scuttled after the First World War, the people who had pinned their faith to the principles of the Atlantic Charter and the United Nations had asked again and again the question, "Why has the United Nations been bypassed?" Our delegate to the United

Nations, Mr. Warren Austin, went before the United Nations Assembly on March 28 and said the things which the President should have said on March 12. Mr. Austin answered some of the important questions which have been troubling us, where Mr. Truman's proposal of intervention was based on one aim of the United Nations, that is, to prevent aggression against a weaker nation. It indicated that our action would be taken on a national basis, depending solely on our own strength and judgment. Mr. Austin's statement to the United Nations put the United States action on a very different basis indeed. Admitting that the United Nations was not ready, he made it clear that our intervention would be in line with the international principles of the United Nations, and that we welcomed the support of the other nations, both morally and financially. He admitted that the United Nations, as presently constituted, was lacking in financial resources. He pledged that our financial aid was on a temporary basis, pending the functioning of the United Nations on a long range basis through the International Bank for Reconstruction and Development. He further advised the Greek Government to apply for a loan of at least $100,000,000 from this source. He promised that our temporary aid would be administered along the lines recommended by the Food and Agriculture Organization of the United Nations, an international commission which has just completed a very fine survey of Grecian needs.

Mr. Austin pointed out that a United Nations commission is at the present time investigating territorial invasions by armed bands on the northern border of Greece. He asked that special efforts be made to expedite their report to the Security Council. And certainly, by implication, he pledged our support in their recommendations.

We see then that belatedly we are harmonizing our plans with the principles of the Atlantic Charter and the United Nations.

CONDITIONAL CAUSES AND
PUBLIC COMMITMENTS

All of the questions have not yet been answered; we hope they can be answered in a satisfactory manner. The conditional clauses have not been enacted into legislation. We hope they can be enacted. The public commitments and assurances from our President and the Secretary of State have not been made. We sincerely trust and hope they will be forthcoming. Unless these conditional clauses can be written into the bill and unless proper collaboration on a multilateral basis can be developed, many of us cannot vote for the bill. Vigilance on the part of every patriotic person will be required to mobilize an enlightened public opinion to point the way down the third road indicated. An enlightened public opinion which will demand that this crisis be handled the "United Nations way."

It may be the deciding factor in the life of the world organization we call the United Nations. It may mean the difference between world peace and world destruction in this atomic age.

If we save the United Nations, it will be because the common people demand that our leaders walk down the third road, "the United Nations way."

42 THE LIMITATIONS OF THE UNITED NATIONS*

Mr. Vandenberg: Mr. President, in response to the urgent recommendations of the President of the United States, the Senate Foreign Relations Committee has unanimously reported the bill (S. 938) entitled "A bill to provide for assistance to Greece and Turkey." It could be alternatively titled "A bill to support the purposes of the United Nations to maintain international peace and security," or it could be titled "A bill to serve America's self-interest in the maintenance of independent governments."

The committee makes this report primarily in response to direct appeals to our Government from heroic Greece which, by her sacrificial World War loyalties, has richly earned the right to perpetuate her proud, historic independence. It does so in response to direct appeals from Turkey, which is the only truly independent nation left on the borders of Soviet Russia from the Baltic to the Black Sea. It also does so in the presence of the overriding strategic fact that the fall of Greece, followed by the collapse of Turkey, could precipitate a chain reaction which would threaten peace and security around the globe. It does so in the profound belief that we Americans have an unescapable stake in all human rights and fundamental freedoms; and that they were better saved—for us as well as others—by adequate and timely support than by waiting for cumulative hazard to magnify the risk. It does so not only in the name of the liberties for which the Allies said they fought two World Wars, but also in the name of the intelligent American self-interest which prefers an ounce of precau-

*Arthur H. Vandenberg, *Congressional Record*, 80th Cong., 1st sess. (April 8, 1947), pp. 3195–98.

tion to a pound of cure, and which believes "that a stitch in time saves nine."

I am not one of those, Mr. President, who conceive that we are launching what has been called, by some, a new doctrine in any such unique sense as did James Monroe a century and a quarter ago. Rather, in my opinion, we are launching a plan which has numerous precedents—although we must frankly and honestly assess the fact that it has new and "broad implications," as President Truman himself declared in his message of March 12. There is no new doctrine in American aid to distressed nations. There is no new doctrine in striving for "the creation of conditions in which we and other nations will be able to work out a life free from coercion" or in "supporting free peoples who are resisting attempted subjugation," again quoting the Presidential message. The pending plan unquestionably broadens our precedents when it enters the Mediterranean—although the Navy and the marines were there in the earliest days of the Republic and in the finest American tradition. The plan broadens geographically, although we long since pronounced the open door for China. It broadens when peacetime military missions, heretofore largely confined to pan-America, enter the Near East. But it is not new in concept. Certainly there is nothing new in our opposition to communism outside of areas where it is officially embraced. We have always done these things. It would be new only if we now were to desert these ideals. In any event, in whatever degree it is new, it is necessary.

But it is much more than a plan for relief of human suffering in Greece and Turkey. Let us be totally plain about it. It is a plan to forestall aggression which, once rolling, could snowball into global danger of vast design. It is a plan for peace. It is a plan to sterilize the seeds of war. We do not escape war by running away from it. No one ran away from war at Munich. We avoid war by facing facts. This plan faces facts. But of course there are other facts to face. No plan can guarantee peace. The most it can do is to take the better calculated risk. That, I believe, is what this plan does. It is a plan, I repeat, for peace. It is a plan to strengthen the United Nations by supporting its objectives in respect to immediate necessities, pending the time when the United Nations can take over.

The Senate, in turn, faces an additional fact. It faces the fact that if we were to reject the plan in its basic purpose we would give the green light to aggression everywhere. Our moral authority and leadership would die on the spot. We would multiply our own hazards. We would weaken the United Nations by multiplying its subsequent responsibilities.

This is not an imperialistic plan. It covets nothing for America but honorable peace in a free world of free men. That is not imperialism. I like what Elihu Root once said of our Monroe Doctrine: "It rests upon the right of every sovereign state to protect itself by preventing a condition of affairs in which it will be too late to protect itself."

That is not imperialism. That is intelligent self-interest. That is what we here propose.

I recall that President Monroe himself declared that the impulse of his "Doctrine" was to prevent the aggressive extension of alien systems "dangerous to our peace and safety." This is not imperialism. It is prudent common sense. It is the pattern of this plan. Curiously enough, one of the things contributing to the birth of the Monroe Doctrine was old Russia seeking to fish in North American waters. Communism thrives on "fishing in troubled waters" today. It is not imperialism to calm the waters. Our purposes are the exact opposite of imperialism. So is this plan. This truth shines through every word of the statement made on March 28 to the Security Council of the United Nations by our American Ambassador:

> The United States . . . does not desire to dominate, intimidate, or threaten the security of any nation, large or small. The United States will support collective security for all nations – large as well as small. The United States respects the rights of all members of the United Nations to follow whatever way of life or system of government they choose, so long as the choice is freely made without intimidation and so long as such nations do not interfere with the rights of other countries or the liberties of other peoples.

I say once more, Mr. President, that we here confront a plan—a special and particular plan. I do not view it as a universal pattern but rather as a selective pattern to fit a given circumstance. We are not suddenly resolved to underwrite the earth. That would be fantastic, improvident, and impossible. What we do is to underscore once more a principle long ingrained in the American character—namely to "support free peoples who are resisting attempted subjugation," again quoting the Presidential message. We point the general direction we propose to go. We do not, we cannot, chart the total course. This plan fits a key, strategic need. Undoubtedly there will be other problems facing other and different needs. For example, our occupational responsibilities in Korea unquestionably will soon demand positive support. It is part of World War II—unless we propose to lose the peace.

It would be a fraud upon our people to pretend that this plan ends all need for aid. Our people prefer the truth. The truth is we do face the fact that Greece and Turkey are not isolated phenomena—even though they involve a unique and emphasized importance. We must face the fact that other situations may arise which clearly involve our own national welfare in their lengthened shadows. Let us harbor no soft illusions. But I emphatically repeat that we do not here set a universal precedent, except in basic self-defensive purpose. We shall always react; but we shall react as any given situation seems to require. Meanwhile, it is to be fervently hoped and prayed that we may have enough foresight hereafter so that we do not always have to react on a "crisis basis."

This plan requires complete candor with ourselves and with the world. It requires prudence lest we overextend ourselves or over-promise others. Equally it requires courage and tenacity of democratic purpose. But I cannot believe it would be intelligent self-interest to deny the plan and thus invite the earth to think that our divided government is impotent. I believe that "standing up" is a better risk than "lying down." I believe that we either take or surrender leadership—and I can find no intelligent, American self-interest in any such surrender.

But the situation, Mr. President, requires something more than is in this bill. It calls for two collateral efforts on our part: First, to strive for the honorable removal of underlying friction, if mutually possible, between the two greatest powers on earth; second, to strive for the closest possible integration of all our plans with the collective responsibilities of a strengthened and matured United Nations which is the world's prime hope for peace.

I shall return to both these propositions before I have concluded. At the moment I now address myself to the specific plan for which the approval of the Senate is now sought.

Aid for Greece is aid for a brave war ally which suffered war invasion; then 4 years of cruel enemy occupation; then bitter internal terrorism which the President identifies as of Communist origin; then Communist-inspired violation of its hard-pressed borders. I have no doubt there also has been terrorism on the right. In any event, Greece is prostrate. British support, assigned to Britain by the Allies as a postwar responsibility, is being withdrawn because Britain herself is in economic straits. In this dire emergency Greece appeals to us to save her political and economic independence. This bill is our response. We are not bailing out the British Empire. We are not perpetuating Greek monarchy. We are making it possible for the Greek people to survive in stability and self-determination.

It is highly important at this point to note that financial and other outside aid for Greece is recommended in a powerful contemporary report of the Food and Agricultural Organization of the United Nations itself—with an appeal to the United States for special aid. The report frankly recognizes this need for special aid from the United States. Then, praising the Grecian tradition of self-reliance, this international report says that "democratic and voluntary methods of future development, rather than compulsory dictation or direction, are in keeping with the century-old characteristics of the Hellenic temperament." Remember, this is the United Nations speaking. From no other possible source could Greece be quite so sure of democratic aid looking toward self-reliance as from the United States. It is a precise prescription from the United Nations itself for the thing we here propose to do.

We need not condone the present Greek regime, though clearly chosen in a free election, in order to come to the aid of the Greeks themselves. We are entitled to expect that the Greeks themselves, responding to the advice they voluntarily have sought from us, will build a more efficient and equitable democracy when relieved of the pressures which have driven them to any sanctuary that has been presently available. But such precious objectives are impossible so long as Greece is torn by externally and internally stimulated civil war. Therefore aid to Greece must include means to develop adequate Greek defense in behalf of lawful peace. In the absence of lawful peace, our aid would be no more than a transient bounty—as has been the case for the last 2 years.

Peace is prerequisite. So is helpful guidance in the establishment of a sound national economy. Greece turns to the United States as the only source of these imminently necessary helps. These comprehensive purposes are the program of the pending bill. Lest there be overemphasis in the wrong place, I hasten to add that our contemplated military mission involves only from 10 to 40 officers and no combat troops. The naval mission contemplates nonbelligerent craft like mine sweepers, in the main. The military effort, though accounting for $150,000,000 of this grant, is to help Greece to help herself to be self-reliant in defense of her self-chosen government, whatever that may be.

The sum of $130,000,000 is for basic reconstruction; $20,000,000 for agricultural rehabilitation; plus $50,000,000 for relief in the general relief bill now pending in the House.

But that is not all. The plain fact seems to be that if the Greeks, in their extremity, are not successfully helped to help themselves to maintain their own healthy right of self-determination, another Communist dictatorship will rise at this key point in world geography. Then Turkey, long mobilized against a Communist war of nerves, faces neighboring jeopardy. The two situations are inseparable. Turkey confronts no such internal extremity as does Greece; but it requires assistance to bulwark its national security. The President says that the maintenance of its national integrity is essential to the preservation of order in the Middle East. If the Middle East falls within the orbit of aggressive Communist expansion, the repercussions will echo from the Dardenelles to the China Sea and westward to the rims of the Atlantic. Indeed, the Middle East, in this foreshortened world, is not far enough away for safety from our own New York or Detroit or Chicago or San Francisco. That is where we come in. Do we face it now or later? Which is the wiser course? Which holds the better promise of honorable peace? Which is recommended by intelligent American self-interest? The President's answer is this: "If we falter in our leadership, we may endanger the peace of the world— and we shall surely endanger the welfare of our own Nation." He adds, "Great responsibilities have been placed upon us by the swift movement of events." God knows these responsibilities are great, no matter what our course. God knows that this would be an infinitely happier land if it were physically possible for us to close our tired eyes, retire within what were our bastions of yesterday, and shut out the external menace of shapes and forms which we abhor. God knows that we painfully search our hearts for wisdom. May His way be the way we choose.

This plan is for 15 months. Can this job be done in 15 months? I do not know. I doubt it; although in 15 months both the United Nations and the World Bank should be able substantially to take over. But I ask neither Congress nor the country to ignore the nature of this obligation. I say again that I trust them to prefer the truth.

In a sense we are a tragic generation, despite our blessings and our place in the sun. We have been drawn into two World Wars. We finally won them both, and yet we still confront a restless and precarious peace. Something has been wrong. It is our supreme task to face these present realities, no matter how we hate them, and to mend the broken pattern if such be within human power.

Therefore, Mr. President, I say again, let us all face facts. The problem involved in this bill—like the problem involved in every other phase of languishing peace — is the persistent controversy between what we loosely call eastern communism and western democracy.

From it inevitably stem persistent difficulties between the Soviet Union and its satellites upon the one hand, and the United States and like-minded non-Communist states upon the other. Still more explicitly, it involves hostility to Communist expansionism and infiltration. This expansionism, in turn, arises, we constantly are told from Soviet fears of resurgent aggression by her neighbors and from fears of encirclement looking toward her destruction. If Moscow really has those fears, she is entitled to have them dependably removed. She cannot be expected to react any differently than we do under like circumstances. Given a fair chance, on a two-way street, we should be able to mitigate those fears because we believe in self-determination for Russians precisely as we insist upon it for Americans and others. We plot no offense against the Soviet Union. We are not hunting world dominion. We are not seeking dictation anywhere. But what we deny to ourselves as a matter of morality we also must deny to others as a matter of conquest.

It may be remembered, Mr. President, that as long ago as January 10, 1945, I discussed this same, identical theme in the Senate. I said then that if Russia pursues expansionism through fear of a reborn Axis, we should offer her a hard and fast alliance against a reborn Axis. We have made that offer. It still stands. It has not been accepted. We can expand that offer. We can sign anything at Moscow which guarantees the independence of the Soviet Union within its own legitimate domain. But there must be two signatures—and they must both be good—better, I regret to say, than signatures at Yalta or at Potsdam. We, in turn, have the reciprocal right to demand effective proof that Moscow is not plotting to encircle us in a Communist-dominated world; that Communist assaults upon us, within and without the United States, shall cease; and that our mutual pledges to the Atlantic Charter and to the principles and purposes of the United Nations shall be reliably honored in behalf of all concerned. I do not mean in words alone. I mean in deeds. I mean the rebirth of international integrity.

It still seems to me, Mr. President, that the great need is comprehensively candid discussions between us, if possible, with all the cards face up upon the table. Although we cannot wait for any such negotiations before proceeding to mend the imminent situation in Greece, yet this is the fundamental objective which I should hope might be pursued. Let us not again drift into misunderstanding of what America means when it speaks. The Greek crisis or the Turkish crisis or any others among potential crises will largely disappear if the mutual will exists between Washington and Moscow. If it cannot exist, even that ominous knowledge is worth having. While we cannot avoid the eternal rivalry of these incompatible ideologies, there ought to be an honorable way to live and let live within the rules of the United Nations. We should mutually strive to search it out on the basis not only of salvaging the ideals of World War I and World War II, but also and particularly on the basis of the self-interest of the two greatest nations on earth—neither one of whom wants any part of another war. But we, for our part, will never find it through equivocation which will be misread as timidity. We shall never find it except as we succeed in convincing Moscow, first, that we have absolutely no ulterior designs; and, second, that we shall not compromise or whittle away the basic human rights and fundamental freedoms which we both have pledged in the most solemn peacetime commitments of which honorable nations are capable. . . .

The United Nations, the voice of collective security, must always be our first reliance and our prime concern as far as possible in every problem of this nature. It must be used to the maximum of practical possibilities. In no available aspect should we bypass its functions. But in no unavailable aspect should we ruin it by assigning to it functions which it does not possess. Such an assignment would destroy it for keeps. Meanwhile, under such circumstances as in the present instance, Greece would sink into the Communist orbit and the fateful chain reaction would set in both East and West.

Under the amended bill, now pending in the Senate, this whole situation is honestly and faithfully assessed. The Foreign Relations Committee has added a preamble which recites the facts. It asserts our belief and purpose that this bill "will contribute to the freedom and independence of all members of the United Nations in conformity with the principles and purposes of the Charter." The committee has added an amendment which stops the functions of this bill whenever the Security Council, without counting vetoes, or the General Assembly finds that "action taken or assistance furnished by the United Nations makes the continuance of assistance—under this bill—unnecessary or undesirable."

Mr. President, far from bypassing the United Nations, this amended bill is the greatest act of voluntary allegiance to it in the whole story of the United Nations. It even goes to the heart and core of the veto controversy. In the first great test which the Security Council ever faced Britain and France demonstrated their good faith by accepting a Council verdict regardless of vetoes in the case of little Lebanon and Syria. We now do so in advance in the case of Greece and Turkey. We accept the untrammeled judgment of the organized conscience of the world on what we do, and we invite it to intervene at its own will. A technical error in the wording of the committee amendment has been corrected. This is not a weasel-worded gesture. This is an act of total faith. Microscopic analysts may try to find hypothetical flaws in it. But no such flank attacks can dull its purpose and effect.

Now let us examine the facts. I speak first of what the United Nations cannot do and what no wise well-wisher will ask it to do. It is not and was never intended to be a relief organization. It has no such funds and was never intended to have such funds. It could get the funds only by an assessment in which we would carry the heavy share and thus face, all over again, the vicious dissatisfactions which we suffered through UNRRA, despite its notable humanities, when we put up our money for others too frequently to maladminister to suit themselves. It has no sustaining military force because the Soviet representatives thus far have declined to permit these plans to materialize. If it had either the funds or the force, their use would depend upon the Security Council. In the Security Council this use would face a veto. Any frank assessment of realities, in the light of experience to date, must concede that the veto would be used by the Soviet Union in any phase of conflict between communism and democracy. These are the facts. There is no way to bypass these facts. Greek independence cannot be saved, at least for the time being, in any such fashion, no matter how adroit the scheme of reference. The implications to which the President refers cannot be met by any attempts, no matter how nobly meditated, to misuse the United Nations as of today. The United Nations itself cannot be sustained by any such misuse. The most we can do at the moment is to leave certain special phases of the problem in United Nations jurisdiction; and to leave an over-all authority in the Council and Assembly to hold us to strict accountability for what we do.

Mr. Sumner Welles recently pointed out what he said will be the line that Soviet propaganda will follow in its efforts to combat the administration's present foreign policy. He cited Izvestia and Pravda—both official Moscow publications—which charge us with destroying the United Nations. He was a good prophet. This argument has met with much popular and often innocent support in the United States. On the one hand, this support is a precious tribute to the faithful hopes of humankind. On the other, it is a cunning backfire to becloud the issue. I know of no better way to destroy the United Nations than to give it a specific job which it is neither intended nor prepared to do. The only better way to destroy the United Nations of which I know is to overuse the veto. Indeed, it is a significant thing that this plan is opposed by two totally opposite and incompatible groups in the United States. As has been well said, it is opposed, first, by those who hope it will not work but are afraid it will, and, second, by those who hope it will work but are afraid it will not.

It is no depreciation of the United Nations to frankly recognize the fact that the Greek petition to us seeks primary relief which the United Nations cannot provide. It is of no small significance, in this connection, that Greece and Turkey, both members of the United Nations, did not themselves apply to the United Nations, but applied direct to the United States.

But, Mr. President, the United Nations does have its important place in this prospectus even as things are today. It is already rendering important aid. Its Security Council has had a commission on the Greek border investigating disturbances between Greece, Yugoslavia, Bulgaria, and Albania. This commission will report within a few weeks. It will establish truth and responsibility at this point of major friction. If a veto does not subsequently intervene, the Security Council may well establish a permanent border commission whose moral authority and whose sanctions may well minimize this phase of the Greek hazard. If the Security Council is permitted to function in this regard, it will greatly simplify the Greco-Turkish problem and greatly hasten success for our own peaceful adventure. Surely it does not destroy or remotely hamper the United Nations, in this phase, if the United States simultaneously is helping Greece to rebuild her own competent independence and helping Turkey to preserve hers. On the contrary, it is what would be called, in American idiom, "team ball."

Nor is that all. The United Nations Food and Agriculture Organization has submitted a 25-year long-range program for Greek economic rehabilitation. And mark this! I repeat that this important instrumentality of the United Nations has specifically recommended that Greece should apply to the United States, among others, for temporary aid in launching this rehabilitation. It frankly recognizes the present limitations within which the United Nations operates. . . .

In my view, Mr. President, the price of noncompliance in the instant case—in addition to all other reasons for prompt passage of this bill—would be the forfeiture of all hope to effectively influence the attitude of other nations in our peaceful pursuit of international righteousness from now on. It would stunt our moral authority and mute our voice. It would encourage dangerous contempts. It would invite provocative misunderstandings of the tenacity with which we are prepared to defend our fundamental ideals. Mr. President, what would you think if you were a citizen of Athens? Where would you be forced to turn in your hopeless extremity? What would you think if you were a citizen of Ankara? What would you think if you were a citizen of any other of the weary, war-worn nations who are wondering this afternoon whether the torch still burns in the upraised hand of Liberty; whether it is hopeless to struggle on toward democratic freedom? And what would you think, Mr. President, if you were the Politburo in Moscow's Kremlin?

The Foreign Relations Committee, without political division, supports the President of the United States. It does so for the sake of the humanities. It does so for the sake of peace with justice. But above all else, it does so for the sake of the Stars and Stripes. [Applause.]

The Bomb

Between 1947 and 1949, the confrontation between the United States and the Soviet Union became increasingly open and rigid. Early in 1948, a Communist-dominated coalition seized power in Czechoslovakia by a bloodless coup. By that time, few Americans had any illusions that the USSR would abandon its goal of world revolution.

As the Soviets expanded and consolidated the Communist bloc, the West in turn formed a bloc on the opposite side of the iron curtain. The main instrument was the European Recovery Plan, more generally known as the "Marshall Plan" because Secretary of State George C. Marshall outlined the idea in a famous speech at Harvard in 1947. Using the precedent of American resistance to Communism in Greece and Turkey, Marshall proposed a program of aid to strengthen all of Western Europe against economic collapse and, implicitly, against Communist revolutions. Inviting the European governments—including the Soviet government—to join (although Stalin had already indicated disapproval), Marshall promised American cooperation. By April of 1948, two months after the Czech coup, Congress had fulfilled the Secretary's promise, appropriating the massive *sum of $5.3 billion for the first year alone (1,300 times the amount of aid for Greece and Turkey). Thus Europe was split into "Marshall Plan countries" and the "iron curtain countries."*

In the center of divided Europe was divided Germany, and within divided Germany was divided Berlin. That unsolved problem not only remained unsolved, but in 1948 brought Russia and the United States close to war. In March the ambassadors of five noncommunist European nations and of the United States announced an agreement, over Soviet protests, which looked toward closer economic integration of the three western zones of Germany, formation of a German federal government, and German participation in the Marshall Plan. In effect, the ambassadors were announcing the independence of Western Germany.

The Soviets replied swiftly and bluntly. In June they halted all land traffic between Berlin and Western Germany. The Berlin blockade was underway. After some debate, American authorities decided to retaliate with an airlift to the beleaguered Berliners. Day after day for eleven months, Western planes transported supplies to the isolated city. The Soviets finally lifted the blockade at the same time as the Federal Republic of West Germany was officially created at Bonn.

Shortly after the blockade began, almost 70 percent of the American public thought that their government's policy toward Russia was "too soft." During these last years of the 1940's, however, the United States had markedly toughened its policy. The Truman Doctrine, the Marshall Plan, the Berlin airlift, the establishment of the North Atlantic Treaty Organization as a military alliance among eleven European nations and the United States—all of these events marked the increasingly muscular posture of the West toward the Soviet Union.

The fundamental premise and reassurance of this policy was that the United States possessed the secret of the atomic bomb and the USSR did not. With their (at least temporary) monopoly of the most powerful, fearful weapon then known to man, Americans could feel more secure in the contest with Communism. In September, 1949, all of this changed: the USSR exploded its nuclear device. "The balance of terror," in Churchill's words, was born. Perhaps more than any other event in the period of 1947–49, the atomic explosion stimulated Americans to assess the "containment" policy and the prospects of Soviet-American war or peace.

The first of the following three articles, an editorial in a popular women's magazine, presents a common attitude toward the possi-

bility of war in the years preceding the Soviet atomic detonation. In the second article, Time *surveys the immediate reaction to the news of that event. The last document, an analysis by Professor Leo Szilard at the University of Chicago, outlines typical liberal-left positions toward Soviet-American relations and disarmament in this period.*

43 IS WAR INEVITABLE?*

The answer, from where we sit, is no. But the most dangerous habit in America today is the habitual talk of an inevitable war with Russia. We hear such talk everywhere—on the street, in stores, in trains and buses, at lectures, at the dinner table, even in church. We even hear of parents who are transferring their sons to military school, so that they will be ready for the war when it comes.

Note that word—"when." The phrase used to be "*if* we fight Russia." With all too many people it has now become "when we fight Russia." At first the talk was of "getting tough" with the Russians. But the recognition that this *might* mean an atomic war still carried with it a sense of shock. By degrees the shock has worn off and the assumption has become that a war is certain. What we began by fearing as a *tragic possibility* we are more and more assuming as an *inevitable fact*—and resigning ourselves to it.

Some of the talk, of course, goes further. There are some people who say we must use the atom bomb against the Russians before they crack its formula and use it against us. This has been well commented on by Chancellor Robert M. Hutchins of the University of Chicago. "If we seriously entertain the idea of a preventive war on Russia," says Hutchins, "we ought first to make our apologies to the Nazis we hanged at Nuremberg."

You may say words are only words. They break no bones and they will never harm us. But this is to take the force of mental habits too lightly. The recent writings on psychosomatic medicine tell us that bodily and mental ills are not separate things, but are deeply interrelated, so that one actually becomes the other. In the same way, the talk of war may become inseparable from the event for which it is preparing the ground. By dwelling so long on it, people may be ready to welcome it as a relief from suspense and as a fulfillment of expectation.

---

* "*Is* War Inevitable?" *Woman's Home Companion,* Vol. LXXV (March, 1948), p. 4.

We are not implying that all is well in our relations with Russia. Obviously it is not. American-Russian relations have deteriorated badly in the postwar years. Former Secretary of State James F. Byrnes, in his book *Speaking Frankly,* has drawn a detailed picture of the fantastic difficulties that American diplomats encounter with the Russians. He has described their uncompromising attitude inside the United Nations, their repeated propaganda blasts at American "imperialist" aims, their unwillingness to go along with the American plan for atomic control, their delaying tactics in international conferences, their use of Communist cells and political strikes in western Europe, the curtain of secrecy which they have drawn between eastern Europe and the rest of the world.

The accuracy of this picture cannot be denied—nor its grimness. It is true that the Russians have thrown their weight around in a way that makes international understanding and cooperation extremely difficult. Incidentally all American leaders and diplomats have not behaved like angels either. In an effort to restrain the expansion of Russian power, many have tightened the screws hard on Russia and its sphere of influence. What is going on looks like a struggle for power between the only two remaining Great Powers in the world. Each fears the power, the ideas, the social system of the other. Only the naïve can shut their eyes to these facts.

But it is dangerous folly to take a leap and conclude that a war is inevitable.

The plain truth, as we see it, is that Russia can gain nothing by fighting America. The Russian casualties in the last war were higher than those suffered by any other nation. The land and the people were ravaged, the houses were burned, the factories gutted, the crops and livestock destroyed, the power dams blown up. The Russians are a proud people and they prefer to hide their weakness. Yet every observer has noted the drastic shortages of man power, materials and machinery in the Russian economy. The recent sharp devaluation of the ruble, in order to deal with an inflation caused by a scarcity of goods, is an index of how hard pressed the Russians are.

The masters of the Kremlin are nothing if not realists. They may talk Marxian theory for home and foreign consumption, but what they practice is cold-blooded realism. They must know that a war against any nation as powerful as America, with our tremendous economic strength and our possession of the newest weapons, would be suicidal. In the showdown they will probably try to avoid, not provoke, such a war. Since we certainly won't provoke such a war, the "inevitable war" has no factual basis *except what it can itself create.* The real danger lies in protracting the "cold war" so long that an inflammable state of mind is created, whereby any international incident might set off a war.

Here we come to the crux of our relations with Russia. By the line of reasoning above, we don't mean that the United States should throw away its arms and let our future security rest on the good will of the masters of the Kremlin. Unfortunately it looks as if strength is the only thing the Russians will respect—at least for some years to come. We must maintain a strong army, a strong navy, a strong air force, a strong program of scientific research.

But at the same time, we must make it clear to the rest of the world, by both words and actions, that these arms are for defense and security only. We are *not* flexing our muscles.

This is a time for the kind of sanity and common sense on which Americans usually pride themselves. The tensions in this world are bad enough without increasing them by irresponsible talk.

What all this boils down to is this:

Nobody can predict the future with absolute certainty. MAYBE we will have to fight Russia some day. But that's still a maybe. This much is certain, however: If we continue to think and act as though war is inevitable, then we WILL have to fight—and no maybe about it.

44 THE THUNDERCLAP *

The dark thunderstorm that had lowered over Washington all morning broke with a crash of thunder and a rattle of hail just as the President's statement was handed to White House reporters: "We have evidence that within recent weeks an atomic explosion occurred in the U.S.S.R."

Washington had known it was coming, just as surely as it had known the storm was coming. Nevertheless, the news hit the nation with the jarring impact of a fear suddenly become fact. The comfortable feeling of U.S. monopoly was gone forever. The fact was too big and too brutally simple for quick digestion. What had been a threat for some time in the future, hard to visualize, easy to forget, had become a threat for today, to be lived with.

---

* "The Thunderclap" and "A Little Something," *Time,* Vol. LIV (October 3, 1949), pp. 7-8, 55. Courtesy TIME; copyright Time, Inc. 1949. [The two articles have been combined into one. Ed.]

Giant Mechanism. The Cabinet meeting, which got the news from President Truman just before it was handed to the newsmen, broke up after an hour-long discussion. In the Capitol, Connecticut's Senator Brien McMahon sat down with his Joint Committee on Atomic Energy and AEC officials behind drawn shades. Michigan's Arthur Vandenberg was asked what he thought of the news. "It's the kind of thing you can't think about on a straight line until you've put it aside for 48 hours," he replied.

Within 48 hours, more facts came out. The explosion in Russia did not equal the intensity of the Alamogordo bomb, much less the later Eniwetok bomb. It had been set off deep in Russia, over land, not under water; the date of the explosion was somewhere around Sept. 1.

All of the facts published or still secret had come from a giant mechanism of men and machines, designed specifically to detect an atomic explosion anywhere in the world. When Intelligence got a tip that the Russians had solved the atomic riddle, the mechanism swung into action.

Patrolling bombers, sniffing at the winds that blow out of Russia, picked up the radioactive cloud. They followed the radioactive trail for days and thousands of miles, gathering the data by which scientists could measure its size, assess its contents. Intelligence officers queried their sources. As the reports came to the capital, half a dozen of the nation's top atomic physicists were gathered there in deepest secrecy. Besides the President and Secretary of Defense Johnson, fewer than two dozen men knew.

They Were Sure. Events moved swiftly. There began a painstaking matching of the scientific evidence with intelligence reports. AEC Chairman David Lilienthal was summoned from Martha's Vineyard, where he was vacationing, for hurried briefing. Secretary of State Dean Acheson was called in. Some time last week the scientists reported to the President: they were sure that Russia had brought off an atomic explosion.

The problem then was what to do with the information. Disclosure might give away the workings of the U.S. atomic detection network; it might be better if the Russians did not know the U.S. knew. But no one wanted to let the Russians make a triumphant announcement at a moment of their own choosing, when the news might become a massive propaganda coup. President Truman decided to announce the news immediately.

As soon as the decision was made, a courier was sent to Secretary of State Acheson at the U.N. meeting in Flushing Meadows so that he would be informed in advance of the public announcement. The British, French and Canadians were also told; Britain decided to make a parallel statement from 10 Downing Street. By next morning, the arrangements were complete and the President's message was published to the Cabinet and the press.

A LITTLE SOMETHING

At 10:50 A.M. one day last week, Myrtle Bergheim, secretary to presidential Press Secretary Charles G. Ross, stuck her head into the White House pressroom. "The Boss says don't go away," said Myrtle. "He might have a little something later."

At 11:02, twelve correspondents were gathered around Ross's big walnut desk. "Close the doors," said Ross. "Nobody is leaving here until everybody has this statement." Then he passed out copies of a mimeographed handout. Merriman Smith of the United Press was first to read enough to catch the gist: "Evidence . . . atomic explosion . . . U.S.S.R." Whistling in surprise, he edged for the door.

The reporters hit the foyer at a dead run, tore through the lobby, and smashed the nose of a stuffed deer on their dash to pressroom telephones. "Bulletin! Bulletin!" shouted Tony Vaccaro of the Associated Press. Said Smith to the U.P.: "Flash!" Bob Nixon yelped at the International News Service switchboard: "Flash, goddammit, gimme the desk!" At 11:05, bells on U.P. and I.N.S. tickers in hundreds of newspapers signaled the big news flash. Three minutes later, the A.P.'s bulletin was on the wire.

No Ballscores.   U.S. afternoon papers rushed out extras with bulletins and big headlines. But compared to the importance of the news, most papers showed a commendable restraint. They followed the advice which Defense Secretary Louis Johnson gave reporters: "I warn you: don't overplay this." Many newspapers gave the story no more play than the devaluation of the pound. (The equally restrained attitude of London's newspapers was summed up by one Fleet Streeter, who made the obvious crack: "Now they've devalued the atom.") The New York *Post Home News* omitted the usual front-page baseball scores, solemnly explained later: "Fateful as the Yankee defeat . . . might prove, we felt the juxtaposition of this news with President Truman's disclosure . . . might have been viewed as savage satire." Next day, many editorials were so determinedly unexcited (the San Francisco *Chronicle:* "Inevitable As Tomorrow") that they succeeded only in being determinedly dull.

Herblock—New York Post-Home News

"... Or Do You Want Me to Do the Talking?"

In their early editions, the New York *Mirror,* the Des Moines *Register* and the Chicago *Tribune* even rated a love bomb over the atom bomb, put their banners on the story of a man charged with engineering an airplane explosion to kill his wife. The *Trib* also smugly reminded readers that Colonel McCormick was already building a bomb-shelter for himself and his staffers. The New York *Daily News* wrote the day's most heartfelt headline, a prayerful play on words: U.S. HAS SUPREMACY, WILL HOLD IT: A-MEN. The Communist *Worker* combined propaganda, craftsmanship and a sly smile: TRUMAN: U.S.S.R. HAS IT; VISHINSKY: LET'S BAN IT.

No Hysteria. As Washington reporters drew blanks on any further bomb news from usually willing sources, the papers fell back on man-in-the-street interviews and unsubstantiated rumors from "reliable Swedish sources." Almost alone the Hearst papers made a try at spine-chilling; the New York *Journal-American* ran a half-page picture showing Manhattan engulfed in atomic "waves of death and havoc." Scripps-Howard's Newspaper Enterprise Association dug up an "exclusive" story: RUSSIA HAS 4 ATOM PLANTS. (N.E.A. got the tip from an "escaped Soviet industrial official.") The New York *World-Telegram's* scareheads on the story overshadowed advice at the bottom of the page, which most of the press had taken: NO REASON FOR ATOM HYSTERIA.

Inevitable Day. Despite the first quick sense of shock, the news made no essential change at all in U.S. relations with Russia. Like U.S. scientists, U.S. planners had well known that the day must inevitably come — and soon — when Russia would have the bomb. "Ever since atomic energy was first released by man," wrote the President, "the eventual development of this new force by other nations was to be expected. This probability has always been taken into account by us."

In spite of that indisputable fact there might be changes on the fringes of U.S. foreign policy. Some looked at Yugoslavia with a new, strategic perspective. Ohio's Senator Robert Taft renewed the argument that the U.S. take strategically placed Spain into the community of nations fighting Communism.

There was also a change in mood and tempo. Military planners were suddenly faced with a whole new timetable of strategic planning. Congressional economizers would have to look at the military budget with different eyes. The whole of the U.S. foreign policy would be subjected to the strain of the new, accomplished fact.

No Panic. By and large, the U.S. accepted the fact with grim concern, but with no panic. In Congress an irresponsible few talked nervously of the desirability of moving some Government agencies out of Washington. A few resurgent isolationists seized on it as a reason for scuttling all international programs from MAP to the Marshall Plan. But most reaction was sober, balanced and a little sardonic. Men told each other wryly: "Better get out your old uniform." Others joked about getting a cabin in the hills. Many talked of a feeling of relief that the period of waiting was over.

The U.S. had entered a new phase of the atomic age in which it would have to live with the Russians' bomb as well as its own. For the first time, U.S. citizens would know, as much of the world had known since 1945, how it feels to live under the threat of sudden destruction—coming like a clap of thunder and a rattle of hail.

45   SHALL WE FACE THE FACTS?*

I have to speak here of matters that lie within the scope of foreign policy. It is with reluctance that I speak of them. For the problem of peace cannot be solved within that narrow scope. The traditional aim of foreign policy is to prolong the peace; that is, to lengthen the interval between two wars. What is the use of postponing war if we know—as we know today—that it will be all the more terrible the later it comes? What we need is not a truce; what we need is peace.

But foreign policy got us into this mess, and foreign policy will have to get us out of it. We have to have a truce in order to have a chance to bid for peace.

Having built up a tremendous pressure around Russia, we dare not now suddenly release it lest we provoke an explosion. But somehow we shall have to find a path from containment to "contentment." It will be a narrow path, and we had better watch our step.

Somewhere along that path we must find the truce that will give us a breathing spell. This paper is concerned only with the first leg of this journey.

MAKING THE PREMISES EXPLICIT

Soviet Russia is a dictatorship no less ruthless perhaps than was Hitler's dictatorship in Germany. Does it follow that Russia will act as Hitler's Germany acted? I do not believe so.

*Leo Szilard, "Shall We Face the Facts?" *Bulletin of Atomic Scientists,* Vol. V (October, 1949), pp. 269–73. Reprinted with permission from the October 1949 issue of the *Bulletin of the Atomic Scientists.* Copyright 1949 by the Educational Foundation for Nuclear Science.

Before the war Germany under Hitler, Italy under Mussolini and Soviet Russia were all dictatorships. Germany under Hitler remained Germany. She had been a militant nation before Hitler, and she will remain a militant nation after Hitler. It is not that the Germans want war, but rather that they like the type of organized action which characterizes a mighty nation at war. Italy under Mussolini remained Italy and would have kept her place if the other nations had shown determination to thwart her aspirations in Abyssinia. Soviet Russia is still Russia. Her policy is Russian policy first and Communist policy second. It is true that Russia dominates Rumania, Bulgaria, Hungary, and Czechoslovakia and that she is using the Communist parties in these countries to secure her rule. Yet she is not putting her foreign policy at the service of Communism, but rather she is using the Communists everywhere as instruments of her foreign policy. The rulers of Russia might very well believe that ultimately Capitalism will collapse and Communism will conquer the world; but that does not mean that Russia has a concrete plan for world conquest, that she has set a timetable for it, or that her day-to-day actions are guided by it.

To my mind anything that Russia has done in the past four years can be fully understood as the action of a nation pursuing her national interests, guided largely, though not solely, by strategic considerations.

These are my premises; my conclusions must necessarily stand or fall with them.

THE REAL CAUSE OF CONFLICT

What is the real cause of the Russian-American conflict? Thucydides gave us the answer over 2,000 years ago when he wrote the *History of the Peloponnesian War.* . . .

The statesmen of Athens tell us that the war was caused by Sparta, and the statesmen of Sparta tell us that the war was caused by Athens, for even in those times war was regarded by the civilized world as an evil and statesmen were anxious to avert the stigma of the aggressor. But Thucydides tells us that "the real reason for the war was that Athens' growing power threatened the security of Sparta."

Today the growing power of Russia threatens America's security, and the growing power of America threatens Russia's security. Is there a solution to their problem? A solution, if there is one, must, of necessity, lie outside of the pattern that governed the actions of Sparta and Athens. The policy outlined in this paper lies outside of that pattern. It requires a move that will make our strategic position more difficult in case of war, but at the same time it will greatly increase our chances of avoiding war. If America and Russia reject moves of this type, they will remain within the same pattern that governed the actions of the Greek city-states, and the result also will be the same.

WHAT ARE THE FACTS?

The first question which we have to examine here is whether the Atlantic Pact can survive in its present structure. What are the facts?

The Russians have exploded one bomb. They might very well have exploded the only bomb they had. But the plant which was used to make that one bomb can turn out others. Within a very short time, one year perhaps, the Russians will have bombs in significant quantity—significant from the point of view of Western Europe. Will the Russians also have the means of delivering these bombs anywhere in Europe? Maybe they do not yet have V-2 type rockets developed to the stage where they can carry their atomic bombs. Maybe they do not yet have bombers fast enough to be able to get through without being intercepted. But clearly the time is not far off, when in case of war Russia will be in a position to deliver bombs anywhere in Western Europe and to deliver them in significant quantity.

If the time thus comes when Paris, Brussels, and Amsterdam face destruction within twenty-four hours after the outbreak of war, and when there is nothing that America can do to protect these cities from such a fate, we shall be faced with a situation which we did not envisage when the Atlantic Pact was concluded.

One might argue that the Atlantic Pact would still offer these countries greater security than they would have without it, since Russia, knowing that the United States would go to war if any of them were attacked, would be less likely to attack them. I am willing to let this argument pass for the moment. But can anyone seriously expect the French, Belgians, and the Dutch thus to accept, for the sake of a lessened probability of war, the absolute certainty that in case of war their cities will be utterly destroyed? Will it be much consolation for them to know that, some ten or fifteen years after their destruction, the United States may be victorious and might then help to rebuild their cities and to reconstruct their devastated country?

SHALL WE LET EUROPE PERISH?

What then is the policy we ought to follow in the face of these realities? It seems to me that there is only one avenue of escape that is open to us, and this is what it is:

We ought to release those countries, who want to be released, from the obligations imposed upon them by the Atlantic Pact. This does not mean that we should abandon them to their fate. We could, for instance, enter into an agreement with France—to single out France for the moment—in which we unilaterally undertake the following obligations:

1. To go to war with Russia if Russia should attack or occupy France;
2. In case of war to respect the neutrality of France as long as her neutrality is respected also by Russia, except if America—in spite of having refrained from using atomic bombs first—is attacked with atomic bombs by Russia or some other nation;
3. To refrain from using atomic bombs, and strategic bombing of any kind, against France as long as no atomic bombs are produced in her territory, even though France may have been forced to surrender to Russia and even though America may be attacked by atomic bombs produced outside of France.

We could enter into similar agreements with Belgium, Holland, and certain other countries in Western Europe.

As long as America is pledged to go to war in case Russia should attack or occupy certain countries, America might have to go to war in fulfillment of such a treaty obligation. Such a war America could bring to a successful conclusion only by ultimately invading Russia. Even though America may not use atomic bombs first, nevertheless, large scale atomic bomb attacks against American cities might occur and result in public pressure on the Government to bring the war as fast as possible to a successful conclusion. The possibility of having to move American troops through Western Europe could not be excluded in such a contingency. In the absence of such an attack on us, we would be pledged to respect the neutrality of Western Europe as long as her neutrality was respected by Russia. Thus we could not count on moving troops through Western Europe and might have to invade Russia through the Balkans, the Near East, the Middle East, or the Far East.

This pledge should be given, but given in the full knowledge that it will greatly weaken our strategic position.

If we pledge ourselves to any nation to go to war in case she is attacked or occupied by Russia, we should make our pledge as unequivocal as possible. A pledge which we fully intend to honor but which leaves some doubts in the mind of a would-be aggressor may increase rather than decrease the danger of war.

We ought to make our pledge unequivocal, but we ought to make it for a period of time which is reasonably limited. For we cannot forever safeguard peace by precariously balancing it with pledges of this sort. In the long run protection against aggression cannot be based on fear of retaliation. It must be based on other motivations.

Within the pattern of the new policy outlined above, we would continue to give economic assistance to Western Europe. We ought even to encourage France, Belgium, and Holland to build up a reasonable amount of armaments of their own [to deter invasion]. . . .

We have so far refrained from mentioning England. England is no less vulnerable to bombs than the rest of Western Europe. But after the fall of France, England decided to fight on in the face of the heaviest odds, and she emerged victorious. England might decide to hold out indefinitely as our ally and, with worse luck this time, perhaps suffer utter destruction in case of war.

Yet England, when she realizes that her geographical position as well as the concentration of her population in London and a few other large cities make her vulnerable beyond endurance, might also wish to be freed from the Atlantic Pact. If she does, we ought to lend her a helping hand rather than try to obstruct a development which is inevitable.

England, if reasonably armed, might speak to Russia much the same as could France, Belgium, and Holland. She might give Russia an assurance to resist, if necessary with force of arms, an American invasion.

By giving her consent and approval to a position of this sort which England might wish to take, America could effectively protect England from a Russian occupation. Clearly in case of a war with America, Russia would have a strong incentive to leave England in a neutral position and thus bar the United States from using England as a base of military operations. It is true that by forcing England's surrender Russia would gain the advantage of being able to use British ports for launching submarines, but this would hardly be as important for Russia as depriving America of the advantage of using England as a base.

In the case of a Russian-American war, the neutrality of France,

Belgium, and Holland might similarly be safeguarded against violation by Russia.

Whether or not Western Europe will perish depends on the attitude America will take on the issue of her neutrality. It is a fortunate coincidence that the neutralization of Western Europe is required for establishing a truce, for reasons of simple humanity and for reasons of expediency. From this triple coincidence, we may derive the hope that within a few years, the neutralization of Western Europe will be an accomplished fact. . . .

CAN WE STOP THE ARMS RACE?

The neutralization of all those nations which are at present caught between the strategic aspirations of America and Russia would remove the most important area of conflict in Russian-American relations. Yet if the arms race is permitted to continue, and particularly if Russian atomic bomb production increasingly threatens the security of the United States, war will ultimately become unavoidable.

Thus the question arises whether, within the pattern of the new policy outlined above, Russia and the United States could agree on some effective method of international control of atomic energy.

International inspection must be an integral part of any such agreement if it is to be effective. Would it have been in Russia's Interest—in the conditions which existed during the past four years—to enter into any agreement on atomic energy that provided for international inspection?

During these past four years we regarded Western Europe as a base for military operations against Russia in case of war. We were engaged in developing long-range rockets and long-range bombers, and we built a considerable fleet of such bombers. In case of war with Russia, it would have been of advantage to us to know the exact locations of the most essential Russian industrial installations, and it was therefore in Russia's interest to keep secret all information relating to them. Thus the Iron Curtain was Russia's most important strategic defense. Such strategic considerations may not have been the only reasons for Russia's desire to maintain secrecy, but they are valid and sufficient reasons nevertheless.

International inspection, if at all effective, is not compatible with the degree of secrecy which Russia was anxious to maintain in the postwar period and which she was successful in maintaining. In the conditions which existed during the past four years it would not have been in Russia's interest to enter into any agreement *limited to the control of atomic energy* which provided for international inspection.

But even if such an agreement had not provided for international inspection, it would still not have been in Russia's interest to be a party to it. Under conditions such as those that existed in the past four years, America could, by using Western Europe as a base, bring the war to Russia's territory. She could do this without atomic bombs, merely by using tanks, heavy guns, long-range bombers, and other conventional weapons. By agreeing to eliminate atomic bombs from national armaments, Russia would deprive herself of the one weapon which might enable her to bring the war to our territory. Russia can not carry the war to our territory by using long-range bombers carrying ordinary explosives, for, to her, the cost of such an operation would be prohibitive.

My thesis is that in these past four years Russia has steadfastly refused to consider any international agreement that would effectively eliminate atomic bombs because, under existing conditions, it was not in her interest to do so.

We must next turn our attention to an issue which is closely related: In the past four years the United States has steadfastly opposed a general reduction of armaments. Why?

Immediately after the war Western Europe was weak and could have been overrun by the Russian army at any time. This might be true even today. But we have been trying to create a situation in which within a few years, Western Europe would no longer be at the mercy of Russia. We hoped to achieve this by arming Western Europe and by maintaining a high level of armaments ourselves. We hoped that such a course of action would enable us to come to the help of Western Europe within a short period of time, if she were attacked by Russia, and that Western Europe would be able to hold out until our help arrived.

Had we then agreed to a substantial general reduction of armaments equally affecting all parties, we would have left Western Europe at the mercy of Russia's enormous reserve manpower. Then, in case of a Russian attack against Western Europe, it would have taken us a long time effectively to enter the war, and in the meantime Russian infantry could have overrun Western Europe.

But the way things are going at present, we may take it for granted that within a short period of time Western Europe will be irretrievably at Russia's mercy in the sense that, if she were attacked by Russia, we could not possibly bring her assistance fast enough to prevent her destruction or prevent her from being forced to surrender. We might then be prepared to neutralize Western Europe and to enter into an agreement with Russia that will stop the arms race by eliminating atomic bombs from national armaments, put limitations on the conventional types of arms, and provide for a substantial reduction of armaments in general.

Such an agreement would still leave Western Europe physically at the mercy of Russia's land armies. But this does not necessarily mean that Western Europe would be in danger of a Russian attack or invasion. Mexico is physically at the mercy of the United States, but she has no reason to fear that the United States will violate her integrity. The United States has not at present any motive for doing so and would hardly have any in the future unless Russia were to make an attempt to prepare Mexico as a base for future military operations against the United States.

While the level of armaments to be maintained by us in peacetime would still have to be adjusted to the level of armaments maintained by Russia and other nations, our ability to win a war would be determined by the level of our arms production during the war rather than by the level of our stockpile of arms at the start of the war. Modern weapons get obsolete very fast. Keeping, in peacetime, a large stockpile of them is a useless drain on any nation's economy.

My thesis is that if we adjust our policy to reality and adopt the proposed new policy, the old reasons, which in the past four years led us to oppose general reduction of armaments, will no longer be valid. An over-all settlement of the outstanding postwar issues may thus become possible. Of these issues, the German problem is perhaps the most difficult. Its solution will remain difficult even if Russia and the United States were to seek it in perfect harmony. But if within the framework of the neutrality of Western Europe, a solution to the German problem and other postwar issues can be found, then general limitations of armaments and the elimination of atomic bombs from national armaments *will* be in the interest of Russia as well as of America.

What particular type of atomic energy control will then be acceptable to Russia?

In the past America pushed for international management of all atomic energy development, delegated to an agency of the United Nations and controlled by a majority vote of that body. This particular solution has some attractive features. But as long as the world remains divided between the allies of Russia and the allies of America, with our allies holding the majority in the United Nations, it will not be in Russia's interest to accept such a solution.

It is conceivable that if the present trend is reversed, countries which are not allies of either America or Russia, and are independent both economically and politically, may gradually become a majority in the United Nations. "International management" might then become acceptable to Russia.

In the meantime, some other form of effective atomic energy control will have to be adopted, if any control is to be adopted at all.

WOULD RUSSIA KEEP HER AGREEMENTS?

The question will be asked, can Russia be trusted to keep any such agreement. The answer is simple. Russia can be trusted to keep an agreement as long as it remains in her interest to do so. We can make Russia keep an agreement if we maintain the conditions in which it will remain her interest to cooperate rather than to abrogate the agreement. It might even be wise to have a provision in the agreement giving both America and Russia the right to abrogate it upon giving due notice. This would at least serve as a reminder that no agreement between nations has much value unless it remains in the interests of the contracting parties to continue the agreement.

Let us remind ourselves at this point that what we are discussing here is a truce and not peace. We shall not have peace until we create a structure in which cooperation will be secured by incentives rather than precariously enforced by fear of punishment. We shall not have peace until we have an organized world community.

The Peloponnesian War occurred fifteen years after Sparta and Athens concluded a peace treaty that was to last for thirty. Russia and America will not fare any better if they conclude a truce and mistake it for a peace.

I have tried to outline a policy which might lead to peace. It may have its faults. Almost certainly it could be improved upon. But what are the alternatives?

We could fight a preventive war against Russia, and there is little doubt that in the years to come this course will be advocated in public by a few, privately by many.

Alternatively, we could pursue the type of policy which we pursued the past four years. It is a policy of "neither war nor peace," and will obviously lead to war. It will probably lead to war when war will be at its worst.

If we want to find a way out of our present predicament, above all let us avoid self-righteousness. Let us not say that we made Russia a generous offer when we proposed the Baruch plan for international control of atomic energy. We would not fool anyone else, but we might fool ourselves. Many of us may be inclined to say that the cause of all the postwar difficulties between America and Russia must be squarely laid at the doorstep of Russia. A "Thucydides" of the twentieth century to whom perhaps will fall the bitter task of writing the history of "The Downfall of the Atlantic Civilization" might see it differently.

In these past four years Russia and America were not at war. They did not exchange shots; but they traded blows. Who struck the first blow? Does it really matter? During the first World War the Hungarian writer, Karinthy, was sitting in his study attempting to write an essay on the causes of that war, when he was interrupted by a loud noise which seemed to come from the nursery. Opening the door, he saw his five children engaged in a free-for-all. "Who started this fight?" he said sternly to Peter, his eldest. "It all started," said Peter, "when David hit me back."

Korea

The policy of containment began with Europe in mind. But in 1949, Americans had to broaden their definition to include Asia, for in that year the Chinese Communists brought their decades of revolutionary activity to a climax and a victory. China, one of the largest nations and by far the most populous in the world, had become a member of the Communist bloc. The "red tide," that vivid feature of so many maps in American magazines after 1946, now spilled awesomely over the globe's surface.

Mao Tse-tung's victory, and Chiang Kai-shek's ignominious retreat to Formosa, provoked one of the bitterest political controversies over foreign policy in American history. The State Department issued The White Paper in defense of its China policies, explaining that even the best efforts of the Truman administration could not save the corrupt and inept Chiang regime. The Republicans reversed the charges, accusing Truman, Secretary of State Acheson, Marshall, and other Democratic leaders of ineptitude and corruption. Some Republi-

cans extended the accusation to treason. By 1950, Senator Joseph McCarthy was launching his crusade against Communists at home, especially in the State Department. The perjury conviction of Alger Hiss, a former State Department official who had played a part in the Yalta Conference and the creation of the U.N., provided welcome ammunition for the attacks by McCarthy, Senator William Knowland of California, and others.

After the Communist victory in China, the Far East remained a volatile site for the drama of Cold War. And because Americans considered China to be merely the largest of Russia's many satellites, rather than an independent Communist state, they made Asia a part of the general problem of containment.

This perspective was strongly reinforced in June of 1950, when North Korean troops invaded South Korea. This peninsula on the eastern edge of Asia had been divided at the end of World War II, the northern part under occupation by Russia's Red Army, the southern part by American military forces. As in Germany, the temporary division became permanent. During 1948–49, the United States and USSR withdrew their troops. Then came the North Korean attack, with Russian support, and the American forces were ordered back to South Korea. Under the aegis of the U.N., the United States was at war—a limited war, one without nuclear weapons and, so it seemed to many Americans, without end.

Even when 200,000 Chinese Communist troops entered the war, after General Douglas MacArthur's forces crossed into North Korea and came close to the Chinese border, the war remained a limited one. Truman set the limits for fear of provoking Russian intervention. In fact, the President eventually dismissed MacArthur for publicly demanding an attack on China and "victory." (This dismissal forms an ironic parallel to Henry Wallace's fate in 1946 for declaring very different views.) Not until 1953 did the fighting stop, and then the status quo ante bellum was restored.

As the following selections suggest, the Korean War prompted American commentators to both alarmed and speculative analyses of American foreign policy. The first selection, by the influential Alsop brothers, appeared in the widely read Saturday Evening Post *and probably typifies the thinking of most Americans at the time. Later in 1950, one of* The Nation's *editors, Freda Kirchwey, tried to extract the larger significance of the Korean conflict.*

46 THE LESSON OF KOREA*

The lesson of Korea is grimly simple. Despite innumerable warnings, we did not do enough to deter Soviet aggression or to contain Soviet imperialism. Since the end of the Second World War, we have been on public notice from such authorities as George F. Kennan that any "soft spot" would tempt the Kremlin to attack. Only a few months ago, Secretary of State Dean G. Acheson told the Congress and the country that the Kremlin would seize any territory that was "within its grasp and reach."

Korea was a soft spot, within the Kremlin's grasp and reach. The strength of the West, and particularly the armed strength of the United States, was too slight to instill in the masters of the Kremlin any healthy fear of reprisals. Hence Korea was attacked.

Such are the obvious, surface facts. Beneath the surface, however, lies another set of facts of infinitely greater significance to every American. Korea is only the first episode of an attempt to bring all Asia and all Europe within the Soviet Empire. The Kremlin's true aim is not merely to seize the rocky hills of South Korea. It is not merely to grab anything that is not nailed down. The real Kremlin goal is to make the living death of the slave society the universal condition of mankind, from the shores of the Atlantic to the islands of Japan, from the icy cliffs of Spitsbergen to the bright sands of Cape Comorin.

Furthermore, expert observers have already discerned the outlines of the well-conceived world strategy by which the masters of the Kremlin expect to reach their staggering goal. The existence of this Kremlin world strategy is solidly testified to by much other evidence than the Korean affair.

Indeed, there are good reasons to believe that the Soviet planners formally communicated the first part of their program to trusted Asiatic communist leaders at a secret conference in Peking nearly nine months ago. This meeting, held under the cover name of the "Asian and Australasian Bureau of the World Federation of Trades Unions," examined in detail the whole military-political situation in Asia and approved a policy of aggression on almost every front. It was then that Korea was probably tentatively chosen as the first point of attack.

---

* Joseph and Stewart Alsop, "The Lesson of Korea," *Saturday Evening Post*, Vol. CCXXIII (September 2, 1950), pp. 17–19, 96, 98, 100.

Korea was chosen, in turn, precisely because it was a territory under American protection. This may be paradoxical. Yet it is the key to the whole problem. In brief, for excellent reasons which will be examined later, the Soviet planners expected no American response to the Korean attack. They hoped, therefore, for a rapid triumph, which would simultaneously show the great strength of the Soviet Union and expose the feebleness of the United States. And this, of course, is precisely the tactic on which the whole Kremlin world strategy is based. Two thirds of the world is to be conquered, not by overt onslaughts of the Red Army, but by carefully prepared, strictly localized, yet violently terrifying demonstrations of unchallengeable Soviet power.

How this can be is hard for most Americans to understand, in this rich, never-conquered, ocean-girdled, self-confident land. Yet the fact remains. In the blood-drained, neurotic world of the bad time after the second great war, brute strength can win battles where no blow is struck.

We should soon have seen the truth of this if the Korean attack had turned out as the Kremlin intended. In Asiatic politics, the desire to back the winner always predominates. Such poor governments as that of Quirino, in the Philippines, or the odd little gaggle of Socialist idealists who preside over the nation-wide riot in Burma, or the distracted administration of Sukarno and Hatta, in Indonesia, are neither deeply rooted nor powerfully led. The spectacle of a Kremlin triumph in Korea would have deeply intimidated the leaders of every new government in Asia. Their whole orientation would have been altered. And so the rot would have begun.

There is a reliable intelligence, moreover, that even as the Kremlin gave the order to march in Korea, plans had already been laid for a second, even more devastating attack on the great soft spot of the Middle East, oil-rich Iran. The subjugation of Iran—a combined operation of the "Azerbaijanian" divisions now training in Russia and the communist-front Tudeh Party within the borders—was projected for this autumn. A success in Iran would two thirds complete the collapse of Asia under Soviet pressure.

We may hope that this Iranian project has been upset by our firm response to the Korean challenge. But we cannot be sure. The plain fact is that a sudden show of American firmness was the last thing the Kremlin anticipated. The effect may be to knock the Kremlin strategy galley west. But precisely because this danger is inherent in our firmness, the effect may also be to make the Kremlin speed

ALEUTIAN ISLANDS

PACIFIC OCEAN

MARIANAS

GUAM

JAPAN

S. KOREA

N. KOREA

FORMOSA

Peking

PHILIPPINES

MONGOLIA

CHINA

FRENCH INDOCHINA

INDONESIA

U. S. S. R.

TIBET

PAK.

BURMA
THAILAND
MALAYA

BRITAIN

FINLAND

GERMANY

Moscow

POLAND,

CZECH.

HUNGARY

YUGOSLAVIA

RUMANIA

AFGHANISTAN

PAKISTAN

INDIA

CEYLON

Berlin

IRAN

FRANCE

SPAIN

AUSTRIA

ITALY

BULGARIA

TURKEY

IRAQ

SAUDI ARABIA

ALBANIA

GREECE

AFRICA

SOVIET UNION

COMMUNIST DOMINATED

THREATENED AREAS

Copyright, Newsweek, Inc., July, 1950

What We're up against

up the whole tempo of its effort far beyond anything previously planned. Before the odds in favor of either of these results can be intelligently calculated, however, it is first necessary to grasp what may be called the Kremlin strategy's tactical pattern.

This pattern is clear. In Korea, the Kremlin meant to start something exactly like the rapid caving of a muddy riverbank under the furious gnawing of a flood. Surrender was to lead, by easy stages, to surrender. Victory in Korea was to be the prelude to victory everywhere. This was emphasized and re-emphasized in every analysis of the Korean attack by the State Department experts. And it was for this reason, and this reason only, that the President gave the order to fight for Korea, which the armed services held long ago to be militarily valueless.

Nor was the fate of Asia the sole consideration in those two anxious days at Blair House before the President made up his mind. In the vast convulsion that the Kremlin is attempting to engineer, the capture of Asia is only a phase, whereas the engulfment of Europe is the final objective. The new Soviet Empire must include Europe's great industrial potential, to balance Asia's hungry man power and unexploited raw materials. Northern France and the Low Countries, steel-rich Sweden, the busy Po Valley and the vital Ruhr—these are the grand prizes in the Kremlin game.

OLD DOC MARSHALL'S POTENT MEDICINE

In Europe, to be sure, we have already proved we can win a great contest with the Kremlin if we only try. The Marshall Plan has promoted an astonishing European recovery. Economic betterment has begun to cure Europe's postwar neuroses and has begun to transform the nations across the Atlantic into powerful potential allies of the United States. Indeed, there is no doubt that the Kremlin adopted its new world strategy, a direct borrowing from Adolf Hitler, precisely because we had already defeated the first postwar campaign for Europe, which was conducted on classic Stalinist lines of revolutionary infiltration and politico-economic disruption.

Yet an American diplomat who watched developments in Paris, the European nerve center, has called the forty-eight hours before President Truman's Korean decision "the worst two days of my life." A man long trained to be sensitive to such things, he saw the politicians beginning to trim their sails a little. He saw the editors walking on eggs in their comment on Soviet aggression. He saw the rich men hurrying to the banks to send away their money, and the poor men sadly reading the headlines and resigning themselves to the worst. After the 1930's, the first sorry signs of submission and appeasement were only too familiar to his eyes.

Remember the 1930's, and you will instantly comprehend what the Kremlin can achieve in Europe. In the 1930's, Hitler took the Rhineland and Austria, the Sudetenland and Czechoslovakia with no shot fired, by the same tactics of terror and power that the Kremlin has now borrowed. The method was to use power to beget terror, to beget appeasement. In the 1950's, Western Europe is far weaker than in the 1930's—immeasurably less well armed, still exhausted by the shock of war, still divided by communist infiltration. Meanwhile, the Kremlin plays the power-and-terror game upon a larger stage than Hitler ever dreamed of. Iran, Burma and Indo-China, Berlin, Vienna and Belgrade are the scenes where the might of the Soviet Union is to be proved and the feebleness of the West is to be shown. The effect in Europe, if countermeasures are not taken, will be utterly paralyzing.

Again, this is no nightmare, this Kremlin plan for Europe, as one of these reporters learned during a long, recent trip of inquiry. The march of the Free German Youth on Berlin this spring was undoubtedly designed as a preliminary power demonstration. It would have come off if the threats of Gerhart Eisler had not been answered by the stoutness of John J. McCloy. And this trifling Kremlin failure means much less than the Kremlin's astute preparations, all over Europe, for great successes later on.

In France, for instance, the communist-front Partisans of Peace are carrying on a deafening propaganda about the horrors of atomic warfare, warning, in huge advertisements, of Paris being incinerated in thirty seconds from 13,000 meters, blaming the Americans as "atomic aggressors," but omitting to state that the Soviet Union also has the atomic bomb. Millions have signed the Partisans of Peace petition for the outlawry of atomic war, while tens of thousands among the more intelligent have begun to listen to the apostles of European "neutrality." Any fool can foresee how these people will react, and how many million others will flock to join them, if the Partisans of Peace propaganda is ever provided with its planned future commentary—by the unveiling of a Soviet strategic air force, backed by a stockpile of atomic weapons, in a Europe without an air defense.

Equally, any fool can foresee how useful, in that time, will be the current transformation of the Western European communist parties into pure paramilitary groupings, with sabotage and disruption as their sole function. And any fool can foresee how, if that time is allowed to come, there will be a sudden urge to leave the Atlantic Pact, to sign "nonaggression pacts" with Moscow; to prove good will by accepting "democratic elements" in the governments, and to prove "neutrality" by total disarmament.

As in the case of Iran, we cannot tell how these Kremlin plans for Europe will be affected by our firm response in Korea. Since terror is the essential ingredient of the Kremlin program, and since a Korea-stimulated build-up of American strength may ultimately dispel this terror of Russian power, the result may be to upset every calculation of the Politburo. But the result may also be to tempt the Politburo to strike far sooner than had been intended, at Berlin, or in Yugoslavia, or elsewhere. For the present, at any rate, there is no doubt that the Kremlin, sooner or later, hopes to break the line in Europe. If the line in Europe breaks anywhere, it will break everywhere. And then, not very long after all the nonaggression pacts have been tremulously signed, the Soviet viceroys will organize their vast domains in the very sourceland of our civilization.

Such is the first part of the lesson of Korea, that this Kremlin world strategy exists beyond question; that it is to be taken completely seriously; and that it must be checkmated at all costs. The problem that confronts us is no antibandit operation in a small and unknown land, which can be carried on with all the customary delights of business-as-usual and politics-as-usual. Our problem is a titanic struggle for world dominion.

ONLY ALL-OUT EFFORT WILL SAVE US NOW

As for the second part of the lesson of Korea, it is as unpleasant as the first. If we treat the Korea war as an isolated antibandit operation, every basic cause of the Kremlin's aggression there will continue to operate with increasing force. Soviet war preparations will go forward with mounting effectiveness—for the British and American intelligences believe that the Kremlin has moved in Korea three full years before the climax of the Russian rearmament. Meanwhile, our own power, by the same token, will grow relatively less with every passing month. Soon or late, another vulnerable flank will be attacked; whether Iran or Burma, or Berlin or Yugoslavia, it hardly matters. Again the iron engine of the Kremlin world strategy will begin to operate. And when that happens we shall have reached the pass to which Baldwin and Chamberlain brought Britain.

We shall have to choose between launching a war of desperation or surrendering in our turn, for let no one suppose it will not mean eventual destruction, in this age of the absolute weapons, to be isolated in our hemisphere with all the resources and all the peoples of all the rest of the world arrayed against us by the Kremlin's hard hand.

If we wish to avoid this future choice, we must face the facts and do something about them. We must rebuild the defenses of the West without an instant's delay. For the true basis of the Kremlin's world strategy is not the vulnerability of the exposed flanks, like Korea and Iran, although this vulnerability plays its part. The true basis of the Kremlin's world strategy, in fact, is the simple predominance of the naked military power of the Soviet Empire over the armed strength of the United States and the free world. The real "soft spot" that invited the Korean attack was not the weakness of the ineffectual Syngman Rhee, *but our own weakness.*

On this point, theoretically responsible American leaders have recently misrepresented so much and dodged so often behind the useful screens of "military secrecy" that the average American must be astonished to learn the danger of our situation. All over this country, people are angrily asking why an overt act of Soviet aggression was needed to disclose the true state of our defenses, and how our defenses got that way.

Curiously enough, the moment when we took the road that has led to Korea can be rather exactly dated. It was in mid-November of 1948. The new budget was about to be closed. Assembled at the White House, in the presence of the President, were James Forrestal, the Chiefs of Staff of the services and other important officials. Forrestal, gray-faced, exhausted by his burdens, already in the last phase before his final tragedy, was the speaker. With all his earnestness, he warned of Soviet war preparations. Slowly and painfully, he presented the case for an American defense expenditure based on the realistic strategic requirements created by Russian rearmament, amounting to $17,000,000,000 in 1949–50.

The President listened coldly. The others present contributed little. And when Forrestal's presentation was concluded, the President quickly gave his decision—strategic requirements would not be taken as the basis of our effort, the Soviet threat would be dealt with by hoping for the best, and defense expenditure would be held under an arbitrary ceiling of $14,000,000,000.

Although almost no one realizes it, American foreign policy was radically changed by this attempt to save $3,000,000,000. From the end of the war until that day in November, 1948, a different rule had been followed. *Whatever was required, we did,* whether it was to aid Greece and Turkey or to launch a Marshall Plan. Furthermore, toward the close of this remarkable period of American policy making, when the conduct of affairs was dominated by Forrestal and Under Secretary of State Robert A. Lovett, the urgency of the defense problem had already been clearly recognized.

The *coup d'état* in Czechoslovakia had rung the alarm, touching off an emergency American rearmament program in the early spring of 1948, when the demobilization mess was beginning to be cleaned up. By the summer of 1948 this emergency program was being transformed into a coherent long-range plan. Lovett, Forrestal and Sen. Arthur H. Vandenberg had laid the groundwork for the Atlantic Pact, to co-ordinate the whole effort of the West and to permit us to contribute to the strength of our allies. By patience and persistence, Forrestal had induced the rival services to be reasonable in their requests and to fit their own programs into the larger Western pattern. The $17,000,000,000 that Forrestal argued for at the White House was the necessary first payment for a continuous, orderly, economical build-up of American and Western strength, sufficient to guard against the threat of growing Russian power.

It is bitter to think today of the influences, so many of them cheap and sordid, that led the President to reject Jim Forrestal's advice. There was Louis A. Johnson, who considered that he had a mortgage on Forrestal's job. There was Maj. Gen. Harry H. Vaughan, who hated the guts of both Forrestal and Lovett. There was Secretary of the Treasury John Snyder, in alliance with the Bureau of the Budget, who seemed to believe that the richest nation in the world could not afford the added expenditure which security so clearly demanded. And there was the pervading atmosphere of blindness and complacency in Washington, typified by some leading Congressional Republicans.

In the last analysis, of course, the final responsibility for the solemn decisions belonged to the President himself. He was suffering, that November, from his election-born attack of euphoric cockiness, and he was in full revolt against his former meek dependence on such men as Lovett and Forrestal. Yet it is hard to be too harsh with Truman, who has generally acted with courage and forthrightness whenever he has been well advised. In the first place, he consulted General Marshall about Forrestal's program; and the general, by then out of touch with defense problems, merely stated that we should be content with an adequate "posture of defense." And in the second place, most of our present peril might still have been averted if Forrestal had been replaced by a man of equal stature. Instead, his successor was the politically minded Louis A. Johnson, hell-bent for election in the role of the great economizer.

. . .

Combat unit after combat unit, of the air, ground and naval forces, was ruthlessly suppressed as superfluous. Aircraft replacement rates were so brutally reduced that our Air Force was condemned to rapid obsolescence, while the fleet and Marine air arms—the latter almost our only element of air power thoroughly trained in close support of ground forces—were hurried to the chopping block. Great gaps, such as our shocking deficiencies in tactical aircraft, first-class tanks, modern antitank weapons and air-warning equipment, were treated as though they hardly existed. The research-and-development program was left to stagnate.

. . .

In order to achieve these cuts, staggering sums were totally wasted in penalty payments for contract cancellations, which were, however, pleasingly press-releasable as "savings." And at each new "saving" accomplished by these methods, Louis Johnson cried again and more loudly that he was making no sacrifice of armed power. Indeed, he repeatedly claimed that we were growing stronger and stronger. When Forrestal laid down his office, we had a respectable, if insufficient, military establishment, and were still increasing our strength, although at too slow a rate. When the Korean war broke out, one man's misstatements had become a leading item in the inventory of our strength. The American people were deceived, but the Kremlin was not. The masters of the Kremlin saw their opportunity, and they struck.

It seems incredible today that this sort of thing can have gone on after the Berlin blockade, after the explosion of the Soviet atomic bomb—which even the Forrestal plan had not provided for—after the fall of China, and after the full, clear disclosure of Soviet purposes in Southeast Asia. Yet the record speaks for itself, except on one point. This is the transformation of the Atlantic Pact, the supposed great instrument of the defense of the whole Western world, into a mere hollow mockery.

Here we come to the third part of the lesson of Korea. It is not only the strength of the United States that the Kremlin watches and measures Soviet power against. America, although unavoidably the leader, cannot undertake the whole task of defending the Western world. Strong allies—a strong Britain, a strong Canada, strong nations in all of Western Europe—are needed to share the burden and guard the long lines of the frontier. Only this broader base of strength can overcome the European fear of Soviet power, which continues to stimulate the postwar neuroses and now makes all Western Europe vulnerable to the new Kremlin world strategy of terror. Only this solid Western strength can neutralize the danger of aggression in the politically confused Middle and Far East. In the existing state of world politics, non-Soviet Asia is essentially an extension of the West. And only the power of the center can protect the otherwise indefensible flanks.

. . .

In addition, the American defense planners were specifically directed by the Secretary of Defense to consider no plans which would either interfere with his "savings" or require an increase of military aid to our allies above the original level of about $1,500,000,000.

. . .

The truth is that when the Korean attack occurred, the Atlantic Pact organization had still failed to produce a workable, agreed, overall plan for the defense of the West. A useful transfer to Europe of American surplus, with a small percentage of new equipment, was occurring under the Military Aid Program. But for an air defense against the growing Soviet strategic air force, with its atomic bombs, Europe still needed scores of fighter-interceptor squadrons, great quantities of antiaircraft guided missiles and guns, a complete air-warning net, bases and emplacements for all these weapons, and men to use them. None of these things existed or were being brought into being.

For a ground defense, Europe needed at least thirty divisions, with all their transport, tanks, antitank weapons and artillery, plus a powerful tactical air force to support the ground troops, plus mine fields and other fixed ground defenses in depth. Almost none of these things existed or were being brought into being, and the line where the ground forces would defend had not even been agreed upon.

Omitting such lesser problems as guarding the sea lanes, Europe finally needed some offensive striking power to balance her defensive forces. Yet the improvement of the Soviet air-defense system, and the continuing failure to build forward bases in North Africa and elsewhere, were daily impairing the effectiveness of our strategic air force. And nothing was being done about this either.

Indeed, in this time after the Korean attack, two years after the conception of the Atlantic Pact and eleven months after its ratification, the defenses of Europe can still be pretty completely summed up in a listing of the small allied occupation forces in Germany, plus the Swiss militia, plus the thirty divisions of Yugoslavia.

And this condition has been allowed to continue, without any serious attempt to remedy it, in the face of three truly awe-inspiring facts. This undefended Europe constitutes a flank of the free world just as exposed as the Middle and Far Eastern flanks and infinitely more important in the Kremlin world strategy. We, in the United States, are formally committed to defend this undefended Europe. And this Europe is the only area, except the United States, where new Western strength can be built up to protect the free world's troubled eastward extension.

Such have been the effects of Johnsonian "economy." It has been even less excusable than the disastrous stupidity that Baldwin and Chamberlain, Sir John Simon and Sir Horace Wilson committed against Britain in the 1930's. But the real question that confronts us now can be put in one sentence: What do we do?

What we do must be conditioned not only by the longer-range factors already described but also by the existing military situation. Here is where the Korean attack has, obviously, produced the most direct effects. For a long time the available forces of our major potential allies have been pretty completely tied down. Almost the whole French professional army has long been committed in Indo-China, leaving little strength even for the German occupation, while Britain's forces are thoroughly engaged, either in Germany or on ordinary but essential empire duties, as in the Middle East or in the antiguerrilla campaign in Malaya. This was less alarming while the forces of America were not committed. But because of our previous disarmament, the Korean attack has now required the total commitment, on this distant and difficult terrain, of all the existing free strength of the United States.

In contrast, except for the occupation army in Eastern Germany—which is in the hardest combat training—no important Soviet forces are committed anywhere. The new satellite armies are certainly sufficient to keep the slave populations in order. The whole Red Army, with all its numerous supporting arms, stands today disengaged, unchallenged and ready to be used tomorrow, if the Kremlin chooses, at any one of the numerous sensitive and strategic points where the Soviets have already indicated aggressive intentions. And in this situation of deadly peril, we further know that the Kremlin has adopted a world strategy aimed to bring all Eurasia within the Soviet Empire—

which will surely be the prelude to the establishment of a Stalinist One World.

Such is the debit side of the balance sheet, which is dark indeed. Perhaps the masters of the Kremlin may have yielded to the strong temptation of these facts; perhaps they will have struck again and again, even in the short interval before these words are printed. Meanwhile, the balance sheet's credit side also must be examined.

First, there is one element of American strength that is not as yet committed—the Strategic Air Force and the stock of atomic weapons. In these categories, the masters of the Kremlin still suffer from deficiencies, although they are working hard to overcome them. Moreover, although they are improving it rapidly, they have not as yet completed the air defense of their homeland. On the recent European trip of one of these reporters, a great British air leader remarked to him, "We may as well face it; there's going to be a very bad time, which we'll have to get through on nerve plus willingness to use atomic weapons if necessary." That time is now upon us.

Second, there is the incompleteness of Soviet war preparations. The effects of the unfinished state of Russian rearmament should not be overestimated; but they should not be ignored either. Besides the more obvious problems of atomic stocks and air defense, already mentioned, transport deficiencies, for example, must also be a powerful deterrent. In the present state of the East-West rail-and-road net, it is even hard to see how Russia could deploy in Western Europe the great armies that would be demanded by a general war.

Third—and this is the most important point of all—the men who should know best from long, firsthand experience, are convinced that a general war is the one thing Stalin and the Politburo still boggle at. The outcome must test the verdict of the experts. But it must be said that the expert view is supported by the nature of the Kremlin world strategy, so elaborately and astutely calculated to secure the effects of a gigantic victory in war by mere local operations, terror tactics and menaces. And it must be said also that the other arguments that the experts offer are equally convincing.

To trace these arguments in any detail would require a second report as long as this one. Suffice it to say that there are two main ones. The first concerns the instability of the slave base of the Soviet power pyramid. After the German attack on Russia, the Russian villages greeted the invaders with bread and salt. Russian men volunteered, literally in hundreds of thousands, to serve in German divisions. Indeed, there is a mass of evidence that Hitler might have used the Russians to beat Russia, if his folly of racism had not led him to proclaim the policy of scorched earth, which in turn stimulated and solidified the Russian resistance. And if this was the situation in the Soviet Union in 1941, what must be the conditions in the satellites today?

As for the second argument, it is founded on personal observation of Joseph Vissarionovich Stalin himself, by such men as W. Averell Harriman, Charles E. Bohlen and Harry L. Hopkins. To all of these, and to many other Americans and Englishmen who saw him in war-time, Stalin repeatedly confessed his bottomless respect for the American industrial potential, when it was mobilized. None of those who have heard him on this subject thinks that the dictator of the new Soviet Empire will wish to court a general war with a mobilized America, however glittering may be the promises of early triumph.

Here, of course, is the final, the conclusive, the quintessential part of Korea's grim lesson. We and the whole free world are in most dreadful danger because we, as leaders of the free world, have ignored the inherent menace of Soviet war preparation. We may hope that the existing deterrents may still operate, for a while, to prevent the further Soviet aggressions that could lead only to a third world war. But we must face the cruel fact that these deterrents will operate at all only if we show ourselves ready to fight Russia herself, if need be, in order to save the cause of freedom in the world. And we must face the further cruel fact that even if we show this willingness, the existing deterrents are, all of them, wasting assets, which will grow less and less effective as the Russian rearmament continues.

In this position to which our own folly has brought us, we have only one recourse. Everything that can conceivably contribute to the strength of the free world must now be done without hesitation, without question, without regard to politics or cost. Whether the need is to extend and improve our intelligence effort, or to set on foot a propaganda, by clandestine means if necessary, to defeat the Partisans of Peace, or to give massive aid to Yugoslavia or vastly to expand our military-aid program—it must be done.

Above all, the whole resources of this country and the whole available resources of our allies must now be mobilized fully and forthwith to rebuild with all speed a solid defense of the West. Even in the short time that is left to us, we can still hope to do the job if we go all out. But in this short time we cannot hope to rebuild the defenses of the West by the flaccid and comfortable methods of the pretended rearmament program that Stanley Baldwin offered Britain after the 1935 election. There will be comfort-loving, complacent souls who will plead for this; they must be dismissed with contempt.

Security for the free world cannot now be purchased cheaply. We must not only steel ourselves for a period of unnerving risks. We must also prepare for a period of heavy personal sacrifices. It is the only way. At least, it is the only way unless we prefer to indulge ourselves for a fugitive instant, and then to see the totalitarian silence and the night of the soul close over this world of ours.

47   DEMOCRACY'S WAY OUT*

Korea is a case history of the illness of our time. There, in the space of a few months, we have seen emerge in acute form all the symptoms of the inner conflict that is convulsing post-war society, and may end in its death. Only if the case is studied with detachment and its meaning put to use, here in America and elsewhere in the world, will society be able to make the adaptations needed for survival.

Korea revealed the basic distrust that existed between Soviet Russia and the West even in 1945. It is untrue to say that only gradually after the war did the Western powers give up their belief in Russia's friendly intentions. Matters have grown worse, but suspicion and latent hostility, dating not from the war but from 1919 and 1920, from 1938 and 1939, caused trouble as soon as the fighting ended. Suspicion and hostility on both sides fixed the line along the Thirty-eighth Parallel that cut Korea into two parts and ruined its chance of normal development. Because of the line and what it symbolized, the Korean people, from the beginning of their so-called liberation, were in bondage to the great rival powers that moved in when the Japanese moved out. This fact conditioned everything which followed.

Americans in the south and Russians in the north set up their contrary versions of "democracy." The Soviet zone reproduced faithfully the pattern established in North China—distribution of land, liquidation of usurers and landlords who resisted the new order, speedy abolition of various old servitudes. A good deal of local self-government was permitted, giving the people who benefited from the revolution a sense of sharing in the running of their own affairs. But

*Freda Kirchwey, "Democracy's Way Out," *Nation*, Vol. CLXXI (December 16, 1950), pp. 622–25, 645.

on top control was tight and tough, and while the Russians kept in the background far more than the Americans did in the south, policy-making was in the hands of men who took their orders from Moscow.

The United States zone reflected the manifold confusions of American foreign policy. At the start the generals in charge displayed a high disregard for the political wishes of the people. A provisional Korean government representing numerous parties was brushed out of the window. And while political parties were permitted, elections planned, democratic safeguards ordained on paper, the old reactionary nationalist leader Syngman Rhee, established in power against the better judgment of a few sensible American officials, was allowed to use the Japanese-trained police to suppress opposition on the left. Numerous liberal-to-left parties that leapt into existence were smashed or driven under ground, active Communists were arrested or killed, along with many moderates who couldn't swallow the Rhee dictatorship. Political assassination became a commonplace. The first election was a stop-gap affair that did not pretend to be representative. The second, under U.N. observation, was worse because it did make such claims. The police terror that preceded it and the absence of left parties and candidates turned it into a bloody farce. The result of the first fairly free election, held in the spring of 1950, was a sweeping repudiation of Syngman Rhee's regime. A limited land reform, forced through by the military government, was still to be put into effect when war struck last summer.

These two political emanations of the Russian and American spirit are symptoms to be studied, for they provide clues to the troubles that soon developed. The Communist blend of reform, social overturn, and popular participation at the "rice roots" under top-level party dictatorship produced, as it has done elsewhere, a tight political texture. It is self-deceiving to pretend that the tyranny inherent in such a set-up promptly breeds disaffection, or that the revolution is just a hoax. The important fact is that, whatever Russia's ultimate purposes may be, *its interests are promoted rather than interfered with by revolutionary change.* With no stake in the survival of free enterprise, it can consolidate its power in the very process of satisfying the most urgent social and economic desires of the majority. Those who get hurt are the few, especially in countries like Korea, with primitive standards of living and of political action.

The American experience offers different clues. Handed a job like the occupation of Korea, Americans, especially military men, have small patience with ideology. Only a few know much about the people they have been sent to rule. Dominated usually by the single desire to get the job done and get out, their tendency is to install, by rule of thumb, certain prescribed democratic procedures and, beyond that, to rely on those local elements most likely to keep everything under control. No technique could be better designed to give a shrewd, landlord-minded politician like Syngman Rhee a free field in which to carry out a program of planned repression under the camouflage of democratic forms—and in doing so to make the name of America a stench in the nostrils of Asia.

The meaning of it all boils down to this: In the present stage of American political development we seem almost incapable of doing what needs to be done in countries ripe for revolution. Where drastic reforms groove smoothly into the policy aims of Russia, they cut across the grain of normal American thinking and interests. To force the rapid expropriation of land, to oust a corrupt, oppressive ruling class, to give power to popular leaders: this would seem reckless, immoral, a surrender to the enemy. And behind these inhibitions is the most damaging one of all—the idea that small brown or yellow people are objects of contempt or, at best, of humorous benevolence; in a word, Gooks.

Perhaps this is the deepest reason for the collapse of the American case in Asia.

The creation of two governments — one at Seoul, the other at Pyongyang—deepened the wound in Korea. Not only did each reproduce the forms and policies favored by its sponsor; each also mirrored the conflict between them. The departure of the occupying forces in 1949 made no difference; the pattern was set by that time. Both North and South knew that reunion was Korea's single hope, but in terms of the cold war reunion could only mean conquest of one by the other. Both used accepted cold-war tactics—denunciations, spying, lies, propaganda overtures, border raids. The fact that Syngman Rhee's regime had been left too weak to indulge in dreams of military glory did not discourage him from threatening North Korea with attack. Kim Il-sung's northern government, with more to back its play, made similar threats. Both sides staged forays across the Thirty-eighth Parallel, but in this the Communist regime was by far the worst offender, according to the U.N. Commission on Korea. Almost a year before the invasion of last June, observant correspondents, including Andrew Roth in *The Nation,* reported that war between North and South was only a matter of months. When the blow fell, only the United States military mission at Seoul seems to have been taken by surprise.

That the North's attack was an "aggression" is disputed only by Communists and their backers. It was an aggression because the Thirty-eighth Parallel, agreed upon by the occupying powers, was also recognized de facto by both Korean regimes. It was an accepted boundary, crossed by the northern army in force. But to say this and nothing more is again to blur meanings. For the attack was more than an aggression; it was also an act of civil war and revolution. Its roots lay in the political conflict that dominated Korea's whole existence.

Shortly before the North Korean army started south, Pyongyang sent a "peace" delegation to Seoul with proposals for reuniting the country through joint action by democratic groups and parties on both sides. According to Communist semantics, this offer may have been in effect an ultimatum: either union and peace on our terms, or else. Whatever it meant, it was not answered. Instead, the emissaries were thrown into prison without charge or trial.

The incident was mentioned in a report from the U.N. Commission on Korea, but no great point was made of it. War washed over South Korea, drowning out minor overtures and instigations. I recall it here not to minimize the aggressive nature of the North Korean attack but to point up its internal, revolutionary aspect. By Syngman Rhee the delegates from the north were regarded—and treated—not as foreign envoys but as native subversives.

And so when the United States and the United Nations moved with unprecedented vigor to check aggression by one state against another, they stepped into the midst of a piece of the Asian revolution. The fact of revolution altered the meaning and effect of the U.N. action from the start. Although military sanctions, proposed by the Americans, won the support of the great majority of members and United States initiative was applauded, especially in Europe, as an indication that Russian-inspired aggression would be challenged no matter where it occurred, the political implications of the decision worried many leaders in non-Communist countries. They realized that a precedent might be in the making which could later be used to justify U.N. sanctions in case of rebellion — described as Russian-inspired—against a colonial power or an oppressive national regime. The nature and behavior of the American-made South Korean government threw doubt on American purposes, and this feeling was augmented by our unilateral "insulation" of Formosa and our refusal to recognize the Peking government. When MacArthur flew to Formosa and issued his unauthorized pronouncement in support of Chiang Kai-shek, suspicion was turned into open criticism, which was not wholly silenced by Mr. Truman's repudiation of the General's remarks. Political worries multiplied as the U.N. forces pushed the Communists back across the Thirty-eighth Parallel, ignoring India's warning that the Chinese had threatened to attack if the war moved into North Korea.

Then MacArthur permitted Syngman Rhee, in defiance of U.N. orders, to take over the administration of liberated areas in the north. For some reason American newspapers, in spite of their impressive bulk, gave little space to this story. But the facts were reported fully in the meager European press; even conservative papers described the hasty, brutal liquidation of supporters of the northern regime by Rhee's police—still the same Japanese-trained force—and by members of his youth organization, a semi-military, wholly fascist body, who were sent north to handle the job of "political reeducation." Farmland was actually restored to the former landlords, and the machinery of revolution set in reverse.

It was a policy hardly calculated to convert North Koreans to Western democratic ideals. Once more, a military action—the drive into North Korea—took on political meanings, only dimly discerned in this country, which touched off sharp reactions among politically conscious Europeans and Asians.

In Washington, even at Lake Success, the belief that China would intervene was generally discounted as the drive toward the northern frontier continued and the North Korean army began to crumble. Even when the first Chinese made an appearance, their presence was minimized, by MacArthur as well as the uninformed public. It was not until the Chinese avalanche began to gather bulk and momentum that questions were raised about the Yalu River power plants, and Mr. Truman and Mr. Lie broadcast hasty reassurances to Peking. By then, assuming time had anything to do with the matter, it was too late.

Whether the Chinese would have gone in if MacArthur had stopped at the Thirty-eighth Parallel, whether they would have launched their great counter-offensive if he had not begun his end-the-war drive on Thanksgiving Day—these questions will be debated long after today's bitter tea has been drunk. But most of the debates will leave out considerations that should be weighed, both to place responsibility for what has happened and, more important, to provide guidance in the future.

When Foreign Minister Chou En-lai, on October 1, said China would not tolerate an attack on North Korea, it may have been eyewash. Perhaps China would have invaded Korea anyhow, though it is hard to see why, in that case, Chou bothered to give the warning. But if MacArthur had stopped at the Thirty-eighth Parallel and declared his mission successfully accomplished, calling for a cease-fire and leaving the task of winding up the war to the new U.N. commission, then an invasion by China would have met solid disapproval throughout the free world. Even if MacArthur, having crossed the border on the say-so of the U.N., had sternly prohibited political reprisals and sent Syngman Rhee's "administrators" back to Seoul he would still have kept the record fairly straight. At least it would not have been so dismally compounded of military and political error as to allow China to claim the sympathy of Asia and a fair part of the rest of the non-Communist world.

I asked an Asian leader at the United Nations whether the successful Chinese drive would not frighten the peoples of Asia. He replied: A success for MacArthur would frighten them more. I said: The terrible meaning of what you say is that faith in the United Nations has been undermined by American policy in Korea. He answered: It was not only America. The other nations acquiesced at critical moments when they should have said no. Their responsibility is in one way greater, for they understand better than America the power and significance of the revolutionary drive in Asia.

Korea is a case history in which one can trace the course of democracy's defeat. Today that defeat is being written in the language of military disaster, and one would be foolish to pretend that the political process described in these pages is the whole story. It is merely the part of the story that is generally left out or distorted by illusions and preconceived ideas. How the present crisis can be surmounted—what agreement may be reached or whether any agreement is possible—is a question beyond the scope of this article. It will be answered in terms of the bargaining position of the contending powers. But unless the meaning of Korea for the rest of the world is understood by the West—by America in particular—the end of the United Nations is in sight, and the prospect of an effective coalition of free nations may as well be abandoned.

First, we must accept revolution as the dominant, inescapable fact of our time. Call it a fever, an infection, anything you want. Certainly it is contagious, but it can spring out of unhealthy local conditions too. It appears in different forms, in varying intensities, depending largely on the economic state of the area affected. Where conditions are really bad, as in Korea, the disease cannot be halted by minor remedies—elections, constitutions, a "recovery" program. Nor can it be cured by methods of suppression, though these are universally popular with political witch-doctors such as Syngman Rhee. In a country like Korea, or in other countries covering two-thirds of the globe, revolution must run its course, helped by radical measures to correct the systemic disbalance which caused it in the first place, and by ameliorative measures to prevent convulsive symptoms likely to cause death.

Images get boring. In plain nonmedical language, Korea proves that when the United States uses its power to prevent revolution where revolution is inevitable, it sets its feet on a road that leads directly toward war. Korea proves that the United Nations will reduce its capacity to stop aggression in the degree to which it permits itself to be used as an instrument of counter-revolution.

Korea proves that the only way this country can help organize a free world possessing enough power to deal on equal terms with Russia—and with Moscow-ruled communism—is to put our own strength behind the forces of change. We must become, and quickly, the new sponsor of revolution, helping the peoples of the world to win all that communism promises or provides—plus liberty.

If we can learn this lesson fast enough we still have a chance to snatch peace out of war and victory out of defeat. For despite Korea, it is most unlikely that Russia and China are set to conquer the rest of Europe and Asia by force of arms. The assumption that they are, now so generally accepted, is a natural product of panic and dismay—but it has little solid evidence behind it. The attack on Korea certainly was *not* designed in advance as a trap for American manpower. On the contrary, there is every indication that no serious resistance was expected, inside or out; South Korea, as the record shows, was expected to fall of its own weakness with no more than an armed "assist" from above the border. Korea, in fact, offers better evidence that Russia and China intend to expand their areas of control, where possible, by exploiting situations ready-made for revolution. The Communist powers would be foolish indeed to invite the vast destruction of atomic war; far better to bide their time and let events, and American policy, prepare the ground for a revolution they can shape and direct.

This prospect is not limited to the underdeveloped areas of Asia. It embraces Europe as well, and eventually will include Latin America. The challenge it presents to this country is a sharp one, for it calls for a drastic overhauling of our foreign policy in the direction of more courageous, aggressive democracy, at a time when the unthinking reactions of people and politicians clamor for the opposite.

We must, if we are to seize a chance which may indeed be the last, rediscover our own democratic beliefs, lost somewhere in the compromises of these years of shifting expediencies. Talk about defending freedom has a hollow ring when we plan to include among its defenders a shoddy leftover like Chiang Kai-shek or the German generals; such cynicism denies us the backing of those who might put some zeal into the job of fighting even for survival. We ditch our professed principles, and along with them goes our security.

The criticisms and positive proposals contained in this issue offer a concrete basis for a policy which might reintegrate our democratic strength. The chance of negotiating a settlement with Russia depends as much upon such political "situations of strength" as upon the frantic effort at mechanical unification and rearmament that has so far borne so little fruit. Let our government turn now to the task of carrying out a Point Four program that is related not only to the magnitude of the need but to the even more necessary attack upon feudal and colonial power; let it risk greatly to build up and stabilize democratic institutions in the newly free areas of Asia; let it reverse its despairing decision to restore German fighting power—at the cost of popular confidence in Western Europe and legitimate panic in the East. By drastic means such as these we can repair the damage our nation has suffered in its own eyes and those of the world and, with renewed hope, begin to apply those positive plans for the peaceful reorganization of the world so ably outlined in this final section.

VI

THE COLD WAR

1953-1965

the question of coexistence

The Death of Stalin

The election of Dwight D. Eisenhower to the Presidency in 1952 ended the 20-year Democratic control of the White House. But this change mattered far less to the development of Soviet-American relations than the end, several months later, of a much longer reign. Premier Stalin died in March, 1953, after dictating Soviet policies for almost 30 years. To most American observers, the coincidental change in leadership of the world's foremost powers signaled the possibility of a new era in the Cold War.

The following selections portray a variety of positions toward the USSR shortly after Stalin's death. The first selection reprints a notable address by Eisenhower one month later. The two subsequent articles present the prevailing view among liberals and conservatives respectively. (At the end of 1954, by the way, David Lawrence was calling for a severance of American diplomatic relations with Russia.)

48 A PRECIOUS CHANCE*

In this spring of 1953 the free world weighs one question above all others: the chance for a just peace for all peoples.

To weigh this chance is to summon instantly to mind another recent moment of great decision. It came with that yet more hopeful spring of 1945, bright with the promise of victory and of freedom. The hope of all just men in that moment, too, was a just and lasting peace.

The 8 years that have passed have seen that hope waver, grow dim, and almost die. And the shadow of fear again has darkly lengthened across the world.

Today the hope of free men remains stubborn and brave, but it is sternly disciplined by experience. It shuns not only all crude counsel of despair but also the self-deceit of easy illusion. It weighs the chance for peace with sure, clear knowledge of what happened to the vain hope of 1945.

In that spring of victory the soldiers of the Western Allies met the soldiers of Russia in the center of Europe. They were triumphant comrades in arms. Their peoples shared the joyous prospect of building, in honor of their dead, the only fitting monument—an age of just peace. All these war-weary peoples shared, too, this concrete, decent purpose: to guard vigilantly against the domination ever again of any part of the world by a single, unbridled aggressive power.

This common purpose lasted an instant and perished. The nations of the world divided to follow two distinct roads.

The United States and our valued friends, the other free nations, chose one road.

The leaders of the Soviet Union chose another.

The way chosen by the United States was plainly marked by a few clear precepts, which govern its conduct in world affairs.

First: No people on earth can be held, as a people, to be an enemy, for all humanity shares the common hunger for peace and fellowship and justice.

Second: No nation's security and well-being can be lastingly achieved in isolation but only in effective cooperation with fellow-nations.

---

*Dwight D. Eisenhower, "Address before the American Society of Newspaper Editors, Washington, April 16, 1953," reprinted in *Documents on American Foreign Relations: 1953,* Peter V. Curl (ed.) (New York: Harper & Bros., for the Council on Foreign Relations, 1954), pp. 27-34.

Third: Any nation's right to a form of government and an economic system of its own choosing is *inalienable*.

Fourth: Any nation's attempt to dictate to other nations their form of government is *indefensible*.

And fifth: A nation's hope of lasting peace cannot be firmly based upon any race in armaments but rather upon just relations and honest understanding with all other nations.

In the light of these principles the citizens of the United States defined the way they proposed to follow, through the aftermath of war, toward true peace.

This way was faithful to the spirit that inspired the United Nations: to prohibit strife, to relieve tensions, to banish fears. This way was to control and to reduce armaments. This way was to allow all nations to devote their energies and resources to the great and good tasks of healing the war's wounds, of clothing and feeding and housing the needy, of perfecting a just political life, of enjoying the fruits of their own free toil.

The Soviet government held a vastly different vision of the future.

In the world of its design, security was to be found, not in mutual trust and mutual aid but in *force:* huge armies, subversion, rule of neighbor nations. The goal was power superiority at all cost. Security was to be sought by denying it to all others.

The result has been tragic for the world and, for the Soviet Union, it has also been ironic.

The amassing of Soviet power alerted free nations to a new danger of aggression. It compelled them in self-defense to spend unprecedented money and energy for armaments. It forced them to develop weapons of war now capable of inflicting instant and terrible punishment upon any aggressor.

It instilled in the free nations—and let none doubt this—the unshakable conviction that, as long as there persists a threat to freedom, they must, at any cost, remain armed, strong, and ready for the risk of war.

It inspired them—and let none doubt this—to attain a unity of purpose and will beyond the power of propaganda or pressure to break, now or ever.

There remained, however, one thing essentially unchanged and unaffected by Soviet conduct: the readiness of the free nations to welcome sincerely any genuine evidence of peaceful purpose enabling all peoples again to resume their common quest of just peace.

The free nations, most solemnly and repeatedly, have assured the

Soviet Union that their firm association has never had any aggressive purpose whatsoever. Soviet leaders, however, have seemed to persuade themselves, or tried to persuade their people, otherwise.

And so it has come to pass that the Soviet Union itself has shared and suffered the very fears it has fostered in the rest of the world.

This has been the way of life forged by 8 years of fear and force.

What can the world, or any nation in it, hope for if no turning is found on this dread road?

The worst to be feared and the best to be expected can be simply stated.

The *worst* is atomic war.

The *best* would be this: a life of perpetual fear and tension; a burden of arms draining the wealth and the labor of all peoples; a wasting of strength that defies the American system or the Soviet system or any system to achieve true abundance and happiness for the peoples of this earth.

Every gun that is made, every warship launched, every rocket fired signifies, in the final sense, a theft from those who hunger and are not fed, those who are cold and are not clothed.

This world in arms is not spending money alone.

It is spending the sweat of its laborers, the genius of its scientists, the hopes of its children.

The cost of one modern heavy bomber is this: a modern brick school in more than 30 cities.

It is two electric power plants, each serving a town of 60,000 population.

It is two fine, fully equipped hospitals.

It is some 50 miles of concrete highway.

We pay for a single fighter plane with a half million bushels of wheat.

We pay for a single destroyer with new homes that could have housed more than 8,000 people.

This, I repeat, is the best way of life to be found on the road the world has been taking.

This is not a way of life at all, in any true sense. Under the cloud of threatening war, it is humanity hanging from a cross of iron.

These plain and cruel truths define the peril and point the hope that come with this spring of 1953.

This is one of those times in the affairs of nations when the gravest choices must be made, if there is to be a turning toward a just and lasting peace.

It is a moment that calls upon the governments of the world to speak their intentions with simplicity and with honesty.

It calls upon them to answer the question that stirs the hearts of all sane men: *is there no other way the world may live?*

The world knows that an era ended with the death of Joseph Stalin. The extraordinary 30-year span of his rule saw the Soviet Empire expand to reach from the Baltic Sea to the Sea of Japan, finally to dominate 800 million souls.

The Soviet system shaped by Stalin and his predecessors was born of one World War. It survived with stubborn and often amazing courage a second World War. It has lived to threaten a third.

Now a new leadership has assumed power in the Soviet Union. Its links to the past, however strong, cannot bind it completely. Its future is, in great part, its own to make.

This new leadership confronts a free world aroused, as rarely in its history, by the will to stay free.

This free world knows, out of the bitter wisdom of experience, that vigilance and sacrifice are the price of liberty.

It knows that the defense of Western Europe imperatively demands the unity of purpose and action made possible by the North Atlantic Treaty Organization, embracing a European Defense Community.

It knows that Western Germany deserves to be a free and equal partner in this community and that this, for Germany, is the only safe way to full, final unity.

It knows that aggression in Korea and in southeast Asia are threats to the whole free community to be met by united action.

This is the kind of free world which the new Soviet leadership confronts. It is a world that demands and expects the fullest respect of its rights and interests. It is a world that will always accord the same respect to all others.

So the new Soviet leadership now has a precious opportunity to awaken, with the rest of the world, to the point of peril reached and to help turn the tide of history.

Will it do this?

We do not yet know. Recent statements and gestures of Soviet leaders give some evidence that they may recognize this critical moment.

We welcome every honest act of peace.

We care nothing for mere rhetoric.

We are only for sincerity of peaceful purpose attested by deeds. The opportunities for such deeds are many. The performance of a great number of them waits upon no complex protocol but upon the simple will to do them. Even a few such clear and specific acts, such as the Soviet Union's signature upon an Austrian treaty or its release of thousands of prisoners still held from World War II, would be impressive signs of sincere intent. They would carry a power of persuasion not to be matched by any amount of oratory.

This we do know: a world that begins to witness the rebirth of trust among nations *can* find its way to a peace that is neither partial nor punitive.

With all who will work in good faith toward such a peace, we are ready, with renewed resolve, to strive to redeem the near-lost hopes of our day.

The first great step along this way must be the conclusion of an honorable armistice in Korea.

This means the immediate cessation of hostilities and the prompt initiation of political discussions leading to the holding of free elections in a united Korea.

It should mean, no less importantly, an end to the direct and indirect attacks upon the security of Indochina and Malaya. For any armistice in Korea that merely released aggressive armies to attack elsewhere would be a fraud.

We seek, throughout Asia as throughout the world, a peace that is true and total.

Out of this can grow a still wider task—the achieving of just political settlements for the other serious and specific issues between the free world and the Soviet Union.

None of these issues, great or small, is insoluble—given only the will to respect the rights of all nations.

Again we say: the United States is ready to assume its just part.

We have already done all within our power to speed conclusion of a treaty with Austria, which will free that country from economic exploitation and from occupation by foreign troops.

We are ready not only to press forward with the present plans for closer unity of the nations of Western Europe but also, upon that foundation, to strive to foster a broader European community, conducive to the free movement of persons, of trade, and of ideas.

This community would include a free and united Germany, with a government based upon free and secret elections.

This free community and the full independence of the East European nations could mean the end of the present unnatural division of Europe.

As progress in all these areas strengthens world trust, we could proceed concurrently with the next great work—the reduction of the burden of armaments now weighing upon the world. To this end we would welcome and enter into the most solemn agreements. These could properly include:

1. The limitation, by absolute numbers or by an agreed international ratio, of the sizes of the military and security forces of all nations.
2. A commitment by all nations to set an agreed limit upon that proportion of total production of certain strategic materials to be devoted to military purposes.
3. International control of atomic energy to promote its use for peaceful purposes only and to insure the prohibition of atomic weapons.
4. A limitation or prohibition of other categories of weapons of great destructiveness.
5. The enforcement of all these agreed limitations and prohibitions by adequate safeguards, including a practical system of inspection under the United Nations.

The details of such disarmament programs are manifestly critical and complex. Neither the United States nor any other nation can properly claim to possess a perfect, immutable formula. But the formula matters less than the faith—the good faith without which no formula can work justly and effectively.

The fruit of success in all these tasks would present the world with the greatest task, and the greatest opportunity, of all. It is this: the dedication of the energies, the resources, and the imaginations of all peaceful nations to a new kind of war. This would be a declared total war, not upon any human enemy but upon the brute forces of poverty and need.

The peace we seek, founded upon decent trust and cooperative effort among nations, can be fortified, not by weapons of war but by wheat and by cotton, by milk and by wool, by meat and by timber and by rice. These are words that translate into every language on earth. These are needs that challenge this world in arms.

This idea of a just and peaceful world is not new or strange to us. It inspired the people of the United States to initiate the European Recovery Program in 1947. That program was prepared to treat, with like and equal concern, the needs of Eastern and Western Europe.

We are prepared to reaffirm, with the most concrete evidence, our readiness to help build a world in which all peoples can be productive and prosperous.

This Government is ready to ask its people to join with all nations in devoting a substantial percentage of the savings achieved by disarmament to a fund for world aid and reconstruction. The purposes of this great work would be to help other peoples to develop the undeveloped areas of the world, to stimulate profitable and fair world trade, to assist all peoples to know the blessings of productive freedom.

The monuments to this new kind of war would be these: roads and schools, hospitals and homes, food and health.

We are ready, in short, to dedicate our strength to serving the *needs,* rather than the *fears,* of the world.

We are ready, by these and all such actions, to make of the United Nations an institution that can effectively guard the peace and security of all peoples.

I know of nothing I can add to make plainer the sincere purpose of the United States.

I know of no course, other than that marked by these and similar actions, that can be called the highway of peace.

I know of only one question upon which progress waits. It is this:

What is the Soviet Union ready to do?

Whatever the answer be, let it be plainly spoken.

Again we say: the hunger for peace is too great, the hour in history too late, for any government to mock men's hopes with mere words and promises and gestures.

The test of truth is simple. There can be no persuasion but by deeds.

Is the new leadership of the Soviet Union prepared to use its decisive influence in the Communist world, including control of the flow of arms, to bring not merely an expedient truce in Korea but genuine peace in Asia?

Is it prepared to allow other nations, including those of Eastern Europe, the free choice of their own forms of government?

Is it prepared to act in concert with others upon serious disarmament proposals to be made firmly effective by stringent U.N. control and inspection?

If not, where then is the concrete evidence of the Soviet Union's concern for peace?

The test is clear.

There is, before all peoples, a precious chance to turn the black tide of events. If we failed to strive to seize this chance, the judgment of future ages would be harsh and just.

If we strive but fail and the world remains armed against itself, it at least need be divided no longer in its clear knowledge of who has condemned humankind to this fate.

The purpose of the United States, in stating these proposals, is simple and clear.

These proposals spring, without ulterior purpose or political passion, from our calm conviction that the hunger for peace is in the hearts of all peoples—those of Russia and of China no less than of our own country.

They conform to our firm faith that God created men to enjoy, not destroy, the fruits of the earth and of their own toil.

They aspire to this: the lifting, from the backs and from the hearts of men, of their burden of arms and of fears, so that they may find before them a golden age of freedom and of peace.

49 ACCOMMODATION*

President Eisenhower's speech to the newspaper editors might have been delivered by Henry Wallace or by Dean Acheson. That is its greatness, and also its weakness.

The greatness of the speech lies in Eisenhower's assumption of world leadership—the one unique and sound reason for his Presidency. He commits this nation, as Wallace, Acheson, Truman and Stevenson could not, to the responsibilities and the restraints which offer our best hope for peace.

In this speech the combination of arrogance and isolationism which dominated Republican attitudes in opposition is absent. The leader of the party whose right-wing equated negotiation and appeasement, moderation and subversion lays aside the flaming promises of "liberation" and *Life's* insistence that peace lies beyond the annihilation of the Soviet state. He declares that it is the imperial expansion of Soviet Communism and not its internal order that threatens war. He calls for the withdrawal of Soviet forces to their legitimate frontiers, not for the destruction of the Soviet regime. He insists that no issue between the free world and the Soviet world is insoluble. He calls for a peace that is "neither partial nor punitive," and fortified "not by weapons of war but by wheat and by cotton; by milk and by wool; by meat and timber and rice."

This general approach should mark the transition of a major party from irresponsible opposition to acceptance of national responsibility. But does it? The Russians—and others—will ask: Is Eisenhower really speaking for his party in Congress, in the press, throughout the

* "Eisenhower's Speech—the Greatness and Weakness," *New Republic,* Vol. CXXVIII (April 27, 1953), pp. 5-7. Reprinted by permission of THE NEW REPUBLIC, © 1953, Harrison-Blaine of New Jersey, Inc.

nation? He calls on the Russians for deeds, not words. But can he advance his own peace program from words to deeds?

The new Administration has no plans to support Eisenhower's offers on Korea and Indo-China. The Pentagon would explode if the Russians should indicate acceptance of Eisenhower's proposal to return to world control of atomic energy and all armaments. The Congress has no intention of lowering tariff barriers to move the wool and the timber, the cotton and the meat on which the world's peace is to be fortified.

Eisenhower calls for deeds, not words. But what is the world to conclude when in the same week in which Eisenhower stated: "We are prepared to reaffirm with the most concrete evidence our readiness to help build a world in which all peoples can be productive and prosperous" he turns down the low bid from Britain for electrical equipment, in support of the Buy American Act?

Eisenhower's Administration promises world prosperity but foresees at best the extension of the feeble trade agreements program. It calls on the Russians to recognize human dignity in all lands, but acts to abandon the Covenant of Human Rights. It seeks to lift the Iron Curtain at Leningrad, but leaves lowered the bars at Ellis Island. While it holds forth the promise of Point Four in happier days, it moves to kill Point Four, now when it counts most.

Eisenhower's speech is important, because his views carry in the government as Truman's never did. Yet the majority of his appointments are of men to whom the philosophy of the April 16 speech is repugnant. Eisenhower's victory over Russian extremism is foreseen in the speech; his battle with Republican extremism has yet to be acknowledged. The speech is regarded as a challenge to the Russians; it is in fact a challenge to the United States.

II

The greatness of the speech is the challenge; its weakness is that the challenge is presented in the framework of the Crusade. For the Crusade marches in the moral realm which Wallace and Acheson shared: the world of good and bad faith; the struggle of right and wrong followed by the conversion; the agreement to be friends; the vision of living happily ever after as crusaders and infidels unite to do good works. There is no such world, and if there is to be peace, it will draw nearer by smaller and less dramatic steps.

Eisenhower is elected to represent America's national interest—an attitude shaped by our geography and economy, our culture and our faith. It is a fair assumption that the Soviet leaders regard themselves as the responsible defenders of Russia's national interest, dominated far more than we like to assume by the same historical forces. Russia's national interest differs from ours and will continue to differ. Now, as always, the aim of diplomacy is to bring the formal attributes of sovereignty into accord with the realities of power and the accepted concepts of justice, and to resolve without the tensions caused by change.

Between the free world and the Soviet world there are deep ideological divisions. But they are not the root cause of the conflicts of the postwar years which have been crystallized and perhaps prolonged by the term *Cold War*. In prewar years the Russians prepared to accelerate and take advantage of the breakdown they regarded as inevitable in other societies. Their efforts caused only marginal conflicts until the war. Then the suicidal aggressiveness of Germany and Japan and the bankruptcy of the Nationalist regime in China opened up huge areas that invited intervention. So the Russians intervened, and so we checked them. The check was limited but violent. It leaves like a scar the suspicion that there is no basis of compromise with the Russians because what is right for them is thereby wrong for us. That leaves a world of tremendous tensions; of apocalyptic wars or sweeping change followed by a wholly altered time. That is the world of Eisenhower's speech. And yet the truth is that tensions will be lowered not by grandiose settlements but by unpretentious and continuous accommodations. For there are times when it is mutually advantageous for adversaries to reach agreement, even if the agreements are in the nature of bets on the final outcome of the contest.

If accommodations are reached, that does not mean that trickery is ended. Always and naturally the Soviet leaders will act in good faith and in bad faith, honoring agreements which are realistic and hitting whenever we are stupid enough to leave ourselves open to the punch. We are now like two wrestlers locked in a body scissor and a toe hold. One, to make the fight more flexible, moves to disengage. That doesn't mean that he kneels to kiss his adversary, nor that, if given the opportunity, he will not thrust a knee in his opponent's groin. But because one wrestler moves to disengage, the other does not conclude that the deadlock must be maintained.

The Soviet regime is overextended and beset by internal disputes. For this reason the Soviet leaders may have concluded that it is in their interests to settle for a truce in Korea or even to seek agreement in Germany or Austria. These agreements alone would not lead to disarmament; every loophole in every treaty would be exploited against us; the agreements would continue only as long as they reflect the balance of power. And yet they would be useful in reducing tensions.

The conflicts concerning Germany and Japan (of which Korea is a reflection) are military and territorial. For that reason they are, in theory, subject to practical accommodations. But the accommodations will not be concluded by the Soviet leaders at Russia's sole expense.

Yet that is what President Eisenhower, when he moves from his general approach to his varied proposals, is asking.

In Korea, Eisenhower proposes free elections for a unified Korea. Apart from the unreality of free elections in a shattered nation, his proposal amounts to a call for surrender which the Chinese and Russians are not likely to accept. Korea is the military highway to China, and its northern border is a sensitive Soviet frontier. Japan discovered that she could influence only as much of the mainland as she was ready to occupy with her own armies. We plan to withdraw and yet retain, in the free world, territory we have not been able to gain in the Korean War.

In Eastern Europe, Eisenhower proposes to put democracy and Communism on open trial in free elections. Following the victory of strongly anti-Soviet émigré groups at the polls, so we assume, the Russians are to put their tails between their legs and retire to lick their wounds. When they can be driven in this manner from Warsaw, they can be driven from Moscow as well.

In Germany Eisenhower proposes free elections to bring into being a united and sovereign Germany. The new Germany will then be free to join a military alliance led by the United States. There is no indication that if Soviet troops should retire to their own frontiers U.S. troops would also withdraw. What incentive then is there for the Russians to conclude these accommodations? While Eisenhower rejects unconditional surrender as a general war aim, he is in fact demanding unconditional surrender in Korea, Eastern Europe and Germany, and without a military victory.

And Eisenhower knows this! Yet, he cannot offer compromises because the speech is directed to America as well as to Russia and his own party in America would repudiate him. He cannot indicate that NATO is ultimately expendable, and that American troops must someday retire from continental Europe, because to do so now would bring Europe's rearmament to a halt and might send her governments in panic to the Russian side.

Eisenhower has rightly committed our government to a limited objective—the withdrawal of the Russian armies behind Russia's frontiers. It will never be obtained by screaming headlines and overdramatized elections. To the Soviet leaders, this kind of setback would be worse than war. The only possible method of achieving Eisenhower's objective is to make the reduction in Russia's political influence in Eastern Europe as gradual, as unobtrusive, as devoid of outward triumphs as possible.

To pursue this patient and quiet course is difficult for any Administration. But it is possible for Eisenhower given his widespread support. It will not leave the Soviet leaders wondering which of his paragraphs are aimed at them and which at his fellow Republicans or domestic minority groups. It will help to convince our allies that this nation can fulfill its world responsibilities without the nervous compulsions aroused by alternatives of a new Garden of Eden or cataclysmic war.

50   THE BIG ILLUSION *

No finer example of American idealism has been presented to the world in our times than the address delivered last week by President Eisenhower before the United Nations General Assembly.[1] It won approval instantly from governments throughout the world, with the exception of the Communist governments at Moscow and Peiping.

But the illusion in the address was its euphemistic premise—that the present government in Moscow is a decent, respectable agent of the people of Soviet Russia, a government worthy of trust, a government capable of negotiating agreements that would be honored by the Soviets.

The simple truth is that the government at Moscow is an unmoral instrument, possessing for the moment the power to mislead hundreds of millions of persons behind the Iron Curtain.

It is often argued that we might as well talk and confer with the Soviet Government, and then, if the Communists spurn our pro-

---

*David Lawrence, "The Big Illusion," reprinted from *U.S. News and World Report,* Vol. XXXV (December 18, 1953), p. 128. Copyright 1953 U.S. News & World Report, Inc.

[1] Editor's note: He proposed that nuclear nations give atomic materials to an international atomic agency for use in peaceful projects.

posals, we will at least know—and the world will know—who is obstructing peace.

What a naive approach! It is as if we haven't had countless pieces of evidence for several years now that the leopard doesn't change its spots. Actually, by our continued conferences we are building up the prestige of the Malenkov government inside Russia. By treating it as an equal, we glorify its standing and strengthen its internal position.

What advantage is there in acting as if the other person were not a criminal—imagining the devil to be a person of innate virtue and of good conscience? Are criminals rehabilitated before or after they have served a term of ostracism imposed by the other members of society?

The fact is that evil is not redressed or eradicated by ignoring its existence. When there are gangsters in the city, we do not "negotiate" with them. There can be no "peaceful coexistence" with criminals. No churchman that we can recall ever rose to defend "coexistence" when some citizens argued that red light districts in our cities should remain because they were segregated and hence did not hurt the main residence districts.

"Peaceful coexistence" as a slogan in the world situation today is a mockery. It is only an alibi for moral cowardice.

Significantly enough, the President in his speech pointed to the danger of a "surprise aggression." He was certainly not referring to any government in the free world. He wisely served warning that the immense atomic power of America would be swiftly and resolutely used in retaliation if such an aggression occurred. He told the people of Soviet Russia what a terrible fate awaited them if their rulers ever chose to make the awful mistake of starting an aggressive war.

These words, however, by themselves can at this time do little more than assist our propaganda campaign as against the Communist propaganda in the "cold war." Sooner or later we must face squarely the big illusion. We must recognize that it is impossible to continue diplomatic relations with a gangster government in Moscow. The people of Soviet Russia must be told in unequivocal language that the peoples of the rest of the world are waiting for them to set up a free government.

For, while it is axiomatic that neither this country nor any international organization should tell a sovereign people what form of government they shall have, it is also fundamental that any form of government which is a menace to world peace cannot earn the respect or recognition that is customarily accorded a decent, civilized government representing a free people. Minor dictatorships here and there in the world are at times disregarded as local phenomena, but when any dictatorship becomes a threat to world peace, its impact is no longer just internal, but external. It then becomes properly a matter of international concern.

We must stop deluding ourselves with the idea of "negotiating" with criminals. We must instead exalt morality. For we cannot end tension merely by making a deal with the unmoral and the unscrupulous.

The time has come to ostracize the unmoral governments that threaten world peace. The first step should be the expulsion of the Soviet Government from the United Nations, followed by the cutting off of all communication and all trade by the free world with the governments at Moscow and Peiping. We can well afford to subsidize those on our side who are financially damaged. It would cost only a fraction of the billions we spend annually on armament.

This is the only policy that presents an effective alternative to war.

We must look, therefore, to peoples — not dictatorship governments—to stay the hand that would drop an atom bomb among human beings anywhere in the world. And when all peoples are represented by governments chosen in free elections, the Eisenhower plan to pool atomic knowledge for peaceful purposes will become practical, and the world can then begin to enjoy an era of enduring peace.

The Geneva Summit

A new era in Soviet-American relations seemed to have emerged after the death of Stalin. The Cold War seemed to be thawing slightly, the two governments were beginning to engage in communication rather than confrontation. No more appropriate symbol of the change can be found than the fact that in 1955 the Soviet and American heads of state met personally for the first time in a decade. The Potsdam Conference had marked the onset of the Cold War; the Geneva Conference, many people hoped, would mark its decline.

During the months preceding the event, the press was filled with sanguine expectations. And in Congress, members of both parties pledged their support and good wishes to Eisenhower's diplomatic mission. There were a few, like Senator Joseph McCarthy, who warned that Geneva would be a "sell-out" to the Communists, but they were sternly rebuked by Republican leaders. Most Congressmen—and probably most Americans—looked to the summit meeting with hope; some even predicted that, as a Connecticut Congressman put it, this might be "world communism's last stand."

Premier Nikolai A. Bulganin had laid the groundwork for a summit conference by signing a treaty reuniting Austria and providing for the withdrawal of all occupation forces. Two months later, from July 18 to July 23, the leaders of the United States, USSR, France, and England conferred at Geneva on the problems dividing them. The main results were general commitment to the ideal of international arms control (which led to a long series of international disarmament talks in months and years to come) and continued Soviet-Western disagreement on the status of Germany.

In the aftermath of the conference a trio of authors, each occupying a different point on the political spectrum, assessed what had or had not been achieved. It is interesting to note in what ways the three evaluations overlap. The first is by Louis Halle, a professor specializing in foreign affairs, the second by William V. Shannon, the Washington correspondent for the liberal New York Post, *and the last by a writer in the right-wing* American Mercury.

51   HOW MUCH CAN WE EXPECT FROM RUSSIA?*

Now that we of the free world have embarked on general negotiations with the Soviet leaders we ought to be clear on what we are negotiating for.

If we tried to explain our position to the inquisitive man from Mars, we would probably begin by telling him that a quarrel had been raging for a number of years in the human family, with much shouting and threatening, and that our objective was to end that quarrel by some settlement on which both sides agreed. Before we told our Martian what terms of settlement we had in mind, however, we would have to tell him what the quarrel was about.

This would not be simple. We could not point to any one issue, such as a disputed boundary or conflicting legal claims, which might be made the subject of a negotiated settlement. The best we could do, off the top of our heads, would be to make some general state-

*Louis J. Halle, "How Much Can We Expect from Russia?" *New York Times Magazine* (September 25, 1955), pp. 13, 30, 32, 34. © 1955 by the New York Times Company. Reprinted by permission.

290 American Views of Soviet Russia

ment to the effect that the conflict was really between two opposed ways of life.

It is this generalized character of the conflict that confronts us with a riddle when we think of negotiating a settlement. How does one negotiate the settlement of an ideological quarrel, as distinct from a quarrel over claims? Can our diplomats expect to negotiate the Russians out of their Communist philosophy? Or are we willing, on our part, to make concessions in our way of life?

If the Martian knows his mundane beans, he is not going to let us get away with any such implications. He will try to pin us down on the specific provisions of a settlement that we consider possible. We might then attempt to meet his challenge by listing particular issues on which we want the Russians to modify their position. We might tell him that we want them to pull their army out of the center of Europe; to liberate East Germany, Poland, and the other satellites; to agree to some scheme for reducing their armed forces; to call off the Communist agents in our midst. Though we may not be able to get a change in their philosophy, we say, we can at least negotiate for their physical abandonment of the forward positions that they now occupy.

But all this is like trying to dictate terms of military defeat to a nation that is undefeated. If the Martian has had any experience of these matters, he will not put his money on our side. We are no more likely to be able to negotiate Russia's physical than her ideological surrender.

Having arrived at this point of frustration, we ought to ask whether the trouble is not that the Martian's questions are being answered in terms which are too categorical. The fact is, we might tell him on second thought, that we do not really expect a "settlement" in any final sense at the conference table.

We do not expect the negotiations to put an end to the conflict. We are not really negotiating for either total agreement between ourselves and the Soviet Union or for the suicide of the Soviet regime. Diplomacy, like politics, is the art of the possible. What we are seeking, we might tell him, is the abatement and limitation, rather than the termination, of a conflict that has become intolerably dangerous to the Russians and ourselves alike.

This, however, still begs the question. Abatement and limitation must take the form of actions on which both sides in the negotiation agree. What actions, asks the Martian?

Again we attempt an answer, based on our second thoughts. The

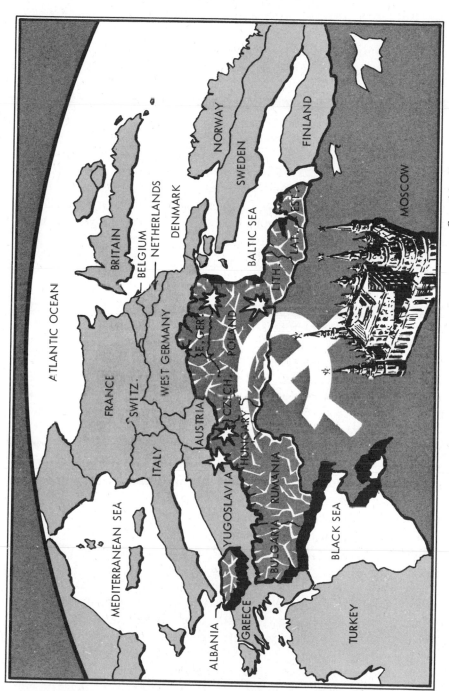

ATLANTIC OCEAN

BRITAIN

BELGIUM
NETHERLANDS
DENMARK

NORWAY

SWEDEN

FINLAND

FRANCE

SWITZ.

WEST GERMANY

E. GERM.

POLAND

BALTIC SEA

LITH.

LATV.

EST.

MOSCOW

ITALY

AUSTRIA

CZECH.

HUNGARY

MEDITERRANEAN SEA

YUGOSLAVIA

RUMANIA

BULGARIA

ALBANIA

GREECE

BLACK SEA

TURKEY

As the Kremlin Views Its Crumbling Empire

292 *American Views of Soviet Russia*

Western negotiators, we have said, are concerned to reduce a danger. That danger arises from two distinct elements which are excessively dangerous only in their combination: the power of the Soviet Union is one, its hostility is the other. The masters of Russia may well have a similar view when they look out at the world from their windows in Moscow: the power and hostility of the free world make a combination that appears dangerous to them. The evident danger for ourselves and the Russians can be lessened by reducing the hostility, reducing the power, or reducing both. The greatest difficulty, in such a situation, is simply to make a beginning.

Fortunately, quite a small beginning has already been made—at Geneva. The two sides appear to have tacitly agreed that hostility is to be diminished first, although our side has insisted that this must lead to an eventual retraction of Russian power as well.

What, to begin with, are the specific actions by which an abatement of hostility can be brought about? The exchange of visits and of ideas is one of them. When two enemies decide to see if they can get along with each other they may begin simply by breaking bread together in their own homes and talking things over. This kind of thing, the importance of which can be overestimated and underestimated alike, has already begun.

We and the Russians are, once again, on speaking terms. Our Ambassador in Moscow no longer finds himself cut off from communication with the government to which he is accredited. A few American visitors are being admitted to the Soviet Union and allowed, within limits, to roam about and speak their minds to the Russian people; a few Russians are being allowed to visit us. We even see atomic scientists of the two worlds tentatively comparing notes. Diplomatic negotiation, which can encourage these exchanges by agreement on specific measures for their facilitation, is itself facilitated by them. This is the beginning.

But the establishment of means for mutual communication cannot, of itself, insure any real or permanent abatement of hostility. It may merely open a channel for Communist duplicity. If it is true that the Russians are unchangeable in their attitudes, now and forevermore, as many believe they are, then the channel will be used by them simply to lull us into relaxing our vigilance. This we would suspect and be prepared to block.

The theory that the Russians are forever unchangeable overlooks two lessons of history, one general and the other specific. The general lesson is that all human societies have always been in a state of change. No generation has been able to keep intellectual fetters on its successors, although every generation has tried.

Marx could not control Lenin's thinking; Lenin could not control Stalin's; and since his own death Stalin has had nothing to say about the thinking of those who have taken his place. The Soviet Union has, in fact, been undergoing continuous ideological change since 1917, just as revolutionary France underwent continuous ideological change between 1789 and the restoration of 1815. . . .

. . . Is there not reason to hope, however cautiously, that we see in Stalin's successors the swing of the pendulum back toward the Westernization of Russian behavior? To the student of Russian history there is something oddly familiar about Khrushchev's European sacksuit and necktie, his ingratiation, his attempt to be accepted as a European statesman. There is a like echo from the past in Bulganin's effort to play the diplomatic game, once more, according to Western rules and manners—as Litvinov played it a generation ago.

More than that, there is something nostalgic about what appears to be a revolution, inside Russia and among the Russian leaders against the arbitrary oriental rule of Stalin. Perhaps his successors, too, feel frustrated by the impediment of the Iron Curtain which he left them.

Herein lies hope that the hostility between the Soviet Union and the free world really can be abated now. It is worth trying. Perhaps we can reach genuine agreement with the Russians on measures for overcoming their Iron Curtain (and also the rather similar drapery that we, in putative self-defense, had begun to raise around our own borders).

If we can see into Russian territory, as they have always been able to see into ours, it will become more difficult for them to mount a surprise attack. A major basis of distrust can thus be reduced.

But the legacy of Stalin cannot easily be negotiated away, even if we suppose equally good intentions on both sides. That legacy includes, in addition to the Iron Curtain, the advanced position of Russia's military power in the heart of Europe. Friendly visits back and forth between the Russians and ourselves, and renewed cooperation in cultural exchanges, will mean little if they do not lead, at last, to a retraction of the military power which looms so darkly over our allies.

Yet this would not be an easy undertaking for the Russian leaders, who were left by Stalin in the position of holding a bear by the tail. East Germany and the occupied nations have been implacably antagonized by the occupation and may seek their revenge if ever they find themselves free again.

Then, too, the Russians undoubtedly fear our power and hostility as we fear theirs. This makes it hard for them to abandon what they may regard as their defensive outposts. It is possible that any Russian leader who advocated a withdrawal might expose himself to fatal charges of disloyalty by his political rivals.

On the other hand, Stalin's successors have made some slight moves in the direction of withdrawal. They have evidently reconciled themselves to the independence of Yugoslavia, and they have backed out of Austria. These were their easiest moves. What remains would be incomparably more difficult.

While we must hope for their withdrawal, we shall get nowhere by pressing them in such fashion that they feel they have to hang on the harder. Our outspoken insistence on liberation of the satellites may only discredit peace-seeking elements in the Kremlin and strengthen irreconcilables.

We must not expect, moreover, that we can get something for nothing. Reciprocal concessions are the coinage of diplomatic bargaining. But it is hard to see what we can give without surrendering our own safety. We have few positions from which we can afford to retreat, and that for a simple reason. The Cold War was precipitated, not by Western but by Soviet aggression. It is the Communist world that has gone beyond bounds.

What the Russians are, in fact, asking us to give up is the complex of defensive arrangements made to meet their threat, chiefly N.A.T.O. and the Western European Union. This is like asking us to take off our armor on the grounds that it endangers them. While they have sword in hand we dare not do it.

We may not doubt, however, that the Russians do have real anxieties over their security, especially when they contemplate the prospective rearming of Germany and Japan. Surely we can offer them guarantees compatible with our own security that will allay these anxieties. Sir Anthony Eden's proposal at Geneva of a five-power pact is suggestive.

On other points, too, concessions by the Russians may make concessions by us possible—always bearing in mind that the reasonableness of Russian behavior is likely to be in proportion to our military strength, which we must therefore keep up. We could afford to discontinue foreign-language broadcasts across the Iron Curtain should there ever be enough ordinary communication between the peoples behind it and those outside so that they had other means of learning the truth.

What, then—to return to the Martian's inquiry—may we expect to obtain from the Russians in the negotiations on which we have now embarked?

Note first what we may not expect. We may not expect an end of the conflict. It will continue beyond any negotiations now in sight, for it is inherent in the differences between our nations. The Russians will continue to be our acknowledged ideological rivals, proclaiming to the world the eventual doom of our system and the triumph of theirs. We may not expect them either to embrace our liberal democracy, to commit suicide, or to draw their own teeth at our demand because we thump the table in making it.

We may expect, however, agreement on measures to reduce the conflict to less menacing proportions, to limit it by certain rules of international behavior—as the conflicts of nations in a state of civilization have always been limited. In fact, we may expect, in the fullness of time, to bring it gradually within the bounds of legitimate intellectual, political, and commercial competition.

The measures by which this may be accomplished over the years may roughly be divided between those that allay hostility and those that confine power. By and large we must expect that the latter will become possible only as the former are successful in re-establishing a measure of trust, although both may be attempted concurrently. Freedom of travel inside Russia, while reducing hostility, would also confine power to the extent that it made surprise attack unlikely.

We begin, then, as we are in fact beginning, with measures for increasing communication and restoring good manners between the two worlds. These may include provisions for tourist travel, exchange of publications, freedom of newspaper correspondents, limitation of official propaganda, and withdrawal of support for subversive activities.

As they are successful, it may become possible to go on to other measures for the limitation of armaments, the unification of Germany, and the restoration of a more normal political and military situation in Europe.

At the same time, we shall inevitably be dealing with Red China, and if the restoration of more civilized relations between ourselves and the Soviet Union succeeds, it is not too much to look for Russian cooperation in keeping the expansive fervor of Peiping within bounds. Occasional restraint on lesser Communist movements may also be expected.

International relations, like life itself, are continuous. Unlike the world of fable, they are not ordinarily marked by a beginning, a middle, and an end. Atomic war, it is true, could mean an abrupt end to our familiar world. Any success, however, must lack either the dramatic suddenness or the finality of such a disaster. The chief thing is to take the first steps.

We ought to tell the man from Mars that we are trying to move in a certain direction rather than aiming at any end now visible to us.

52   THE GENEVA ILLUSION *

It is becoming increasingly clear that the journey of the Western leaders to Geneva was a journey to the land of illusion. If it was not a mistake to go there, it was at least a mistake to go there and talk in the dreamlike language of the Russians. For their dream is our nightmare.

Walter Lippmann, perhaps our most sagacious commentator on foreign affairs, has recently begun to register the new mood of Western unease and disillusionment in a series of columns following his return from a post-Geneva trip to Europe. Even Mr. Lippmann, however, manages to cling to the central and fatal illusion engendered at Geneva and given a gleaming, transient life there. "The Summit Meeting at Geneva in July," he writes, "was a public recognition by both sides that they could not use thermonuclear war or the threat of it to settle the struggle between them. This did not mean that the struggle was over. It meant that the struggle would become a diplomatic contest."

British Foreign Secretary Macmillan expressed the same sentiment in his catch phrase: "There ain't gonna be any war."

If only this were true! All of us would like to see the shadow of thermonuclear war lifted from mankind and the East-West struggle confined to the diplomatic arena, that old familiar jousting ground where we could be assured that no matter what the outcome of the conflict we might lose prestige and some share of our power but not civilization and life itself. The shadow, however, has not lifted. A dozen men in Moscow retain, now as before, the power to make war at any moment in any manner they choose. The rendezvous by Lake Geneva, the bonhomie, the suave rhetoric, and the new-found politesse do not alter that grim circumstance. Behind this Potemkin

*William V. Shannon, "The Geneva Illusion," *Commonweal,* Vol. LXIII (November 25, 1955), pp. 191-93.

facade, all is darkness. What little we know of the careers of the members of this Soviet directorate does not encourage the belief that they are susceptible to the same humane aspirations and restraints which actuate the Western figures with whom they negotiate.

Consider for a moment Khrushchev, who has climbed to power with the blood of millions of Ukrainian peasants dripping almost literally from his stubby fingers, or Bulganin, the old political general who has probably purged more soldiers of the Red Army in his time than there were battle dead in General Eisenhower's American forces in World War II. Risk and ruthlessness, terror and death are integral to their mode of life. It is a brave man who would dare to say that such men may not sometime take the biggest risk of all.

In his first "Fireside Speech" in 1952 Adlai Stevenson stated another and more profound premise, "What is the lesson of history and of all human experience? What is the primary law of life? You struggle and you survive—you fail to struggle and you perish. The ways of the world are marked with the bones of peoples who hesitated. . . ."

It is from this tragic insight into the nature of the human condition that our thinking and our actions in foreign affairs must spring. To some, this may be a disheartening, even psychically demoralizing conception. Yet it is only the hard truth—writ large—that each of us will one day die. It is difficult to see why we should nourish fantasies about our collective fate when we acknowledge our individual mortality.

Our civilization may survive but history offers no guarantee. One cannot, of course, disparage the motives of those who stress the horrors of modern warfare, but neither can we succeed with a policy which rests ultimately on a paralyzing fear of hydrogen weapons, for we have no way of knowing that our adversaries are restrained by the same fear. In the endless thrust and parry of international diplomacy the Russians may well exploit this fear without ever actually having to take the supreme gamble. If we act on a premise that is untrue we shall find ourselves continually leading from weakness, a course of action as disastrous at the conference table as at the bridge table. A conception of foreign policy that excludes the tragic dimension may assuage the pain which the burdens of the Cold War exact, but can only serve to undermine our moral strength in the long years ahead.

To recall the realities Geneva obscures is not to argue that the Western leaders should not have gone to Geneva at all. If the Soviet junta wishes to talk, there is no reason why we should not always be willing to listen and to talk in turn. The fears long expressed in some quarters that the Soviets would necessarily convert such a meeting into a propaganda and political success are nothing more or less than a scandalous self-indictment of our own diplomatic incapacity. But the Soviets do, in fact, appear to be well on their way to capitalizing on the Geneva conference. They would find it difficult to do otherwise for theirs is a success by American default. President Eisenhower and his associates at Geneva appear to have journeyed there not with a policy but with a preoccupation. Mr. Eisenhower went to extraordinary lengths to reassure Western Europe and the uncommitted neutrals, on the one hand, and the Russian leaders if possible, on the other, that the United States has only peaceful intentions. The former deserved no such reassurances, and the latter were not impressed by them.

It seems almost impossible for Americans to get over the obsession that they should be loved, or at least well-liked, as well as respected by their allies. Rome in the third century and Britain in the nineteenth were not well-liked by their neighbors, and neither is America in the twentieth. The duty a great power owes to itself and its allies is to be strong and firm and give a lead, not to court what is at best an evanescent popularity.

The Russians sought the Geneva meeting; it is they who lead from weakness. It is their agriculture, after all, which is in chronic crisis, their ruling hierarchy in rapid flux, their captive satellites restive, their population starved for peace and consumer goods, their war machine still a narrow half-step behind our own in technological efficiency. They, not we, are shopping for fake peace and breathing space. They, not we, should have made the concessions.

For a decade, this nation has pursued a policy of containment looking toward prospective negotiations from "situations of strength." Once the moment did present itself, once Stalin did die, once farm collectivization in the satellites did fail, once the Soviets did abandon their hold on Austria and their cold war against Yugoslavia, once the rulers in Moscow did make tentative overtures for a truce, the American government wavered and retreated.

Mr. Eisenhower, for reasons best known to himself, chose at this critical moment to pander to sentimental fancies and a degrading desire for comfort at home, and the most dangerous, wrong-headed notions of British Bevanites and Paris neutralists abroad. He gave priority in the Geneva discussions to emphasis on the futility of atomic and hydrogen warfare, and to proposals for disarmament. These may have been useful strokes in psychological warfare, but they did not deserve first place in any practical discussion of the business at hand. If thermonuclear war is not a feasible policy, the hard-headed Russians are well aware of that and do not need Mr. Eisenhower to tell them so. Disarmament is the supreme fruit of mutual confidence. When no such confidence exists it can only follow and never precede the settlement of major outstanding issues, such as the division of Germany, the fate of satellite States and Russia's meddling in the Near and Far East.

Many Europeans can still argue that the Russians in the year 1955 are hostile to the West because they genuinely misunderstand our motives and genuinely fear capitalist encirclement and attack. Yet, what is this but a mere revival of Mr. Henry Wallace's threadbare arguments of a decade ago? Surely the long siege of confusion which this country endured from 1945 to 1948 on this precise point must have taught us something.

What course of action might we more wisely have followed in Geneva in place of Mr. Eisenhower's homilies on the futility of war, the peacetime uses of atomic energy, and the utopian scheme of aerial inspection?

It would seem clear to all that the satellite States are the crucial ground for settlement between East and West. Militarily and politically, there can be no security for Western Europe as long as the Red Army is thrust into the heart of the continent. Morally, the United States cannot countenance any solution that leaves the Poles, Czechs, Hungarians, and other peoples who once shared our freedom and civilization forever enslaved.

The President might properly have reminded Khrushchev and Bulganin of this burden on their conscience and on ours. He might have called the roll of Benes and Masaryk and Maniu, of the members of the London government-in-exile of Poland lured to their death in Moscow, and of the countless other Eastern European democrats. He might have reminded them of the broken pledges of free elections made at Yalta. He might have observed that America was not going to embark on a war of liberation to free these peoples but that it is not going to forget them either.

This suggested speech would have cast a chill on the jollity of the occasion, but how much is a smile worth? It would have reasserted our moral position and intensified the pressure on the Soviet hierarchy to make tangible, if limited, concessions. It might even have reawakened the soggy conscience of certain Western Europeans who feel that nothing is at stake in this vast struggle except the safety of their own skins. Finally, it would have underlined the point that a strong nation, like a strong man, does not fail those weak who depend on it.

The Geneva Conference already looms in retrospect as but an episode in the fateful drama and not its penultimate climax. If, as has been argued here, it was a bungled episode and a missed opportunity, it was not a fatal engagement, and there will be future opportunities. What are needed now are radical new initiatives in both political and economic directions. The Atlantic, already shrunk to the size of a large lake, is becoming in the jet age a small pond. We must draw even closer politically to Britain and France, abandon our archaic trade policies, and together devise a common Atlantic policy to liquidate North African colonialism and solve the chronic economic instability of our two smaller partners. In Africa and Asia, we need a Point Four and economic-assistance program conceived in terms of immediate as well as long-term political objectives, scaled in billions rather than millions of dollars and executed with the urgency of a "crash" mission. These are things we urgently need to do. But America is not likely to undertake such programs in a year of political drift, especially since all issues are hopelessly obscured by the Geneva haze.

53   DISASTER AHEAD?*

The master fact in the world situation – a fact which is conveniently overlooked by most American writers and commentators – is that Russia's prime objective in its present maneuvers is the winning of time. And a short-sighted American leadership is giving Russia and her satellites this all-important objective.

In doing this they are perhaps signing the death warrant of this republic. Time is a matter of life and death to world Communism. While a peace-blinded American people drown themselves in the vodka of "peaceful existence," Communism cynically prepares for the world showdown which it sees in the years ahead. That showdown will come when Communism finds itself strong enough to strike.

Let us consider how world Communism is using the priceless factor of time to its strategic advantage. Four basic but related activities

*Eric Tarnley, "Disaster Ahead?" *American Mercury* (Torrance, Calif.), Vol. LXXXI (December, 1955), pp. 36–40.

are being furthered by the time gift which America is so irresponsibly offering. These are:

1. The liquidation of opposition in the Communist countries.
2. The upbuilding and consolidation of their productive resources in preparation for a future world war.
3. The perfecting of intercontinental ballistic missiles.
4. The infiltration of their agents into strategic positions in our nation in preparation for conquest.

An analysis of these four Soviet operations will place the actual present situation realistically before us.

The liquidation of anti-Communists in the Iron Curtain nations is steadily strengthening the Red leaders and eliminating the possibility of a revolt of the peoples. The existence of widespread unrest behind the Iron Curtain has been authenticated by all responsible reports which have reached us. In the case of Red China it was spectacularly instanced by the 14,209 Red Army prisoners of war who, after the Korea armistice, chose to go to Formosa rather than return to the Communists. The Free World has millions of friends behind the Iron Curtain. Their presence is a powerful threat to the Red rulers in the event of war—they are the Achilles heel of the Communist leadership.

Unfortunately, unless we do something about it, this resistance factor within the Red world is certain to diminish and well-nigh disappear as the years pass. Without outside aid and encouragement, the anti-Communists will grow disheartened and give up the struggle.

In Red China, as recently as 1952, a total of 1,000,000 guerrillas were reported to be operating clandestinely behind the lines in Mainland China, many of them directed by short wave from Formosa. Most of these resisters have now about given up the fight. Few enclaves of rebellion are still operating. In the case of China, irresolute American policies are primarily responsible for this shrinkage of the resistance. Instead of aiding and encouraging the 1,000,000 who were ready to fight our battle, Washington permitted them to wither on the vine.

Such irresponsible disregard of long range strategic factors has been characteristic of American policy throughout the Cold War. Our words have often been realistic, but our deeds have been stupid.

Aside from Communist repression, one factor which is certain to wipe out much of the anti-Communist opposition in the Red countries is the disappearance of the pre-Communist generation. The mortality tables work for Communism. We may expect few resistance leaders from the youth generation which has grown up, or is growing up, indoctrinated under Communism.

The time to encourage resistance to Communism in the satellite nations is now while there are still millions of potential resisters. This irrefutable fact was recognized by the United States in 1952 by the passage of the Kersten Amendment. It has been given lip service by the many Americans who have generously supported the Crusade for Freedom. Unfortunately, little has been done by those in authority to implement it, as "Liberation" has been replaced by "co-existence" as the slogan of the Administration.

World Communism is also winning on the level of consolidation of its resources, territory and personnel in preparation for World War III. The program target of the Communist nations in this field is the consolidation of Russia, China and most of Asia and North Africa into a single co-continuous economic unit—prosperous, teeming with a technically trained productive population, and invincible to outside attack. Such a vast coordinated population mass, if unchecked, will inevitably dominate the world.

A preliminary step toward this grandiose objective is the development of wide-scale East-West trade. The Communist rulers have estimated that they can shorten their preparedness timetable by several years if they can induce the Free World to strengthen the Red economy by strategic goods and exchange of know-how.

We are witnessing the first rumblings of this inauguration of East-West trade in the present obscene scramble of British, French and American traders for Communist trade. The propaganda for East-West trade has become the principal activity of the pro-Communist stooges in all the Free countries. It is snowballing as the months pass.

Even the United States, which does not need Soviet trade, is swallowing the Moscow bait. Washington is steadily weakening the ban on shipment of strategic goods—a ban which was not effectively enforced. The Department of Commerce reports that during 1954 we carried on a trade with the Iron Curtain countries of $1,615,000,000. This was five times the total for 1953.

The importance to the Reds of the imports which they are obtaining from the United States and the other free nations can only be gauged in the light of the projects which Russia and Red China are now feverishly pushing.

One of these projects is transportation. Communist blue-prints call for a great modern communication system which will interconnect Siberia, and its burgeoning war industries, with the untapped resources of Red China. An important link in that network—a railway between Alma Ata in the Uzbek Republic of Southeast Siberia and the Sinkiang border—is already nearing completion.

Another Red master project, still on the planning boards, is a railway connecting Urumchi and Kashgar, spanning the whole vast province of Sinkiang. Another line which will connect with this trunk is now under construction from Lanchow to Pingfan. These are but geographic names to the average reader but in terms of logistics they mean a continuous rail route between the wealth of Northwest China and Siberia. When they are completed, the Russian and the Chinese economy will be interconnected into a single throbbing productive machine.

An American export policy, which blindly disregards the danger of vastly strengthening the economy of an enemy who is pledged to our destruction, will lead to disaster.

Another Communist program which looms like a baleful shadow on the backdrop of our American future is Soviet atomic development. We know little or nothing about this development except that it is far advanced. And yet our American leaders at Geneva seriously proposed that we exchange our atomic know-how with Russia!

Given the respite of time, and aided by the blind co-existence policies of the free nations, the Communist bloc in a relatively few years will have lifted its economy to a height comparable to our own. And this will be the signal for World War III. We of the Free World will have been in the unique position of having helped to fabricate our own destroyer.

However, the Communists, on their strategic chessboard, have worked out an alternative plan which, if successful, can bring us to our knees more quickly. They will use intercontinental ballistic missiles.

The intercontinental ballistic missile is a pilotless rocket designed to reach America in less than one hour, from Russian launching platforms. It does not need to be guided all along its course to the target. It is the ultimate weapon of world conquest.

The American people must not deceive themselves concerning Soviet ability to perfect this weapon. With the aid of German rocket experts and scientists, who were prevented from coming to America, it is within possibility that the Russians will have intercontinental ballistic missiles in from two to five years. If they have the help of traitors in our midst, they may be able to shorten this period even further.

We can understand the present Soviet zeal for "Peace" in the light of this ballistic missile possibility. Russia needs only to reassure the Free World by two to five years of pretended peacefulness, and she will have the weapon of world conquest in her hands. Even if the United States, in the meantime, should have perfected the same weapon, Russia still will have the advantage because she can strike first.

American political ethical concepts make it unthinkable that the United States should strike the first offensive blow in a world war. The Soviets expect, with the help of traitors within the United States, to paralyze the American capacity to resist, before an effective counterattack can be mounted. In this expectation they are probably right unless we awaken.

Certainly, with this possibility before them of crushing America by a pushbutton attack, the Communists will not be likely to risk an old-style war in the interim. They will play the sure thing. For this reason, their present "Peace" overtures become understandable.

But Russia has yet another weapon in its arsenal to reinforce her others. This is the weapon of skillful infiltration of the enemy. It is the weapon of placing her agents and dupes at the choke points of the American war apparatus. The practiced skill of Communism in accomplishing this stealthy task has been shockingly revealed to the American people during the last eight years.

The present particular targets of Red infiltration in America are the Department of Defense, the Atomic Energy Commission, the Central Intelligence Agency, the National Security Council, and all major defense plants and communications centers. How far the Communists have succeeded in placing their stooges in these agencies is extremely difficult to ascertain. Only the most effective security system, supported by all American officials, can throw a screen around our sensitive agencies which can halt the infiltrators.

Unfortunately, with suicidal perversity, a great army of so-called "Liberal" Americans, aided by columnists, radio and TV commentators and by many of the nation's intellectuals, are furiously engaged in a campaign to discredit the security system.

The same Left-wing writers and publicists who are most insistent upon an American policy of appeasement and co-existence with Russia are loudest in their denunciations of anti-Communist vigilance in our government. They are the most scornful in their denial that there are spies and infiltrators in high places, and the most outspoken in their abuse of government anti-Communist agencies. All of which, wittingly or unwittingly, plays dangerously into the hands of Russia's long range plans.

But there is a psychological danger in the present appeasement and co-existence thinking of so many of the American people. The time comes when appeasement becomes a compulsive habit.

Many Americans will be still appeasing when the guided missiles begin to drop and the knives of the traitors are plunged into our backs.

The Left-wing irresolution, in the face of Communism, is a doctrinal drug which eventually destroys its victim. Russia, sustained by its fanatical faith, may well believe in its final victory as it contemplates those who have been deciding American and British policy during the post-war years. The Russians may well believe that they are heading for a painless conquest.

In view of their past performance, it would not be surprising to find some of our Left-wing writers and public figures arguing on decision day that "Peace" with world Communism, after all, is not so bad, and that the real enemies who must be liquidated are the wicked anti-Communists who have provoked Russia. The irrationality of the co-existence mind leads inexorably to such an absurdity. For appeasement is a habit-forming narcotic.

America is approaching the most dangerous period of her long contest with world Communism. It is a period in which we may lose our whole fight for survival because of the delusions which are in our own minds. The sands in the hourglass are fast running out for American anti-Communist policy. If, in our hunger for peace, we allow Communism to win the precious battle for time, we face the strong prospect of actual annihilation.

It is for these total stakes that Communism is now maneuvering shrewdly with the weakly-chosen statesmen of the Free World.

Sputnik

During the two years following the Geneva summit conference, Soviet-American relations remained on a rather cordial plateau, although not without some jolts. The most serious crisis developed in the fall of 1956, when Hungarians and Poles used Communist Party Secretary Nikita Khrushchev's de-Stalinization campaign as an opportunity for loosening Moscow's domination over their countries. In Hungary, the attempt became outright revolution by the "freedom fighters" against the Soviet-backed regime in Budapest. Russian troops and tanks soon crushed the uprising with ferocious bloodshed. Meanwhile, the United States government did nothing to aid the rebels, despite Secretary of State John Foster Dulles' earlier proclamation of a "liberation" policy toward the Soviet satellites. American intervention might have meant war with the USSR, and the Eisenhower administration would not risk that.

Those bloody weeks in Eastern Europe provoked a crise de conscience *for Americans. But the excitement remained considerably less intense than after another Soviet action the following year: the launching of the first earth satellite into space. Americans had already been alarmed when Khrushchev announced in August the successful launching of an intercontinental ballistic missile; that feat accentuated what would soon be called the "missile gap." Then in October came Sputnik, sensationally symbolizing Russian technological progress. It would be three months before the United States would launch its own satellite, 15 months before the United States successfully fired an ICBM. As the silvery object encircled the earth with a halo of "beep-beeps," a furor of anxiety erupted within the United States. In the course of the post-Sputnik debate, Americans once again—as so often in their history—reexamined fundamental aspects of their way of life, from military to moral. Perhaps not since the time of the First Five-Year Plan had the USSR aroused Americans to such a degree of self-doubt.*

Walter Lippmann extracted the diplomatic and philosophical significance of Sputnik in two of his columns, one written immediately after the Soviet feat, the other after the United States launched its Explorer satellite. The final selection presents excerpts from a discussion on the Senate floor by several Democrats, primarily Henry Jackson of Washington and Mike Mansfield of Montana, on the inadequacies of the (Republican) defense program.

54   EXPLORER, SPUTNIK, AND THE MOON *

The few who are allowed to know about such things, and are able to understand them, are saying that the launching of so big a satellite

*Walter Lippmann, "The Portent of the Moon," Today and Tomorrow (October 10, 1957), and "Explorer and Sputnik," ibid. (February 4, 1958), both reprinted in The Essential Lippmann, Clinton P. Rossiter and James Lare (eds.) (New York: Random House, 1963), pp. 66–70. Acknowledgment is made to Walter Lippmann for permission to reprint these passages from The Essential Lippmann © Copyright 1963, by Walter Lippmann.

signifies that the Soviets are much ahead of this country in the development of rocket missiles. Their being so much ahead cannot be the result of some kind of lucky guess in inventing a gadget. It must be that there is a large body of Soviet scientists, engineers, and production men, plus many highly developed subsidiary industries, all successfully directed and co-ordinated, and bountifully financed.

In short, the fact that we have lost the race to launch the satellite means that we are losing the race to produce ballistic missiles. This in turn means that the United States and the Western world may be falling behind in the progress of science and technology.

This is a grim business. It is grim, in my mind at least, not because I think the Soviets have such a lead in the race of armaments that we may soon be at their mercy. Not at all. It is a grim business because a society cannot stand still. If it loses the momentum of its own progress, it will deteriorate and decline, lacking purpose and losing confidence in itself.

The critical question is how we as a people, from the President down, will respond to what is a profound challenge to our cultural values—not to the ideal of the American way of life but to the way in fact we have been living our life. One response could be to think of it all in terms of propaganda, and to look around for some device for doing something spectacular to outmatch what the Russians have done. The other response would be to look inward upon ourselves, and to concern ourselves primarily with our own failings, and to be determined not so much to beat the Russians as to cure ourselves.

The question then might be defined in this way: why is it that in the twelve years that have passed since the end of World War II, the United States which was so far in the lead has been losing its lead to the Russians who at the end of the war were so nearly prostrate? Mr. Khrushchev would say, no doubt, that this is because communism is superior to capitalism. But that answer really begs the question, which is not why the Soviets have moved ahead so fast but why we, who had moved very fast, have not been moving fast enough. For while our society is undoubtedly progressive, it has not in the postwar years been progressive enough.

I do not pretend to know the whole answer to what is for us and for our future so fateful a question. But I venture to think that even now we can discern certain trends that since the World War have appeared in American life and must be taken into account.

We must put first, I think, the enormous prosperity in which, as the politicians have put it to the voters, the private standard of life is paramount as against the public standard of life. By the public standard of life I mean such necessities as defense, education, science, technology, the arts. Our people have been led to believe in the enormous fallacy that the highest purpose of the American social order is to multiply the enjoyment of consumer goods. As a result, our public institutions, particularly those having to do with education and research, have been, as compared with the growth of our population, scandalously starved.

We must put second, I think, a general popular disrespect for, and even suspicion of, brains and originality of thought. In other countries, in Germany and in most of Europe and in Russia, it is an honor, universally recognized, to be a professor. Here it is something to put a man on the defensive, requiring him to show that he is not a highbrow and that he is not subversive.

What McCarthyism did to the inner confidence of American scientists and thinkers has constituted one of the great national tragedies of the postwar era. It is impossible to measure the damage. But the damage that was done was very great. It was done in the kind of thinking where the difference between creation and routine lies in the special courage to follow the truth wherever it leads.

With prosperity acting as a narcotic, with Philistinism and McCarthyism rampant, our public life has been increasingly doped and without purpose. With the President in a kind of partial retirement, there is no standard raised to which the people can repair. Thus we drift with no one to state our purposes and to make policy, into a chronic disaster like [the] Little Rock [school desegregation crisis]. We find ourselves then without a chart in very troubled waters.

. . .

The American satellite Explorer has made us all feel better, having given tangible proof that the science of rocketry is known in this country and that our experts possess the art of making and guiding rockets. The event has confirmed the testimony of those who have been saying that the Russians have a considerable lead but that we are in the race.

Explorer is, therefore, a good popular antidote to the panicky view that we are in mortal danger. But it does not wash out the main portent of Sputnik—which is not that the Russians launched a satellite first, and that their satellite is very much bigger and heavier than Explorer. The main portent is that, starting at the end of World War II with their country devastated, their technology far more primitive than our own, the Russians have achieved a *rate* of scientific and technological development which is faster than our own. What they did with the Sputnik shows not merely that they have mastered a particular specialty but that they have generated a tremendous momentum in the physical sciences and their application.

Though Explorer is in the sky, there is no reason to think that the comparative rate of development is now back in balance, much less that it is in our favor. We are still the bigger and the stronger. But they are still moving forward the faster.

There is, therefore, much for us to do, and as I see it we must move forward simultaneously along three broad paths. The first is that we have to find out how to make the government much better able than it is now to take and to carry out long-range decisions. There is little doubt that American progress in missiles has been retarded by bureaucratic confusion presided over by political appointees who did not understand the issues they were supposed to decide.

Undoubtedly, this requires a reorganization in the Pentagon. But the trouble will not be cured in the Pentagon alone. The White House and the relevant committees of Congress have at least an equal responsibility.

The second path we must take is even broader. It is the transformation of American education which on the average and by and large is declining in quality as the quantity of those to be educated grows larger and larger. Our schools and colleges are overwhelmed by the growth of the population they are supposed to educate, and they are under enormous pressure—for the most part irresistible—to lower their intellectual standards. There is an ominous tendency in American education to teach more and more students less and less of the great disciplines which form an educated man.

It is in this, more than in the ups and downs in the military balance of power, that there lies the deepest danger to our American society. We can most surely defend ourselves against conquest or domination. What we have to worry about is that with the declining level of education, with the vulgarization of the cultural standards in our mass society, we shall become a big but second-rate people, fat, Philistine, and self-indulgent.

The third path on which we must travel is to learn to adjust our minds to the hard facts of life—particularly to the fact that our Western society, of which we are the strongest member, is no longer paramount, is now only an equal, among the great societies of the globe.

Britain and France have had to learn in this generation what Sweden and Spain learned in earlier days—that they are no longer the main centers of power and influence for all mankind. At the end of World War II for a few short years the United States was the paramount center of power and influence in the world. Our conception of our role, as we have formed it in the postwar years, has had as its fundamental premise the paramountcy of the Western society led by the United States. This was a fact. But it was transitory.

The postwar era is ending and the great reality to which we have now to adjust our thinking is that we are an equal but not a paramount power.

55 CONGRESSIONAL CRITICISM *

Mr. Jackson: Mr. President, I should like to make a few undramatic suggestions on some down-to-earth defense needs. I want to stress the things we need to do immediately to stay alive.

In a subsequent speech I shall discuss the parallel efforts we should make to speed advanced weapons projects and other long-range programs that may win us the race to the stars. But first things first. There are some things we have to do on earth in 1958 if we are to go to the moon in 1968.

My remarks today will take the form of a series of constructive recommendations. This is in accord with the policy I have tried to follow over the years in pointing out deficiencies in our defense program and in proposing remedies.

History may prove that some of the steps I am suggesting were unnecessary. But we cannot await the verdict of history. Gone are our two precious allies in past wars—time in which to mobilize, and distance to protect our homeland. Today, whatever force is required, either to deter war or to win it if deterrence fails, must be on hand—ready at all times. No longer can we afford the luxury of second guessing our requirements. In the missile age, it is the first guess that counts.

The aggressor will always have one grave advantage over us. He can prepare to strike when he wants, where he wants, and how he wants. We have to prepare to meet aggression in many different forms, and not at times or places of our own choosing.

---

*Henry Jackson and Mike Mansfield, *Congressional Record,* 85th Cong., 2nd sess. (January 30, 1958), pp. 1343-47.

Mr. President, what are we now failing to do that we should be doing—in the air, at sea, and on land?

In particular, I want to make the following seven recommendations:

First. We should produce more B-52 heavy bombers and KC-135 tankers, faster.

The Russians are at present well ahead of us in the IRBM-ICBM race. The Soviet missile program has proceeded much faster than we expected 3 years ago. Our own missile program has proceeded more slowly than was expected. More Soviet missiles sooner. Fewer American missiles later. This is the fact and the outlook before us.

The one and only way to fill the gap is by more long-range manned bombers. Ultimately manned bombers will supplement ballistic missiles, but they cannot supplement missiles which we do not have.

This year, next year, and the year thereafter, we must work with what we have in hand. This is the B-52, and the KC-135 tanker that keeps it airborne.

The B-52 is now the world's most advanced operational long-range bombing plane. In its existing version, and in its advanced version—the B-52G—this plane must and will be the mainstay of our retaliatory force for the critical years ahead.

Yet in the face of this fact, what have we done? Incredible as it seems, we have been cutting back and stretching out our programs, when every day that passes urgently calls for more B-52's, sooner. The fact is we still have as many wings of the obsolete B-36 as we have of B-52's, while our medium-range bomber, the B-47, becomes more obsolescent every day.

The record contains impressive and uncontradicted evidence that our position in manned bombers is seriously deficient.

In 1956 General LeMay, then commander in chief of the Strategic Air Command, testified that "Under current intelligence estimates and approved plans and programs the Soviet long-range air force will be relatively stronger than the Strategic Air Command by 1960 at the latest."

General LeMay went on to say: "If present plans and programs, as I understand them, are unchanged and our estimates of Russian airpower are correct, I think there is grave doubt that the Strategic Air Command would present an effective deterrence in that time period (1958-60)."

Mr. Mansfield: Mr. President, will the Senator yield?

Mr. Jackson: I am happy to yield.

Mr. Mansfield: The Senator has stated that the Russians are at present well ahead of us in the IRBM–ICBM race. Could the Senator give us some idea as to just how much ahead of us the Russians are at this time in those two fields?

Mr. Jackson: The Soviets have operational intermediate range ballistic missiles. We do not.

The Soviets probably have some operational intercontinental ballistic missiles. We do not.

Mr. Mansfield: Would the Senator mind explaining the ranges of the IRBM and ICBM?

Mr. Jackson: The Soviets have intermediate range missiles in the range area of 1,000 nautical miles.

Our specifications for these missiles call for 1,500 miles for IRBM's and 5,000 miles for ICBM's.

Mr. Mansfield: Will the Senator tell us, further, how the IRBM and the ICBM travel?

Mr. Jackson: The IRBM probably would traverse a distance of 1,500 nautical miles in 13 minutes. At its maximum speed, I believe it reaches about Mach 14 prior to reentering the atmosphere.

The intercontinental ballistic missile can traverse 5,000 miles in about 33 minutes. It probably reaches a maximum speed, prior to reentry into the atmosphere, of Mach 21.

When I use the term Mach, that means the speed of sound.

Mr. Mansfield: Do I correctly understand that on the basis of the information which the Senator has just given the Senate, the United States is within 15 minutes of any missile takeoff from the Soviet Union or contiguous territories?

Mr. Jackson: Yes; the Soviets have that capability, or will have it soon. In addition, the Soviets have a fleet of more than 500 submarines, some of which have missile-firing capability.

Mr. Mansfield: The Senator from Washington has been diligent in this particular field, and more than diligent in pointing out the deficiency which this country suffers in comparison with the Soviet Union so far as submarines are concerned.

On the basis of the startling statement which the Senator has made this afternoon, is it safe to assume that in case of another great emergency, this country would no longer be the privileged sanctuary it was in the first two World Wars?

Mr. Jackson: Very definitely the No. 1 target of the Soviet Union in an all-out war will be the United States. If the United States is destroyed, all of our allies will fall with it. We will be the No. 1 target in an all-out war.

Mr. Mansfield: Then, to recapitulate, we are within 15 minutes, on the basis of ICBM speeds, of any missile takeoff from the Soviet Union. We will no longer be a privileged sanctuary in case of another world conflagration. We will no longer have time to mobilize our manpower, gird our industry, and develop our resources. Is that correct?

Mr. Jackson: That is correct. We have had two fortunate allies in past conflicts—time and space: time to mobilize and space to protect our shores from enemy attack. These two allies, together with the great industrial capability of this country, have made possible our victories in the last two terrible wars. . . .

Mr. President, since General LeMay gave his testimony, our manned-bomber programs, far from being increased, have been reduced.

The truth is that the Soviet Union is speedily diminishing our lead in manned airpower and, at current rates, will outdistance this country in the very near future.

And now the budget requests before Congress call for not a single penny for more B-52's, beyond the 11 wings already programed.

General White, Air Force Chief of Staff, recently told Congress: "If we don't get more money, we will be unable to reorder B-52's except at very great expense, because the production line goes to pieces; and I feel that until we know more about these ballistic missiles and until we know about the B-58 we should have the insurance of keeping that line open."

General White went on to say he had "taken every step I know" to obtain an additional $615 million for another wing of B-52's and for the KC-135 tankers to support them, only to have the Secretary of Defense refuse his request.

Mr. President, I am not sure that the $615 million is enough. My own belief is that at least $1 billion could now be profitably budgeted for this purpose. But of this much I am sure: The Air Force request constitutes the irreducible minimum required for our national safety.

Second. We should step up the production schedule for the B-58 medium-weight supersonic bomber.

The B-52—even in the advanced version—by no means represents the last word in manned bombers. Even more advanced manned weapons systems are bound to come. We can be sure of one thing: Moscow is hard at work on new high-performance aircraft.

At present we have one hopeful new plane sufficiently developed to go into production. The possible successor to the B-47—the B-58

—exists in prototype; and seven B-58's have been delivered for testing purposes. Currently planned programs bring the total number of B-58's on order to less than 80.

In my view, we can get the new B-58's more rapidly than present plans allow. Recently, when General White was asked whether they are producing the B-58's as rapidly as they could, he replied: "I am sure they are not. It may take some money."

Mr. President, if we tool up faster for the B-58, we shall have more of them sooner. I am hopeful that Congress will promptly budget funds for this purpose.

Mr. Mansfield: Mr. President, will the Senator from Washington yield to me?

The Presiding Officer (Mr. Bible in the chair): Does the Senator from Washington yield to the Senator from Montana?

Mr. Jackson: I am happy to yield.

Mr. Mansfield: During the course of the very excellent speech being given by the distinguished Senator from Washington, I did not hear him use the expression "lead time," but I understood him to make indirect references to it. Can he state just what is the difference, as between the United States of America and the Soviet Union, so far as the lead time in the production of both planes and missiles is concerned?

Mr. Jackson: We know that in the case of the B-52 as compared with the Soviet Bison bomber, the Russians were able to cut their lead time to half as much as ours—in fact, I prefer to call it "leg-time."

I cannot state any precise figures as to the missiles; but I can say that it is quite clear that the Soviets took many calculated risks, made their decisions promptly, and were able to get the jump on us, in connection with the development and production of both the IRBM and the ICBM.

Mr. Mansfield: Mr. President, will the Senator from Washington yield further to me?

Mr. Jackson: I am happy to yield to the distinguished Senator from Montana.

Mr. Mansfield: Referring to the production of the B-52 in comparison with the production of the Bison bomber, the Soviet counterpart of the B-52, can the Senator from Washington give an approximate figure, in years, as to how long in the way of lead time it took to develop the B-52, on the one hand, and the Soviet Bison bomber, on the other? Can the Senator give a rough figure as to that?

Mr. Jackson: My rough guess is that in our case it was about 10 years from the initial development phase to the point of obtaining operational capability.

Mr. Mansfield: From the planning boards?

Mr. Jackson: Yes; compared with 5 years for the Soviets.

Mr. Mansfield: If that statement is a correct one—and I assume it is—then it appears to me that by the time the 10 years taken up in our lead time is over and the finished product becomes operational, it also becomes obsolete.

Mr. Jackson: There is that danger.

It has been clear to many of us for a long time that the Soviets realized that, if they were ever to defeat the United States and the rest of the Free World, they would have to defeat us at our own game. The strength of our position over the years has been our industrial, our scientific, and our technical capability. The Soviets have demonstrated dramatically, with sputnik and with other devices, that they are out to seize our trump card and to beat us at our own game. We have dramatic proof that they have been doing exactly that.

Mr. Mansfield: I can understand the Senator's point, when he states that in the matter of lead time the Soviet Union is beating us at our own game, because we have always boasted of our industrial know-how and of the fact that we could get things done on a big production basis.

What is the reason for the difference of 5 years—again referring to the B-52's and the Soviet Bison bombers; what is the reason for this 5-year lag behind the Soviet Union, insofar as we are concerned, in view of all the facilities we have at our disposal?

Mr. Jackson: I think there has been a basic assumption in the United States—one which extends all the way to children who, at the age of 5 or 6, enter grade school—that we are superior in anything involving industry, science, or technology. If I were to give one, over-all reason for our difficulty, it is that we have a national superiority complex.

When it comes to the mass production of anything in the way of industrial goods for domestic consumption or the mass production of arms with which to defend our country, the average American, when asked, "Who can turn out the most?" will reply, "The United States of America." There has been a feeling that the Soviets are only a few years from a feudal society, so how could they ever match the United States of America?

Our difficulty is a national superiority complex. The sooner we learn humility, the stronger the United States and the rest of the Free World will be.

Mr. Mansfield: I thank the Senator from Washington.

Mr. [Stuart] Symington [of Missouri]: Mr. President, will the Senator from Washington yield to me?

Mr. Jackson: I am glad to yield.

Mr. Symington: For some years the distinguished Senator from Washington and I have been listening to statements which have attempted to justify our passing over quantitative superiority to the Soviet Union, on the ground that we were qualitatively superior, on the ground, on the sea, and in many respects, in the air. Will not the distinguished Senator from Washington, who has made so thorough a study of this subject, agree that what sputnik did, more than anything else, was to expose the fallacy of the claims of our being qualitatively superior, as a justification for our having passed over quantitative superiority?

Mr. Jackson: I agree completely with what the distinguished Senator has said. It is quite obvious that if we, with only 8 percent of the world's population, are to maintain a military posture which will assure our survival, we certainly have to overcome the numerical disadvantage, through qualitative superiority. The Soviets realize this; and the Soviets have centered their attack on the very area in which we have maintained supremacy in the past.

In my trip to the Soviet Union in 1956, I found first-hand corroboration of that objective. This is the obvious course for the Soviets to pursue if they wish to win.

Mr. President, I come now to my next point:

Third. We should further expedite the dispersal of our strategic striking force, we should take steps to harden existing bases, and we should redouble our efforts to provide early warning against enemy planes and missiles.

Our Strategic Air Command bases are now the No. 1 target for Soviet attack, because our SAC represents our means of retaliation against Russia. Moreover, as the Kremlin expands its stockpile of nuclear weapons and improves its means of delivering bombs, our bases become more and more vulnerable.

By either this year or next year, our entire system of overseas bases will be exposed to Russian IRBM attack. This year, and even more in the years thereafter, the strategic airbases in our own country will become exposed to Soviet ICBM assault. Meanwhile, vital bases here at home are now open to enemy missiles from the sea.

Confronting this hazardous prospect, what have we done to disperse our bombers, to protect them on existing bases, and to assure them the earliest possible warning so they can get off the ground before they are hit?

The answer is we have done far too little.

SAC dispersal programs have proceeded at a leisurely pace. We have taken no decisive measures to harden our bases by protecting our bombers from indirect hits. At the present time the retaliatory force on which our safety depends stands on ramps above ground. An H-bomb that misses its target by a wide margin will still wipe out a force that is so exposed. Early warning and detection systems against manned aircraft are far from peak efficiency. Interservice rivalry has kept us sitting on our hands for the past 2 years in developing an early warning system against the ICBM.

New budget requests now before Congress provide for dispersal of SAC at a faster rate and for improvement of our early warning and detection programs. Again, however, I think an insufficient effort is planned.

SAC is the only deterrent, retaliatory force we have on hand. Nothing is more urgent than safeguarding it against destruction or neutralization by surprise attack. Surely, substantial funds to speed this effort are warranted. . . .

Fourth. We should increase the number of operational missiles that will be available by immediately ordering additional IRBM's and ICBM's.

It may be true that we cannot now shorten the time in which we will get our first operational ballistic missiles. Certain irreducible items of technological lead time are working against us.

We can, however, hasten the time at which we will have significant numbers of operational missiles. We can take the calculated risk of going into mass production before every minute item of the missile has been tested.

In the Manhattan project in World War II we constructed production facilities at Hanford without knowing for sure that the facilities could do the job. Had we waited until every phase of the bomb was tested out, our achievement of that decisive weapon would have been long delayed.

Test missiles are fine, but only operational missiles in abundance will pay off as a deterrent.

General Schriever, Commander of the Air Force Ballistic Missile Division, recently said that the capabilities now exist to start building more units of the Thor and Atlas than are in presently approved programs. He said a further stepup in production schedules is possible by using our current production base, with only some rounding out.

I consider wholly inadequate the budget requests now before Congress to accelerate production rates for ballistic missiles. These missiles are supposed to have the highest national priority. If that means anything, it means that we must execute that priority at every stage of their preparation, including production.

Fifth. We should revise upward our program for producing Polaris missile-launching submarines, and lay down a minimum of 15 keels immediately.

I have previously proposed that we build 100 Polaris missile-launching submarines at the earliest possible date. These submarines afford the opportunity to increase radically the effectiveness of our IRBM. After all, an IRBM launched from an ocean platform can have the same target coverage and the same military effect as an ICBM launched from our own country.

The problem we face in keeping the peace is to convince the enemy that, even if he strikes first, we will be able to strike back just as hard, perhaps harder.

If we kept 50 Polaris submarines at sea at all times, constantly on the move, hard to find, and next to impossible to destroy, we should have a formidable deterrent to Soviet attack. No matter how effective an enemy might think a sneak attack against our cities and land bases might be, he would know he could not avoid a crushing return blow by our underseas force.

I think it very likely that the Polaris system, if set up in strength, could become the Free World's main deterrent, retaliatory force.

The 1958 supplemental budget provides funds for our first three Polaris missile submarines, and we are told money for six more will be requested. This number falls short of what we should order this year. We can move more rapidly toward the objective of 100 such submarines by starting 15 of them immediately, 6 more than are presently contemplated.

Mr. Symington: Mr. President, will the able Senator yield?

Mr. Jackson: I am happy to yield.

Mr. Symington: The Senator stresses the Polaris missile. Nearly everybody connected with its development has also emphasized the importance of that missile. Will the Senator not agree with me that if we do not have the submarines to launch the missile, the missile cannot perform its intended mission?

Mr. Jackson: The statement of the Senator is correct. It is very important that we take parallel action on both the missile and the submarine. In other words, we are facing a situation in which we shall probably, unless we do something about it, have Polaris missiles without their launching platforms; namely, nuclear-powered submarines. The missile is only half of the weapon system. Unless we have the · means to launch it we lose its deterrent value.

Mr. Mansfield: Mr. President, if the Senator will yield, may I ask the other half of that question? Do we have the Polaris missile?

Mr. Jackson: The answer is "No." If all of the schedules work out as planned, we will make good progress on the Polaris missile.

Mr. Mansfield: Then, if we do not have the Polaris missile, why should we build Polaris missile submarines?

Mr. Jackson: The objective, of course, is to produce the Polaris missile on a schedule that will tie it in with the submarine, so that the missile can be married to the submarine on a concurrent basis.

Mr. Mansfield: What the Senator means is that the two items, the Polaris missile submarine and the Polaris missile, should be developed simultaneously.

Mr. Jackson: The Senator is correct.

Sixth. We should radically accelerate our antisubmarine warfare programs and provide for a Vice Chief of Staff for Undersea Warfare.

The Soviet Union has the largest undersea fleet in the world—over 500 submarines, many with missile-launching capability. Admiral Rickover told Congress this year that if the Russians were to commence building atomic submarines now at a fraction of the rate they have been building conventional submarines we would even lose our present lead in nuclear submarines—and as early as 1961.

At the current building rate we will have only about 15 nuclear submarines in operation before 1961.

Moscow may not yet have the equivalent of the Polaris submarine system, but she can build it soon. When that day comes most of the United States will be within range of nuclear attack from the sea.

In the face of this threat, are we doing enough to keep our ocean lifelines open? Are we preparing to safeguard our mainland from missiles launched from Soviet submarines?

The truth is our antisubmarine methods are still mainly conventional and of little value against the unconventional threat. We have only begun to develop the new ships, train the new men, and achieve the needed breakthroughs in detection techniques.

Rear Adm. Rawson Bennett, Chief of Naval Research, has testified before Congress that "at this point we are not in the very rapid state of advance in antisubmarine warfare."

Thus far antisubmarine warfare has relied on a strategy of attrition. Even when the target was a conventional submarine, the detection and kill record has been low. Now with the coming of the nuclear submarine every difficulty is multiplied.

We need to aim for 100 percent detection and 100 percent kill. The frightful destructive power of one enemy submarine makes anything less inadequate. One submarine alive can mean one American city dead.

The 1959 budget includes a request for some additional money for antisubmarine warfare, but the increase is not very substantial.

Once more, I believe we are shortchanging a vital program. We must win the race for discovery of new detection techniques. We need to order more attack and hunter-killer submarines that can sink Russian submarines. There is every justification for budgeting ample funds for these purposes.

I also want to repeat my earlier suggestion for the appointment of a Vice Chief of Staff for Undersea Warfare to help get the effort into higher gear, and maintain it that way.

Seventh. We should build up the Army to 18 divisions and fully modernize its equipment – the pentomic division should really be made pentomic.

The greatest threat we face is all-out Soviet attack, but this is not the most likely threat—today. As long as American power can still devastate an aggressor, Moscow may refrain from an all-out blow.

The Kremlin doubtless prefers to inherit the world, if it can, rather than demolish it. Our most probable immediate military danger is the limited Soviet probe and penetration carefully calculated not to arouse this country to a showdown.

This being their likely tactic, we require modern mobile forces prepared to prevent local engagements from getting out of hand. As Gen. Maxwell D. Taylor, Army Chief of Staff, said in 1956: "If the small war breaks out, we must suppress it promptly, because that small war may easily lead to the great war which we are all trying to avoid."

In the light of this requirement what have we done? Illogically and disastrous as it is, we have relentlessly cut our Army from 20 divisions, to 18, and then to 15 at the end of this fiscal year. Now Congress is asked in the 1959 budget to give its blessing to a 14-division Army.

This further cut is proposed despite testimony by such men as General Gavin, Chief of Army Research and Development, that even with the present number of army divisions we are not in a position to fight a limited war.

Eight of our divisions are deployed overseas, three are really training organizations, leaving us with a striking force of three or at the most four divisions. This is an absurdly small force to compare with the 175 Soviet divisions.

These Soviet divisions are poised to threaten such critical areas as the Middle East, Southeast Asia, and Europe. We ask the nations who are under the muzzles of Soviet guns to resist the powerful forces across their frontiers; we pledge our assistance. Yet we would be hard pressed to move only one division by air transportation, and these countries, and the Soviets, know this fact.

The Army has recognized the need to adapt to the nuclear age. It has reorganized its active divisions under the pentomic concept to provide greater mobility, greater striking power, and faster reaction to the changing conditions of battle.

These new pentomic divisions, however, are still shackled to World War II equipment. At the rate modern equipment is being provided it will be several years before the new divisions are anything but paper pentomic.

General Taylor, Army Chief of Staff, recently testified: "I do not believe that the Army can modernize to the extent I consider necessary without a significant increase over the funds received in recent years."

But this is not all. Congress is asked in the 1959 budget to reduce Army Reserve components. A case might be made for holding down the Regular Army if we had enough Army Reserve divisions equipped and trained to constitute combat-ready units. But it makes no sense whatsoever to cut back the Regular Army and simultaneously deal a body blow to the Reserve program.

Clearly, we should provide this country with a modern Army, equipped to fight on today's battlefield. Its strength should be restored to 18 active divisions as a minimum; the rate of modernization should be speeded up; and the Reserve forces program should be assured steady support.

Mr. President, one final point. In matters of national security—in matters, in other words, affecting freedom's life and death—it is not the business of the executive branch or Congress to shy away from necessary programs simply because they demand sacrifices of our people. It is the business of both branches of Government to tell the people honestly and clearly what is needed for our survival, and to fight for programs that will meet those needs.

Berlin

Sputnik posed an indirect challenge to the United States. In November, 1958, Premier Khrushchev levied a direct challenge. Asserting that the post-World War II occupation agreements had become outdated, he declared that in six months the Soviet Union would sign a separate peace treaty with East Germany and hand over its power in Berlin to Walter Ulbricht's Communist regime. Thereafter, the Western Powers would have to deal with East Germany over the status of Berlin. In reply, the United States insisted on its treaty rights and promised to "maintain the integrity" of West Berlin. Thus, once again the specter of war hung over the unresolved situation in the heart of Europe.

The renewed Berlin crisis lasted for three years, subsiding intermittently, then reaching a climax in the summer of 1961. Khrushchev soon lifted his six-month deadline, but that did not affect the basis of the East-West stalemate. Three questions were at stake: the independence of Germany, the reunification of Germany, and the status of Berlin. Since 1949, two German governments had been in existence, each increasingly allied with one of the Cold War blocs. The rearmament of West Germany and her membership in NATO were particularly aggravating to the Kremlin. Khrushchev therefore sought to separate West Germany from the West by proposing peace treaties between the World War II victors and each of the German governments. These documents would provide for the removal of occupation troops along with the independence and disarmament of both Germanies. Then the two governments themselves could negotiate German reunification. The Western Powers, on the other hand, proposed independence only after reunification by means of free elections in East and West Germany. As for Berlin, Khrushchev suggested the withdrawal of military occupation forces and the conversion of West Berlin into a "free city." Here too the West would consider a settlement of Berlin's status only after German unification.

This was the diplomatic deadlock, and it survived a series of negotiations between Russia and the West after 1958. First the foreign ministers met in Geneva, conferred at length, but failed to make any progress. Then the Soviet Premier himself came to the United States in September, 1959, toured the nation, and concluded his visit with two days of talks with President Eisenhower at Camp David. The resulting statement by the two leaders raised hopes for resolving the crisis. All international disputes should be resolved peacefully, the communiqué declared; in particular, negotiations over Berlin (which Eisenhower termed "an abnormal situation") should be reopened without any deadline imposed on them. The American press exultantly spoke of a "spirit of Camp David."

Another summit conference was scheduled for Paris in May, 1960. But shortly before the leaders arrived, the Soviets shot down an American U-2 plane flying over Russian territory on a reconnaissance mission. Khrushchev used the event as a reason for accusing the United States of bad faith and for disrupting the summit conference. He apparently had begun to doubt that the West would make concessions on Berlin, and the U-2 flight enabled him to save face. Eisenhower's scheduled visit to the USSR, in return for Khrushchev's American trip, was abruptly canceled. And in October, the Soviet leader set April, 1961, as the deadline for signing a separate peace treaty with East Germany.

By that time a new man occupied the White House, but the old deadlock remained. John F. Kennedy met with Khrushchev at Vienna in the spring of 1961, but they simply reaffirmed their antithetical positions on Berlin. When the Premier returned to Moscow, he repeated his ultimatum and renewed his deadline. President Kennedy, in turn, told the American people in a nationwide television address that the United States would fight, if necessary, to defend its rights in Berlin and the freedom of the West Berliners. But he also went one step beyond this familiar assertion: he called military reserve units to active duty.

With the three-year-old crisis at an acute point of tension, war seemed imminent. There had been those like George Kennan and Poland's Foreign Minister Adam Rapacki who had offered plans for "disengagement" and neutralization in Eastern Europe. But that idea had won little support and, in the tense summer of 1961, seemed utopian. Many Americans, with the President's encouragement, turned to a more despairing alternative: the construction of fallout shelters. Most Americans simply waited for whatever might happen.

It happened before dawn on August 13. The East German government closed the border between East and West Berlin across which

*three million Germans had fled from Communism since 1949. During
the next few days, the East Germans began erecting the concrete
blocks and barbed wire of the Berlin Wall. The Western Powers protested but took no action. In one blunt gesture, Khrushchev completed the isolation of East Germany. He followed with an even more
ominous gesture two weeks later, announcing that the USSR would
resume nuclear testing in the atmosphere. This decision ended the
test moratorium to which both the United States and Russia had
been voluntarily subscribing for three years.*

*Thus, Soviet-American relations reached their lowest point since
the death of Stalin. The hope of "peaceful coexistence," which
Khrushchev had personally and explicitly endorsed in 1959, now
seemed in jeopardy, if not altogether absurd.*

*The following articles illustrate some of the highlights of American
reactions to the Berlin crisis. Hans J. Morgenthau, the noted political
scientist at the University of Chicago, outlines the basic issues in a
brief article written soon after Khrushchev's first ultimatum.*

*The subsequent two essays, published in 1959 and 1960 during
the middle of the long crisis, discuss the general characteristics and
implications of the Soviet-American confrontation. Chalmers M.
Roberts was on the staff of the* Washington Post, *while Stanley Millet
taught social sciences at Briarcliff College. The next pair of articles
expresses the prevailing American mood just before and just after the
Berlin Wall was erected, as compared to the minority position taken
by Norman Cousins, editor of the* Saturday Review.

*Finally, the well-known historian of Communism in America and
Cuba, Theodore Draper, offers a general interpretation of the role of
the Berlin crisis within the larger drama of the Cold War.*

56   SEPARATING THE ISSUES*

The Russian policies which have created the Berlin crisis, and the
reactions to them which can be expected from the West, re-enact—in
a more threatening setting—the fundamental conflict which has pitted
East against West since the end of World War II. This conflict is the
very core of the Cold War.

---

*Hans J. Morgenthau, "Separating the Issues," *New Republic,* Vol. CXL (May 11, 1959),
pp. 13–14. Reprinted by permission of THE NEW REPUBLIC, © 1959, Harrison-Blaine of
New Jersey, Inc.

The fundamental issue which has divided East and West has been the legitimacy of the territorial status quo as it had been established in 1945 by military conquest. The Soviet Union has always considered the line of demarcation of 1945 as the permanent and legitimate boundary between two spheres of influence, one dominated by the Soviet Union, the other by the United States. Stalin envisaged the postwar world divided into two such spheres, and he and his successors have many times—publicly and privately—tried to obtain Western recognition of the legitimacy of the two spheres and their boundary. The West has consistently refused to consider the actual boundary as anything more than a provisional line of demarcation which a definitive settlement must redraw considerably farther to the east, preferably so as to coincide with the frontiers proper of the Soviet Union.

Berlin is the symbol of this unresolved conflict. The Western foothold deep in the Soviet sphere, derived from the legal claim that Berlin is potentially the capital of a united Germany, symbolizes the provisional character of the boundary now running 100 miles west of Berlin. The utter precariousness of the Western position in Berlin, unenforceable on the spot and at the mercy of Russian discretion, reflects the relative permanence, as a matter of political and military fact, of the boundary dividing both Europe and Germany. In the measure that the prospects for that permanence increase and the practicality of unification fades away, Berlin comes to symbolize even more the actual weakness of the West rather than the soundness of its legal claim.

It is against this background of the symbolic function which Berlin has fulfilled in the Cold War that one must consider the alternative policies which are at the disposal of the West. The Russian attack upon the Western position in Berlin implies a commitment to the permanence of the division of Germany. The West can counter this attack by standing firm, by not giving an inch, by pretending that nothing has changed since 1945. This is the position West Germany and France have taken.

The West can go to the other extreme by starting from the assumption that, with Germany being divided in virtual permanence, the Western position in Berlin has become an anachronism. In order to make that position tenable it is then necessary to restore the expectation of German reunification upon which the Western position was originally based. This can be accomplished only by an over-all negotiated settlement with the Soviet Union. The British Government has taken this position, and it must be added in passing that Macmillan follows here in the footsteps of Churchill, as Khrushchev follows in Stalin's. Churchill advocated such a settlement in more than 40 speeches which, in so far as they were reported at all, were dismissed in this country as election propaganda—as are his successor's proposals today.

The third alternative open to the West coincides by and large with Mr. Lippmann's position. It consists of a shift in the legal basis for the Western presence. That shift would go in the direction of internationalizing that legal basis by putting it under the auspices of the United Nations and perhaps also that presence itself by adding neutral contingents to those of the Western allies. Berlin would then symbolize less the unity of Germany than the interest of the international community in a Western enclave in the Communist world.

Of the three alternatives for Western policy, the first is the easiest to choose. It requires little thought and no action at all. It will look heroic and might see us through this crisis while leaving us unprepared for the next one, without contributing anything to the settlement of the conflict of which the current crisis is a mere surface manifestation. The second alternative requires a full measure of statesmanship, great daring, and the taking of considerable risks. It can easily be dismissed as impractical, and so it might well turn out to be. For what has the West to offer the Soviet Union in exchange for at least the first genuine steps toward the unification of Germany? But since genuine over-all negotiations have never been tried— to put forward proposals which on the face of them cannot be accepted by the other side is not to negotiate—it has still to face the test of its practicality.

Mr. Lippmann's proposal requires the willingness and ability to negotiate on the limited issue of the Western position in Berlin. By separating that issue from the problem of German unification, it reconciles Germany's division in relative permanence with the Western presence in Berlin. Such a formula might solve the present crisis and forestall another one over the same issue. It is a formula for dealing with a symptom. It does not pretend to deal with the disease itself. Yet this disease, uncured and even unattended, will erupt again into symptoms of a different kind, each likely to be more serious than the preceding one. Today, the inflexibility of the French and West German Governments hamstrings Western policy. Tomorrow, the flexibility of the two Germanies—one armed with nuclear weapons, the other controlling the accesses to Berlin—might well threaten the world with destruction. Perhaps it is impractical to suggest that the thinkers and statesmen of the world concern themselves with so grave an issue. Yet the very impracticality of the suggestion is a measure of the decline of statesmanship on both sides of the line that divides East and West.

57 THE SEARCH FOR A POLICY*

The Berlin crisis has become the focus of a much larger and more complex question: the future military posture of the United States vis-à-vis that of the Soviet Union. There was more than just lampooning in the Gridiron Club's song at the spring dinner this year. To the tune of "I've Never Been in Love Before," the newsmen sang:

> *We've never been behind before;*
> *Now all at once we are. . . .*
> *It costs too much to try.*
> *The tortoise passed us by;*
> *We're second in the sky.*
> *At last we've stopped*
> *The craze we once were in.*
> *We've really never been*
> > *Behind*
> > *Before.*

But whatever the outcome of the momentous argument over American military preparedness may be—and the outcome will set the limits of power for whoever becomes President in January, 1961—the Berlin crisis must be faced here and now. It is generally agreed here in Washington that negotiations with the Soviets will be under way before Khrushchev's initial May 27 deadline. But there agreement ends. For there is really a fundamental lack of accord, both inside and outside the administration, over the prospects for negotiation.

The prevailing view in the capital is that Khrushchev created the Berlin crisis because of the weakness of the Soviet position in eastern Europe, especially in East Germany. This line is akin to that of Chancellor Konrad Adenauer. The theory is that West Berlin, that island of freedom and luxury inside East Germany, makes Communist consolidation of the satellites impossible; and hence Khrushchev has moved to liquidate West Berlin. Khrushchev probably thought he

*Chalmers M. Roberts, "Guesswork, Loose Talk, and the Search for a Policy," *Reporter*, Vol. XX (April 2, 1959), pp. 24-25. Copyright 1959 by The Reporter Magazine Company.

could get the city cheap, that the specter of nuclear war cast by Soviet missile blackmail would force a western retreat. If he discovers otherwise, so the theory goes, he will back down.

Another view is that Khrushchev, though cocky over Soviet military power, is really seeking an accommodation with the West in Europe, partly to gain time to overtake the United States economically and partly to press forward at points of western weakness in the Middle East, Africa, Asia, and Latin America. This view considers Khrushchev's demands that the West recognize the *status quo* in Europe as indicative that he may be willing to pay a price of some sort for such recognition, and that he is using Berlin to pry forth a serious western offer for a European settlement.

Official policy has, in fact, become an amalgam of both lines of thought. The administration is going to negotiate; that is clear enough. The question is how far it is prepared to go and what kind of proposals it can agree on with its allies—Britain, France, and West Germany above all. The flurries in Washington, Paris, and Bonn over Harold Macmillan's visit to Moscow all related to this question. So did Macmillan's visit to Washington.

JUST THINKING OUT LOUD

Part of the confusion in Washington is an inevitable concomitant of a democracy making up its mind. But part also is due to the illness of John Foster Dulles. His absence has robbed the West of its most resourceful spokesman. Regardless of Macmillan's efforts to fill the vacuum, the leadership of the West inevitably lies in Washington, not in London. With Dulles ill, President Eisenhower has become the western spokesman; but his words have been confusing and imprecise. And in the absence of Dulles's precision in policy pronouncements, every man—and especially members of Congress—has become his own foreign-policy expert.

Everyone of importance has pronounced himself in favor of standing firm over Berlin. But no one is really sure just what that means. The Senate's Democratic whip, Mike Mansfield of Montana, got himself out on a limb by calling for direct negotiations between East and West Germany, to Khrushchev's glee and Adenauer's alarm. In fact, the senator was intent on trying to wake up Washington and the nation to the Berlin crisis. When he found he had gone too far, Mansfield did his best to crawl back from his limb.

The most alarming loose talk, however, has come from within the administration. Defense Secretary McElroy was the first to say that any war over Berlin would doubtless be nuclear. Like the President, he was reacting in part to Democratic criticisms of administration defense policies. Mr. Eisenhower is not a man who likes criticism. And at his extraordinary press conference on March 11 he appeared in the role of General Eisenhower, angered by the needling of buck-private members of Congress. His voice was full of scorn at those who challenged his earlier declaration that "I think I am more able" than the critics to decide what is needed for defense. There was a steely glint in his eyes when he said the individual members of the Joint Chiefs of Staff each has "his own reservations when he wants what he wants." In a sense, the President also seemed to be mad at himself. Because he is not the most articulate of men, he gets frustrated, then angry, when he realizes he can't make his listeners understand or accept what seems to him a simple fact.

The morning of the press conference the Washington *Star* had carried a dispatch from West Berlin saying diplomats there felt the only way to deter Khrushchev from trying to impose his own settlement was by giving him "the clearest warning of the danger of nuclear war." At the conference the *Star's* White House reporter asked the President whether the United States is "prepared to use nuclear war if necessary to defend free Berlin." It was in response to this query that Mr. Eisenhower said, "Well, I don't know how you could free anything with nuclear weapons"—having just said there would be no ground war in Europe because the West is so greatly outnumbered.

The President added his expression of disbelief "that anyone would be senseless enough to push that to the point of reality ...," i.e., that Khrushchev would push things in Berlin to the point of conflict. This statement was taken by his critics as indicating an overhopeful view. And coupled with a no-ground-war and nuclear-war-is-too-terrible attitude, what did it leave? Only negotiations. But on what terms? The circle of confusion was made complete.

Ironically Secretary Dulles, who has been the apostle of firmness, had begun to show signs of flexibility before he was hospitalized in February. On his last trip to Europe, his aides reported that he had won Adenauer's consent at least to consider the idea of thinning out the rival East-West forces in central Europe. This idea is still alive in Washington, certainly in London, perhaps even in Paris and Bonn.

But the problem is not so much whether troops should be thinned out, or whether there should be a nuclear free zone as suggested by the Rapacki Plan, or whether there should be some other form of what is generally termed disengagement. The problem is how to get Khrushchev to pay something for any of these changes—and they would be major changes—in western policy. Specifically, the problem as seen in Washington is how to get Khrushchev to agree at least to steps toward German reunification.

Khrushchev has said "No" to reunification so often and has demanded some form of disengagement so many times that the basis of any East-West conference, whether among foreign ministers or heads of government, has been shifting. For a decade or more the West could simply reject Soviet terms and make the rejection stick. But this is no longer true. That fact underlies the alarm expressed today by the administration's critics.

The reason, as the critics see it, is the change in military posture. The 1959 Berlin crisis, they feel, really dates from the first Sputnik. Khrushchev is using his new power and using it effectively. Moreover, the administration won't concede its mistakes, won't concede that its concentration on budget balancing has robbed it of diplomatic power. This is perhaps the most alarming feature of all.

IS THERE A "DULLES PLAN"?

It was against this background of alarm and confusion that the President necessarily took to radio and television on March 16 to state his and America's case. Fundamentally, of course, he said nothing to alter the fact that American weaponry is on the downgrade relative to Russia's. Showing a list of missiles, present and future, did not silence the critics on this long-range issue. But Eisenhower did bring some order out of the chaos of his press conference when he talked to the world about Berlin and about negotiating with the Kremlin. He stated well the reasons for firmness, and he did it without saber rattling.

As to negotiations, the President took the road toward the summit and removed some of the impediments as he did so. Instead of the oft-repeated demand for real progress by the foreign ministers first, this time Mr. Eisenhower spoke only of "developments that justify a summer meeting at the Summit." That should make it much easier to get the heads of state together at a conference table—and to swallow the perilous Berlin issue in larger discussions about Germany and European security.

In addition, the President said that the United States is not only willing to listen to "new ideas" but will present some of its own. There has been talk here in Washington that Dulles has been putting pencil to paper in the hospital to produce those ideas, perhaps even a "Dulles Plan" to cap his career.

Viewed in the context of the larger issue of the relative Soviet and American military postures, the Eisenhower speech indicates that Soviet might is forcing the first real break in a decade in American policy for Europe. In terms of the immediate Berlin crisis, the result may well be to minimize the possibility of armed conflict.

Both Moscow and Washington appear to be trying to avoid words like "deadline" and "ultimatum," even if the press and the senators keep using them. Perhaps this is a hopeful sign; perhaps the Berlin crisis will not lead to a passage at arms after all. It does appear to be leading to a conference table at which the stakes are tremendous, but where the West's pile of chips is far less imposing than it was at the last East-West meeting.

58 A ROAD TO PEACE*

We have lived so long with the cold war that our very capacity to think about foreign policy has atrophied. Foreign policy is the major issue in the Presidential campaign, and everyone agrees that "fresh approaches" and "bold new plans" are necessary. But of new policies themselves, or of fresh approaches that might be tested, we have heard scarcely a word. Our political thought is so tightly imprisoned in primitive anti-communism and narrow strategic concepts that the only serious debates over foreign policy which our public life has sustained in recent years have been concerned with military expenditures and with espionage. For the rest, we seem content with containment, collective security pacts and, as the current phrase has it, an adequate defense posture. That is to say, we accept the structure built for the cold war, the very structure which the events of the past spring and summer have called into question.

But these are paradoxical times. If the free world has been unable to break free of stale commitments, such has not been the case in the unfree East. The Khrushchev proposals to bring the cold war to an end through peaceful coexistence are just such an attempt at a radi-

---

*Stanley Millet, "A Road to Peace," *Nation,* Vol. CXCI (September 10, 1960), pp. 127–30.

cal reformulation of Russian foreign policy and of the principles upon which that policy has been based since the end of the Second World War. Within the context of Soviet political thought the Khrushchev proposals are heretical. By asserting that the Western "imperialists" no longer necessarily seek war and that it is possible for the Communist world to live in peace with them (dare an American politician make an equivalent assertion about the Communists?), Khrushchev has attacked sacred doctrine itself. That imperialism inevitably breeds war has, after all, been a cardinal principle of Leninism.

Paradox piles on paradox. It appears now that the Great Debate over foreign policy has taken place, not in the United States where speech is free, but in the totalitarian Communist world. Such, it is evident, was the main business at the conference of Communist parties in Bucharest last June. And at that conference the debate apparently was resolved in favor of Khrushchev's policy of détente.

Despite the intransigence of Soviet policy in recent weeks, the Khrushchev proposals are still said to stand. They are still as relevant to our predicament as they are to that of the Russians. The alternatives posed by them are the only alternatives which face both of us: either détente and an end to the cold war, or containment and deterrence with the inescapable risk that the whole system of pressure and counter-pressure may collapse at any moment. And if our own public discussions have failed to turn up reasonable terms for détente, we are left with only the Khrushchev proposals to consider.

Do the Khrushchev proposals in fact point the way to an agreement? The five years which have passed since they were first offered have set his arguments in perspective. In sum, he has proposed that the cold war be ended on the basis of the existing *status quo,* and that future conflict between the two systems be carried on through peaceful means alone. The principal specific issues which must be settled to bring the cold war to an end are defined as disarmament, the German question and the related question of Berlin.

In his early speeches, Khrushchev invariably gave prominence to the German question. This, he said, was the "question of questions" between East and West. More recently, he has reversed the order, and called disarmament the crucial question. The reversal of importance is unfortunate, and it is equally unfortunate that all of the Western statesmen have joined him in thrusting this issue into prominence. It is unfortunate because disarmament is the least promising issue through which to seek a détente between East and West. Precisely because of the terrible character of modern military technology, negotiation over purely contentious questions must be avoided. And, until political conflict is eliminated, disarmament talks will yield only contention, never solutions. As long as fundamental political conflict persists, disarmament discussions necessarily take place on the basis of a search for military advantage, that is to say, on the basis of irreconcilable interests. Even when disarmament is considered in the abstract, it is clear that only the most insignificant agreements affect both parties with reasonable reciprocity, so different are their situations, geography, development, and the like. In practice, both Russia and the United States have been seriously interested only in such measures of disarmament as conserve their advantages as they see them, and the record amply justifies the recriminations made by both.

Following the Khrushchev theses, then, we are left with only Germany and Berlin as issues through which a détente might be reached. But the Berlin question, however grave it has become in its own right, is only an appendage to the German question. Khrushchev deliberately raised it as a lever with which to force a more satisfactory solution to the German question. At the carefully prepared press conference from which the Berlin question was launched in November, 1958, the *Pravda* reporter asked why it was necessary to press the matter of Berlin at that time. Khrushchev replied that negotiations over Germany were at an impasse because the West refused to recognize realities—and he made it clear that the *de facto* existence of two Germanys was the particular reality he then had in mind—so Russia had no choice but to bring about an end to the occupation of Berlin. The uncertain line which the Russians have followed since suggests that the strong stand taken by the United States came as a surprise to Khrushchev. But we did take a strong stand, declaring last April that we regarded our position in Berlin as a *casus belli;* Khrushchev answered in kind only a few weeks before the May Summit meeting and, if Khrushchev's interests in Berlin had really been what he made them appear to be, that city would have brought us closer to war with the Soviet Union than we were in 1949.

There are lessons as well as risks in the Berlin question. The Russians insist on the termination of Western rights in Berlin. We insist on their continuance. So posed, there is no compromise, and again we are confronted with an issue in which the interests of the sides are irreconcilable. Russia has a geographical advantage in this dispute; hence the tactical insistence upon a time limit for the solution of the question. But there is no real urgency in the Berlin matter for the Soviet Union. The pressure is entirely artificial. The only real solution for the Berlin question lies in a solution to the German question, and it was for this purpose that the dispute was manufactured. All the compromises which we have so far proposed—the reduction of occupation forces to token strength, the control of propaganda and espionage, the recognition of an East German "presence"—are beside the point and useless. Khrushchev will drive us to the recognition of East Germany if he must risk war to do it.

These are bold tactics, but boldness is a side of the Russian Premier that must never be lost sight of. He is not only a daring politician; he has a positive appetite for the dramatic. Witness not only the Berlin dispute, but the performance at the Paris Summit meeting and, boldest of all, the attack upon Stalin at the 20th Party Congress. Khrushchev is par excellence the statesman of the "brink," and in tense times is a real danger if pushed too hard.

The Berlin dispute, then, offers no hope for détente. What of the German question? In form, it is the classic type of dispute—a conflict over territory lying between the parties—which permits resolution through compromise. Is it so in substance as well? The answer becomes clear when the issues are examined.

At first glance, the Khrushchev position seems no different from that held by the Russians since the appearance of the two German regimes: unification through a federation of the two existing Germanys. Nor has our own position changed materially. We insist upon unification only through free elections. The Russian position contemplates not only the "neutralization" of Germany, but the extension of Russian influence deep into Western Europe. The Western position contemplates not only the disappearance of the East German regime (based on a reading of German sentiment toward Russia) and a united Germany allied with the West, but the contraction of Russian influence at least to the borders of Poland. The essence of the German question is thus revealed to be a conflict over spheres of influence in Europe, and it is a conflict that reaches to the very heart of the cold war.

But the Khrushchev proposals create a new setting for this dispute and offer, at last, the possibility of its resolution. Khrushchev has insisted that the cold war can be ended if both sides will accept existing realities. And this means acceptance by both parties of the division of Europe between East and West with which the Second World War ended, and which has since been consolidated by the years of the cold war. It means also a settlement along the line of the Iron Curtain—a recognition by the West of the existing system in Eastern

Europe in return for a recognition by the Soviet Union of the restriction of that system to Eastern Europe. In a word, a recognition by both sides of what *is* the case in Europe, what has been the case in Europe for more than fifteen years, and what neither the Russians nor we will permit to change, even if we must go to war to preserve it. Our attitude in the Berlin question and Russia's actions in Poland and Hungary in 1956 amply demonstrate that determination. Russian willingness to accept this situation has already been shown by recognition of the West German government; the parallel course for us, pointing the way to the end of the German question and the Berlin question, lies in our recognition of the East German government, with all that that implies.

Is such a settlement in our interests? Although detailed arrangements will be very difficult to arrive at, an accommodation on the basis of an exact reciprocal regard for the strategic interests of both East and West can, in principle, be found. No other outstanding issue has this advantage. Moreover, a German settlement should include not only recognition of the East German government but a retreat from our Potsdam position and a recognition of the existing borders of Poland. In this way, the freedom of action of West Germany might be preserved.

More important, any relaxation of Western pressure upon the satellite system must necessarily result in a relaxation of Russian pressure on these states. Thus, a Western guarantee of Poland's present borders promises not only freedom of action for Germany but for Poland as well. The history of the Hungarian uprising in 1956 might have run an entirely different course had the future of Germany been settled at the time when Nagy held power. Indeed, recognition of the satellite system of Eastern Europe and "disengagement" through some reciprocal withdrawal of American and Russian forces stands as the *only* present path to possible freedom for these states: the heavier the Western military pressure on the Soviet Union, the heavier must the Russian yoke rest upon the states of Eastern Europe. Whatever kindness we can do for these countries can be done only through détente with the Soviet Union.

Of course, the Khrushchev proposals are also to the advantage of the Soviet Union (else they would never have been offered). But this very fact serves to answer Western skeptics who argue against a détente on the ground that the Russians cannot be trusted. Even the most implacable Russophobe must admit that the Russians can be trusted to uphold an agreement which serves their interests.

Two further considerations arising out of the Khrushchev proposals must be touched on. His offer is for a European settlement only. China and the problems of the Far East are referred to no more than protocol would seem to require. This aspect of his proposal may be, in the final analysis, the most significant. It may well represent more important evidence of the divergence between the policies of the Soviet Union and those of Communist China than do the ideological disputes about which we have heard so much of late. It suggests the possibility that Khrushchev may be concerned to secure his western flank. And, if we insist on thinking in strategic terms, by the same token but with more immediate urgency, it permits us to secure our flank in the West. The earth is round, and it is we who are encircled in the cold war.

But Khrushchev's offer of a purely European settlement also suggests that he wishes to settle differences among the nuclear powers. These are—for the present—the European powers as well. Once again we find an interest in common with the Soviet Union. At the moment détente with Russia is the only move that offers to us and to the world the possibility of restricting nuclear weapons to the present holders.

Finally, we must consider the kind of peaceful coexistence that Khrushchev proposes. He has been clear about this: by peaceful coexistence, he does not mean an end to conflict between the two systems. The "ideological struggle," as he puts it, is to continue. The battle between capitalism and communism for control of the world is to be carried on by all means short of violence between the two major representatives of these systems. War, as a revolutionary method, is to be abandoned; conversely, Khrushchev asks that war as a "counter-revolutionary" method be abandoned. This conception of peace has been rejected by the United States, although it may be the best that we can manage. And would acceptance be entirely against our interests? Our official doctrine does not require war to defeat communism. Dare we have so little confidence in the power of our system to prevail in non-violent conflict with theirs? In Europe, in any case, the risk is not very great. There are the most stable states in the world, and little is to be feared there from subversion.

Moreover, need we continue to think in the artificial antinomies of Communist analysis—either capitalism *or* communism? The post-war world has shown itself to be astonishingly rich in the creation of new social forms, and political lines have never been drawn according to the simple prescriptions of Marxism-Leninism. The future will be, as the past has been, a time of change and upheaval. We cannot avoid change, nor can we stifle it. But we can influence the direction and quality of change; Khrushchev's proposal confers upon us at least as much chance to influence change as it does upon him. Both of us have in common an interest to see that no effort to influence the course of the future will lead to war.

59 GETTING SET FOR TROUBLE*

The war of nerves which may end in some form of shooting before its climax is reached has kept on expanding in recent days.

Nikita Khrushchev on July 9 again threatened to blow up those who do not give him his way. That same day he made a big display of his latest heavy bombers. This time he rattled his military aircraft rather than his missiles.

The Soviet dictator also announced that he was rescinding plans to reduce his armed forces by 1.2 million men. Instead he said that he was going to increase military spending by 30 per cent and warned that if Western nations add one division of troops to their defense he will add 100 to his.

Khrushchev was talking at his toughest.

A U.S. Call-up? President Kennedy on July 10 directed that another study be made of the U.S. military position. He asked that a report on that study be ready within two weeks.

It was made known to Congress that a further increase in funds would be requested for military purposes.

All of this led, on July 11, to a statement by Roswell L. Gilpatric, Deputy Secretary of Defense, that the Defense Department is considering a call-up of reserve forces.

August 1 was being mentioned as the time when moves might begin that could build up to later trouble of a serious nature.

On August 1, the Soviets say, they plan to put East Germans in charge of the air corridor from West Germany to West Berlin. Aircraft would be required to register with East German authorities before they could make flights.

The East Germans on July 12 charged that two divisions of troops had been flown from West Germany to West Berlin. The Commu-

* "Getting Set for Trouble" and "How Americans Feel about Standing Up to Khrushchev," *U.S. News and World Report,* Vol. LI (July 24, 1961), pp. 31-35. Reprinted from *U.S. News & World Report.* Copyright 1961 U.S. News & World Report, Inc.

nists' statements about the movement of troops were characterized by Western officials as "nonsense."

Senator Hubert H. Humphrey of Minnesota, who is close to the Kennedy Administration, said in West Berlin on July 10 that the problem of Berlin might find its way into the United Nations for consideration.

Khrushchev in Moscow on July 11 replied that the Soviet Union "would not recognize" any decision of the United Nations that went against Soviet wishes, but "would uphold its rights, relying on force."

Communist rulers of East Germany at about the same time began to harass people of East Berlin who have jobs in West Berlin. These East Berliners were denied the right to buy electrical appliances and some other products in the stores of the Communist-controlled part of the city. . . .

In Washington, the White House prepared an *aide mémoire* setting out in detail all of the moves made by the Soviet Union in violation of agreements covering the rights of Allied forces in Berlin. The record was being made clear as a prelude to other moves.

Khrushchev's growing threats have forced a reappraisal of U.S. military policy. Military opinion appears to be swinging away from the view that any future shooting in Europe will lead immediately to the use of nuclear weapons. Nuclear weapons will be in the background, but actual shooting for limited objectives can be done by ground troops, using conventional weapons and relying on conventional air support.

It is this altered view of the military problem that has led to a somewhat "agonizing reappraisal" of U.S. strength. What this reappraisal has disclosed is not found reassuring. Military manpower is being squeezed to a point that is regarded as entirely inadequate to deal with the threat posed by Communist forces.

President Kennedy on July 14 was reported to be considering a request to Congress to declare a national emergency. That would permit the Administration to call up the Standby Reserve as well as the Ready Reserve of the National Guard and the reserve forces of Army, Navy and Air Force.

By July 15, it was clear that the U.S. was preparing for a showdown on Berlin.

· · ·

The American people, by a margin of nearly 3 to 1, are ready to call Khrushchev's hand in Berlin.

If this means war, then these same people are prepared to risk it rather than to be pushed around any more.

In a survey of opinion across the country, members of the National Staff of *U.S. News & World Report* talked to hundreds of Americans from coast to coast. Here is what those people said the U.S. should do about Berlin:

Make a strong stand risking war if necessary	71%
Be firm but cautious avoiding war if possible	15%
Yield rather than fight in defense of Berlin	14%

At the same time, other staff members went over mail that has been received by members of Congress. They discovered the same attitude expressed there.

If Nikita Khrushchev thinks that his recent threats and his boasts of Soviet military power are frightening the American public, he's wrong.

The survey shows only a small minority of Americans are ready to yield in Berlin rather than take any risk of war.

Instead of fear, the prevailing mood in this country today is one of anger. Mention Russia to almost any American, and he gets angry.

This phrase you hear time and again: "We're going to have to lick the Russians."

"Get rid of them—knock them in the head," was the urging of a hydraulic engineer in Carson City, Nev.

"Poke Khrushchev in the nose," said a woman operating a news-stand in Columbus, Ohio. In that same city, a Negro porter said: "I think we ought to call Khrushchev's bluff. I'm getting sick of listen-to him."

"Russia is a bully," said a worker in a garment factory in Brooklyn, N.Y. "We didn't take guff from Japan or Germany in the last war. I wouldn't take it from Russia now."

Everywhere you go you find Americans who are tired of giving ground to the Soviets. Said a logger's wife in California:

"We've been backing up so long we've lost face in the world. And we at home have lost faith in our Government. I'm ashamed of our endless backing up. We're as strong as they are. Why don't we act accordingly? I want this country to show leadership, not just react to what the Communists do. Yes, I realize war's a possibility. But we can't go on endlessly giving in."

Across the country, in Fall River, Mass., a business executive expressed the same idea:

"You can't let yourself be kicked around all the time by a bunch of gangsters. There was a time we had guts. Now we go to wars and refuse to win them. We should have stopped the Communists years ago."

In Madison, Wis., a retired official of the State Government said:

"We've been soft. When you're soft, they take advantage of you. The reason that Russia gets ahead of us is that in the U.S. there are too many pussyfooters, too many straddlers, and too many who will take something with their hands behind their back."

"We've been kicked around long enough," said a supervisor in a Bronx manufacturing concern. "We should stand firm against the Communists all over the world."

One person after another tells you that the time has come for U.S. to stand up to Russia. . . .

An advertising man in Omaha, Nebr., declared:

"If they shoot down our planes, we should just start dropping bombs on Russia and get it over with. We would have to go into Russia and Red China. If Truman had let [General] MacArthur go into Red China we wouldn't have that worry today."

A few Americans are ready to take the initiative and hit Russia first—instead of waiting for Russia to start it. A fisherman in Lapush, Wash., expressed that idea in these words:

"The one that pushes the first button is going to win the next war. If I were President, I'd start pushing the button right now."

"Time to Draw a Line."   The idea most often expressed is that this country should now draw a line and warn Russia not to step over it.

A department-store owner in Des Moines, Ia., summarized this thinking:

"The only thing Khrushchev understands is power. We should draw a line and tell him, 'Don't come across.' I don't want to see another war, but if we give way, he'll keep nibbling away at us.". . .

"We Can't Withdraw."   A minister in Napoleon, Ohio, expressed an attitude found often: "We have commitments to West Germany. We can't withdraw from those commitments."

A Virginia banker agreed: "Berlin is now a matter of principle." An attorney in Des Moines, Ia., said: "We've let Khrushchev maneuver us into a position where the decision on Berlin is a major one, and we can't afford to back down." And a Stanford, Calif., housewife said: "All along, we've made Berlin the place where we said we'd stand. We can't back down on this one."

Berlin is regarded by a number of Americans as the last chance to make a stand. This view was expressed by a State legislator from Akron, Ohio:

"We gave in too many times in the past. This is one time we can't give in. We've gotten to the break-off place. There's no place to go if we back up now."

Many people are found not to be overly excited about Khrushchev's latest Berlin threats. They figure he is bluffing—and that if his bluff is called he will choose not to fight. . . .

Better Now Than Later.   If it turns out that Khrushchev really is itching for a fight, then it is the opinion of most Americans that it would be better to have the fight now than later.

A receptionist in Carson City, Nev., put it this way: "The only way to stop Khrushchev is with bullets. Better today than in five years when they've already got everything."

A Nevada businessman predicted: "The longer we delay a showdown, the tougher it will be for us."

"By giving up more ground any place in the world we only create more risk of war later on," said a Perry, Ia., banker.

In Columbus, Ohio, a businessman looked at it this way:

"If we fail to act on the principles we believe in—as the European nations failed to act against Hitler in the mid-'30s—then this young generation will eventually have to fight a war on the enemy's terms."

One who favors an early showdown was a medicine wholesaler in North Carolina, who said: "Let's get in a fight over Berlin now, so we won't have to fight in the U.S. later."

You find very little support among Americans for a policy of appeasement. The feeling is that the U.S. already has appeased Moscow too long. . . .

Faith in U.S. Might.   If it comes to a showdown fight with Russia, most Americans express confidence that this country will come out on top.

"Khrushchev doesn't scare me," said a retired grocer in Bristol, Conn. "I'll put American boys up against the best he's got, anytime—if it came to that."

Said a sand blaster in Scranton, Pa.:

"Khrushchev's nibbling us to death. I say let's get this situation straightened out. And I don't think we'd come out second best. But if we did, I'd rather die a quick death than a slow one.". . .

A Minority View.   Not everybody, of course, is willing to fight for Berlin. There is a minority in America which believes that this country should avoid, at almost any price, the horror and destruction of a nuclear war.

"Did you ever stop to think what another war would mean?" asks a woman teacher in Phoenix, Ariz. "It could mean the destruction of our planet."

Some Americans see no reason to die for Germans, whom this country has fought in two world wars. A railroad man in North Hero, Vt., expressed this view:

"I wouldn't lift a finger to defend Berlin. The sooner we talk our way out of there the better, because sure as anything the Germans are going to get us into a new war in Europe. What would I fight for? Not for Europe, that's sure."

And a California saleswoman said: "The Germans wouldn't go to bat for us. They never have."

Women, as might be expected, are somewhat less ready to risk war than men. A New Rochelle, N.Y., housewife spoke for many women when she said: "I don't want to see my boys go into service. We should put a firm foot down someplace. But we should try and do it without a war. Once you do that, we're all finished."

A Look to the Future.   Yet you find many women, as well as men, who are ready to take a strong stand against the Russians—and back it up, even if it means war.

Like the Atlanta, Ga., housewife, who said:

"If we don't wake up soon we will be slaves. We've gotten so soft the Communists are going to take us over. Right now, I would give up my lovely home and go fight for freedom. I don't want to be a slave."

Or the housewife in Amarillo, Tex., who said:

"We have so much to lose we should stand up and protect it. I'm concerned as to what kind of world my children will live in. I want it to be a good world."

60   THE POWER AND THE HONOR *

Darkness falls from the air. Khrushchev's nuclear debris over North America, on its way around the globe, redeclares the Cold War's

---

* "The Power and the Honor," *Life*, Vol. LI (September 15, 1961), p. 4. Life Magazine, September 15, © 1961, Time Inc.

ubiquity. His brutal intransigence on Berlin redeclares its seriousness. The Cold War may turn hot any week.

We have been told that nobody can win that hot war—and there is still reason to hope and pray that it can be avoided. But the Berlin crisis makes one thing clear, even to Americans who have long preferred not to face it. The Cold War will have a winner. And it will have a loser.

Winner and loser may or may not be decided in Berlin. As Assistant Secretary of Defense Paul Nitze stated last week, our best Berlin tactics may be to apply counterpressure elsewhere. But Berlin is one test of our readiness to fight for freedom, and that readiness is one qualification for victory in the Cold War.

"There is no question about Berlin—we'll fight," says President Kennedy. Khrushchev has heard this. Why then does he talk and act as though he does not believe it?

Khrushchev must be aware that the American people are willing to face nuclear war for Berlin. He may even know about our spontaneous boom in shelter-building, and that people like Eleanor Roosevelt, who used to think shelters "foolish," are now in favor of them. He cannot doubt our ability to wage nuclear war, or to erase his cities.

Can he doubt that we have a good reason to fight for Berlin? Perhaps he thinks that what he calls "the common sense of the Western statesmen" will make us give way at the last minute. So let us re-examine why we are willing to fight.

Our paramount reason is our commitment, in solemn agreements of long standing, to defend those allied rights in Berlin on which the liberties of its people depend. Such a commitment is reason enough for a great nation to do what it has said it will do. Khrushchev understands this reason in a cloudy way, but only when it is translated as American prestige—*not* as American honor. President Kennedy's immediate problem is to make Khrushchev understand the importance of our commitment more exactly. Unlike prestige, honor cannot be served by some face-saving device. Honor is an aspect of our power.

For the first 10 years of the Cold War—from the Truman Doctrine until Sputnik—the U.S. was far more powerful than Russia, both in fact and in men's eyes. Soviet gains in that decade were made, so to speak, on our mistakes or our sufferance. But since Russia achieved parity in nuclear weapons, the U.S. has been militarily just as vulnerable as Russia, and this new rough equality of power gives an advantage to the offensive side. Since his first Berlin "ultimatum" in 1958, Khrushchev has been basing his offensive demands on this new power relationship.

"Times have changed now," he said last week, "the Soviet Union has changed, and its economic, political and military might is much greater." According to one American who has argued with him, Khrushchev thinks it is immoral to have power and not exploit it. If his new power does not earn him new concessions, currently Berlin, he will feel somehow robbed. He will continue to feel that way, being a Communist, until "the International Soviet shall be the human race."

The new power balance which Khrushchev is exploiting is clearly dangerous to peace, to freedom and to the security of the West. In the not very long run, it will have to be replaced by a world in which the Communists are drastically and increasingly out-gunned, out-numbered and out-powered. That development would mean victory in the Cold War.

How do we go about getting this safer balance? Since forms and vehicles of power are changing, the ultimate victory may depend on anything from the third grade curriculum to moon-shots, and we shall have to cultivate continuous excellence on many new frontiers. But two older sources of Western power require immediate attention.

The first is our NATO alliance. Khrushchev said last week that Britain, France and Italy are in effect his hostages, since a few bombs on each could take them out of a nuclear war. There is some uncomfortable truth in his reckoning. Europe has distressingly lagged in its contribution to Western defense. The NATO forces and strategy, overdependent on SAC, have been losing credibility for several years.

Washington has recently initiated some corrective measures. Not only is the U.S. range of deterrents being given more flexibility but NATO ground forces are being substantially increased. To encourage still greater increases by the Europeans, some 40,000 more U.S. troops have been ordered abroad and more could usefully follow.

Europe's potential in wealth and manpower would be ample to redress the power situation if mobilized. Said *Paris-Match* recently, "On the day when the Russians have to measure themselves, in their struggle for the future, not only against the U.S. but also against Europe, the course of history will begin to change."

A second source of U.S. power that needs attention is world opinion. We have made a considerable investment in cultivating this amorphous and uncertain power, but not always of the right kind. Tito's meeting of "nonaligned" leaders in Belgrade last week illustrates the point.

The kind of world opinion worth cultivating will hear any argument except one: might makes right. The Belgrade leaders, claiming to be "the conscience of the world," had a chance to say something meaningful about the Berlin crisis and at least to reprove Khrushchev's use of nuclear terror. Instead they produced a lot of irrelevant eyewash about colonialism. The might-makes-right argument, apparently, was the only one they heard.

"A decent respect to the opinions of mankind" does not require us to be guided by foolish opinions. Our duty rather is to clarify our own policies, letting our own conscience be our first guide. We are now credited with a propaganda victory (short-lived) because Khrushchev, not we, ended the nuclear test ban. Perhaps we would have earned more respect, even in Belgrade, had we ended it months ago with a good explanation of our reasons. They were better reasons than the ones Khrushchev gave.

Honor and reason are on our side in the Cold War. As the Berlin crisis makes urgently clear, we also need the power and will to carry us to victory.

61 NO EXTERMINATION WITHOUT REPRESENTATION*

In the front pages of this issue, Mr. Joseph Alsop, one of America's most knowledgeable and respected world affairs observers, defines the national survival challenges facing President Kennedy. The key question involved in these challenges, as Mr. Alsop sees it, is whether the President is justified in risking national suicide on the Berlin issue.

It is possible that the question may be even broader than this. The essential question facing President Kennedy—and also Chairman Khrushchev—may go even beyond the issue of national survival. That question is whether any nation has the right to engage in war against the human race in the pursuit of its national aims or needs.

The central meaning of nuclear war is precisely that it is not a contest just between the contending nations. The effects of a nuclear war today will extend to a large part of the earth's population. This does not mean that the human race will necessarily be exterminated in a modern war. It is possible that large areas in the southern latitudes may be spared. But it is also likely that a substantial portion of the population in the northern latitudes will be condemned. The radioactive poisons pumped into the air and carried by the winds

*Norman Cousins, "Berlin: No Extermination without Representation," *Saturday Review,* Vol. XLIV (August 5, 1961), pp. 20, 40.

would convert the atmosphere into a lethal canopy over the most densely populated regions of the world.

President Kennedy, therefore, is confronted with a question that is not limited to the future of the United States. He is confronted with a question concerning human destiny. It is a profoundly moral question. How far should a nation go in upholding its national interests? What is the ultimate responsibility of an American President? Is it just to the nation? If the answer is yes, then is there anything in the history or values of that nation which connects it to a purpose or to values higher than its own welfare? What is the highest good? Does the human community have any claim on the American purpose?

To repeat, how far should a nation go in upholding its national interests? Is a policeman justified in firing into a crowd in an effort to kill a murderer? Is any nation justified in firing into the body of humanity in an effort to kill an enemy?

It is natural and urgent that the United States consider these questions. The United States is not just a national enterprise. It is a human enterprise. It was founded for a very special purpose. That purpose was not just to create a nation but to create a set of ideas by which free men could come into their own, the theory being that government exists in order to protect the natural rights of man.

It is not in the American grain, therefore, to take the cynical view and say that our job is to look out for ourselves and let the atomic chips fall where they may. Those who argue that moral judgments are extraneous where the national interests are concerned may have in mind the history of nations in general, but they do no particular justice to the ideological origins of this nation.

Inevitably, it will be asked at this point whether this means that the United States has no alternative but to back down on the Berlin issue. It will be said that Mr. Khrushchev may be gambling that the United States will be unwilling to risk a nuclear showdown over Berlin; indeed, he may be counting on it. Are we therefore to become paralyzed by nuclear jitters while Mr. Khrushchev proceeds to take over place after place under the cover of our fears? On the other hand, if the Soviet knows we mean what we say when we say we will not retreat, come hell or high atomic water, may this not in fact be the only way of saving Berlin and preventing what would ultimately be a nuclear war anyway?

This is a strong argument, but it misses two essential points.

The first point is that it is all well and good for the United States to say we don't want to live in a world in which Berlin will fall under

Communist control, to be followed, piece by piece, by most of the rest of the world. But at least let us not make decisions that affect others without consulting them. At least let there be no extermination without representation. If we believe that all men are involved in the issue over Berlin—as they may well be—then let our approach reflect that fact. Let us carry the case before the entire human community. Let us mobilize our facts in the most dramatic form in an attempt to put the potent force of world public opinion to work in the present crisis. The only thing greater than nuclear force is an aroused world conscience. And if we hold back from doing this because we have little confidence that we can persuade the majority, then there is something wrong with our moral imagination.

The second point, closely related to the first, is that it is dangerously untrue to say that the only choices before us are national suicide or national surrender. The vital alternative is a massive attempt through the United Nations to relate the crisis of Berlin to the larger crisis facing the world. That larger crisis is represented by the absence of effective law in the relationships of nations, and the likelihood of aggression in a situation in which nations are allowed to decide for themselves what their security requires.

Mr. Khrushchev has warned that he will not be intimidated by what the United Nations may decide. If this is the case, then this should be the central issue, rather than Berlin alone. If the Soviet wishes to take the position that it is stonily opposed to any attempt to settle differences among nations on the basis of world law and world will, then the entire human community should consider the implications of this fact. In any event, the issue of Berlin is not just whether the United States is right or the Soviet Union is right. The issue is whether the contending nations have the right to proceed without regard for the lives and opinions of others. Mankind is involved and mankind has a right to be consulted. There can be no more hideous arrogance than is represented by a policy that involves other peoples without their fullest participation in any determination.

Not until the United Nations is made central in any attack on the Berlin problem, and not until the power of world public opinion is tapped, can we or anyone say that the only alternative to Soviet intransigence in Berlin is nuclear force.

At the beginning of his article, Joseph Alsop speaks of the courage and nobility of the Athenians in confronting the Persians. He points to the organic connection between magnificent dreams and magnificent boldness. The relevance of that analogy cannot be doubted. But there is another analogy that comes to us from ancient Greece. There came a point where the peoples of the Greek world—separated by differences of ideology, politics, language and custom—could not survive unless the Greek states themselves created a structure of law binding on all. The failure to act on this challenge cost Greece its life.

62 BEYOND BERLIN*

The differences between the Soviet Union and the United States have become increasingly intractable. One is reluctantly reminded of the agonizing situation that prevailed in Europe in 1938 or even 1939. More than one survivor of the 1930's has been struck by the startling resemblance between the conflict over Danzig and that over Berlin. Even some of the same words have come back to haunt us. The Soviets want to make West Berlin into a "free city"; the last "free city" was Danzig—hardly an auspicious precedent. In the spring of 1939, a notorious French appeaser, Marcel Déat, wrote a then scandalous article, *"Mourir pour Dantzig?"* Why should Frenchmen die for a faraway city that was one of the First World War's most abnormal legacies? Four months later, war broke out. It is impossible today to think of Déat's article as anything but a historical curiosity; serious students hardly bother to dispute whether the war was fought over Danzig, except possibly as the symbolic expression of a larger conflict. And yet, change a few names and details, and Déat's article could be—and virtually is being—written today as a contemporary document on our own dilemma.

The central issue posed by Danzig yesterday and Berlin today is the relationship of limited and unlimited aims in the policy of expansionist and apocalyptic powers. Nazi Germany pursued limited and unlimited aims simultaneously, and this conjunction was intrinsically responsible for the transition from appeasement to war. Limited aims can be negotiated, but how is it possible to negotiate unlimited aims? To be sure, no power proposes to negotiate unlimited aims, but when it has them, it presents its limited aims in such a way that they set in motion a train of events of unlimited extension. Limited aims simply become unlimited aims on the installment plan. Thus piecemeal appeasement cannot be practiced to the bitter end without falling over into full-scale collaboration, and a thin but decisive line separates the

* Theodore Draper, "Beyond Berlin," *Commentary,* Vol. XXXII (November, 1961), pp. 382–90. Reprinted from *Commentary,* by permission; copyright © 1961 by the American Jewish Committee.

true appeasers from the true collaborators. At some point, the appeaser must draw back, even if too late, in disillusionment; the collaborators are appeasers without end.

It is not necessary to equate Nazi Germany and Soviet Russia to recognize that, in this respect, they present us with similar problems. *Mourir pour Berlin?* has the same ominous implications today that *Mourir pour Dantzig?* had twenty-two years ago. Now, as then, we must ask ourselves: Does the Soviet Union also pursue limited and unlimited aims? Is the Soviet Union appeasable? What are the limits of appeasement? And when does one cross over into collaboration?

One's understanding of Soviet aims depends to some extent on which Soviet documents one reads. In the Soviet messages primarily directed at the non-Communist world, such as the Khrushchev Prize interviews granted to journalists, some things never appear. But in other documents, primarily intended for the Communist world, some things always appear.

I have chosen three of the fundamental declarations of the second type which have emanated from Moscow in the past year. They are the "Statement of the 81 Communist Parties" of December 5, 1960; the exceptionally important speech by Nikita Khrushchev of January 6, 1961; and the "Draft Program of the Soviet Communist Party" of July 1961. They are much too long and complex for justice to be done to them here, but I wish to point out some basic ideas in all of them that I believe cast light on the deeper springs of Soviet policy and action.

The keynote was struck in the Statement of the 81 Communist Parties last December. Again and again it proclaimed that the world had entered a "new stage" in which the "balance of forces" had changed in favor of the Soviet system. This idea was expressed in various ways: "the superiority of the forces of socialism over those of imperialism," "the world socialist system is becoming the decisive factor in the development of society," "today it is the world socialist system and the forces fighting against imperialism, for a socialist transformation of society, that determine the main content, main trend, and main features of the historical development of society," "an increasing change in the balance of forces in favor of socialism," and "the superiority of the forces of socialism, peace, and democracy is becoming increasingly obvious." Some of these expressions are vague and general, some precise and concrete, but the former take on new meaning in terms of the latter and other statements of the same kind.

Khrushchev's speech of January 6 was, in effect, an extended commentary on the Statement of the 81 Parties. The speech advised Communists, in a manner that might benefit everyone else, to grasp the connection between the theoretical and practical aspects of the "new stage": "The question of the character of the era is by no means an abstract or a narrow theoretical question. The general strategic line and tactics of world Communism, of each Communist Party, are closely related to it."

Khrushchev divided the period since the October 1917 Revolution in Russia into two stages. The first had lasted as long as the Communist system was confined to the Soviet Union. The second had begun with the expansion of the Communist system outside the Soviet Union. That expansion, he explained, had reached a point at which "the balance of forces in the world arena [has] undergone radical changes in favor of socialism," or as he put it in another passage, "the ever-increasing change in the correlation of forces to the advantage of socialism."

The Draft Program of the Soviet Communist Party presented last July contained the characteristic themes of the Khrushchev "era." A world war could be averted, it said, but this possibility was linked to "the growing superiority of the socialist forces over the forces of imperialism." War in general, and especially a thermonuclear war, must be prevented, but a certain type of war, "liberation wars against imperialism," was encouraged. "Peaceful coexistence" was acclaimed, but it was also characterized as "a specific form of class struggle." Socialism could be ushered in without civil war or armed violence, but a "non-peaceful transition to socialism" could not be ruled out.

II

In the abstract, of course, the Communists have always held that history was working in their favor. But the present stress on the new "balance of forces" is not meant to be understood abstractly. The new balance, according to Khrushchev, has already come into existence, politically, economically, and militarily. Khrushchev himself made the distinction between the old saying that "history was working for socialism" and a new one that "socialism is working for history."

In the final analysis, however, the crucial test of Khrushchev's thesis is military in nature. For all the importance of political and economic factors, the Soviet Union could not afford to take real risks without sheer military superiority. As long as the military balance was admittedly unfavorable, Soviet policy aimed essentially at splitting potential enemies to prevent the formation of an international anti-Soviet coalition. The German-Soviet treaty at Rapallo in 1922, the Franco-Soviet Pact of 1935, and the German-Soviet Pact of 1939, were high points of the policy, which prevailed as long as Stalin lived.

In the present phase, however, the Soviet leadership feels strong enough to defy and intimidate the entire non-Soviet world. It still treats the United States with the respect befitting a strong enemy, but for the once great powers of Europe, which it formerly sought to play off against each other, it barely troubles to conceal its contempt. The new stage fundamentally derives from Soviet progress in nuclear weapons, a development which has made Khrushchev, in many respects, far more aggressive and adventurist than Stalin ever was.

The new Soviet rocket diplomacy was tried out for the first time during the Suez crisis in 1956 by Khrushchev's immediate predecessor, N. A. Bulganin. His threat to intervene, however, seemed belated and unnecessary in view of the more-than-enough pressure put on Britain and France by the United States. Nevertheless, by now, the incident has been magnified by Khrushchev into the first major triumph of the new Soviet policy. In his January 6 speech, Khrushchev gloated. "The Soviet government's stark warning to Eden and Guy Mollet stopped the war," and, "We interfered and stopped their aggression." The failure of the United States to intervene in the Indochinese war was put in the same category by Khrushchev.

Far more representative of the new period, however, is Khrushchev's own intervention in the Cuban crisis in 1960. In July of that year, after the United States had cut the Cuban sugar quota and the Castro regime had retaliated with a decree foreshadowing the expropriation of all United States property in Cuba, Khrushchev seized the occasion to announce that, "figuratively speaking, in case of necessity, Soviet artillery men can support the Cuban people with their rocket fire" if the United States attacked Cuba. The Cuban leaders proceeded to exploit this threat for all it was worth. Che Guevara declared: "Cuba is today a glorious island in the center of the Caribbean, defended by the rockets of the greatest military power in history." In October 1960, Khrushchev seemed to tone down the Soviet commitment by explaining to the Cuban editor, Carlos Franqui, that it had been "really symbolic." But Franqui refused to be satisfied and insisted: "If the threat does exist, if this threat is carried out, are rockets adequately prepared?" To which Khrushchev replied: "Unquestionably. You have it right." He ended by expressing the hope that the Soviets would not have to use their rockets. But Guevara returned to the charge in January of this year: "It is well known that the Soviet Union and all the socialist countries are disposed to go to war to defend our sovereignty and that a tacit agreement has been established between our peoples."

Since then, rocket threats, real or implied, have become a staple of Khrushchev's diplomatic conversation. He has entertained the British Ambassador in Moscow with information of just how many nuclear bombs it would take to destroy England. The Italian Premier has been regaled in much the same way. After listening to Khrushchev at a Soviet-Rumanian friendship meeting in Moscow on August 11, the Moscow correspondent of the Paris *Figaro* observed: "This notion of the present power of the USSR, which has changed the relationship of forces in the world, visibly obsesses M. Khrushchev" (*Le Figaro,* August 12-13, 1961). Six days later, after the wall sealing off East Germany had been erected, Walter Ulbricht, the East German Communist leader, exulted that the act "had demonstrated to the world the actual power relationship in Germany." And no one has ever accused Ulbricht of originality.

III

Soviet policy always confronts us with the problem of linking the limited and unlimited, the concrete and the abstract, the immediate tactic and the long-range strategy. The Soviet leaders themselves link them only with the greatest difficulty, and not always successfully. The problem is, of course, even more difficult for outsiders, but at least we must think in these terms if we are to think about Communist policy as the Communists themselves think.

At the present moment, Soviet policy expresses itself in all these ways, some apparently lending themselves to one interpretation, some to another. There is the proposal to make West Berlin into a "free city," or at least free of Western troops and protection. There is the demand for the recognition of the East German Communist regime. There is the renewal of nuclear tests and reiteration of more or less thinly veiled nuclear threats. There is the concept of the "new stage" in which the "balance of forces" has changed in favor of the Communists. There is Soviet propaganda on behalf of "peaceful coexistence." And there is the Chinese Communist emphasis on war which seems to make the Soviet Communists the more "moderate" and "peaceful" wing of world Communism.

Is it possible to fit these elements into a coherent pattern? There is one school of thought which creates a pattern by a process of elimination. It considers some Soviet statements, especially the more aggressive and expansionist, to be "ritualistic" and, therefore, of no practical significance. It interprets "peaceful coexistence" as if the Soviets had unconditionally decided to renounce the use of force. It attributes major importance to the theoretical dispute between the Russian and Chinese Communists on the relation of war and revolution, and construes it to mean that the Chinese stand for an aggressive, the Russians for a non-aggressive, Communist tendency.

Without going into the danger of wishful thinking in relegating the more aggressive Soviet expressions to the realm of "ritual," there can be no doubt that the basic concept of the "new stage," on which Soviet policy now admittedly rests, has nothing remotely ritualistic about it. The proposition that the "balance of forces" has changed in favor of Communism represents a distinctly new departure in the Soviet assessment of the world situation. It has begun to turn up regularly in fundamental Soviet documents because the Soviet leaders wish to hammer it into the heads of their followers as well as their foes. Indeed, judging from the Soviets' past willingness to resort to force when necessary, one might make a stronger case for the ritualistic character of the Soviets' "peace-loving" protestations. But that would be too easy a retort, because there is a sense, I believe, in which Soviet policy is both "aggressive" and "non-aggressive," "pro-war" and "anti-war."

Of all Soviet propaganda slogans in recent years, "peaceful coexistence" has undoubtedly been the most successful. Who could be against it without opening himself up to the charge of being an imperialist madman and reactionary warmonger? Yet the slogan has always suffered from an inherent contradiction which the Soviets have never attempted to resolve. The operative word is "coexistence," not "peaceful," because coexistence today must be peaceful or not at all. But before two parties can agree to each other's coexistence, they must first be reconciled to each other's continued *existence*. And this is precisely what the Soviet leadership will not or cannot accept. Indeed, it professes to be certain that the "complete triumph" of Communism is closer than ever before, and it makes no secret of its determination to accelerate the inevitable. At best, then, "peaceful coexistence" means that the Soviets intend to put an end to rival social orders by peaceful means if possible and to coexist with them only as long as necessary. The slogan is, if anything, a description of the present, not a prescription for the future. This is a very different matter from what "peaceful coexistence" seems to suggest, and the formula derives its effectiveness from the way it permits the Soviets to have their cake and eat it, too.

We thus come back in another form to the seemingly "aggressive" and "non-aggressive," the "pro-war" and "anti-war" character of Soviet policy in the "new stage." I put these words in quotation marks because they are relatively meaningless or misleading by themselves; they enjoy no independent existence but are rather alternative means to a larger end which may be achieved one way or the other.

Altogether too much has been made, therefore, of the so-called ideological difference between the Soviet and Chinese Communist leaderships. We know from experience that struggles for power within Communist movements must take ideological forms; if there were no ideological differences, they would have to be invented. This is just as true of struggles between national movements as it is true of struggles within these movements. With or without ideological differences, the Soviet and Chinese Communist leaderships could be expected to agree on spheres of influence only with the greatest difficulty. The Soviets have never accepted the concept of spheres of influence within the Communist world. As the Statement of the 81 Parties puts it, "the Communist Party of the Soviet Union has been, and remains, the universally recognized vanguard of the world Communist movement, being the most experienced and steeled contingent of the international Communist movement," and there is no room in these words, upon which the Soviets undoubtedly insisted, for dividing the Communist world into a Chinese sphere in the East and a Soviet sphere in the West. The Chinese would unquestionably be satisfied, for the present, with such an arrangement, but in view of Soviet unwillingness, they have invaded the West as far as the Albanian and other Communist movements to show that two can play at the same game. If ideological differences were the only ones at stake, they could be patched up with relative ease, but it is the struggle for power within the Communist world—for two "vanguards" instead of one—that has envenomed them.

I am not impressed by the determining character of the ideological dispute because it is so abstract in character and so far removed from the everyday realities of Soviet and Chinese Communist policies. The Soviets are not necessarily conciliatory because they profess to believe in "peaceful coexistence," and the Chinese are not necessarily incorrigible because they scoff at it. Both are conciliatory and incorrigible as the opportunity offers and their interests dictate. The notion that the ideological dispute over "peaceful coexistence" makes the Soviets "peace-loving" and the Chinese "war-like" is an oversimplification that verges on political innocence.

What, then, is the Sino-Soviet ideological dispute about? The answer takes us close to the heart of the "Berlin crisis," the renewal of nuclear testing, the message of the most important Soviet documents in the past year, and all the rest. The missing link is not hard to find, because it is a prerequisite of Soviet strategy that it should not be kept a secret.

For the Soviet leaders, and most of all Nikita Khrushchev, have been trying to pound into us the belief that we have entered a "new stage" of history in which the odds have turned against us. Why fight? Why resist? "Of course," said Khrushchev in his speech of January 6, "as yet we are unable to completely exclude the possibility of wars, for the imperialist states exist. However, the unleashing of wars has become a much more complicated business for the imperialists than it was before the emergence of the mighty socialist camp. Imperialists can unleash a war, but they must think hard about the consequences." So it is Khrushchev's business to remind us unceasingly and in the most forceful ways of the consequences.

This is the purpose of the legend that, as far back as 1956, the Soviet Union was strong enough to issue a "stark warning" to Britain and France, and, forthwith, they capitulated. It is the purpose of the legend that the Soviets were responsible for a similar victory in North Vietnam. It is the primary purpose of all the stark warnings that have issued from Moscow in connection with the Berlin crisis. If warnings do not suffice, nuclear tests are even more instructive. And if the non-Communist world learns the lesson that Khrushchev is trying to teach it, it will always behave in the way that Khrushchev says it behaved during the Suez and Indochinese crises—*it will capitulate.* I am not now concerned with the merits of these cases, but only with Khrushchev's use of them.

The essential difference on war and peace between the Russian and Chinese Communists, then, boils down to different estimates of the practical possibilities. The Chinese, who do not have a nuclear bomb and have not been able to achieve their aims in Formosa despite some rather forceful efforts, see no reason why they should spread illusions about "the peaceful road to socialism" or expect Western capitulation. The Soviets, who possess nuclear bombs and have far more successfully pursued a short-of-war policy, can afford to be, or appear to be, more optimistic. The Soviet leaders are not less aggressive than the Chinese, but they have more reason to believe that they can achieve their ends not by war but by the threat of war, not by "devastating blows" but by the threat of devastating blows, not by nuclear bombs but by the threat of nuclear bombs. Since the Soviet leaders have by no means excluded the possibility that the threat will not be enough, the purely doctrinal debate would surely be muffled or even hushed up, if other more practical and material considerations of power were not involved.

Despite the intensity and sometimes the longevity of some Communist factional struggles, it is remarkable how often the victor, once firmly established, has taken over the position formerly identified with the loser. The present archetype of Soviet aggressiveness, Stalin, came into power a paragon of moderation, and "socialism in one country" was once considered the betrayal of all expansion of the Soviet system outside Russia. The "non-aggressive" Khrushchev is just as much a fable as the non-aggressive Stalin used to be; there was more than one Stalin, depending on circumstances and opportunities, and there is more than one Khrushchev, for the same reasons. There has also been and will continue to be more than one Mao, whose internal difficulties now seem to be swaying him to appear to be more sweetly reasonable in his foreign relations.

IV

Negotiating with a power which has limited aims is the traditional function of diplomacy, but negotiating with a power which has unlimited as well as limited aims is an infinitely more difficult and thankless task. It is this duality of Soviet policy which makes the present "Berlin crisis" and all other such tests of strength and wars of nerve so extraordinarily tortuous and treacherous. The limited aims themselves vary enormously in scope, from the sealing off of East Germany to stop the flow of refugees into West Berlin and West Germany, to the *de facto* or diplomatic recognition of the East German Communist regime, to the permanent partition of Germany by formal adoption of the Soviet thesis of the "two German states." Yet the Soviets have tied all three together in the Berlin knot.

The first of these aims was relatively easy to accomplish; it merely required a wall of concrete blocks which the Western powers protested against but had no intention of penetrating. The second is more difficult inasmuch as it requires the cooperation of the United States to make it an accomplished fact. To make the United States somewhat more cooperative, the Soviets have applied pressure at this point—the threat that a separate Soviet "peace treaty" with East Germany would cut off access to Berlin to be reestablished only through negotiation and agreement with the East German regime. And the last aim entails such potential danger that the Soviets would like to take out a political insurance policy before going through with it.

For, if history teaches us anything, it is that a nation like Germany cannot be permanently divided without retribution. The price may be paid in the next generation, not in this, but it will be paid. In an age when the most artificial congeries of tribes demand and obtain national recognition, it is folly to imagine that a historic nation in the heart of Europe can be split up indefinitely. I am not suggesting that, in the present conflict of interests or state of public opinion in the East and West, the reunification of Germany can or should be put on the order of the day; I am convinced, however, that there is only one thing worse than the present unnatural division, and that is to make it any worse than it is. The Soviet leaders well know that they are playing with fire, and they are determined, therefore, to take out an insurance policy by making the West accomplices in the deed. In the long run, of course, the Soviets have no intention of confronting the German people as the historic enemies of their national unity; the day the whole of Germany shows signs of moving into the Communist camp, the Soviet Union will unquestionably emerge as the noisiest and crassest defender of German national unity.

This wide assortment of "limited" aims gives the Soviet leaders plenty of room to bargain and to maneuver. Beyond any or all of them, however, is the Soviet determination to hold on to the initiative in world affairs and to set such forces in motion that one Soviet advance leads to another, one Western retreat to another. If all the Soviet demands were accepted tomorrow, nothing would be "normalized," nothing "regularized." If the arrangement really guaranteed "free access" to West Berlin, it would continue to threaten the East German regime as an outpost of freedom and refuge from totalitarianism; and if the arrangement proved to be illusory, the gradual asphyxiation of West Berlin would afflict the West with a trauma of guilt and shame far more dangerous in its ultimate effect than the present predicament. If the West recognizes Ulbricht's regime, it will not make life in East Germany any easier or sweeter; it will merely

358 American Views of Soviet Russia

make Ulbricht more arrogant and insufferable. If the West conducts negotiations with Ulbricht—that most servile, shameless, and bankrupt of the old German Stalinists—we may be sure that the process of arriving at an interpretation of "free access" to West Berlin that does not disturb the interests and sensibilities of the East German rulers will be most painful. At every disputed point, the West will face the choice of capitulating or returning to the crisis atmosphere— and the wiseacres will not be slow to point out that, once having decided to negotiate, the West should have realized that it "could not have its own way." If Germany is permanently dismembered now, the operation will have to be carried out by the Soviet Union and the United States without a semblance of consent by the German people who will have something to say about it sooner or later. Anyone who thinks that it is possible to recognize the East German Communist regime under duress, be forced into a compact for the permanent dismemberment of Germany, remove West Berlin as an embarrassment to the East German regime, without whetting the Soviet appetite for more, is living in a fool's paradise.

It cannot be emphasized too strongly that the entire issue has been distorted and confused by making it appear to be exclusively or predominantly related to West Berlin. In reality, the Soviets are using West Berlin as a back door to impose their ultimate will on Germany as a whole, or as small change to obtain a vastly strengthened position in Germany as a whole. They are attempting to subordinate the fate of Germany to that of Berlin or at least to use this bargaining technique. However abnormal or irregular the present status of Berlin may be, the fact remains that it cannot be normalized or regularized unless the fate of Berlin is subordinated to that of Germany. And if the world is not yet ready to face openly and honestly the German problem, it should not prejudice the case by dealing with it in this backdoors, shamefaced fashion, or above all delude itself that it is settling or solving anything of substance.

V

The Soviets have driven so hard and so far since the end of World War II that they think—or they consider it politic to think—that they have come in sight of total victory by "peaceful," piecemeal submission to their demands. The victory they envisage can only be a victory by capitulation, and it is for this reason that Khrushchev could say in his January 6 speech that "the slogan of the struggle for peace appears as a companion of the slogan of the struggle for Communism."

Ironically, the latest battle cry of some nuclear pacifists, "Better red than dead," contains a little more truth than poetry. Those who think in these terms have already lost the power of decision. They can only throw themselves at the mercy of the biggest nuclear power or the one that makes the biggest threats—or perhaps the one most likely to carry them out. It is, of course, far from clear that the military balance is actually as one-sided as the Soviets would like us to believe; more likely, the Soviets are ahead in some fields, the United States in others; and the most responsible Western military opinion still firmly believes that, on balance, the Western alliance enjoys a decided military advantage. The Soviets can claim an advantage in the "balance of forces" not because they have nuclear weapons and the West does not have them, but because they are willing to use their "nuclear deterrent" against the West in a way that the West has not been willing to use against them.

Thus it is most significant that the slogan is not "Better red-white-and-blue than dead" or "Better anything than dead." Why, if both the Soviet Union and the United States are equally capable of mass destruction, should the choice be limited to "red" and "dead"? What would have been the reaction if Eisenhower had intimated in 1956 that the Hungarian rebels could count on the support of American rockets as Khrushchev intimated in 1960 that the Castro regime could count on Soviet rockets? In fact, what would happen if the President of the United States (1) called in the Polish, Czech, and Rumanian ambassadors, and told them how many nuclear bombs would be necessary to level their countries to the ground, ancient monuments included; (2) designated these three countries as "hostages"; (3) announced the active support of "liberation wars against Communism"; and (4) promised to give nuclear protection to any rebellion against Communist rule?

I think it is clear that we are not dealing here with a genuinely pacifist position; it is rather a form of pseudo-pacifism that is politically motivated by the appeasement of one side—Soviet Russia. But the appeasement of a power with unlimited aims is never enough, and these pacifists have already taken the long step toward collaboration. The moral and political tension in "Better red than dead" is so hard to maintain that it is always in danger of falling over into the shorter version, "Better red."

All this, however, is not only politically one-sided; it is also, to a large extent, politically irrelevant. In the existing state of Western society, some may be prepared to surrender in advance, but the decisive majority is not. The real option, therefore, is simply and nakedly, "alive or dead," not "red or dead." And this embraces everyone, including the reds, whom it deprives of any special advantage.

But as long as the Soviets base their policy on a supposedly advantageous "balance of forces," they are bound to be tempted by the prospect of progressive Western capitulation, with incalculable, unthinkable consequences for the future of mankind. As long as the dread of these consequences emboldens the Soviets and unnerves the West, the "balance of forces," whatever it may be objectively, tilts in favor of the Soviets subjectively. As long as the West does not find a way to demonstrate that the Soviets are wrong about their "balance of forces," the equilibrium will not be restored. And without a new equilibrium, a new starting point is unlikely to emerge.

The problem is, of course, far more difficult to solve than to state. Yet one of our greatest hazards is that we are not yet agreed on the nature of the problem. Of one thing we may be sure: however difficult and delicate it may be today, it will be far more dangerous and costly tomorrow. The Soviet stress on the "balance of forces" is relatively recent; we are still in the exploratory, probing phase of the "new stage." One of the factors being explored and probed most incisively is our own frame of mind. Objectively, the balance has hardly changed as much as the Soviets say it has. In any case, something more than words is needed to convince us. The Berlin crisis is, above all, an object lesson to provide the skeptical with a living demonstration of how the allegedly changed "balance of forces" operates. In effect, we are being invited to confirm the latest Soviet dictum. We have only begun to hear about it, but a few more practical demonstrations and it will become the incessant drum beat of Soviet propaganda. That will be the moment of supreme peril. We are not yet there, but a major change in the heart of Europe could easily get us there.

Disarmament or Deterrence?

Ever since the mushroom clouds billowed over Hiroshima and Nagasaki, the fear of nuclear weapons and the hope of controlling them preoccupied the American government and people. When the

Soviets detonated their first atomic bomb in 1949 (followed four years later by a hydrogen bomb, eight years later by an ICBM), the issue of disarmament became the center of intense and anxious controversy. This controversy resounded in innumerable books, articles, classified government studies, Congressional debates and hearings, and peace marches.

It also took place across conference tables among representatives of the world powers. Throughout the 1950's, under the aegis of one or another organization and in one or another place, delegates from the USSR, the United States, and other leading nations met to discuss the feasibility of arms control. Three main topics were at stake: an effective system of inspection to control the new weapons; a reliable method of preventing surprise attacks; and a ban on testing nuclear devices. On the first two topics, the Soviets were apparently intractable, since they feared that any inspection within their borders would be a disguise for Western spying. Instead, they proposed immediate and total abolition of all nuclear weapons without any meaningful guarantees against "cheating." The United States, on the other hand, was determined to join disarmament with inspection, rather than trust the USSR.

On the third topic a test ban there was more progress, although again the issue of inspection divided the two great nuclear powers. In 1958, Khrushchev announced that Russia would unilaterally suspend its nuclear tests. The United States followed suit, but persuaded the Soviets to confer on an international test ban and on means for detecting violations. During the next three years, various conferences were held over tedious months, but all ended without agreements. The Soviet resumption of tests in 1961—highlighted by the detonation of a monster 100-megaton bomb—seemed to close the question entirely. Within a few months, President Kennedy announced renewed nuclear testing by the United States.

Nevertheless, the international conferences on arms control continued, patiently going over the same or new arguments, introducing ever more sophisticated and ingenious proposals in hopes of somehow producing a consensus that never appeared. However futile the process may have appeared at times, it persisted on the momentum of urgent apprehension. Nuclear war was too frightful a prospect for the nations to give up hope of controlling nuclear weapons.

That prospect almost became reality in the fall of 1962. At that time, the United States discovered that Khrushchev was secretly installing in Cuba launching sites for intermediate-range missiles.

Immediately, Kennedy set up a naval blockade on all offensive weapons bound for Cuba and demanded that the Soviet Union dismantle the missile bases or face severe consequences. After several days of fearful tension, Khrushchev backed down: he agreed to withdraw the missiles in return for Kennedy's promise to lift the blockade and not to invade Cuba. As one American official put it, the two nations had been "eyeball to eyeball."

After the Cuban crisis, the quest for arms control gained new and more hopeful momentum. Perhaps because of increasingly troubled relations with the Communist Chinese leaders (who were working to create their own nuclear device), the Soviet Union finally agreed in mid-1963 to a treaty banning atmospheric (but not underground) tests of nuclear weapons. This was the first definite step toward arms reduction since the Cold War had begun. Despite the misgivings of many American scientists and politicians, the United States—along with every other major nation except France, Communist China, and Cuba—signed the test ban treaty.

In the next set of documents one can discern some of the major positions in the arms-control debate during 1961-63, although the complexity of the question requires a selective and, in many respects, superficial sampling.

First of all is the abridged transcript of a three-hour symposium, arranged by Commentary *in May, 1961, on the moral and practical aspects of total war. Participants included Sidney Hook (Professor of Philosophy at New York University), H. Stuart Hughes (Professor of History at Harvard and a third-party "peace candidate" for the U.S. Senate in 1962), Hans J. Morgenthau (Professor of Political Science at the University of Chicago), and C. P. Snow (English scientist and author). Norman Podhoretz, editor of* Commentary, *served as moderator.*

President Kennedy's decision of March, 1962, to resume nuclear testing, which he justified in a nationwide television address, won the approval of most Americans—but not all. The article by James R. Newman, editor of Scientific American, *outlines some of the criticisms directed at that decision. Fifteen months later, Kennedy gave a celebrated address at American University in which he announced not only a moratorium on his nation's nuclear tests, but the resumption of Soviet-American negotiations toward a test-ban treaty. The speech marks an important chapter in American attitudes toward Russia.*

63 WESTERN VALUES AND TOTAL WAR*

Norman Podhoretz: The problem we've selected for discussion this afternoon is a very, very broad one, "Western Values and Total War," but we're going to try to focus on several slightly narrower themes, the main one being the question of whether or not, in a situation that threatens thermonuclear war, there is an inherent contradiction between the job of preserving and extending the liberal democratic heritage and the job of protecting the national interests of the various countries in the Western bloc who presumably represent that tradition.

There have been, crudely speaking, two schools of thought on the question of the nature of thermonuclear war, and most political positions follow ultimately from one or the other of these two sets of assumptions. The first school of thought—which is represented perhaps most prominently by Herman Kahn and certain members of the RAND Corporation—believes that the possibility of thermonuclear war has changed nothing in kind but merely in degree. In other words, this school of thought is willing to contemplate the use of nuclear weapons and to calculate the point at which a civilization might rebuild itself after a thermonuclear war.

The other school of thought—which has been represented recently by Karl Jaspers—begins with the assumption that thermonuclear war is different in kind, not merely in degree, from all other forms of violence and armed conflict between nations. This school of thought believes that one cannot speak of preserving civilization, freedom, or values by resort to nuclear warfare, and therefore would consider that nuclear warfare must be ruled out as an instrument of national policy. I think spokesmen for this school might argue that we can conceive of preserving a nation *physically* even after a thermonuclear war, but that it is absurd to speak of preserving values—moral values, political values—and certainly impossible to speak of preserving a civilization like our own. I wonder, Professor Hook, whether you would begin by commenting on this opposition that I've rather crudely described.

Sidney Hook: The situation that Mr. Podhoretz has laid out for us is even more complex and difficult. I do not know how great the destruction will be in the event of war. I don't think anybody knows

*Sidney Hook, H. Stuart Hughes, Hans J. Morgenthau, and C. P. Snow, "Western Values and Total War," *Commentary*, Vol. XXXII (October, 1961), pp. 273–304. Reprinted from *Commentary*, by permission; copyright © 1961 by the American Jewish Committee.

because so many contingencies are involved. We can grant that in any case the upshot will be horrible. The main question to me in this context is the moral one—what price are we prepared to pay for the preservation of freedom in a world in which such things may happen? However, when we discuss this question, we must bear in mind the following: On the eve of the Second World War it was widely predicted that a world war would lead to the end of all civilization because of the use of poison gas. And for all I know, there existed at the time well-grounded possibilities that the use of gas would make human life impossible on this planet with as much or even more plausibility, in a technical sense, than the use of thermonuclear weapons. Despite these predictions, two things happened. Those who felt that the values of the West were worth preserving against the onslaught of fascism took the risk of war, despite the fact that they weren't sure that gas warfare wouldn't bring an end to mankind. And secondly, to the surprise of many, gas warfare was not used. Hitler was a madman; yet this madman realized that if he used gas he would provoke reprisals which would mean the end of the national existence of Germany. From this, I draw the following conclusion: If we surrender the deterrent—which is widely recommended by many—we invite the conquest of the world by Communist totalitarianism. And no matter how we define Western values, they are certainly incompatible with that system of organized terror. If we hold on to the deterrent, then, since Khrushchev is not a madman and does not want a war which would mean the end of Soviet existence, and since the Communists make a fetish of history—survival is the be-all and end-all for them—it might be possible, by preserving peace through the retention of the deterrent weapon, to work out a multilateral form of controlled disarmament, thus permitting the nations of this world to make their own decisions concerning the kind of life they wish to live.

I conclude this introductory statement with a reminder about our theme. I had hoped that we would begin with a discussion of the nature of Western values. As I read the history of Western culture it seems to me that survival at all costs is not among the values of the West. It was Aristotle who said that it is not life as such, or under any conditions, that is of value, but the good life. The free man is one who in certain situations refuses to accept life if it means spiritual degradation. The man who declares that survival at all costs is the end of existence is morally dead, because he's prepared to sacrifice all other values which give life its meaning. But our alternatives today are not limited to surrender to Communism or universal destruction by war. We can count upon the sanity of the men in the Kremlin—they're very sane and realistic. If we do not abandon our deterrent weapons, I believe that in time we can work out an alternative which will avoid the extremes described by our chairman.

Podhoretz: Mr. Hughes, you are one of the many people Mr. Hook was referring to who have advocated the abandonment of the deterrent as an instrument of national policy, and I know that you have a rather different view of the alternatives before us. So perhaps you'd care to comment on the statement just made.

H. Stuart Hughes: Yes, one thing I'd like to say at the start is that I'm not a pacifist, but as a historian I find very few wars worth fighting. I would almost limit those worth fighting to the Second World War. I would definitely not include the American Revolution, the American Civil War, or the First World War. You may say that I include the one war I fought in, but that's just how it happened. My position would be a non-pacifist one, but one extremely skeptical of wars in any case, and totally skeptical of wars of mass destruction. Where I differ from some of my friends is in feeling that the great change came not with the dropping of the atomic bomb on Hiroshima, but in 1943, when we began the terror bombardment of Germany. There's where I think the character of war changed and the use of weapons of mass destruction began.

Now, I think here one should apply a type of reasoning such as the theologians have always used. Presumably any war worth fighting— e.g., the Second World War—is in theological and moral terms a just war. I would argue to this day that the Second World War was a just war. But if I understand the theologians correctly, a war can only be considered just if the means are proportionate to the evil to be eradicated. Now it seems to me the means used against Hitler were proportionate until the terror bombing; and you did not need the terror bombing to win that war. It was both morally and technically stupid and wrong. I cannot see any way of fighting Communism by general war in which the means would be proportionate to the evil. I happen to think that Communism has a great deal of evil in it, but less than Nazism had. On this basis, then, I throw out all comparisons with the 1930's and Munich. I know this is the classic argument and I think people who hold my position should be prepared for it. We sound like appeasers. Well, we accept that charge and say that the situation is different. Remember, appeasement was not originally an ugly word. It became such after 1938.

If I may go on a moment more—I hope disarmament will come up eventually, but I want to leave that out for the present—it seems, then, we have to face the old "Red or Dead?" question, as Bertrand Russell and others express it in England. Which do you want, to be red or dead? To speak very crudely, I'm on the red side of this, and I gather Mr. Hook is on the dead side. But let me just suggest in this connection that people who hold my views do not think that they are inviting Soviet conquest and do not believe in surrender. We believe that the enemy should be met with real force, but real force on a human scale which would give men the old alternative of making a personal choice as to whether they wanted to die. If the Communists were to invade, I would like to take up a gun and fight. But that would be my personal choice. It wouldn't involve all sorts of neutrals, the animal world, unborn generations, etc. So, my point of view is: yes, we should be prepared to fight and to fight hard—but with conventional weapons, by guerrilla warfare, militia-type organizations, passive resistance, underground activity. And the most important task for this country is to begin to study these methods. I went just a month ago to the international congress in Milan on the history of resistance organizations during the Second World War, and I regard this as a most important type of study—to find out how you resist as human beings without weapons of mass destruction. I say these things to distinguish my position from a doctrinaire pacifist position or from a position of simply saying, "Let us let the red hordes wash over us."

Podhoretz: Mr. Morgenthau, would you rather be red or dead, or neither? Is there a way of escaping this gruesome alternative?

Hans J. Morgenthau: I certainly would rather be neither, if I have a choice. I don't want to address myself at the moment to the grim question as to whether or not to surrender the nuclear deterrent. But I want rather to discuss the fundamental philosophic question—whether it is possible to defend the values of Western civilization by nuclear war. I'm indeed inclined to answer this question in the negative, while admitting the possibility, or even perhaps the likelihood, that we will have to fight a nuclear war. This likelihood is the measure of the dilemma we are facing and of the political and moral bankruptcy we are suffering because of our inability to devise a third alternative to those which have been mentioned—both of which are to me equally unacceptable.

I think a revolution has occurred, perhaps the first true revolution in foreign policy since the beginning of history, through the introduction of nuclear weapons into the arsenal of warfare. For from the beginning of history to the end of the Second World War, there existed a rational relationship between violence as a means of foreign policy, and the ends of foreign policy. That is to say, a statesman could ask himself—and always did ask himself—whether he could achieve what he sought for his nation by peaceful diplomatic means or whether he had to resort to war. A statesman, up to the beginning of the nuclear age, was very much in the position of a labor leader who asks himself, "Can I get what I want by the peaceful means of collective bargaining or do I have to resort to industrial warfare in the form of a strike?" To use another metaphor, the statesman in the pre-nuclear age was very much in the position of a gambler—a reasonable gambler, that is—who is willing to risk a certain fraction of his material and human resources. If he wins, his risk is justified by victory; if he loses, he has not lost everything. His losses, in other words, are bearable. This rational relationship between violence as a means of foreign policy and the ends of foreign policy has been destroyed by the possibility of all-out nuclear war.

I cannot accept the analogy with gas warfare. Before the outbreak of the Second World War, the possibility of gas warfare was infinitely more marginal than is the possibility of nuclear war today. Certainly, the United States today must rely primarily on the nuclear deterrent in defense of its national interest; and when the chips are down, it will be faced with either retreat or resort to nuclear war. No such simple, stark alternative existed before the Second World War with regard to either retreat or gas warfare. Gas warfare was one weapon among many from which nations could choose. Furthermore, it was not a rational deduction but practical considerations which made gas warfare appear inadvisable to Hitler. In the period of the *Blitzkrieg,* gas warfare was unnecessary because the German armies overran their neighbors on all sides, and afterward the initiation of gas warfare would have been suicidal for Germany. The question hardly arose for the Allies because they were engaged in a war of movement and therefore resort to gas warfare was also senseless for them. Furthermore, because they were so engaged, they would have had to kill not only the German armies but the populations of the occupied nations as well. So there is, I think, quite a difference between the fact that all belligerents refrained from gas warfare in the Second World War and the possibility, if not the likelihood, of nuclear war in the future.

However, the fundamental question is, in view of this disproportion between the means of violence and the ends of foreign policy, whether it is still possible today to defend the values of any civilization by resort to nuclear warfare. For if you assume—as even the most optimistic analysts such as Herman Kahn have assumed—that in a third world war fought with nuclear weapons, fifty, eighty, or a hundred million Americans would die, and nine-tenths, let me say, of the economic capacity of the United States would be destroyed, you must be possessed not only by an extreme optimism but by an almost unthinking faith to believe that civilization, any civilization, Western or otherwise, could survive such an unprecedented catastrophe. For the fundamental error in the reasoning to which I'm referring, it seems to me, lies in the assumption that the moral fiber of a civilization has an unlimited capacity to recover from shock. I would rather assume from individual personal experience as well as from the experience of history that there is a breaking point for a civilization, as there is a breaking point for an individual man. For, after all, when we speak of civilization we are speaking of an abstraction; we are really speaking of man in the mass, of Americans in the mass. Would Americans in the mass be able to hold to the values of Western civilization in the face of such an unimaginable, unprecedented catastrophe?

We are of course all guessing here, but I would dare to make the guess that Western civilization would not survive such a catastrophe. If this estimate is correct, then obviously an all-out nuclear war in defense of Western civilization is a contradiction in terms, an absurdity. I must say that this absurdity may occur, but if it should occur, I would still say that it was an absurdity.

Hook: I think that both of my colleagues have been inconsistent.

Podhoretz: With each other, or each with himself?

Hook: Not with each other, but with themselves. Mr. Hughes maintains that he'd rather be red than dead, and then tells us that of course he's prepared to die fighting against Communism. And he talks about means of underground warfare against totalitarianism without any regard for the great qualitative difference which totalitarianism makes where opposition is concerned. There is no underground in the Soviet Union, Mr. Hughes—you probably learned that at the congress you attended. One of the reasons there is no underground in the Soviet Union is that the Kremlin organizes its own opposition in order to destroy it. And this introduces a qualitative change of enormous magnitude.

But I want to go back for a moment to a very interesting thing Mr. Hughes said about mass bombing, which for him represented the great turning-point in history. He asserted that the use of weapons must be proportionate to the end. He deplored the mass bombings of Germany which, of course, the English did not initiate—Coventry preceded the mass bombings of Germany—and condemned them on the ground that they were strategically and militarily unnecessary. Some people with excellent hindsight have criticized the use of the atomic bomb at Hiroshima on similar grounds. I frankly don't know whether these criticisms are justified by military and strategic considerations or not, but my question to Mr. Hughes is this: suppose the only way in which the West could have prevented the world victory of Hitler was by this mass bombing of Germany? Would you have been in favor of it or not? Mankind paid the price of forty million dead to get rid of Hitler. It sounds macabre to make comparisons and weigh lives against values, but it seems clear that Mr. Hughes, who justifies the Second World War, thinks that forty million dead was not too high a price to pay for a free civilization. My contention is that both of my colleagues have overlooked the disproportion between the two alternatives of surrender and willingness to resist. Professor Morgenthau said that we might soon be confronted by a choice between the preservation of the United States—that is, the preservation of our freedoms—and the use of a nuclear deterrent. He didn't clearly indicate what his position would be if that were our choice. There was some intimation that he believed, if that were really our choice, we should have to surrender. . . .

Morgenthau: That is not what I meant to say.

Hook: I'm glad I misunderstood you on that point. But if we decide against surrender, then the question is: how can we best preserve ourselves? You face the same problem as Mr. Hughes. If conventional weapons won't prevent Khrushchev from taking the world, and if the only thing that can prevent him is the nuclear deterrent, should we use it or surrender? I don't see how we can avoid that point.

The main thing I want to stress, however, is that it is a mistake to make an easy equation of the alternatives between surrender on the one hand and resistance and the cost of resistance on the other. For if we are prepared to take the risk of fighting for freedom, then we must prepare ourselves in such a way that the costs are diminished. Here we're dealing with speculative notions. The one thing we can be sure about is that if we surrender, Communism, with all its evils, will take over the world. But if we are prepared to fight, then we may not have to fight, for the reasons which I have indicated; and if the enemy is foolish enough to attack us—which I don't believe for a minute he will do if we keep the deterrent—then, if we are prepared, the losses may not be as great as some anticipate. There are questions involved here whose answers are indeterminate. I challenge the accepted notion that all life necessarily must be impossible by virtue of any kind of nuclear combat independently of what we do. After all, Germany seemed finished at the end of the Second World War.

I would like my colleagues to address themselves to the question: whether when the chips are down they are prepared to sacrifice the integrity and existence of the free world to Communism? And further, whether they have done justice to two considerations: first, that our willingness to fight for our freedom may be the best way of preserving it, just as sometimes in personal life one's willingness to lose one's life may be the best way of defending his life; second, that for the Communist world nothing exists but history. Survival, I repeat, is the *summum bonum* for Communism, whereas the West, buttressed in part by belief in immortality, whether as a myth or fact, has always maintained that there are certain values which are more important than life itself. To the Communist world there is nothing worse than defeat. That is why Lenin always emphasized the importance of what he called the policy of strategic retreat, and its correlative maxim: avoid provocations! That is why the Communists will never start a war which they have reason to fear they will not survive. Consequently, in the light of all this, I say to Mr. Hughes that his position invites the Communists to take over the world. And when they do so, he has no guarantee even then of survival. He does not know whether or not the Chinese will use atomic weapons against the Russians. He may end up both red and dead.

Podhoretz: Mr. Hughes, would you agree that the renunciation of the deterrent would automatically, or even probably, result in a Communist take-over?

Hughes: I would say we would only be honest in answering that Soviet take-over in certain areas might be invited. . . .

Podhoretz: Might be invited by unilateral disarmament?

Hughes: By some sort of unilateral renunciation of thermonuclear deterrence. I dislike the term unilateral disarmament without qualification because it sounds as though one is going to strip down to one's underwear shorts tomorrow, and that is not it. It would be a question of starting a movement in this direction. Renouncing deterrence as an instrument of foreign policy might, I think, invite or at least facilitate Soviet penetration of certain areas, particularly in the underdeveloped world, but these areas are largely indefensible anyway.

Podhoretz: What about Western Europe, Berlin?

Hughes: No, I do not think so. I think in Europe deterrence has not deterred anything. Let's leave out Khrushchev as more rational, perhaps more humane, than Stalin, and get back to Stalin before 1953. What deterred Stalin from taking over Western and Central Europe? I would argue it was not our monopoly of atomic weapons, but the conviction that these would be very hard countries to rule. He was having enough trouble already. . . .

Podhoretz: . . . You are saying, then, that you don't think one ought to assume that the Russians would move into Berlin, for example, if we renounced thermonuclear deterrence? Do I understand you correctly?

Hughes: Exactly.

Podhoretz: Mr. Morgenthau, what is your reaction to all this? Do you believe, as a leading exponent of the school of *Realpolitik*—you have been called that, anyway. . . .

Morgenthau: I have been called lots of things.

Podhoretz: Well, that probably more often than other things. Anyhow, do you think it's plausible to assume that the Russians have been deterred by American strength in the past ten years?

Morgenthau: I have absolutely no doubt. I am convinced that the Russians were deterred from advancing. I don't believe for a moment that the Russians today are imposing upon themselves a certain self-restraint because they are afraid that Western countries may be difficult to digest. After all, if you consider that since the end of the Second World War, in election after election, one out of every four Italians has voted the Communist ticket, it shouldn't have been very difficult for the Communists to digest Italy. In 1946 or 1947 it would have been relatively easy for the Russians, short of American deterrence through the threat of atomic war, to take over Italy and other such countries, not necessarily by sending the Red Army in but by letting the best organized and largest political group within those countries do the job.

Podhoretz: Mr. Morgenthau, what then is your own position? I think that Mr. Hook was asking a few minutes ago what choice you would make.

Morgenthau: I would fully agree with Mr. Hook that I would not surrender. I would rather fight if I'm forced to fight a nuclear war.

But I would be fully convinced of the utter absurdity, of the utterly suicidal character of such a war. It would be an absolutely senseless war, but it would be imposed upon us because it would be one of the two alternatives which not only Western statesmanship but the statesmanship of the world would have left to us.

Hook: If I understand you, then, Mr. Morgenthau, you're prepared to be heroic even if foolish. I maintain (though I don't like to use these phrases) that if we're prepared to be heroic, we will not have to be foolish.

Morgenthau: Let me say a word about heroism. I believe the advent of nuclear power has also changed the character of heroism. I don't believe that it is appropriate to quote Aristotle in this context, because when Aristotle speaks of the value of life as over against the value of the good life, he does not contemplate—nor could he have contemplated—the mass extermination of large segments of a civilized population. He had in mind individual acts of heroism—Leonidas being slain at Thermopylae and Socrates drinking the hemlock. Those are deaths which carry a meaning. They are deaths which were worth dying, as it were, but the extermination of eight million New Yorkers within a fraction of a second is an entirely different type of thing. I see no meaning in the reduction of tens of millions of people to atomic dust, of the monuments of a civilization to radioactive rubble. I see no meaning at all, I see no heroism at all in this.

Hook: Then why do you want to resist it?

Hughes: I think Mr. Hook is logical and I think I'm logical, although we disagree; but I do not see your point about fighting a senseless war. If it is senseless, then why fight it?

Morgenthau: The other alternative is also senseless, but perhaps somewhat more. I'm not trying to be facetious.

Podhoretz: Mr. Morgenthau, I think we'd all like to know what the sensible alternative might be. You spoke earlier of diplomatic means of conducting conflict between nations. Now the only diplomatic means we've heard about this afternoon so far are in the nature of military policy. Are there other diplomatic means that might get us out of this awful dilemma?

Morgenthau: The way out of the dilemma is to transcend the two equally unacceptable alternatives of surrender or fighting a suicidal atomic war, and that means taking nuclear power out of the arsenal of individual nations altogether.

Hughes: By multilateral disarmament.

Morgenthau: Not necessarily by multilateral disarmament, but some kind of supra-national agency which we may call world government, because this is what it would be. . . .

C. P. Snow: . . . And yet it's not easy to see how this country or the Soviet Union can get rid of nuclear weapons at once. I think we might hope that there will be a scaling down. That seems to be possible. It seems to me extremely important that this country should build up conventional weapons in a way that it has—very erroneously in my view—neglected to do since 1945. Both qualitatively and quantitatively this country is hopelessly behind the Soviet Union in that particular field. As to the constant use of this particular nuclear thinking not only as a threat but as a kind of support to society, my general inclination is that we probably have to damp that down or we're simply going to die on our feet.

Hook: I gather then, Sir Charles, that you are not urging a policy of unilateral disarmament on the part of the West.

Snow: No, I have never.

Hook: This mood of thinking in England which you describe, and with which I can sympathize, is shared very widely, by Macmillan as well as Gaitskell. On the basis of it, it's still possible to elaborate alternative policies.

Snow: Yes, oh yes. I don't think it's an all-or-nothing situation in that kind of way. There are really two different sets of conditions. One is, I think—coming down again to the sort of things military theorists talk about—that between this country and the Soviet Union at the moment there is a relatively stable balance which would not be affected either by the increase or the diminution of nuclear weapons on either side by quite a large factor. I would think that either country during the next decade is going to have enough material to do the other devastating harm.

Podhoretz: The so-called technological breakthrough that would put somebody far ahead is highly unlikely?

Snow: That's highly unlikely. In fact, if you've got the stuff and you've got any means of delivering it, then technological breakthroughs don't count. No, I don't believe in that. What I'm more worried about immediately is the rapid coming into possession of these weapons by large numbers of people. Because that seems to me to alter the dangers of accident, error, and so on quite out of proportion to the number of bombs. The number won't be very much greater, because the gross number of these weapons is so large in American and Russian hands that the six or eight powers that are going to possess them, or already possess them, won't alter them appreciably. But they do enormously alter the possibilities of some of these things going off, and I bet—in fact I've stated that I'm sure that they will go off, unless we can contain this dispersion. Whether their going off in a particular circumstance is going to start the whole holocaust, of course, is a matter partly of luck. It depends where the chance happened, in what circumstances it happened, in what hands these things were. The optimistic theory is that just as there is a fairly stable locking between this country and the Soviet Union, there will equally be lockings between, say, Israel and Egypt, and what not. That, I confess, I am far less confident about. Secondly, I would have thought that if this country and the Soviet Union go on regardless, increasing their armaments in this particular way, the position which may be stable now is bound to become unstable. I can't imagine an arms race of that type going on for very long without becoming unstable.

Hook: Unless there were countervailing considerations, I would agree with you. If one speaks in terms of a long-run building up of weapons, at some critical point it would lead to a denouement; but as Keynes said, in the long run we shall all be dead. But suppose we take into account the possibilities of modifying the trend. There are so many contingencies, as you pointed out, that enter the situation. They depend upon what we do to control tests, and limit the extension of the bomb with respect to the $N+1$ countries. But I've always been puzzled, to be perfectly frank with you, Sir Charles, about the theory of probability you were using in your speech before the AAAS [American Association of Atomic Scientists] when you predicted that there was almost a mathematical certainty that in ten years these things would go off.

Podhoretz: I think the term used was "statistical certainty," wasn't it, Sir Charles?

Snow: What I was actually prophesying—and I prophesy it here and now again—was that some of these things will go off. I didn't say that a thermonuclear war need break out, and that is why I was qualifying it here. It depends enormously on the particular way in which this accident happens. For instance, if by some unfortunate chance, a nuclear bomb went off in or over New York this afternoon, I wouldn't think that would give us much hope of avoiding the worst. We would have to show great prudence and wisdom for that sort of contingency not to bring about the thermonuclear war. And similarly, if by any chance one went off over Moscow, my expectations wouldn't be very cheerful. But I can imagine that somewhere in the remoter parts of Asia Minor, so to speak, one could go off, by accident or by some mad action, which wouldn't have decisive results. That, I think, needn't lead to a nuclear war.

Morgenthau: It's not only a matter of accidental nuclear war. Once nuclear weapons have been dispersed to an indefinite number of nations, the very mechanics of mutual deterrence as they exist today, stabilizing within certain limits the international situation, would disappear.

Snow: I agree.

Morgenthau: For if tomorrow an atomic bomb exploded in New York, everybody would know whose atomic bomb it was, and the retaliation would be swift and devastating. For this reason we don't need to worry about an atomic bomb going off tomorrow in New York.

Snow: Except by chance.

Morgenthau: Well, that possibility is extremely slim. We don't need to worry about that. But if you imagine for a moment, as we must, that within five or ten years ten nations have atomic weapons and tension exists between the United States and, let me say, two or three different nations, and an atomic bomb goes off in New York—against whom are you going to retaliate? Are you going to blow up the whole world in order to make sure that the culprit doesn't escape? Furthermore, you will then have a new refinement of diplomacy, trying to make it appear that the atomic bomb originated from some country other than the one which actually dropped it. You will then have a very interesting new Machiavellian situation, which I suppose you will not survive for long. Before you came in, Sir Charles, I painted a rather glum picture of two different types of absurdity with which we are confronted. I think that the situation will not only be more difficult to handle in diplomatic and military terms but will also be intellectually and morally infinitely more grave than it is now, once the atomic club is wide open and an indefinite number of nations have joined.

Hook: How can we prevent the extension of nuclear weapons to the $N+1$ countries? Have you any ideas, Mr. Morgenthau, about procedures? In the next ten years if scientific knowledge is dispersed throughout the world, even if the Soviet Union and the United States were to renounce the use of thermonuclear weapons, what's to prevent some small nation from. . . .

Morgenthau: You are absolutely right. You see, this is really my main argument against unilateral nuclear disarmament. It may work in a bi-polar nuclear situation. But it is bound not to work when you have a multi-polar situation, when you have five or ten nations, because it doesn't do the United States any good to renounce for itself the use of atomic weapons, when the nine other nuclear powers don't renounce such use.

Hughes: It may be true that it is going to be too late even for a unilateral solution. This is the really nightmarish possibility. But it seems to me, Mr. Morgenthau, that you and Sir Charles . . . are in positions that are very close to each other, and you lead yourselves almost up to unilateralism and then stop short of it by describing the present situation as impossible. Actually I think you differ with Sir Charles, Mr. Morgenthau, in believing the present situation is less stable than he does. I would say that your arguments finally reduce to the absolute necessity of breaking the circle, the vicious circle, of mutual distrust between us and the Soviet Union, and doing it fast, and arriving at what amounts to an American-Soviet alliance for the preservation of the peace and the denial of nuclear weapons to other nations. And I would maintain that the only way that circle can be broken, and broken fast, is by a dramatic act of renunciation on one side or the other. Since we are not sitting in the Soviet Union, it has to be done here. Q.E.D.

Podhoretz: Well, that's a dramatic point at which to end the discussion at the table and throw the floor open to questions from the audience. . . . Mr. Joseph Kraft.[1]

Kraft: I have a question for Mr. Hughes. One of the few things on which there was general agreement was that it would be useful to have some kind of international control over thermonuclear weapons. The question is this: If the United States renounced the use of thermonuclear weapons in any believable way, wouldn't it be removing one of the few incentives for the Russians to enter into a control agreement?

Hughes: I don't know. This is a really "iffy" question, but I maintain that one of the fallacies we commit in the ordinary conventional-wisdom discussion of the Soviet Union is to believe that the only argument they understand is force. I think it's been implicit around this table that the Russians, at least under Khrushchev, understand other arguments. My guess is that to renounce thermonuclear weapons would be worth more in terms of breaking the vicious circle of mutual distrust—and I apologize for using the phrase again— I think this would be more effective in bringing about an agreement

---

[1] Mr. Kraft is a free-lance political journalist.

than continuing with deterrence. It may be that I am very wrong, and I think this is where a really crucial choice-point comes. I've made my choice, but I can see there's an extremely logical argument for the other one.

Podhoretz: I suspect that Mr. Hook would like to provide that logical argument.

Hook: Logic, of course, isn't sufficient, but it's necessary. In these questions we are dealing with historical evidence. Mr. Hughes has spoken about faith in the Soviet Union and implied that distrust is unreasonable or vicious. But I submit, Mr. Hughes, and as a historian you will agree, that—I take the risk of repeating Santayana's *bon mot*—"Those who have forgotten the past are doomed to repeat it." We can base ourselves only on probabilities. Whether we have faith or distrust in the Soviet Union depends upon the record of its performance. When Henri Spaak at one UN meeting turned to Molotov, who had charged the West with mistrust, and said, "What else can we have in the light of your behavior since the Second World War?" it seemed to me he was phrasing what was in everybody's mind. In 1948 Bertrand Russell urged the West to use atomic bombs against the Soviet Union if it wouldn't accept reasonable conditions of international atomic control. The U.S. at that time had a monopoly of atomic power. If it had been guilty of the imperialism the Soviet Union charged it with, it would have dropped the bombs. But in an act which was unprecedented in the history of hostile nations, the U.S. offered to surrender its monopoly of these weapons to an international authority with the sole provision that measures be taken to prevent bombs from being dropped on the U.S. Every nation of the world accepted this proposal save the USSR. Do you really think it's unjustified to be mistrustful of the USSR? The experience of all Western nations with the Soviet Union justifies a profound mistrust.

Hughes: May I say that this is really off the subject. Let me just say once and for all, because I'm so often misunderstood, that I agree with everything you say about Communist tyranny. We don't have to argue that old one again.

Hook: But we were talking about *trust.*

Hughes: No, but I was talking about trust only on the narrow question of attitude toward thermonuclear weapons. What seems to me has to happen is that the U.S. and the Soviet Union must come to a realization of their mutual interest in having a world totally free of thermonuclear weapons. Now, I think that even in terms of absolute power-political, totally unscrupulous, unprincipled Soviet behavior, this makes sense. They would do better in the world competition without nuclear weapons than by having this nightmare hang over them. I don't really think we'd be giving up much.

Hook: That's all very well, but let us examine your notion of trust, not on the broad historical level but on the narrow level of weapons control. I ask you, Mr. Hughes, what is your evidence—you must have some evidence—that we can reasonably have trust great enough to justify a policy of unilateral disarmament, that the Soviet Union will accept our opening gambit? If it were England we were dealing with, there'd be no question about it. If it were any other non-Communist country in the world, we could have reasonable trust. Look what happened in Geneva at the conference to prohibit further bomb tests. All the concessions since last year have been made by the Americans. The Russians repudiated the agreement made previously that the enforcement group would be headed by a neutral. They have insisted upon a built-in veto by specifying a three-man control which parallels Khrushchev's proposal for the UN. In the light of this action in the narrow sphere of weapons control, I ask you, Mr. Hughes, what are the grounds of your faith?

Hughes: I think they think we don't mean it, and we think they don't mean it. On the test-ban issue, I believe that they've become bored. They want the big discussion. But again, this seems to me rather irrelevant. The main point, it seems to me, is that there need be no ethical ground for faith or belief in benevolent intentions. The main point is, looking at it from the angle of Moscow, that the subversion of non-Communist peoples could progress far more readily and far more predictably if there were no thermonuclear weapons around. This throws off all the Marxist calculations of the future.

Morgenthau: I must disagree with this prediction, for if there were no thermonuclear weapons, the U.S. would not be compelled to pursue the same kind of abstentionist and cautious policy which it has pursued consistently vis-à-vis Communist expansion. It is exactly because it fears thermonuclear war evidently more than does the Soviet Union that it finds itself in this situation. Remove that threat and limit the use of violence to conventional weapons, and any number of wars would have broken out in the world, in some of which the U.S. would have been fully involved. . . .

Podhoretz: . . . Mr. Irving Kristol.[2]

Kristol: I have a question to the panel in general on this matter of

---

[2] Mr. Kristol has been an editor of *Commentary*, co-editor of *Encounter* in London, and editor of the *Reporter*.

faith in the Soviet Union. I think I see what Mr. Hughes is getting at and I don't think this question has been adequately discussed. What Mr. Hughes is saying, if I understand him correctly, is that it does not make sense from the Russian-Communist point of view to have a world in which there is a threat of thermonuclear destruction; that from the Communist point of view it makes sense to enter into a nuclear disarmament agreement. The question, therefore, is why don't they do it? I personally think they don't do it because they are Communists, because they are not rational, because there are elements of mythology in Communism which dictate their policies. But I should like to hear what the members of this panel think.

Hughes: I think they don't do it because they think we don't mean it. And so we have to do something dramatic to show that we mean it.

Morgenthau: It is of course obvious that the Russians as rational beings have the same interest as everybody else in not being destroyed in a nuclear war. But there is a very long step from this simple recognition of a rational interest to political action putting this rational interest into practice. The statesmen of Russia are no more motivated by one simple rational consideration than anybody else. We all have contradictory motives; we all are torn by different tendencies, and so are the Russians. On the one hand, Mr. Khrushchev knows that a nuclear war would make an end to the Bolshevik regime in Russia, if not to the very national existence of Russia. But on the other hand, he says to Walter Lippmann that there are neutral nations, but no neutral men. I shall never surrender the security of the Soviet Union to a non-Communist, he says, any more than you would surrender the care for your security to a Communist.

So you have here two incompatible positions within the mind of the same man. And the question arises, how do you transcend these two incompatible positions? Mr. Hughes says we ought to make a dramatic gesture, which would really be an unprecedented act of renunciation, in order to show the Russians the right way. This assumes that Mr. Khrushchev is motivated by nothing but his rational interest in surviving in the present world. But he is certainly also very much motivated by the specter of a Communist world which he firmly believes the process of history is bound to bring about. Presented with such an opportunity, I must say my faith in Mr. Khrushchev's rationality in terms of survival would certainly yield to my distrust of Mr. Khrushchev as an apostle of Communism.

Hook: Mr. Kristol's question as to why the Russians don't accept a disarmament treaty brought from Mr. Hughes the rejoinder, "Because they don't believe we mean it." Now that's a little ambiguous. First of all, we did make a dramatic gesture at the time of the Acheson-Lilienthal proposals. We made it, and the Communists rejected it. Will Mr. Hughes say that we didn't mean it? If he does, again I would like to ask for evidence.

Hughes: Incidentally, I didn't say we didn't mean it. I said they *thought* we didn't. That's a different thing.

Hook: Oh, well, that just puts the question further back. Why did they believe we didn't mean it? What could we do to make them believe that we mean it, short of surrendering to them? We made them this offer and they turned it down. I doubt that they thought we didn't mean it. There is another plausible explanation. It's this: the Russians do not fear that we will use the nuclear weapon. On several occasions, I believe, they have actually implied that it's morally impossible for the West to use the nuclear weapon without being provoked. Mr. Morgenthau indicated another line of thought that moves them. If they know their flank is covered, so to speak, that they needn't worry about an atomic Pearl Harbor on our side, why should they forego the position of strength that they get from a war of nerves? I think Khrushchev is counting upon the growing hysteria in the West. And by hysteria I don't mean fear—intelligent fear is a good thing—I mean blind fear. He's counting upon the growth of hysterical fear in the West to force it to retreat again and again. Obviously that's the logic—or psychology—of the situation. If you say to the Russians, "Short of war we will use all means to stop you," what's to prevent them from closing their iron fingers around Berlin? Step by step they will march on, or to use an analogy of Kissinger's, we can lose a football game by a series of five-yard dashes as much as by one end-run. If the Communists can count upon our hysterical fear of world destruction, then they can sit pretty. And they *are* sitting pretty. They *are* winning the world. They're winning the world because we haven't worked out other alternatives. However, they can't be finally sure of winning the world until we surrender the deterrent....

64   TESTING—WHAT DOES KENNEDY MEAN?*

For the past week I have been examining the text of the President's March 2 speech on the resumption of testing. This has not

*James R. Newman, "Testing—What Does Kennedy Mean?" *New Republic,* Vol. CXLVI (March 26, 1962), pp. 11–13. Reprinted by permission of THE NEW REPUBLIC, ©1962, Harrison-Blaine of New Jersey, Inc.

been an exhilarating exercise, but I was moved to it for several reasons. That the decision to resume testing is iniquitous is perfectly clear to me, but I had to settle for myself the question whether Kennedy's arguments are in fact as confused as they sounded on delivery. Second, while I have in recent years become quite accustomed to large sections of the press exhorting Americans, in the name of survival, to join hands, close ranks, lock elbows, and march bravely off the edge of the cliff, I was appalled at the uniformly self-righteous and self-congratulatory tone of ensuing editorial opinion. And, third, I had to try to make sense of the spate of news "analyses," both before and after the event, which repeatedly emphasized the President's "agony" and "anguish" in making his decision.

Regarding this last piece of blather, may I say at once that it never occurred to me, nor, I suppose, to anyone else who is not completely demented, that Kennedy is a monster. He may not, to adopt a phrase of the late Sir Lewis Namier, have conspicuous capacity to imagine the past and remember the future; he may be too immersed in the stir and bustle of the present to have adequate perspective; but he is a man like other men, not unmindful of his humanity, no stranger to sympathy. It would not have crossed my mind that he could make a decision which is likely in the long run to cost thousands of lives, to spawn widespread disease and suffering, to mutilate future generations of children, and certain to deepen the despair and darken the hopes of mankind for peace—that he could take such a step without sorrow and inner conflict. One requires no instruction on this point by pundits or publicists. Prick the President and he will bleed; no doubt. Observe, however, that this is a necessary but not a sufficient qualification of leadership.

To return to the speech: careful scrutiny exposes it as a low yield device. It rolls, rumbles and reverberates; the crackerjack, the potted phrases, the humble supplications, the mood words, the organ tones: all are here. "Mortal hands," "Free World," "awesome responsibilities," "prevent the nuclear arms race from mushrooming out of control," "hope and prayer that these grim unwelcome tests will never have to be made," and so on. But comb out the fustian and what remains? What did Kennedy say that he has not said before? What fresh thought did he contribute? What light did he focus on dark questions? That he spoke truths is clear; and truth is always welcome. But truth can be misused, made the stalking horse to error; and one detects a collapse of reason between the worthy premise that the "world [must] be made safe for mankind," and the bizarre

382 American Views of Soviet Russia

conclusion that this is to be accomplished by making bigger battle axes and trying them out on the necks of anonymous innocents.

I am not disposed to burden you with a minute content analysis of the President's speech, but a few samples may be permitted.

The main argument, of course, is that the U.S. must maintain an effective quantity and quality of nuclear weapons to deter "a nuclear strike, or an overwhelming ground attack upon our forces and allies." Kennedy accepts this without question. Many persons agree with him, many do not. This is not a self-evident truth, no more than it is self-evident, say, that the death penalty deters murder. The President gives no sign that he appreciates even the possibility of a doubt as to the effectiveness of terror in preventing terror. One would feel more secure if one thought he had misgivings about this thesis.

REVENGE, NOT PREVENTION

There is an even more serious point to be considered in connection with the deterrence philosophy. Deterrence is, at best, a primitive, muddled concept, confusing alike to those who swear by it and those who repudiate it. I propose an analogy. What is a parachute tester? A man who tests parachutes? No. He is a man on whom parachutes are tested. Consider: if the parachute opens during the test his services are in a sense unnecessary; if the parachute does not open he is dead. And so, roughly, with deterrents. For these are devices to be tried out *on* us, not *for* us; of unknown value when unused, and useless when used. No wonder, therefore, that when men purport to argue for weapons which will prevent war, they end inevitably with a passionate plea for weapons which will make war more terrible. Here, at least, one is on safe ground; revenge, not prevention. Again and again Kennedy betrays his confusion on this score.

Take the second paragraph of his speech: The U.S., he says, must have weapons "so deployed and protected as to be capable of surviving any surprise attack [who is to survive, we, or the weapons?] and devastating the attacker." What has this to do with deterrence? The next sentence pretends to answer: "Only through such strength can we be certain of deterring a nuclear strike. . . ." But the sentence after that tips the President's hand: "Only through such strength can we in the Free world—*should the deterrent fail* [my italics]—face the tragedy of another war with any hope of survival." What does this mean? We deter or we do not deter. If we fail to deter, how can deterrent weapons help us to survive? They may help a dying country to destroy its assassin, a thought to comfort us on our exit, but they have even less to do with survival than the Administration's puny shelter program.

More in the same vein: "Were we to stand still while the Soviets surpassed us—or even appeared to surpass us—the Free World's ability to deter, to survive and to respond to an all-out attack would be seriously weakened." What has our "deterrent" to do with the Soviets' ability to attack us? What has a "deterrent" to do with responding to an attack? What has a "deterrent" to do with the fact that the Soviets "appear to surpass us"? Indeed, what does the word "appear" signify in this context? "Appear" to whom? To us? To the Soviets? To the Basques? What is the President talking about?

Next item. "Our friends around the world," says Kennedy, "know we are not deciding to test for political or psychological reasons. . . ." Can he be serious? We are testing, according to Kennedy, to acquire information which will enable us to improve our weapons so that they can "penetrate" the Soviets' antimissile system (assuming they have one), and "to achieve such a system for ourselves" (assuming this is possible). Are we planning to attack the Soviets? We are not. Our "peaceful intentions are clear." We are merely defending ourselves against the danger of Russian attack. Why then do we need missiles to "penetrate" their defense system? The answer is that the Russians must be made to understand that if they wallop us we will wallop them right back. Our deterrent must, as Kennedy said, be "credible." The Soviets must be persuaded that we can in fact match deed to threat. We must, in short, bring them to their senses. They must either agree to our terms at the next Geneva disarmament conference, or come round after we have impressed them with our determination and our nuclear proficiency. But what is involved in this persuasion other than a mixture of politics and psychology? Deterrence is to a cold war what slaughter is to a hot war: a continuation, if I may quote a quaint adage, of politics by other means. Kennedy knows this; we know it; the Soviets know it; also everyone knows that everyone else knows it. Whom is the President fooling?

One further point. The tests we threaten to carry out are described by Kennedy in almost ecstatic terms: they will "restrict the radioactive fallout to an absolute minimum, far less than the contamination created by last fall's Soviet series. Moreover, we will hold the increase in radiation in the Northern Hemisphere, where nearly all such fallout will occur, to a very low level." (I hear a noise behind the arras, which sounds like the father of some bomb or other.) The recent Soviet tests surprised the scientists, because of the remarkably low incidence of fallout. It may be, as the President says, that our tests will improve on this. Yet there will be fallout, which will add to the radiation to which men are exposed; and, as leading geneticists have made irrefutably clear, *any* increase augments the mutation rate, which in turn leads to deaths, stillbirths, malformations, disease. From this statistical fact there is no escape, though there are some who regard the bill as of small moment since the bulk of the payments will be deferred.

To claim that, because U.S. tests will be held over "the open sea," they will "rule out any problem of fallout in the immediate area of testing," thus implying that the Soviet tests, which were conducted in the Arctic, created just such a problem, is disingenuous. Leaving aside questions of amount, altitude of shots or wind and weather conditions, fallout over Novaya Zemlaya is no different from fallout over Christmas Island. No one supposes that tests have been or will be conducted over populated places. Moreover, as Kennedy knows, fallout over the test area itself is only part of the story. Radioactive debris spreads and circulates in time over an enormous area, and these secondary effects raise many difficulties and dangerous health problems imperfectly understood and impossible to solve.

Nor does the fact that our tests will take place over the Pacific—a soothing name—make them more peaceful than tests conducted over the Arctic. The truth is simple: the Soviet tests were immoral; ours are immoral; neither promotes life; both promote its extinction.

As for Kennedy's statements that he finds it "deeply regrettable" that any radioactive material must be added to the atmosphere, "that even one additional individual's health may be risked in the foreseeable future"; and that, "however remote and infinitesimal those hazards are judged to be, I still exceedingly regret the necessity of balancing these hazards against the hazards to hundreds of millions of lives which would be created by any decline in our nuclear strength" —these are examples of bathos. "This hurts me more than it hurts you," may be suitable sentiment for father when he punishes his son with a strap; but Kennedy is not my father, not the father of his country, let alone the father of mankind. I am not moved by his "regrets"; I regard them as an inadequate solatium for the poisoning of the air. Instead of oratory about human freedom and decency, I suggest that if we want to do something to promote peace we begin by being peaceful.

65 TOWARD A STRATEGY OF PEACE*

"There are few earthly things more beautiful than a University," wrote John Masefield, in his tribute to the English universities—and his words are equally true here. He did not refer to spires and towers, to campus greens and ivied walls. He admired the splendid beauty of the university, he said, because it was "a place where those who hate ignorance may strive to know, where those who perceive truth may strive to make others see."

I have, therefore, chosen this time and this place to discuss a topic on which ignorance too often abounds and the truth is too rarely perceived—yet it is the most important topic on earth: world peace.

What kind of peace do I mean? What kind of peace do we seek? Not a *Pax Americana* enforced on the world by American weapons of war. Not the peace of the grave or the security of the slave. I am talking about genuine peace, the kind of peace that makes life on earth worth living, the kind that enables men and nations to grow and to hope and to build a better life for their children—not merely peace for Americans but peace for all men and women, not merely peace in our time but peace for all time.

I speak of peace because of the new face of war. Total war makes no sense in an age when great powers can maintain large and relatively invulnerable nuclear forces and refuse to surrender without resort to those forces. It makes no sense in an age when a single nuclear weapon contains almost 10 times the explosive force delivered by all of the Allied air forces in the Second World War. It makes no sense in an age when the deadly poisons produced by a nuclear exchange would be carried by the wind and water and soil and seed to the far corners of the globe and to generations yet unborn.

Today the expenditure of billions of dollars every year on weapons acquired for the purpose of making sure we never need to use them is essential to keeping the peace. But surely the acquisition of such idle stockpiles—which can only destroy and never create—is not the only, much less the most efficient, means of assuring peace.

I speak of peace, therefore, as the necessary rational end of rational men. I realize that the pursuit of peace is not as dramatic as

*John F. Kennedy, "Toward a Strategy of Peace: Commencement Address at American University, Washington, D.C., June 10, 1963," reprinted in *Documents on American Foreign Relations: 1963*, Richard P. Stebbins (ed.) (New York: Harper & Row, for the Council on Foreign Relations, 1964), pp. 116-23.

the pursuit of war, and frequently the words of the pursuer fall on deaf ears. But we have no more urgent task.

Some say that it is useless to speak of world peace or world law or world disarmament—and that it will be useless until the leaders of the Soviet Union adopt a more enlightened attitude. I hope they do. I believe we can help them do it. But I also believe that we must re-examine our own attitude, as individuals and as a nation, for our attitude is as essential as theirs. And every graduate of this school, every thoughtful citizen who despairs of war and wishes to bring peace, should begin by looking inward—by examining his own atti-tude toward the possibilities of peace, toward the Soviet Union, toward the course of the cold war, and toward freedom and peace here at home.

THE POSSIBILITIES OF PEACE

First: Let us examine our attitude toward peace itself. Too many of us think it is impossible. Too many think it unreal. But that is a dangerous, defeatist belief. It leads to the conclusion that war is inevitable, that mankind is doomed, that we are gripped by forces we cannot control.

We need not accept that view. Our problems are manmade; there-fore they can be solved by man. And man can be as big as he wants. No problem of human destiny is beyond human beings. Man's reason and spirit have often solved the seemingly unsolvable, and we believe they can do it again.

I am not referring to the absolute, infinite concept of universal peace and good will of which some fantasies and fanatics dream. I do not deny the values of hopes and dreams, but we merely invite dis-couragement and incredulity by making that our only and immediate goal.

Let us focus instead on a more practical, more attainable peace, based not on a sudden revolution in human nature but on a gradual evolution in human institutions—on a series of concrete actions and effective agreements which are in the interest of all concerned. There is no single, simple key to this peace, no grand or magic formula to be adopted by one or two powers. Genuine peace must be the prod-uct of many nations, the sum of many acts. It must be dynamic, not static, changing to meet the challenge of each new generation. For peace is a process, a way of solving problems.

With such a peace there will still be quarrels and conflicting interests, as there are within families and nations. World peace, like community peace, does not require that each man love his neighbor; it requires only that they live together in mutual tolerance, submitting their disputes to a just and peaceful settlement. And history teaches us that enmities between nations, as between individuals, do not last forever. However fixed our likes and dislikes may seem, the tide of time and events will often bring surprising changes in the relations between nations and neighbors.

So let us persevere. Peace need not be impracticable, and war need not be inevitable. By defining our goal more clearly, by making it seem more manageable and less remote, we can help all peoples to see it, to draw hope from it, and to move irresistibly toward it.

COMMON INTERESTS OF U.S. AND SOVIET UNION

Second: Let us reexamine our attitude toward the Soviet Union. It is discouraging to think that their leaders may actually believe what their propagandists write. It is discouraging to read a recent authoritative Soviet text on military strategy and find, on page after page, wholly baseless and incredible claims—such as the allegation that "American imperialist circles are preparing to unleash different types of wars . . . that there is a very real threat of a preventive war being unleashed by American imperialists against the Soviet Union . . . [and that] the political aims of the American imperialists are to enslave economically and politically the European and other capitalist countries . . . [and] to achieve world domination . . . by means of aggressive wars."

Truly as it was written long ago: "The wicked flee when no man pursueth." Yet it is sad to read these Soviet statements—to realize the extent of the gulf between us. But it is also a warning—a warning to the American people not to fall into the same trap as the Soviets, not to see only a distorted and desperate view of the other side, not to see conflict as inevitable, accommodation as impossible, and communication as nothing more than an exchange of threats.

No government or social system is so evil that its people must be considered as lacking in virtue. As Americans we find communism profoundly repugnant as a negation of personal freedom and dignity. But we can still hail the Russian people for their many achievements—in science and space, in economic and industrial growth, in culture and in acts of courage.

Among the many traits the peoples of our two countries have in common, none is stronger than our mutual abhorrence of war. Almost unique among the major world powers, we have never been at war with each other. And no nation in the history of battle ever suffered more than the Soviet Union suffered in the course of the Second World War. At least 20 million lost their lives. Countless millions of homes and farms were burned or sacked. A third of the nation's territory, including nearly two-thirds of its industrial base, was turned into a wasteland—a loss equivalent to the devastation of this country east of Chicago.

Today, should total war ever break out again—no matter how—our two countries would become the primary targets. It is an ironical but accurate fact that the two strongest powers are the two in the most danger of devastation. All we have built, all we have worked for, would be destroyed in the first 24 hours. And even in the cold war, which brings burdens and dangers to so many countries—including this nation's closest allies—our two countries bear the heaviest burdens. For we are both devoting massive sums of money to weapons that could be better devoted to combating ignorance, poverty, and disease. We are both caught up in a vicious and dangerous cycle in which suspicion on one side breeds suspicion on the other and new weapons beget counter-weapons.

In short, both the United States and its allies, and the Soviet Union and its allies, have a mutually deep interest in a just and genuine peace, and in halting the arms race. Agreements to this end are in the interests of the Soviet Union as well as ours, and even the most hostile nations can be relied upon to accept and keep those treaty obligations, and only those treaty obligations, which are in their own interest.

So let us not be blind to our differences, but let us also direct attention to our common interests and to the means by which those differences can be resolved. And if we cannot end now our differences, at least we can help make the world safe for diversity. For in the final analysis our most basic common link is that we all inhabit this planet. We all breathe the same air. We all cherish our children's future. And we are all mortal.

THE PURSUIT OF PEACE

Third: Let us reexamine our attitude toward the cold war, remembering that we are not engaged in a debate, seeking to pile up debat-

ing points. We are not here distributing blame or pointing the finger
of judgment. We must deal with the world as it is and not as it might
have been had the history of the last 18 years been different.

We must, therefore, persevere in the search for peace in the hope
that constructive changes within the Communist bloc might bring
within reach solutions which now seem beyond us. We must conduct
our affairs in such a way that it becomes in the Communists' interest
to agree on a genuine peace. Above all, while defending our own
vital interests, nuclear powers must avert those confrontations which
bring an adversary to a choice of either a humiliating retreat or a
nuclear war. To adopt that kind of course in the nuclear age would
be evidence only of the bankruptcy of our policy—or of a collective
death wish for the world.

To secure these ends, America's weapons are nonprovocative,
carefully controlled, designed to deter, and capable of selective use.
Our military forces are committed to peace and disciplined in self-
restraint. Our diplomats are instructed to avoid unnecessary irritants
and purely rhetorical hostility.

For we can seek a relaxation of tensions without relaxing our
guard. And, for our part, we do not need to use threats to prove that
we are resolute. We do not need to jam foreign broadcasts out of fear
our faith will be eroded. We are unwilling to impose our system on
any unwilling people, but we are willing and able to engage in peaceful competition with any people on earth.

Meanwhile we seek to strengthen the United Nations, to help solve
its financial problems, to make it a more effective instrument of
peace, to develop it into a genuine world security system—a system
capable of resolving disputes on the basis of law, of insuring the
security of the large and the small, and of creating conditions under
which arms can finally be abolished.

At the same time we seek to keep peace inside the non-Communist
world, where many nations, all of them our friends, are divided over
issues which weaken Western unity, which invite Communist intervention, or which threaten to erupt into war. Our efforts in West
New Guinea, in the Congo, in the Middle East, and in the Indian
subcontinent have been persistent and patient despite criticism from
both sides. We have also tried to set an example for others—by seeking to adjust small but significant differences with our own closest
neighbors in Mexico and in Canada.

Speaking of other nations, I wish to make one point clear. We are
bound to many nations by alliances. Those alliances exist because

our concern and theirs substantially overlap. Our commitment to defend Western Europe and West Berlin, for example, stands undiminished because of the identity of our vital interests. The United States will make no deal with the Soviet Union at the expense of other nations and other peoples, not merely because they are our partners but also because their interests and ours converge.

Our interests converge, however, not only in defending the frontiers of freedom but in pursuing the paths of peace. It is our hope—and the purpose of Allied policies—to convince the Soviet Union that she, too, should let each nation choose its own future, so long as that choice does not interfere with the choices of others. The Communist drive to impose their political and economic system on others is the primary cause of world tension today. For there can be no doubt that, if all nations could refrain from interfering in the self-determination of others, the peace would be much more assured.

This will require a new effort to achieve world law, a new context for world discussions. It will require increased understanding between the Soviets and ourselves. And increased understanding will require increased contact and communication. One step in this direction is the proposed arrangement for a direct line between Moscow and Washington, to avoid on each side the dangerous delays, misunderstandings, and misreadings of the other's actions which might occur at a time of crisis.

We have also been talking in Geneva about other first-step measures of arms control, designed to limit the intensity of the arms race and to reduce the risks of accidental war. Our primary long-range interest in Geneva, however, is general and complete disarmament, designed to take place by stages, permitting parallel political developments to build the new institutions of peace which would take the place of arms. The pursuit of disarmament has been an effort of this Government since the 1920's. It has been urgently sought by the past three administrations. And however dim the prospects may be today, we intend to continue this effort—to continue it in order that all countries, including our own, can better grasp what the problems and possibilities of disarmament are.

The one major area of these negotiations where the end is in sight, yet where a fresh start is badly needed, is in a treaty to outlaw nuclear tests. The conclusion of such a treaty—so near and yet so far—would check the spiraling arms race in one of its most dangerous areas. It would place the nuclear powers in a position to deal more effectively with one of the greatest hazards which man faces in 1963, the further spread of nuclear arms. It would increase our security; it would decrease the prospects of war. Surely this goal is sufficiently important to require our steady pursuit, yielding neither to the temptation to give up the whole effort nor the temptation to give up our insistence on vital and responsible safeguards.

I am taking this opportunity, therefore, to announce two important decisions in this regard.

First: Chairman Khrushchev, Prime Minister Macmillan, and I have agreed that high-level discussions will shortly begin in Moscow looking toward early agreement on a comprehensive test ban treaty. Our hopes must be tempered with the caution of history, but with our hopes go the hopes of all mankind.

Second: To make clear our good faith and solemn convictions on the matter, I now declare that the United States does not propose to conduct nuclear tests in the atmosphere so long as other states do not do so. We will not be the first to resume. Such a declaration is no substitute for a formal binding treaty, but I hope it will help us achieve one. Nor would such a treaty be a substitute for disarmament, but I hope it will help us achieve it.

PEACE AND HUMAN RIGHTS

Finally, my fellow Americans, let us examine our attitude toward peace and freedom here at home. The quality and spirit of our own society must justify and support our efforts abroad. We must show it in the dedication of our own lives, as many of you who are graduating today will have a unique opportunity to do, by serving without pay in the Peace Corps abroad or in the proposed National Service Corps here at home.

But wherever we are, we must all, in our daily lives, live up to the age-old faith that peace and freedom walk together. In too many of our cities today the peace is not secure because freedom is incomplete.

It is the responsibility of the executive branch at all levels of government—local, State, and national—to provide and protect that freedom for all of our citizens by all means within their authority. It is the responsibility of the legislative branch at all levels, wherever that authority is not now adequate, to make it adequate. And it is the responsibility of all citizens in all sections of this country to respect the rights of all others and to respect the law of the land.

All this is not unrelated to world peace. "When a man's ways please the Lord," the Scriptures tell us, "he maketh even his enemies to be at peace with him." And is not peace, in the last analysis, basically a matter of human rights—the right to live out our lives without fear of devastation, the right to breathe air as nature provided it, the right of future generations to a healthy existence?

While we proceed to safeguard our national interests, let us also safeguard human interests. And the elimination of war and arms is clearly in the interest of both. No treaty, however much it may be to the advantage of all, however tightly it may be worded, can provide absolute security against the risks of deception and evasion. But it can, if it is sufficiently effective in its enforcement and if it is sufficiently in the interests of its signers, offer far more security and far fewer risks than an unabated, uncontrolled, unpredictable arms race.

The United States, as the world knows, will never start a war. We do not want a war. We do not now expect a war. This generation of Americans has already had enough—more than enough—of war and hate and oppression. We shall be prepared if others wish it. We shall be alert to try to stop it. But we shall also do our part to build a world of peace where the weak are safe and the strong are just. We are not helpless before that task or hopeless of its success. Confident and unafraid, we labor on—not toward a strategy of annihilation but toward a strategy of peace.

Postlude

In the fall of 1964, Premier Khrushchev was ousted from office by his Politburo colleagues. Whether this change in leadership signaled a new phase in Soviet-American relations—or whether the policies of Communist China, the American military presence in South Vietnam, or some other, unforeseen factor proves more influential in those relations—must be left to future historians. Prophecy is not the obligation and not usually the temptation of those who tell the story of the past.

Nevertheless, Professor Paul Seabury of the University of California has written an essay, published in 1965, which serves well as both a retrospect on Soviet-American relations and a modest prospect of how they may evolve in the future.

66 THE COMMUNIST CHALLENGE AHEAD*

Wars which are not wars in the classical sense bedevil our minds and our times. Men with hearts and consciences pray that this limited yet limitless conflict known as the cold war will not lead to all-out war. But the rational mind remembers past wars which had known beginnings and known ends. The rational mind also remembers that the principal wars of the recent past accomplished very important things—for better or worse. No matter how horrible they were, they involved clear contests, and they achieved definitive solutions: the defeat of Nazi Germany, for instance. They also had their known ends—in a railroad car, a chandeliered hall, or on a battleship deck. The prospect of their impending conclusion made it possible for men to plan for futures in which these specific conflicts no longer existed. Such futures often were called—and sometimes too optimistically— the "post-war world."

Because it has been difficult for Americans to agree among themselves about the nature of the present cold war, it also has been difficult to agree when it began; hazardous to conclude that it has, or has not, abated; and certainly impossible to say that, thus far, our actions in it have definitively "solved" anything. For these reasons, it is extremely difficult to talk about the desirable features of a "post-cold war world." Since we must assume that thermonuclear weapons will indefinitely remain in the hands of the great powers, including Russia, "no-win" policies do have something to recommend them. "No-settle" policies may also be necessary; if war can no longer be the ultimate arbiter, many conflicts will not be definitively settled in our own time. Conflict may be moderated, contained, or tinkered with by diplomacy and by provisional understandings, but not "solved." In time, perhaps, some of these conflicts may gradually disappear, like Lewis Carroll's Cheshire cat; though one might be hard-pressed to identify the moment at which the smile (or the grimace) actually could no longer be seen or no longer mattered very much.

Whether we continue to describe the relationship between America and Russia, between the West and the Communist bloc, as a cold

---

*Paul Seabury, "America and the Communist Challenge," in *The Crossroad Papers: A Look into the American Future,* Hans J. Morgenthau (ed.) (New York: W. W. Norton, 1965), pp. 141–51. By permission of W. W. Norton & Company, Inc. Copyright © 1965 by W. W. Norton & Company, Inc.

war, it is clear that since the 1962 Cuban crisis the original structure of that cold war has been very much changed. The "grand structure" of American policy has certainly not been abandoned, but developments such as the increasingly strained relations with de Gaulle's France have modified it very substantially; and, as in the case of Southeast Asia, its fundamental assumptions have been seriously questioned. Since 1962, the crisis points of policy (such as Vietnam, Cyprus, and South Asia) may still be described in cold-war language; they may still be dressed in cold-war pyjamas and sent upstairs to the same Procrustean bed. But they have recently had a way of throwing off the sheets and climbing out.

How different is this present climate of thought about American foreign policy from that of a decade ago. In the 1950's, a foreign diplomat once described John Foster Dulles' policy as having the architectonic clarity of a Gothic cathedral. One might not have liked it very much, especially its Calvinist gargoyles, but at least one knew what it was and had some understanding of why it was. This also remained true of policy in the early Kennedy Administration. For in 1961, also, there were clear outlines of an emerging design, attuned to the crisis as it then existed. But Cuba in 1962 seems to have been a very important watershed. Its swift terrors, its brief shock were as psychologically immense as those of a full-fledged war. To stand "eyeball to eyeball," as Mr. Rusk then put it, was to become suddenly aware both of an obliterable humanity commonly shared with an opponent and of a boundless common predicament. Perhaps this was the Third World War, acted in terrifying charade, and the test-ban treaty its provisional armistice.

I

To discuss the future problems and opportunities of American relations with the Soviet Union and the Communist bloc, we must engage in two kinds of thinking: first, we must reexamine the principal characteristics of Soviet and Communist conduct which from the late 1940's were repugnant to us and which constituted a threat to ourselves and to the broader Western community of which America is a part. We must, secondly, attempt to distinguish among our various "policy aspirations" concerning these characteristics. For while it is unhappily true that American policy can only marginally affect most of these, it is the better part of wisdom to acknowledge that, even if our influence were greater, we would still be at a loss to face with candor the question of what kind of Russia and what kind of Communist bloc (or post-Communist bloc) world it is that we would wish, and that might be a "sign" to us that our Cold War with them had indeed no further purpose to serve.

We must distinguish among four aspects of Soviet-Communist society and behavior which have provoked America and the West to fear them and to undertake countermeasures of containment. Since the late 1940's, there have been the troublesome problems of the growth of Soviet power, both absolute and relative; the related matter of Soviet territorial expansion and imperialism; the ideological challenge of Marxist-Leninist (and, more lately Khrushchevian and Maoist) doctrine to American liberal values; and, finally, the behavior and aims of the Communist movement seen in its broadest dimensions. One aspect of our predicament in dealing with the Soviet Union during this Cold War arises from the fact that large numbers of fearful Americans have remained unable or unwilling to make these distinctions, and thus have discerned only an amorphous, yet presumably monolithic threat to our society and its values. The second aspect of this predicament lies in the fact that, for those who were able to distinguish among these features, it was difficult to find agreement about which of them constituted the principal and controlling *causa belli frigidi,* that America and the Western community might wish to see altered, modified or eliminated in the Communist world.

Let us start with the problem of Soviet Russian power, whose relative and absolute enlargement was so poorly anticipated by American policy-makers during World War II. For there certainly can be no doubt that this sudden event, a product of that war, was made all the more disconcerting in the face of a politically prostrate Europe, as well as the disintegration of the great European overseas empires and the collapse of the traditional societies of the non-Western world.

When discussing Soviet Russia's power in the years immediately after Hitler's defeat, we must bear in mind that the power of this empire would probably have been as immense a problem for us even if Russia had never known Karl Marx or his Russian disciples. Just as German unification in 1870 severely strained the European state system, so now on a global stage this constellation of Russian power was bound—irrespective of its special ideological features—to arouse very deep misgivings and fears. This is especially true of those nations in its proximity which had previously experienced Russian domination or the possibility of it. In this respect, an authoritarian Tsarist

Russia, even one with Kerensky-like features, would have posed problems somewhat similar to those of Stalin's Russia. Had either of these
been responsible for establishing the scope of Russian empire, for
governing its enormous land mass and diverse peoples, their actions
in important ways would surely have resembled those of a Stalin. So
also, a post-Stalin or even post-Communist Russia (were this ever to
come to pass) would pose similar problems for Russia's neighbors and
for the whole system of international politics.

Related to this matter of Russian power were the imperialistic
aspects of Russian expansion in the post-Hitler years. Again we must
remember that these cannot exclusively be attributed to Soviet ideology or to Soviet totalitarianism. If we were fancifully to assume
that, in World War II, for instance, a "generals' plot" had overthrown
Stalin and the Communist Party and then led Russia to victory in
Europe, many of the difficulties which gave rise to the cold war in
Eastern and Central Europe and the Far East would still have obtained: the problem of Poland and Germany, for instance, and the
other areas of Eastern Europe which the Red Army "liberated." We
speak in ironic tones of Communist imperialism when describing
these expansionist tendencies of Soviet Russia. But Europeans with
long memories (and, today, Chinese Communists) remember that
such tendencies existed long before Karl Marx went to school. They
could be aspects of any Russian political system. The most intractable of them would include, in any future time, the question of
whether, in Central Europe or in Asia, we wish a roll-back by Russia,
whether under Communist rule or not; also, the question of what
kind of a roll-back would be consonant with legitimate Russian security interests, with justice to the peoples now experiencing Soviet
imperial rule, and with an enduring international tranquility. Certainly, while most Americans profess still to believe in Woodrow
Wilson's formula of national self-determination, none of us should
insist that such a formula be recklessly waved as a flag, or imposed
in doctrinaire manner on the map of Europe or even of Asia without
thought for its consequences.

Viewed from a Central European vantage point, the prudence of
being aware of this aspect of Soviet expansionism becomes especially
clear. Certainly, further Soviet expansion here would be intolerable
to us. But whatever the chances of Soviet retrenchment, the West as
a whole—and American policy in particular—has today no formula,
satisfactory either to all of its Allies or to the peoples of Eastern
Europe, to substitute for the present condition of Russian domina-

tion. Certainly, we have no formula which could possibly assuage non-German fears about the enlargement of German power and national aspirations which any German reunification would entail. Nor for that matter does the West have any means of assuring East Europeans — including Russians — that future German independent thermonuclear capabilities would make their lives any more placid and secure. In point of fact, one difficulty in coping with the Communist bloc in Europe arises from the fact that Western leaders have not publicly been willing to acknowledge that the shrill protests from Russia and its satellite regimes about German military revival reflect, at least in part, deep and quite legitimate concerns of thoughtful non-Communist Europeans, including some Germans as well.

II

I deal with these matters of Russian power and Soviet imperialism first in order to stress the fact that in important ways they must be distinguished from the ideological issue which has been so prominent in the conflict between America and Russia. Of course, it was from the beginning this ideological element which deeply aggravated Soviet-American tensions and which continues to do so. Certainly, no one could say that the United States started this quarrel; or that it can do much by itself to abate it. The trouble is that it has struck such sensitive neuralgic points in American culture that it has caused many of us to ignore these other equally troublesome features of Russia's position in the society of nations.

It seems strange that it has been in America (where the internal threat of Communism has been least present) that these ideological aspects of the Soviet threat aroused the deepest popular indignation— so much so that all else seemed at times to pale into insignificance. One explanation of this, strangely, is a wholly negative one: at no time before or after 1917 did traditional Russian expansionism directly collide with vital American interests. The cultural incompatibilities between non-Slavic and Russian cultures never directly troubled Americans much; most of us still today understand them very imperfectly.

One should recall that, long before the Russian Revolution, the principal irritants in Russo-American relations were already ideological. What most aggravated Americans about Tsarist Russia was that it seemed to represent the worst that the Old World had to offer. Its very existence seemed to confirm America's claim to newness, progressivism, and social modernity. Whether, after the Bolsheviks seized power, one took seriously their incantations about the dismal failures of American capitalism, the most aggravating feature of the litany was not its tone of hostility. Nor were the absurd falseness and irrelevance of the charges and prophecies the explanation for the American reaction. What perhaps caused our emotional response to them to be so strong was that they presented a serious philosophical challenge to American liberalism.

Their claim to have "leapfrogged" America in the race of historical progress and the quest for utopia was what hurt most. What was also annoying to Americans was that so many other peoples—the European proletariat especially—now turned their attention away from Jefferson's and Horace Greeley's America to watch a newer social experiment. Had it really succeeded, it would have robbed American culture of its most precious pretension—its claim to a monopoly of social perfection.

This ideological aspect of the cold war accounts in large measure for a serious ambivalence in American thought about what kind of a future Soviet society and Communist bloc we would be willing to co-exist with. If it were merely a matter of Russian power and Russian expansion—or "Communist imperialism"—which troubled us, the remedies would be a bit simpler to find. But it is also the symbolic character of the system which has boggled us.

Our ideological concern with the symbolic character of Soviet Russia presents us with this dilemma: would we really want to see significant improvements in the quality of Soviet life—more civic freedom, higher living standards, greater permissiveness in relations between Russia and other bloc countries—if these were obtained *within* a Communist world? It could be argued, for instance, that (if the Soviet system were actually to begin to fulfill its proclaimed norms) it would be more attractive ideologically and a more plausible threat to the claims and promises of the "American way of life." Changes such as these have been occurring in some parts of the Communist bloc—and in Yugoslavia also. Yet, because of this very ambivalence in American attitudes, we have done precious little cheering as they took place. Our capacities to derive benefit from such changes have been very small indeed, even though the emergence of a polycentric Communist bloc composed of consumer-oriented economies might greatly reduce the threat of Russian power to us. Some observers, furthermore, have argued that Soviet successes in fulfilling its "Socialist norms" might result in conservatizing its leadership. Fat Communists may be preferable to lean and hungry ones, if one has to make the choice.

Americans have not been able to make up their minds which of two alternative expectations they should welcome—Soviet internal successes (with attendant conservatization of Soviet purposes) or Soviet internal failures (with prospects of Communist collapse). This fact may, of course, have only a marginal effect on the outcome of the Soviet experiment. But surely one cannot forever be torn between regarding Soviet society as provisional, or even doomed to some cataclysmic fate, and regarding it as being capable of gradual accommodation to the habits and practices of a civilized world. It is clear that, if a Western window is to open in the Iron Curtain, this will happen because of a conscious decision by the Soviet elites. But it certainly will not take place as a consequence of prison riots in the Communist world. The warmth of a Western sun, rather than the puffing of Congressional resolutions about "captive nations," could cause the coat of totalitarianism to be shed.

III

The present disarray within both the Western alliance and the Communist bloc, whatever its various causes, heightens our awareness of the distinction among these various aspects of the Soviet problem. Is an increasingly powerful Russia to be feared and opposed simply because it happens to be powerful, and regardless of improvements in the quality of its internal life or its external behavior? If, as some Westerners have held, the cold war arose primarily because of a power disequilibrium between the Communist world and the West, would a perceptible redressing of this imbalance be the occasion to say that our principal aims have been attained? One remembers the laconic expression of Dean Acheson a decade or more ago: what was necessary, before significant negotiations to end the cold war, was a "comfortable surplus of power" in the Western world.

Even if one assumes that the West has today in fact recouped its power *vis-à-vis* Russia, one must see that this recovery severely inhibits any important solely bilateral *détente* between America and Russia. The recovery of Western power since the 1950's has meant also its diffusion within the West; one now faces the ironic fact that Russia and America today have far less leverage to accomplish together major settlements in Europe or elsewhere, were they jointly to decide to do so. Even "good Yaltas" will no longer be possible.

Ironically, also, one inhibiting feature of this new situation is that significant direct Soviet-American contacts risk tarnishing America's reputation as leader of a Western coalition and weakening the credibility of American promises to its European allies. The dilemma is that bilateral attempts to reduce tensions between America and Russia aggravate tensions within the Western alliance. While one might take comfort from the fact that this dilemma exists for them as well, the point is that the broad diplomatic opportunities which once existed in a tight bipolar world of Moscow and Washington no longer exist. One may welcome the relaxation of tensions and the waning of ideological warfare, but the possibilities of directly treating the *objective* zones of cold-war danger—Germany and East Europe especially—seem no nearer in this new situation than they were when the West was weaker and more vulnerable politically.

IV

One might welcome polycentrism in world politics on both sides of the Iron Curtain. One should remember that, in the 1940's and 1950's, it was a principal American objective to restore power and influence among nations in the non-Communist world, and thereby to reduce their dependence on us. The classic concept of the free world held by American statesmen has been one of plurality and diversity. As blocs lose their cohesiveness, opportunities for new contacts arise. As ideological politics ceases to have the cementlike function of binding the world in two camps, America may have to face the fact that it is no longer the sole custodian of Western civilization. This may be bad for the *amour propre* of American statesmen and utopian idealists, but it follows from our own stated aspirations.

But to return to the central theme—our expectations about the Soviet future. It would be fascinating if, as some have wished, the styles and character of Soviet and American life would converge. Thereby, it has been argued by some, the antagonisms arising from real sociocultural differences between us might subside. Yet much naive and wishful thinking has gone into this "convergence-reconciliation" thesis. The Appomattox Courthouse of such a reconciliation would be a miracle kitchen like the one Nixon showed Khrushchev; some followers of Erich Fromm would place it in a psychiatric clinic. Yet it remains to be proved that such a convergence is either necessary or sufficient to effect a reduction in cold-war tensions. Likeness does not necessarily make for friendship among nations any more than it does among individuals.

It might be the better part of wisdom to search out the conditions for reconciliation with the Soviet world in more mundane quarters. It may have occurred to important decision-makers on both sides during the Cuban crisis that, if they had blown each other to smithereens, many people in other parts of the world might have jumped in fright, yawned or sighed—but not wept. The principal zones of conflict between us and the Communist world now lie in areas of revolutionary upheaval far removed from the centers of our most vital interests and theirs—that is, in the underdeveloped world. Wisdom might consist in seeing that these upheavals do not explode and involve both of us; in assuming a common responsibility for a more orderly assimilation of these revolutionary societies into a stable yet just world. Neither America nor Russia is predestined to rule the globe; but together they could obliterate it. Together now, irrespective of ideological differences, they might seek to preserve both it and themselves.

SUGGESTED ADDITIONAL READINGS

The following bibliography is a highly selective one, with the purpose of suggesting the most interesting, informative, and accessible secondary studies pertinent to the preceding documents. For primary works, one should consult the footnotes and bibliographies in the books below, particularly those listed in Section II.

I. SOVIET-AMERICAN DIPLOMATIC RELATIONS

Brennan, Donald G. (ed.). *Arms Control, Disarmament, and National Security.* New York: Braziller, 1961.

Browder, Robert P. *The Origins of Soviet-American Diplomacy.* Princeton: Princeton University Press, 1953.

Clay, Lucius. *Decision in Germany.* Garden City, N.Y.: Doubleday, 1950.

Davison, W. P. *The Berlin Blockade: A Study in Cold War Politics.* Princeton: Princeton University Press, 1958.

Dawson, Raymond H. *The Decision to Aid Russia, 1941: Foreign Policy and Domestic Politics.* Chapel Hill: University of North Carolina Press, 1959.

Feis, Herbert. *Between War and Peace: The Potsdam Conference.* Princeton: Princeton University Press, 1960.

——. *Churchill—Roosevelt—Stalin: The War They Waged and the Peace They Sought.* Princeton: Princeton University Press, 1957.

Kennan, George F. *Russia, the Atom, and the West.* New York: Harper, 1958.

——. *Russia and the West under Lenin and Stalin.* Boston: Little, Brown, 1961.

——. *Soviet-American Relations, 1917-1920,* 2 vols.: *Russia Leaves the War* and *The Decision to Intervene.* Princeton: Princeton University Press, 1956, 1958.

Kissinger, Henry A. *Nuclear Weapons and Foreign Policy.* New York: Harper, 1957.

Lukacs, John A. *A New History of the Cold War.* Garden City, N.Y.: Doubleday Anchor, 1966.

McNeill, William H. *America, Britain & Russia: Their Co-operation and Conflict, 1941-1946.* New York: Oxford University Press, 1953.

Schelling, Thomas C., and Halperin, Morton H. *Strategy and Arms Control.* New York: Twentieth Century Fund, 1961.

Snell, John L. (ed.). *The Meaning of Yalta: Big Three Diplomacy and the New Balance of Power.* Baton Rouge: Louisiana State Press, 1956.

Williams, William A. *American-Russian Relations, 1781-1947.* New York: Rinehart, 1952.

——. *The Tragedy of American Diplomacy.* New York: Delta, 1962.

II. AMERICAN ATTITUDES TOWARD SOVIET RUSSIA

Aaron, Daniel. *Writers on the Left: Episodes in American Literary Communism.* New York: Harcourt, Brace, & World, 1961.

Bailey, Thomas A. *America Faces Russia: Russian-American Relations from Early Times to Our Day.* Ithaca: Cornell University Press, 1950.

Draper, Theodore. *American Communism and Soviet Russia.* New York. Viking Press, 1960.

Feuer, Lewis S. "Travelers to the Soviet Union, 1917-1932: The Formation of a Component of New Deal Ideology," *American Quarterly,* Vol. XIV (Summer, 1962), pp. 119-49.

Filene, Peter G. *Americans and the Soviet Experiment, 1917-1933.* Cambridge, Mass.: Harvard University Press, 1967.

Howe, Irving, and Coser, Lewis. *The American Communist Party: A Critical History (1919-1957).* Boston: Beacon Press, 1957.

Lasch, Christopher. *The American Liberals and the Russian Revolution.* New York: Columbia University Press, 1962.

Warren, Frank A., III. *Liberals and Communism: The "Red Decade" Revisited.* Bloomington: Indiana University Press, 1966.

III. AMERICAN PUBLIC OPINION AND FOREIGN POLICY

Almond, Gabriel A. *The American People and Foreign Policy.* New York: Harcourt, Brace, 1950.

Bailey, Thomas A. *The Man in the Street: The Impact of American Public Opinion on Foreign Policy.* New York: Macmillan, 1948.

Buchanan, William, and Cantril, Hadley. *How Nations See Each Other: A Study in Public Opinion.* Urbana: University of Illinois Press, 1953.

Cohen, Bernard C. *The Press and Foreign Policy.* Princeton: Princeton University Press, 1963.

Markel, Lester, *et al. Public Opinion and Foreign Policy.* New York: Harper, 1949.

May, Ernest R. "An American Tradition in Foreign Policy: The Role of Public Opinion," in *Theory and Practice in American Politics,* William H. Nelson (ed.). Chicago: University of Chicago Press, 1964.

——. "American Imperialism: A Reinterpretation," *Perspectives in American History,* Vol. I (1967), pp. 123-83.

Rosenau, James N. *National Leadership and Foreign Policy: A Case Study in the Mobilization of Public Support.* Princeton: Princeton University Press, 1963.

——. *Public Opinion and Foreign Policy: An Operational Formulation.* New York: Random House, 1961.

Smith, M. Brewster, Bruner, Jerome S., and White, Robert H. *Opinions and Personality.* New York: Wiley, 1956.